Faulkner's *Intruder in the Dust:*

A Critical Study of the Typescripts

Patrick H. Samway, S. J.

Faulkner's *Intruder in the Dust:*

A Critical Study of the Typescripts

Patrick H. Samway, S. J.

The Whitston Publishing Company
Troy, New York

William Faulkner's manuscripts and typescripts are under copyright and
may not be quoted without the permission of Mrs. Jill Faulkner Summers, c/o Manuscripts Department, Alderman Library, The University
of Virginia, Charlottesville, Virginia. The copyright for this book does
not apply to any material quoted from Faulkner's typescripts. I am
grateful to Mrs. Summers for allowing me permission to photograph the
three pages of manuscript and typescript reproduced in this book.

The sketch of Faulkner by José Melik is reproduced with the permission of the National Portrait Gallery, The Smithsonian Institution,
Washington, D. C.

Excerpts cited from the letters of Harold Ober are Copyright © 1980
by Richard Ober and Nathaniel Ober and reprinted by permission of
Harold Ober Associates, Incorporated.

for my families in

Buffalo

New York City

Rochester

Spencerport

Syracuse

Sunday mmnnr
Spnmg
enly May

It was just noon when the sheriff reached the jail with Lucas Beauchamp tho the whole town C the whole county too in that matter; had known since the night before that he had killed a white man.

He was there, waiting. He was the first one, standing lounging trying to look occupied or at least innocent, under the shed in front of the blacksmith's across the street from the jail where his uncle wnld be less likely to see him if in rather when he should come the same from his office to the courthouse.

Because he knew Lucas Beauchamp too — as well that is ae any white person know him. Better than any maybe unless it was another Edmonds on whose place Lucas lived 17 miles from town because he had eaten a meal in Lucas' house. It was in the early winter 4 years ago; he had been only 12 then and it had happened this way: Edmonds was a friend of his uncle; they had been to school together at the state University where his uncle had gone to Harvard and then to Europe and the day when Edmonds had come in to see his uncle on some county business C his uncle was county attorney, and had been for years) and had stayed the night with them and at supper that evening Edmonds had said to him:

'Come out home with me tomorrow and go rabbit hunting.' Then to his mother: 'I'll send him back in tomorrow afternoon. I'll send a boy along with him.' Then to him again: 'a good hunter. He's got a rabbit dog.

'He's got a dog.' his uncle said.

~~So the next mnng he and Aleck Sander went home with~~ ~~had gone home with Edmonds, who sent the one of his~~ ~~tenants along to show them where to hunt C so that he~~ ~~and Aleck Sander by themselves couldn't have found~~

"We are like searchers in a house of darkness,
   A house of dust; we creep with little lanterns,
Throwing our tremulous arcs of light at random,
Now here, now there, seeing a plane, an angle,
An edge, a curve, a wall, a broken stairway
Leading to who knows what; but never seeing
The whole at once. . . We grope our way a little,
And then grow tired. No matter what we touch,
Dust is the answer—dust: dust everywhere."
                    (*The House of Dust,* Conrad Aiken)

"I am the best in America, by God."
                    (Letter from William Faulkner
                    to Robert Haas, [April] 1939)

"Le romancier alors est celui qui aperçoit qu'une
   structure est en train de s'esquisser dans ce qui
   l'entoure, et qui va poursuivre cette structure, la
   faire croître, la perfectionner, l'étudier, jusqu'au
   moment où elle sera lisible pour tous."
                    (Michel Butor, *Répertoire* II)

7 Feb. 1949

Dear Bob;

Here is the insert for INTRUDER re our
recent correspondence.

Page 156 as set down through end of the
paragraph, Stevens' speech ending: ' .... hide from
one another behind a loud lipservice to a flag.'

            (INSERT---NEW MATTER)
        'But what will happen?' he said. 'What will we
do and he do, both of us, all of us. What will become of him
---Sambo?'

        'I just told you,' his uncle said. 'He will
disappear. There are not enough of him to resist, to repel,
to hold intact his integrity even if he wished to remain a
Negro. In time he would have got equity and justice without
even asking for it. But by insisting on social equality, what
he is actually demanding is racial extinction. Three hundred
years ago he didn't exist in America; five hundred years from
now he will have vanished and will be no more. Oh, he will
still exist here now and then as isolate and insulate phenomena, incorrigible, tieless, anachronic and paradox; archaeological and geological expeditions will stumble on him occasionally by individuals and even intact nests in caves in remote
Tennessee and Carolina mountain fastnesses or Mississippi and
Alabama and Louisiana swamps or, generations ago lost and unrecorded, in the mapless back areas of Detroit or Los Angeles
tenement districts; travellers passing through the rotundas
of the Croydon or Le Bourget or La Guardia airports or the
supra transfer stations of space ships will gape at him intact

                    156. A.

with banjo and hound and screenless mudchinked cabin and
naked piccaninnies playing with empty snuff-bottles in the
dust, even to the washpot in the backyard and his bandana-
turbaned mate bending over it, as the Union Pacific railroad
used to establish tepees of authentically costumed Blackfoot
and Shoshone Indians in the lobby of the Commodore Hotel.
But as a race he will be no more; his blood will exist only
in the dusty files of genealogical societies for the members
of what will then be the Daughters of the Founding Fathers
or the Lost Causes to wrangle and brag over as the Briton
does over his mystic trace of Norman, so that in five hundred
years or perhaps even less than that, all America can paraphrase the tag line of a book a novel of about twenty years
ago by another Mississippian, a mild retiring little man
over yonder at Oxford, in which a fictitious Canadian said
to a fictitious self-lacerated ~~Mississippian~~ Southerner in a dormitory
room in a not too authentic Harvard: "I who regards you
will have also sprung from the loins of African kings".'

(RESUME; P 156)

Now they were there and not too long be-
hind the sheriff. For though the car etc etc CONTINUED

B.

TABLE OF CONTENTS

PREFACE xiii

I.   BACKGROUND MATERIAL TO *INTRUDER* 1

II. THE ORIGINAL DRAFT 59
     Chapter One 66
     Chapter Two 76
     Chapter Three 84
     Chapter Four 92
     Chapter Five 101
     Chapter Six 115
     Final Chapter 119

III. THE SETTING COPY 123
     Chapter One 125
     Chapter Two 129
     Chapter Three 142
     Chapter Four 150
     Chapter Five 161
     Chapter Six 164
     Chapter Seven 173
     Chapter Eight 178
     Chapter Nine 179
     Chapter Ten 213
     Chapter Eleven 224

IV. AN EVALUATION OF *INTRUDER* 229

APPENDIX A 285

APPENDIX B 363

APPENDIX C 389

INDEX 395

PREFACE

A few years ago, perhaps longer now than I wish to remember, I asked Professor Joseph L. Blotner, who was then writing his biography of William Faulkner, what direction he thought Faulkner studies would take. Expecting an answer related to biography, I was surprised when Professor Blotner said that, at least for the foreseeable future, he thought the important work in Faulkner criticism would center on Faulkner's manuscripts and typescripts. From conversations I have had with other Faulkner critics, it is quite clear that Professor Blotner is not alone in his views. Yet, it took a while for me to realize palpably the import of Professor Blotner's comments; anyone who spends weeks and months reading Faulkner's manuscripts and typescripts cannot help but experience the thrill and satisfaction of appreciating even more the genius of Faulkner's creative imagination. My own experience in this has given me a respect for the Faulknerian world, not only in its sweeping historical, social, and literary dimensions, but in the specificity of individual words and phrases.

In the last few years, Faulkner criticism has grown tremendously; as expected, some of it is excellent and some a bit repetitious. Few have the time, energy, and resources to keep up with all that is being published on Faulkner in this country and abroad. I make no pretensions in this regard. Yet, I am convinced that if criticism on Faulkner's works is not based in some ultimate way on a knowledge of his books as he wrote them, that is on both the text and context of his works, then criticism will deal with a Yoknapatawpha County even more complicated than even Faulkner would have wished. As scripture scholars know so well, the hermeneutics of criticism about theological texts must be based on a reverence for all the dimensions of the text. Many scholars have often mentioned that until we have accurate editions of Faulkner's works, and at least one series of texts that are fully annotated, then we will have to deal with a diminished appreciation of what Faulkner has bequeathed to us. In this respect, the French have set an example; the first volume of Faulkner's works in the *Bibliothèque de la Pléiade* series, published by Gallimard and presented and annotated by Professor Michel Gresset, is excellent proof of such reverent scholarship.

While writing this study of *Intruder in the Dust,* I have become convinced of the validity of Professor Blotner's insight. A knowledge of the composition of any one of Faulkner's works, including *Intruder,* can only lead to greater literary enjoyment, basically because it means an investment of time and energy into what one intuits is already a worthwhile venture. I have tried to explain the composition of *Intruder* logically and chronologically so that it would be useful to both student and scholar. By following an analysis of the *Intruder* typescripts chapter by chapter, the way Faulkner wrote them, the reader can best appreciate the density of this novel as it gradually developed into a work of art. I firmly believe in continuing what Professor Regina K. Fadiman has called "process criticism" in her book concerning the revisions of *Light in August.* Although the first edition of any novel represents and is the final artistic product, especially if the galleys and page-proofs have been corrected and approved by the author, the history of the text—its genesis in the mind of the writer insofar as it can be determined, its possible sources, its relationship to events and situations during the time the novel was written, and its relationship to other literary works especially by the same author—all give the reader a sensitivity and perspective that can often be valuable in appreciating parts of the novel or the work as a whole. The critical norms that we finally use in judging a work of art should enhance our appreciation of the work and not detract from it.

To anyone who has tried to decipher Faulkner's small, meticulous penmanship or has tried to discern patterns of development amid assorted pages of typescript, whether in Austin, Charlottesville, New Haven, or New York City, it is evident that no one, absolute methodology will be adequate in dealing with what Faulkner has written. From what we already know about certain stories and novels, Faulkner varied the way he wrote these stories and novels depending on time, place, and personal pressures. The excellent articles and books by Fredson T.

Bowers, James B. Meriwether, and James E. Thorpe are most helpful in explaining general methodological considerations and in encouraging the researcher to look at the unique nature of individual texts. As with other novels written by Faulkner, *Intruder* reflects both in general and specific ways the historical and literary environment of its day.

Since Faulkner conserved paper as much as he could by using the reverse sides and by writing in between the lines of pages he had discarded, he has not made the job of the textual critic easier since someone pouring over the manuscripts and typescripts will never know what he will find until he has actually finished. Yet, because the typescript pages of *Intruder* are complete, or very nearly complete, they do give in one instance a clear idea of Faulkner's creative procedure in writing a novel. In addition, *Intruder* has correspondences with *A Fable* and *The Reivers* since all three novels involve horses, youth, and grown-ups in juxtaposition to one another; Faulkner was writing the horse race section of *A Fable* when he took time off to write *Intruder* in 1948 and his letters reveal that before writing *Intruder* he was already formulating the story of *The Reivers.* As will be shown, too, *Intruder* has a most unusual textual relationship with *Absalom, Absalom!*. Thus, one aspect of the methodology I have employed in studying *Intruder* is to explain the general way Faulkner wrote this novel as well as to highlight some of the unique relationships it has to other literary texts.

The first chapter of this book orchestrates what I consider important background material related to the creation of *Intruder*. In general, I have tried to show how Faulkner viewed the coming-to-being of this story as related to other events and situations in his life, some of them quite prosaic. Though *Intruder* provided a respite from the arduous task of writing what Faulkner at one point considered his major literary work, there seems to be a rather long history to *Intruder,* a characteristic of Faulkner's imagination that can be seen more dramatically in the composition of the Snopes trilogy. The second and third chapters of this book analyze both the original draft and the final version, or setting copy, of *Intruder* that was eventually sent to the printers. Finally, the fourth chapter provides an interpretation of the novel, looking not only at the original and final versions, but to other sources which seem to be important in a consideration of this particular novel.

. No interpretation of any novel is ever complete or exhaustive, not at least if the language of literature is living and continuously evokes new responses. Faulkner's world, whether
localized in Yoknapatawpha or beyond, is essentially dynamic
and the reader who enters this world soon realizes that he can
come back time and time again and understand the various
stories and novels from ever-shifting perspectives. As John
Dewey reminds us in his *Art as Experience,* an aesthetic experience does not have a machine-like predictability:

> The work of art, however, unlike the machine, is not only the
> outcome of imagination, but operates imaginatively rather than
> in the realm of physical existences. What it does is to concen-
> trate and enlarge an immediate experience. The formed matter
> of esthetic experience directly *expresses,* in other words, the
> meanings that are imaginatively evoked; it does not, like the ma-
> terial brought into new relations in a machine, merely provide
> *means* by which purposes over and beyond the existence of the
> object may be executed. And yet, the meanings imaginatively
> summoned, assembled, and integrated are embodied in material
> existence that here and now interacts with the self. The work of
> art is thus a challenge to the performance of a like act of evocation
> and organization, through imagination, on the part of the one who
> experiences it.

Thus, for someone who reads one of Faulkner's novels attentive-
ly, his response should not be characterized by passive receptivi-
ty, but by imaginative envolvement so that he knows and understands what it means to be human, to break through the ontic
to the ontological as Heidegger would put it. And each year, as
the reader grows and the patterns and nuances of his life change
and are changed, his enjoyment of even the same novel will be
altered and, hopefully, deepened. This is the power of fiction.
This is the power of the creative imagination.

In writing this book, I am indebted to many people, especially Mrs. Jill Faulkner Summers for allowing me access to
her father's manuscripts and typescripts; to Professor Joseph
L. Blotner who encouraged me to start this project and most
graciously granted me access to the material he had gathered for

his biography of Faulkner; to Professor James B. Meriwether for supplying me with information concerning the contracts of *Intruder;* to Professor Louis D. Rubin, Jr. whose criticism I appreciated and whose knowledge of Southern literature I deeply admire; to the late Mr. Linton R. Massey for giving me permission to read some restricted Faulkner material; to the staff of the Alderman Library at the University of Virginia, particularly the Curator of Manuscripts, Mr. Edmund Berkeley, Jr., and the Curator of the American Collections, Miss Joan St. C. Crane, as well as to Miss Anne E. H. Freudenberg, Mr. Gregory A. Johnson, Mr. Michael Plunkett, Mrs. Lucille Richards, and Mrs. Anne Stauffenberg Southwell; to Mrs. Jean Britt for her excellent typing; to my Jesuit community in Syracuse for providing me with a Le Moyne Grant to finish this book; and lastly, I would like to thank my friend, Benjamin S. Forkner, of the University of Nantes, France, for generously sharing both his Muscadet and his love of Southern letters—especially those Faulknerian thoughts of glamorous fatality, of silver pennons in the air, and the dying fall of horns along the mythic road to Roncevaux.

I

BACKGROUND MATERIAL

Although Faulkner wrote *Intruder in the Dust* during "three months" in the winter and spring of 1948, it was a story he had thought about for a long time, and one which gradually took shape during the mid-1940's as he worked on the various Gavin Stevens' stories and what he ventually thought would be his masterpiece, *A Fable*. After its publication on September 27, 1948, Faulkner thought highly of the book, at least for a while. When Mrs. Mary Betsy Waddle, a long-time friend of the Faulkners, visited Rowan Oak, the Faulkner home in Oxford, Mississippi, in the late 1940's, Faulkner presented her with a copy of *Intruder* and told her, "I consider this book. . .the best I have ever written."[1] Later, when Faulkner met some of the citizens of Nagano, Japan, in 1955, they asked him which of his books they should read first. Faulkner replied, "I would suggest—the title is *Intruder in the Dust*. I suggest that because that deals with the problem which is important not only in my country, but, I think important to all people."[2] By no means do these two references mean that *Intruder* was Faulk-

---

[1]For a further treatment of Mrs. Waddle's views on *Intruder*, cf. *William Faulkner of Oxford*, eds. James Webb and A. Wigfall Green (Baton Rouge: Louisiana State University Press, 1965), pp. 141-142.

[2]William Faulkner in *Lion in the Garden*, eds. James B. Meriwether and Michael Millgate (New York: Random House, 1968), p. 166. Faulkner liked *The Sound and the Fury* and called it his "best failure" (*Faulkner in the University*, eds. Frederick Gwynn and Joseph Blotner, New York: Vintage, 1959, p. 61). In 1958, he suggested that anyone who wishes to read his books should begin with *Sartoris* (*Faulkner in the University*, p. 285).

ner's favorite or that he could continue to recommend it as the first book people should read if they were interested in his works.

While *Intruder* rarely makes the "top ten" list of Faulkner's works, it is important both from a textual point of view, since the typescripts are complete, and from a thematic point of view, since it is a relatively late Faulkner novel and illuminates many of Faulkner's earlier works. In this study, I propose to analyze *Intruder* from three perspectives: 1) to correlate in chronological order all the pertinent material relating to the composition of *Intruder;* 2) to evaluate the typescripts of the novel as found in the Alderman Library of the University of Virginia at Charlottesville, in order to appreciate the imaginative genesis of this work; 3) to analyze the novel in light of the findings made in an evaluation of the typescripts. The first chapter of this study will incorporate many letters written to and by Faulkner; unless noted otherwise, I have corrected Faulkner's typographical errors (actually few in number) and have included material which bears on the composition of *Intruder,* both the novel and the movie, at least up to the early months of 1949, when for all practical purposes, Faulkner ceased any public discussion of this novel.

During the 1940's, Faulkner remained very busy working on what he originally entitled *Who?* (later changed to *A Fable*), composing the material for *Go Down, Moses and Other Stories,* writing the Gavin Stevens' stories, collaborating in Hollywood on screenplays, working on his farm, and trying to solve the never-ending battle with the Internal Revenue Service. As Michael Millgate has observed, these were not years of inactivity, "but they were years during which his [Faulkner's] reputation reached a low ebb, and from which he emerged, with the publication in 1948 of *Intruder in the Dust,* as apparently a different kind of novelist, much more ready to commit himself to specific statements on contemporary issues."[3] While the physical writing of *Intruder* did not occupy more than a few months of Faulk-

---

[3]Michael Millgate, *The Achievement of William Faulkner* (New York: Random House, 1966), p. 210.

ner's time, the genesis of this story is complicated by the more than eight years Faulkner took in bringing this story from the "lumber room" of his imagination and actually setting it down on paper.

After working on the galleys for *The Hamlet* in January 1940, Faulkner submitted to Harold Ober, his agent in New York City, in February two stories ("Gold is Not Always" and "The Fire on the Hearth") involving Lucas Beauchamp, the main character in *Intruder*.[4]   On March 18th, Ober received another story, "Pantaloon in Black," this time not involving Lucas, but Rider, a black man who is grief-stricken at the death of his young wife, Mannie.[5] The white townsfolk misinterpret Rider's actions as he releases the grief and anxiety he feels. Rider eventually enters a crap game, catches a white man, Bird-song, cheating with loaded dice, and slits Birdsong's throat with a razor. Birdsong's relatives waste no time in lynching Rider. Faulkner's treatment of Rider is sympathetic as can be seen in the deputy sheriff's wife's reaction to her husband's views. Thus, while Faulkner was writing stories about Lucas, he also wrote about lynching and the internal, emotional struggles a black man faces under tremendous social and psychological pressure.[6]

The original contract for *Intruder* was signed May 6, 1940 and provided a temporary solution for Faulkner's financial difficulties.[7]   Earlier on April 30th, Robert Haas, another of

----

[4]The Harold Ober-William Faulkner correspondence (hereafter cited as "Ober files") from January 1940-January 1952 is listed as Item 8969 in the Massey-Ober Collection in the Alderman Library at the University of Virginia.   I am grateful to the late Mr. Linton R. Massey for allowing me access to this material.

[5]Ober files.

[6]The question of source-material is a difficult one. It will be treated more comprehensively in the last chapter of this book.

[7]This contract, signed by William Faulkner and Robert Haas, pro-

Faulkner's agents in New York, received a letter from Faulkner: "I need $1,000.00 now, to pay debts and current bills. I want $9,000.00 more, say $400.00 per month over two years."[8] After the exhilaration of finishing *The Hamlet,* Faulkner intended to write more short stories and spend at least six months on another novel. "I wrote six short stories by March 15, trying to write the sort of pot boilers which the [Saturday Evening] Post pays me $1,000.00 for, because the best I could hope for good stories is 3 or 4 hundred, and the only magazines to buy them is Harper's etc." During the spring months he had spent some time mortgaging mares and colts to pay for food and some basic necessities of life. Faulkner continued this letter:

> Now I have run out of mules to mortgage. I can raise the thousand on the assignment. By the time I have paid the income tax assessment and a note at the bank here, that will be gone. And I will still have to keep trying to write trash stories which so far are not selling even fifty percent., because I am now like the gambler who simply has to double and pyramid, the poker player who can neither call nor throw in his hand but has got to raise. I have a blood-and-thunder mystery novel [possibly *Intruder*]

---

vided that Random House would pay Faulkner 15% of retail price of every copy sold, less returns of the first printing, and 20% for all copies sold thereafter. It also noted that Faulkner would receive an advance of $2,000: $1,500 had already been paid and the rest would be payable on demand. Information supplied by the microfilm archives at Random House in New York City (hereafter cited as "Random House microfilm archives"). The Random House files concerning William Faulkner have recently been transferred to the University of Virginia and are in the process of being catalogued. Letters, either originals or Xerox copies, in the Random House files at the University of Virginia which I have quoted will be cited as "Random House files." The Random House Collection at Columbia University has nothing of value concerning the composition of *Intruder.*

[8]Information supplied by Professor Joseph Blotner. Unless otherwise noted, all references to Faulkner's biography and his correspondence are based on material in Professor Blotner's extensive files (hereafter cited as "Blotner's files"). I have relied mostly on Xerox copies of Faulkner's correspondence.

which should sell (they usually do) but I don't dare devote six months to writing, haven't got six months to devote to it. I have another in mind in method similar to THE UNVANQUISHED, but since the chapters which I have written and tried to sell as short stories have not sold, I haven't the time to continue with it.

Faulkner then asked if Random House would consider a contract assuring him of $1,000 plus $300 a month. Haas replied by saying that he had a plan that would possibly help the situation. He thought that Faulkner should expect about $3,000 per book based on the quality of a book such as *The Hamlet* and the projected sales for that book.

Thus, as Joseph Blotner notes, the contract for *Intruder* was part of a package deal for Haas suggested, "a new, three-book arrangement under which they would pay him $1,000 now and another $2,000 during the next twelve months. In the two succeeding twelve-month periods they would send him regularly $250 a month. He [Haas] knew that Faulkner had wanted $9,000 over two years instead of four, but he had hoped that this plan—which was as far as they could go—would help to keep his troubles under control."[9] Faulkner's reply is interesting because it shows that at the same time he was thinking of writing a mystery story, he was thinking about the plot of what would later be called *The Reivers,* thus establishing a tenuous relationship between these two books. Faulkner begins with an *apologia:*

> Every so often, in spite of judgment and all else, I take these fits of sort of raging and impotent exasperation at this really quite alarming paradox which my life reveals: Beginning at the age of thirty I, an artist, a sincere one and of the first class, who should be free even of his own economic responsibilities and with no moral conscience at all, began to become the sole, principal and partial support—food, shelter, heat, clothes, medicine, kotex, school fees, toilet paper and picture shows—of my mother, an inept brother and his wife and two sons, another brother's widow and

[9]Joseph Blotner, *Faulkner: A Biography* (New York: Random House, 1974), II, 1043.

child, a wife of my own and two step children, my own child; I inherited my father's debts and his dependents, white and black without inheriting yet from anyone one inch of land or one stick of furniture or one cent of money; the only thing I ever got for nothing, after the first pair of long pants I received (cost: $7.50) was the $300.00 O. Henry prize last year. I bought without help from anyone the house I live in and all the furniture; I bought my farm the same way. I am 42 years old and I have already paid for four funerals and will certainly pay for one more and in all likelihood two more beside that, provided none of the people in mine or my wife's family my superior in age outlive me, before I ever come to my own.

Faulkner agreed to the contract Haas proposed with only a few minor changes: most of all, he wanted the thousand dollars and thought that when the regular stipend began to arrive he would be more at ease and would begin a new novel:

I think I have a good one. . . . It is a sort of Huck Finn—a normal boy of about twelve or thirteen, a big, warmhearted, courageous, honest, utterly unreliable white man with the mentality of a child, an old negro servant, opinionated, querulous, selfish, fairly unscrupulous, and in his second childhood, and a prostitute not very young anymore and with a great deal of character and generosity and common sense, and a stolen race horse which none of them actually intended to steal. The story is how they travel for a thousand miles from hand to mouth trying to get away from the police long enough to return the horse. All of them save the white man think the police are after the horse. The white man knows the police have been put on his trail by his harridan of a wife whom he has fled from. Actually, the police are trying to return the boy to his parents to get the reward. The story lasts a matter of weeks. During that time the boy grows up, becomes a man, and a good man, mostly because of the influence of the whore. He goes through in miniature all the experiences of youth which mold the man's character. They happen to be the very experiences which in his middle class parents' eyes stand for debauchery and degeneracy and actual criminality; through them he learned courage and honor and generosity and pride and pity. He has been absent only weeks, but as soon as his mother sees him again, she knows what has happened to him. She weeps, says, 'He is not my baby anymore.'

This story, which also contains elements of the horse race story in *A Fable*, also foreshadows some of the elements in *Intruder*, especially the growth of a young boy who becomes friends with an old Negro and the use of a horse to further the plot. Haas sent a check for a thousand dollars with the contract by return mail.

Faulkner, however, did not settle down to write this novel. In May 1940, he suggested that he collect and publish some of the magazine stories he had written since 1933 and add one or two new ones should they be needed to fill out the volume. He thought he could assemble this collection of stories in about a month. With the beginning of the war, Faulkner became depressed and lamented the fact that he was so busy borrowing money from Random House that he had so little time to write. "But I can still write. That is, I haven't said at 42 all that is in the cards for me to say. And that wont do any good either, but surely it is still possible to scratch the face of the supreme Obliteration and leave a decipherable scar of some sort." He now owed about $1,300 in back taxes and requested Haas to send him the $500 they had agreed on, with the monthly stipend beginning in July. To show his good will and to encourage Faulkner in writing the stories he had in mind, Haas sent the check on June 4, 1940, and said that Faulkner could have an additional $1,000 in monthly installments. In fact, another advance of $1,000 could be sent but Haas would prefer that they not take this route.

When Faulkner received the $500 from Haas, he realized that he had received a total of $2,000 in advances on a new novel he owed Random House. Though he had the germ of a story in mind, or what could even be considered the germ of several stories, Faulkner was not psychologically ready to attempt this work. Rather, he wanted to have the collection of stories count as a novel instead. Thus, he wrote to Haas and according to Blotner this "letter constituted their option on the volume of collected material, in return for which he wanted to draw further advances against his general royalty account of at least $200 a month for perhaps twelve months. . . . Haas tried to meet this new turn. The arrangement actually constituted a new advance of $2,400 on a book of stories, he wrote by return mail, 'a pretty steep advance for a collection,' and he hoped that they could let the original agreement stand, fixing on a new advance of, say, $1,500 when he was ready to do the collection."[10] If this arrangement were not agreeable to both parties, then Haas would again try to find a more suitable one.

As these letters went back and forth between New York and Oxford, Mississippi, the story of *Intruder* began to take on more importance. In a three-page letter, single spaced, Faulkner continued to explain his financial situation and the literary plans he had in mind. He regarded the $1,000 advance on the new novel as temporary, though welcomed. In addition, he would need approximately $9,000 more to give him financial security for the next two years, or at least $5,000 for one year. If he did not receive this, then he would have to liquidate his property and he would not hestitate to do this if it were the only way to remain solvent. His bargaining power, he felt, lay in the promise of his literary output in the next two years, provided of course that he not have those pressures which would take him away from his writing. He believed that he could write the novel he had mentioned to Haas, plus "5 short stories already written, two others planned, both of which might sell, one of which is a mystery story, original in that the solver is a negro, himself in jail for the murder and is about to be lynched, solves murder in self defense. Of these I can make a more or less continuous narrative, somewhat after THE UNVANQUISHED. 6-12 months." Thus, it would appear that this murder mystery could be written either as a novel or as a short story and included in a series of short stories with some type of thematic unity. Though Faulkner had allowed Haas a glimpse into his lumber room, he had not reached a satisfactory solution for his financial difficulties.

As Faulkner began thinking about the plot of *Intruder,* he almost made a serious mistake, one that might have meant the end of this story before it had ever been written. Because of his eagerness to find a solution to his financial problems, he contemplated changing publishers, a practice he had which occasionally got him into serious difficulties. He wrote Haas that he considered selling the collection of stories elsewhere:

---

[10]*Faulkner*, II, 1047.

"But if I must sign a longer contract in order to get this sum, let me have your blessing to ask enough in addition to buy back from Random House the contract I recently signed. This notion springs from the fact that, years ago, before I knew you, before I ever anticipated a connection with Random House, a publisher intimated to me that I could almost write my own ticket with him. This may not even hold now. But it is one thing more I can try before I decide to liquidate my property and savings." In the autumn of 1931, Harold Guinzburg of Viking Press had met Faulkner in New York and made the offer then. On June 10, 1940, Haas wrote that he appreciated Faulkner's financial situation, but that there were limits a book company must respect. Faulkner's average earnings from *Absalom, Absalom!*, *The Unvanquished*, *The Wild Palms*, and *The Hamlet* were approximately $3,371 per book and this did not warrant such an advance as Faulkner had asked for. Haas did not see how he could prevent Faulkner from searching out other publishers and he would let him know the legal details of such a switch should Faulkner decide to sign elsewhere. Faulkner then contacted Viking Press and said that he would come to New York City and settle details, thus paving the way to terminate his relationship with his sixth publisher.

Bennett Cerf of Random House wrote to Faulkner saying that he was very upset at the possibility of Faulkner terminating his relationship with Random House. He would be willing to modify their arrangement again so that Faulkner would receive $250 a month for the coming year. Faulkner held his ground, however, and said he would come to New York City and try and resolve everything; he did not like blackjacking one publisher into advancing the money when the second company was unwilling to make the advance. When Faulkner met Guinzburg in New York City on June 25, 1940, they decided that Guinzburg should see Cerf on the following Monday and that Faulkner would receive from Haas the additional $1,000 he had been promised before returning to Oxford. On July 3, 1940, Guinzburg wrote Faulkner and said that he was withdrawing his offer because the amount he would have to invest would be larger "than a conservative business approach would have warranted." He realized that he would be making advances to Faulkner without much assurance of literary production in addition to buying the plates and stock of *The Hamlet* from Random House. Though

Faulkner never terminated his contract with Random House, this did not mean the end of his contractual difficulties.

In the summer of 1941, Stephen Longstreet, a former New York cartoonist who became a Hollywood scriptwriter, informed his friend, William Faulkner, that he had found an agent who would further his career in Hollywood. On Thursday, May 22, 1941, an M-G-M memo notes that William Herndon had tried to make a contract with them for Faulkner at $500 a week for twelve weeks. After this, through some type of arrangement, Faulkner gave permission to Herndon to try and sell the stories in *Go Down, Moses* to the various movie companies, thus getting Faulkner into a contractual situation that became increasingly bothersome during the following years, especially during the writing of *Intruder.* In mid-July 1942, Faulkner said he declined to sign a contract with Herndon and in a telegraph to Harold Ober wrote: "I CONSIDERED HE [HERNDON] VOIDED ANY AGREEMENT BETWEEN US BY FAILING THIS. HAVE NOT HEARD FROM HIM SINCE FEBRUARY OF THIS YEAR." While it became clear that Faulkner did not consider his arrangement with Herndon as binding, Herndon, on the other hand, was reluctant to give up such a potentially valuable client.

Ober agreed to try and sever the Faulkner-Herndon relationship. But the situation did not improve and on July 17, 1942, Faulkner wrote to Ober that he was sure Herndon would cause trouble if he did not remain Faulkner's agent in Hollywood. Ober still thought the situation could be altered and that he and H. N. Swanson, his West Coast agent, could handle Faulkner's business on the Coast. Faulkner, however, thought that a personal approach might be more profitable and said that he would see Herndon in Hollywood and try to extricate himself from their arrangement. In late July, Faulkner was in Hollywood and found that Herndon had negotiated a long series of weekly options, 13-13-26-26, followed by a series of fifty-two week options, with Warner Brothers. Faulkner agreed to these options and thus became more obligated to Herndon than before. Before returning home for Christmas that year, he worked on two films, "Liberation Story" and "Background to Danger," based on Eric Ambler's *Uncommon Danger.*

At this point, because of the pressures of writing scripts in Hollywood, Faulkner seems to have pushed the story of *Intruder* into the back corners of his lumber room. Yet 1943 was an important year, because it was the year he began writing his fable, a novel that leads directly into the writing of *Intruder* and has important thematic ties with it. In January 1943, he finished the film "Life and Death of a Bomber" and began work on three others during the succeeding months, "Deep Valley," "Country Lawyer," and "Battle Cry." During that summer, he met two partners, producer William Bacher and director Henry Hathaway, who in an off-handed manner suggested to Faulkner that he consider the story of the Unknown Soldier as Jesus Christ. Faulkner had previously read Humphrey Cobb's *Paths of Glory* and the creative imagination began to stir again. On a leave from Hollywood, Faulkner wrote to Ober from Oxford on September 30, 1943, "I am working on a thing now. It will be about 10-15 thousand words. It is a fable, an indictment of war perhaps, and for that reason may not be acceptable now. I am writing it out in a sort of synopsis."[11] By November 17th, Faulkner had sent in fifty-one pages of his fable to Ober with a carbon to Bacher and Hathaway. Ober was impressed with the story.[12]

Though living in Oxford, Faulkner was still under contract to Warner Brothers and was paying ten per cent of his studio income to Herndon. It seems, however, that the *Intruder* story still lingered in the back of Faulkner's mind. In a letter to Ober written from Oxford in December 1944, Faulkner wrote, "I am 47. I have 3 more books of my own I want to write. I am like an aging mare, who has say three more gestations in her before her time is over, and doesn't want to spend one of them breeding what she considers, (wrongly perhaps) a mule."[13] In the same letter, Faulkner told Ober that he wanted to get Hollywood out of his system. By Christmas, the fable was taking definite shape

---

[11]Ober files.

[12]*Ibid.*

[13]*Ibid.*

as a book and a definite Christ analogy was beginning to emerge. Thus, for the time being, the *Intruder* story took second place to the composition of the fable.

Faulkner, however, did not keep us his interest in his own writing. In early February 1944, he returned to Hollywood and worked on "God is My Co-Pilot" and a film version of Hemingway's "To Have and Have Not." By mid-May, he had not done any work on his fable since he had arrived in Hollywood and because of the war ("war is bad for writing"), he did not know when he would get back to it. In May, he helped with the script of "The Damned Don't Cry." From June until September, his wife and daughter visited him in Hollywood and provided a change of pace from the two scripts he was working on, "Fog Over London" and "Strangers in Our Midst." From late summer until mid-December, he wrote and rewrote with Miss Leigh Brackett the film script of Raymond Chandler's *The Big Sleep,* interrupted briefly for some writing of "Mildred Pierce." While working with Howard Hawks on "The Big Sleep," Hawks asked Faulkner why he didn't write a detective story. Faulkner replied, "I've been thinking of a nigger in his cell trying to solve his crime." When Faulkner returned home to Oxford in December, he took "The Big Sleep" with him to rewrite parts of it. Though this script dealt with detectives and murder, it did not seem to stimulate his interest in that other murder mystery he had been thinking about for some time. It seems most unlikely that "The Big Sleep" is the source for *Intruder.*

In January 1945, the ebb and flow of Faulkner's writing career reached a new intensity. On January 10th, he wrote to Cerf and Haas: "I am doing a thing which I think is pretty good. Unless I am wrong about it, have reached that time of an artist's increasing years when he no longer can judge what he is doing, I have grown up at last. . . . Well, I'm doing something different now, so different that I am writing and rewriting, weighing every word, which I never did before; I used to bang it on like an apprentice paper hanger and never look back." On January 16th, Haas wrote back and encouraged Faulkner to continue with his new idea, no doubt a renewed interest in his fable. "Well, it is good to know that you are steamed up on the new idea, and we certainly want to do all we can to cooperate."[14]　In two letters to Ober, received on January 24th and March 21st, Faulkner informed him that he has written sixty pages of the fable and that he had reduced the 100,000 words he has written to about 15,000.[15]　In June 1945, Faulkner returned to Hollywood and wrote to Ober about this time that he was rewriting the fable. "It's a novel now and not just a lot of rhetoric as when I sent it to Bob [Haas]." He asked Ober to return to him the previous portions he had sent him as he wanted to incorporate the new sections into the old.

Gradually, the fable was becoming one of the most complicated stories Faulkner was ever to write.　In Hollywood his contract had been renewed for fifty-two more weeks at $500 a week.　He worked on George Perry's novel, *The Southerner,* his own story "Barn Burning," which was never produced, and in July, completed the script of "Stallion Road."　On August 22nd, Ober received a letter telling him that the Herndon relationship was more upsetting than ever and that he was sick of being in Hollywood.[16]　Warner's lawyer, R. J. Obringer, investigated the situation more thoroughly and it was determined that Herndon had a very strong position.　Only a $10,000 settlement, at $100 a week for two years, would tempt him to allow Faulkner to break his contract with him.　Faulkner again went into depression; he had no time for his own work, was required to do more work on "Stallion Road," and refused to meet Herndon's exorbitant request.　Thus, on September 21, 1945, he left for Oxford without permission from Warner Brothers.

The familiar surroundings of northern Mississippi seemed to have put Faulkner into a better framework for getting back to his own literary interests.　During the fall, Malcom Cowley had been in contact with Random House and made arrangements with them whereby they would obtain the rights to the works of Saki if Viking Press could bring out a *Portable Faulkner* under

---

[14]*Ibid.*

[15]*Ibid.*

[16]*Ibid.*

Cowley's direction. Faulkner agreed to such an arrangement and on October 5, 1945, he wrote to Cowley telling him that he was back writing the Gavin Stevens' stories, this time about a man who planned to commit murder by means of an untameable stallion ["Knight's Gambit"].[17] By Christmas he had sent in sixty-five pages of his fable, rewritten three times in order to get them just right. Also, his "An Error in Chemistry" won second prize in the *Ellery Queen Mystery Magazine* contest and he was awarded $250 plus the sale price of $300. As with the previous year, Christmas in Oxford made him reflect on what was most important to him.

On January 5, 1946, Faulkner wrote to Ober: "In France, I am the father of a literary movement. In Europe I am considered the best American and among the first of all writers. In America, I eke out a hack's motion picture wages by winning second prize in a manufactured mystery story contest."[18] The stay in Oxford prompted him to evaluate even more his creative roots in the South, as he expressed it in a letter that month to Cowley:

> Also, as regards material [for writing], the South was the fortunate side. That war [Civil] marked a transition, the end of one age and the beginning of another, not to return. Before it in his wars man had fought man. After it, machine would fight machine. . . . Of course that doesn't explain why the North didn't use the material too. It's not enough to say that perhaps the machine which defeated his enemies was a Frankenstein which, once the Southern armies were consumed, turned on him and enslaved him and, removing him from a middle class fixed upon the land, translated him into a baronage based upon a slavery not of human beings but of machines; you cant say that because the Northerner writes about other things. Maybe the carpet-bagger is to blame, maybe it is the new blood which he brought into the South after 61 which produced the literature, and as soon as something happens to cause

---

[17] William Faulkner in Malcolm Cowley's *The Faulkner-Cowley File* (New York: Viking, 1967), p. 35.

[18] Ober files.

vast throngs of Southern middle class to move into the North, a belated Northern literature about the Civil War will spring up. Or maybe the South will be able to write all the literature about the Civil War we need and what we want is a new war, maybe a group of Dismal Swamp or Florida Everglade Abolitionists will decide to free the country from machines and will start a movement to do so, followed by a vast influx of Tennessee and Mississippi and Virginia carpet-baggers, and then the North will have a war to write about.[19]

As Faulkner was again thinking, in a way similar to Gavin in *Intruder,* in literary terms about the South, he received a visit from Thorsten Jonsson, from Stockholm's daily newspaper, *Dagens Nyheter,* who intimated to "Moon" Mullin, of the Oxford *Eagle,* that Faulkner might possibly win the Nobel Prize for Literature. Both the renewed interest in the South and intimation of literary recognition did not, however, feed and clothe his family. At this point, he had less than $500 in his bank account and he was unhappy about returning to Hollywood and writing scripts that had a good chance of not being produced. Ober and Haas thought if they could see Faulkner's contract with Warner's they could possibly find out how to release him from this obligation and encourage him to get back to writing those novels he had talked about.

Unfortunately, Faulkner could not find the contract and he was most reluctant to borrow money from Random House. On March 4th, Ober received a letter from Faulkner in which Faulkner stated, "I have at least one book in mind that I want to write too much to do justice to one I dont particularly want to write."[20] This criptic sentence, written shortly after he revised "Knight's Gambit," suggests that at this point he was not particularly anxious to write either *Intruder* or the *Knight's Gambit* volume he had suggested earlier. Ober and Haas persuaded Faulkner to remain in Oxford as mid-March approached. Blotner believes "Ober was working on the twin assumptions that Warner

---

[19]*Faulkner-Cowley File,* pp. 79-80.

[20]Ober files.

Brothers could not claim ownership in the book rights of the fable and that anyway it was not the kind of book they would want to film. If William Bacher was free of Twentieth Century-Fox as far as his share of the fable went, and if Bacher would agree to giving Warner Brothers first look at the completed manuscript, Ober felt they would consent to Faulkner's staying home for three more months to finish the book."[21] Faulkner wrote in return, "I myself have made the only request of Warner I intend to make of him, which was to cancel my contract. I took this step mainly since the studio has been lying to me ever since I got there in 1942, about destroying this contract and giving me a better one." Ober wrote to Jacob Wilk at the New York office of Warner Brothers and asked if Faulkner could finish the fable story.

On March 28th, Wilk informed Ober that Jack Warner agreed to let Faulkner finish the novel and the studio did not want the movie rights. On the same day, Ober wrote to Faulkner, "As I wired you this morning, Warner Brothers are now convinced that it would be best for you to finish your novel."[22] Random House said they would advance Faulkner the money to finish the novel. Warner Brothers prepared a quit claim on the novel and Faulkner got his advance from Random House.

Faulkner was able to resolve these contractual difficulties; on March 15, 1946, he signed a revised contract with Random House which covered the *Intruder* novel. Though Random House has no record of this revised contract, Ober wrote to Howard Rinheimer of New York City on September 20, 1951, and mentions this contract: "I am inclosing a copy of William Faulkner's contract with Random House, which he sent me in 1946. He thinks this is the contract under which his book, *Intruder in the Dust,* was published."[23]   On April 2, 1946, the legal counsel for Warner Brothers, R. J. Obringer, wrote to

---

[21]*Faulkner*, II, 1209-1210.

[22]Ober files.

[23]*Ibid.*

Faulkner and said that Mr. Warner had no objection to Faulkner finishing his novel and having it published.[24]   Later, on April 23rd, Faulkner wrote to Cowley thanking him for *The Portable Faulkner:* "The job is splendid. Damn you to hell anyway. But even if I had beat you to the idea, mine wouldn't have been this good. By God, I didn't know myself which I had tried to do, and how much I had succeeded. . . . Random House and Ober lit a fire under Warner, I dont know how, and I am here until September anyway, on a dole from Random House, working on what seems now to me to be my magnum o."[25] Faulkner again returned to his fable, a book judging from the hundreds of pages of typescript, must have taken superhuman effort to write and revise. Faulkner's legal troubles seem quite miniscule compared with the psychic and creative energy he was putting into this work.

By May, Faulkner had sent fifty more pages of his fable to Haas and on June 26, 1946, Ober wrote Faulkner saying he had received from Haas 150 pages of this latest novel.[26] The pages began to mount up. By July 3rd, Faulkner wrote Ober saying he was still working on the fable and five days later Ober wrote saying he had received pages 122-178 and he was adding these to the rest from Haas.[27] Thus by the end of July 1946, Ober had 178 pages of this fable. Faulkner began to see the totality of the novel and in a letter received by Ober on August 12th, Faulkner said he expected to finish the novel by January 1947 or thereabouts.[28]   By August, Ober had received 200 pages and by October 250 pages. And then in late October, Faulkner stopped working on this story. On November 18, Ober received a letter from Faulkner indicating that he would take a four-week respite

---

[24]*Ibid.*

[25]*Faulkner-Cowley File,* pp. 90-91.

[26]Ober files.

[27]*Ibid.*

[28]*Ibid.*

from the novel because of his involvement with a film script.[29] Encouraged by Ober's letter of December 10, 1946, ("The arrangement with Warner's is that you are to continue with your novel until you finish it."), Faulkner went back to his own writing in mid-December.[30] Thus Faulkner could write Cowley before the end of the year: "Am on Random House's cuff, to write a book, wont go back to Cal. until Random House gets tired and money ceases. I shall get back to work at it, now that the weather's too bad here to hunt."[31] There seemed little or no let-up from the demands of this novel.

Faulkner continued to struggle with his fable while remaining in Oxford. On March 24, 1947, Ober received a letter from him saying that he was sending the revision of pages 229-275 of the fable. "I know every word in the book now but I dont write as fast as I used to. It will take another year, probably two."[32] Faulkner continued to remain in Oxford during the spring and summer of that year. On June 9th, Ober received a letter saying Faulkner was still revising his novel.[33] Ober received another letter from Faulkner on July 16, 1947: "At present I have about 400 consecutive pages, plus notes. I believe the book will run at least 1000."[34] Faulkner thus projected that he would finish the novel in 1948; he thought the best plan would be for him to go back to Hollywood in January 1948 and work there for six or eight months. These plans were tentative and no decision had to be made immediately. In late August, Faulkner wrote from Oxford to Haas:

---

[29]*Ibid.*

[30]*Ibid.*

[31]*Faulkner-Cowley File*, pp. 97-98.

[32]Ober files.

[33]*Ibid.*

[34]*Ibid.*

The mss. is going all right. Slow though but so far I have not let that worry me much. I mean having to write it on credit like this. I am now in the middle of a hundred page new chapter which itself is a good story, a complete novelette, about a white man and an old Negro preacher and the preacher's 14 year old grandson who stole a crippled racehorse and healed its broken leg and spent the year dodging from one little back country track to the next racing the horse before the police ever caught them, then the white man shot the horse. They did it not to win money but because (the horse was a valuable champion) its owner would have retired it to stud because of its ruined leg while the thieves knew that what the horse wanted to do was to run races; a champion: a giant among horses.

On August 26, 1947, Ober wrote Faulkner, "Bob Haas just called me up and read me a paragraph from your letter to him, saying that you are half-way through that part of your novel about a racehorse and a white man and an old Negro preacher."[35] Thus about four months before Faulkner began writing *Intruder*, he was deeply into a section of his fable that dealt with an elderly Negro and two assistants, an English groom and a black boy; he would use similar characters in his mystery story.

Many critics of *A Fable* have tried to appreciate, often not with great success, the function of this racehorse story in the context of the entire novel. In early September 1947, Faulkner tried to explain the purpose of this story to Haas: "It describes what caused a man to do or be capable of doing in one single act which carries on the story of the mss. itself. The reason may be 1. This is perhaps the last book I'll write and I am putting all the rest of it into it, or 2. It may contain the germs of several more books." In early fall, Faulkner found that the writing was not as rapid as he had earlier imagined. He wrote to Haas: "This stuff is taking me longer than I ever had to take writing before; I get tired, stale, begin to worry about its slowness while I am drawing money against it and I begin to worry about the money (unearned). Then I think of Hollywood; that

---

[35]*Ibid.*

after all, I can go back there and get out of arrears again." On October 7, 1947, Ober received a letter from Faulkner saying "at very best another year to finish the book, maybe more, maybe it will take five more, I dont know. You yourself have an idea of the amount of rewriting I seem to have to do to get it right."[36] A week later, Faulkner had reason for encouragement: Robert Linscott of Random House told him that the *Partisan Review* might purchase the racehorse story for $1000. Faulkner finally finished this section, ninety pages in all with what he thought was a sustained tone throughout. He gave permission for *Partisan Review* to make any stylistic changes they wanted to, knowing that when the book came out from Random House, he would insist on the original form as he wrote it.

Random House and the *Partisan Review* were not the only people interested in Faulkner's latest endeavor. On October 28, 1947, Ober wrote to Faulkner, "I have been looking for the portion of your book, about the horse. When do you think you can get it to me?"[37] Ober wanted to send it out to such magazine's as *The Saturday Evening Post* and *Collier's*. On November 3rd, Ober wrote to Faulkner saying that he had received pages 120-y to 120-z-42 of the novel.[38] Eleven days later Ober, who had been in communication with Random House, received word that Faulkner had forwarded the ninety-page horse race story.[39] This was sent to the *Partisan Review*. On November 26th, Faulkner learned after returning from a hunting trip that the *Partisan Review* had rejected the story. Philip Rahv of the *Partisan Review* regretted the decision, particularly because he had raised everyone's hopes before reading the manuscript.

For a while, Faulkner misunderstood the nature of this rejection; he thought a revision of the story would make it

---

[36]*Ibid.*

[37]*Ibid.*

[38]*Ibid.*

[39]*Ibid.*

acceptable. On December 1, 1947, Ober received a letter from Faulkner: "As I wrote before, it could well begin with the lawyer's arrival in the town, and what he found there and tried to do with it. I could write a page or so of synopsis, explaining who stole the horse and what his reason seemed to be, and what became of him and the horse up to the moment when the lawyer reached the town, then let the piece carry on from there. This would cut the piece to 60 pages [from 90]. If this is still too long, I suggest they simply lift what they wish where they wish and print it simply as a fragment or fragments from a work. Though the last 60 pages are a complete story in a way: an anecdote anyway of a mob (man at his basest) performing an act of right and justice despite himself, because of base motives. They freed two thieves not because of pity for them but because they would defend at all costs man's right to get that much money, no matter how."[40] It should be noted where Faulkner himself places the emphasis of this story—on the base motives of the mob, the matter of justice is secondary. This preoccupation with the base motives of the mob was a theme he used in *Intruder* too.

The refusal from *Partisan Review* continued to bother Faulkner and he reflected on what might be wrong either with the story or with the readers. In a letter which Ober received on December 9th, Faulkner wrote: "I have an idea that this may have been PR's reason [for refusing the story] : The world has been so beat and battered about the head during the last few years that man is in a state of spiritual cowardice; all his bottom, reserve, strength has to go into physical stamina and there is nothing left to be very concerned with art. That that magazine does not exist now which would have printed sections from Ulysses as in the 1920's. And that the man crouching in a Mississippi hole trying to shape into some form of art his summation and conception of the human heart and spirit in terms of the cerebral, the simple imagination, is as out of place and in a way as a man trying to make an Egyptian water wheel in the middle of the Bessemer foundry would be."[41] Faulkner saw the model

---

[40]*Ibid.*

[41]*Ibid.*

he was working on as somehow analogous with Joyce's innovative masterpiece, and so he did not pity himself, but recognized that the cerebral imagination at work in this fable would not be appreciated by a generation preoccupied by the basic facts of human survival. Faulkner wanted Ober's opinion: "What is your opinion of this stuff? Will anybody read it in the next say 25 years? Are Random House by taking me on absolute faith as they have, wasting their money on it? My own time doesn't count; I dont believe I am wasting it or I would have stopped before now. There is nothing wrong with the book as it will be, only it may be 50 years before the world can stop to read it. It's too long, too deliberate." Then came the realization that the horse race story had been rejected outright.

No author likes his material to be rejected, especially when he considers it part of his *magnum opus*. Perhaps what Faulkner needed to do during this time was to make his cerebral vision of man and the forces within man working to achieve honor, pity, compassion, and pride more vivid in a shorter, more visual story. Temperamentally, the rejection of the horse race episode might have been one of the factors that prompted him to write *Intruder*. Another might have been the death of Ned Barnett, the Faulkner handyman who had been with the family for years. During Christmas time, Old Ned went to Ripley, Mississippi, and Faulkner went back to the town of his grandfather to attend to the last rites of this faithful black man who resembled, in many ways, the character of Lucas Beauchamp. By the end of January 1948, Ober had nearly 500 pages of the fable. Faulkner had been exhausted by the writing of this novel and he had much more to do before it was completed. He thought he would take some time off and write something short.

During 1948, Faulkner stayed in Oxford most of the time with only a brief trip to New York and Connecticut in the fall. On February 1, 1948, he wrote to Ober:

> On Jan 15th I put the big mss aside and I now have 60 pages of an approximate 120 page short novel set in my apocryphal Jefferson. The story is a mystery-murder though there is more relationship between Negro and white, specifically or rather the premise being that the white people in the south, before the North or the govt. or anyone else, owe and must pay a responsibility to

the Negro. But its a story; nobody preaches in it. I may have told you the idea, which I have had for some time—a Negro in jail accused of murder and waiting for the white folks to drag him out and pour gasoline over him and set him on fire, is the detective, solves the crime because he goddamn has to keep from being lynched, by asking people to go somewhere and look at something and then come back and tell him what they found.

I should finish it in another 3 weeks. Please tell Bob [Haas] about it; it might make him feel better about me. Tell him I suggest sending it first to you for possible magazine serial sale, then he will have it for a book. 120 pages is short, but it will make a book wont it?

I hope this idea will please Bob. I've been on Random H's cuff for a long time now.[42]

Thus Faulkner has shifted the theme he had been dealing with in the horse race story and expressed it in *Intruder* in terms of responsibility to the Negro by the white people. The black man in the fable is a preacher; in the story nobody preaches. This is in keeping with the original draft of the novel where nobody does preach, at least in the ecclesiastical sense, such as the preaching Reverend Shegog does at the end of *The Sound and The Fury*. But the setting copy, the second version of this story, has Gavin reflecting on the condition of the South in such a way that he could be said to be preaching, because the tone he assumes has a ministerial quality about it. Faulkner also suggests that the lynching of the Negro will be by setting him on fire, a device he used in *Sanctuary* with Lee Goodwin.

It is difficult to determine the exact pace at which Faulkner wrote *Intruder,* though it looks like he started off by writing approximately four pages a day. On February 9, 1948, he wrote to a neighbor, Mr. Russell, and suggested that they settle their mutual problem. Mr. Russell's cows had been wandering onto Faulkner's property and Faulkner wanted this stopped. A draft of this letter on [110 (V)] occurs in the fifth chapter of the

---

[42]*Ibid.*

original draft of the *Intruder* typescripts.[43]   Since this letter
occurs on the verso of the eighty-fifth page that Faulkner typed,
it is somewhat reasonable to assume that the letter and the
composition of this page of typescript occurred about the
same time. At this time, too, H. L. Mencken, the literary wit
and newspaperman from Baltimore, wrote requesting that Faulkner send some of his novels to a German professor at the University of Berlin who was preparing some lectures on Faulkner.
On February 22nd, Faulkner asked Haas to take care of this task.
He also mentioned that the Bureau of Internal Revenue wanted
$1,700 in back taxes for 1944 and that he needed $500 for state
income taxes by March 15th:

> I have finished the first draft of the new mss. Am rewriting it
> now, a little more of a book than I thought at first so the rewrite
> will actually be the writing of it, which will take some time yet.
> I wont set a date; I'll just work at it.

> Am arguing with the Rev dept over 1944 additional income tax.
> They owe me about $2200.00, claim I owe them $3900.00 I may
> have to pay the 3900 before they pay me the 2200.00. Also must
> pay income 1947.

> I imagine I can put the feds off for a while even after assessed,
> though the int. will climb. But if necessary, can I have this 3900
> plus about 500 for state? or (2) can I have difference between 39
> and 22 hundred, plus 500 for state?

> In either case, can I have extra 500 before March 15th to pay
> state? Will need this regardless.

> Can you do anything about the enclosed from Mencken?[44]

True to his schedule, he had been writing about four pages a day

---

[43]The numbers in brackets refer to the typescript pages of *Intruder*
that are found in the Alderman Library of the University of Virginia. See
Appendix A for a complete explanation.

[44]Random House files.

steadily and by February 22nd had finished approximately 120 pages of the first draft. The second and final version would be more than twice the length of the first. Judging from the final pages of the first draft, it looked like Faulkner was eager to start over again and give the novel a coherence it lacked the first time through.

On February 24th, Haas replied to Faulkner's letter:

> It was nice to get your note and to learn that the new book is going to be even more of an opus than you had planned. Keep me posted, won't you please, about the completion date, as we'd like to get it out just as soon as we can.
>
> As to the finances, sure, Bill, if you need it we will send you the $3,900. I don't have to tell you, however, that I'd like it even better if it were only $1,700. The $500 that you need right now state tax is enclosed.
>
> All this brings to mind the fact that you will recall we gave you a $2,000 advance back in May, 1940, for a novel. This is all right, too, but with your permission I'd like to transfer this sum to your general account, which I think is fair in the circumstances. So unless you let me know to the contrary, I'll fix it that way. O.K.?

A postscript notes that Haas is taking care of the material Mencken wanted.

Later that month, Ben Wasson, an old friend of Faulkner's and Hodding Carter, the editor of the Greenville *Democrat-Times,* visited Faulkner. They wanted The Levee Press to publish the horse race story and Faulkner consented to a signed limited edition as it would mean additional income for him. Faulkner told Haas that each copy of this edition would cost $2.50 and he would receive 25% of that. "I want to do it mainly to confound the people who say nothing good [can come] out of Miss. The Press is less than a year old, is already getting known even though in slightly precious circles, like the Yale reviews etc. Its foundation is Carter's Greenville daily newspaper. His name is familiar to you, probably, lecturer, liberal champion of Negro [against] injustice though no radical, no communist despite Bilbo and Rankin." Faulkner included a report on *Intruder:* "New mss is bigger than I thought. It is a good story, not just a document.

It's going to be longer than I thought, possibly over 200 pages in place of 130. It's going all right." Thus Faulkner appears genuinely pleased with this latest novel, though he must have been growing tired after writing constantly over such a long period of time.

On March 3rd, Haas wrote to Faulkner: "In your last note, you said that you were still uncertain as to when you might complete the story of the negro in jail. Is the date any clearer in your mind now? Don't think for a moment, please, that I am trying to put on any pressure. I wouldn't dream of doing that. All I am thinking about is the mechanics of lists, catalogues, and such. Advance informaion is always helpful, but I know you will get it to me just as soon as you can." On the bottom of this letter, Faulkner made the following comments and returned the letter to Haas:

> Yes, all right about the contract.

> This novel should certainly be ready for fall list. See no reason why you should not have it say by June 1st, but I seem to write so much slower, have to do so much more rewriting before sentences come exactly right than I used to, that I am a little afraid to commit myself.

> By the way, first time in my experience, I cant find a title. I want a word, a dignified (or more dignified) synonym for 'shenanigan,' 'skullduggery'; maybe legal-quasi-latin word, for title like this:

> Shenanigan
> Skullduggery   IN THE DUST
> Jugglery

> Maybe Saxe can think of one. The story is: a murdered man is buried. When someone [digs] him up to prove how he was killed, another man's body has been substituted for him. When the law opens the grave to find out what goes there, there is nobody in the coffin at all.

A day later, Haas replied to Faulkner's query about the titles for the new novel: "Thanks for your notations on the second page of my letter to you of March 3. I appreciate your agreement regarding royalty rates. I am delighted that you think the manuscript will be along by June 1st. I haven't any doubt that we will be able to think of a title that will satisfy you, if you yourself don't beat us to the gun. I'll tell Saxe about the problem, and, if you don't mind, would like to do a little thinking about it myself. It would be fun."[45]   Haas eventually listed five suggested titles of his own:

Imposture in the Dust
Masquerade " "   "
Strategem " "   "
Pattern " "   "
Cabal " "   " 46

With these eight possible titles, Faulkner at least had some words to think about. He had previously used the title *Flags in the Dust* as the original title for *Sartoris*, but the word he wanted this time had to have a certain character about it and he would wait a while longer before making a final decision.

On April 6th, Ober wrote to Faulkner, "I haven't heard from you lately. How are you getting along with the short novel."[47]   In addition to his writing, Faulkner had been considering a suggestion of Malcolm Cowley's that he bring out a collection of short stories and so he had asked Haas to draw up a list of possible titles. On April 9th, Haas received a letter from Faulkner:

> Yours received. The short story volume is all right. I agree, better be stuff not in a book yet. I will go over your list carefully later; think a few changes in your starred list, one or two on it I dont consider first rate and I think one or two omitted which I do. Will attend to that later for this reason.

---

[45]*Ibid.*

[46]*Ibid.*

[47]Ober files.

I'm on the last chapter in the present mss. It will be about 275 pages in all [actually the last page is numbered 281], maybe more. I believe I will have it in to you before May 15th, so it can be the next published. Then the short stories.

I thought first this one would be about 120 pages. It has grown with rewriting, which is why it has taken longer than I thought, as I finished first draft in 6 weeks. You should have it in plenty of time for next spring, as your letter fixed, that is '49 pubn.

I will see to proper copyright of Levee Press piece.[48]

Thus the dates of the composition of *Intruder* become fairly clear:

January 15, 1948—the start of the original draft.

February 9, 1948—written up to p. 85 of original draft.

February 22, 1948—finished original draft and started on the final version (which became the setting copy).

April 9, 1948—working on last chapter of final version.

On April 23rd, Haas received the following letter from Faulkner:

The mss. is finished and goes to you by express within the next day or so.

I'm sending it to you instead of Ober because I still dont have a title, haven't found that word yet which means substitution by sharp practice IN THE DUST.

Please think again, ask Saxe, Don [Klopfer], Bennett, anyone, think of other titles besides ? IN THE DUST if necessary. JUGGLERY is the nearest I know, but harsh ugly word. Just thought of IMPOSTURE, not too it.

---

[48]Random House files.

INTRUDER? in the etc.

Let me know what you think of the book. It started out to be a simple quick 150 page whodunit but jumped the traces, strikes me as being a pretty good study of a 16 year old boy who over-night became a man.

Will take a few days off from writing, then will write you about what I had better do, that is if Random H. will continue to carry me on the other mss. or what to do.[49]

Faulkner could now relax. He had written a book in an extra-ordinarily short amount of time and now he could turn his attention to other matters.

Towards the end of April Faulkner wrote to Haas reviewing the matter of an appropriate title for the newly completed novel:

No, I mislaid the original of suggestions.

I like CABAL for its shortness, but the substitution wasn't a mutual plot. This is true of MASQUERADE.

Temporarily will hold to Imposture, but make it:

IMPOSTOR IN THE DUST

? INTRUDER IN THE DUST ?

SLEEPER IN THE DUST Sleeper in the sense of the forgotten chip on the poker or roulette table, only slumber and death too synonymous; nobody would recognize the other significance.

? MALFEASANCE IN THE DUST ? too long.

? SUBSTITUTION IN THE DUST ?

Since looking at it, I am beginning to like MALFEASANCE.

---

[49]*Ibid.*

?   MALAPROP IN THE DUST   ?   too esoteric?

MALPRACTICE IN THE DUST

TROUBLE IN THE DUST

6 hours later: I believe INTRUDER IN THE DUST is best yet. I cant think of a single good synonym for sleight of hand, which is actually what we want. If anyone thinks of anything better, do so.

Tuesday [April 27] —Still like

INTRUDER IN THE DUST.[50]

Faulkner had finally arrived at a title that suited him, although he was still open to further suggestions.

As ever, he still had to meet his creditors and pay his income taxes. Warner Brothers had told him he could finish his fable if he wanted to before resuming his Hollywood obligations. In early May he wrote to Bennett Cerf:

As Bob probably told you, I was victim of additional income tax assessment for 1944 recently, and Bob agreed that rather than me going back to Cal. on movie pay, I would stay here and keep at mss. and stall the people off. I will owe them $360 or 70 odd June 15th. The whole sum is about $2000.00 but for now they demand the 370 by 15th. Will you send me additional say $375.00 to meet that one?

I would like to come up this fall, haven't seen anybody to talk to in 8 years now. I will have to borrow money to come on though, unless a studio buys the book. No, I have never even seen Mrs. Cerf. Dont know how you are as a husband but Random House has been a good papa to me so maybe you are all right in that capacity just as the least porter in the vatican partakes a little of heaven too.

---

[50]*Ibid.*

Thus, at this point in his life, Faulkner was beginning to think about establishing personal relationships in New York, ones that would be helpful to him when he needed friends.

With the recent experience of having the *Partisan Review* reject the racehorse story, Faulkner gave considerable attention to the form of *Intruder* should it be serialized in a magazine. In late April he wrote to Ober:

> I sent Bob the finished mss. last week, asking him to let you see it with idea of magazine serial sale.
>
> As it is now, it is a mystery story plus a little sociology and psychology. If a mag wants a simple story, we can eliminate chapter IX, take the story from where old Gowrie says '. . .take our son home.' and go straight to the jail that night when the boy and his uncle see the sheriff and Lucas leave to trap the murderer, cut out all except the essential story line of the three people waiting in the lawyer's office, as it is written as the lawyer explains and sums up just what happened. The book can end with that chapter, X, with Miss Habersham's speech: 'That will be nice.' or the last Chapter, XI, can be included as is, or pared down to its essential story matter, which is to show that the sheriff and Lucas were successful, Lucas vindicated, murderer caught, etc.
>
> I suggest this as a point you can offer if editors balk at mss. for popular consumption as is. This paring, editing, as you see, will leave it a simple story of movement.
>
> You can add that I will do this work myself.
>
> Will you telephone Bob and tell him the jist of this?[51]

In all probability, as Faulkner was writing to Ober with instructions concerning a possible magazine sale, Haas was worried about the plans Faulkner had in mind. Should he try and get the novel serialized and then publish it or would Faulkner prefer

---

[51]Letter in Professor Blotner's files. I did not find this material in the Ober files, as might be expected.

to have the novel published and forego any serialization?

In a letter written to Haas, apparently on April 28th, Faulkner explained his plans:

> Your wire just came. These two enclosures explain themselves. I agree to any publication date you like of course. But would like the extra money from a magazine sale if possible. The letter to Harold explains itself regarding such a sale. If you agree to let him try to sell it for mag. publication before you print, forward the letter to him when you send him the mss. This is of course in case a mag. ed. will want the mss. changed, simplified to bare story.
>
> I'm glad you like the mss.
>
> I will assume you will continue to send the monthly check until we have a chance to get together about it.
>
> I will not get seriously or steadily back at the other mss. until this year's planting, farming, is done, about July 4th, though I shall work at it from time to time.
>
> I hope Bennett will like it too. He must be mad at me. I haven't heard hide nor hair of him in years.
>
> Am inclined for INTRUDER IN THE DUST.[52]

Thus, soon after finishing writing the novel, Faulkner had selected a title, one that he would not change.

Early in May, while Ober waited for Haas to send him the manuscript so he could offer it for sale to a magazine, Faulkner took an opportunity to write to Cerf and resume an ever-increasing bond between these two men:

> I dont quite like BEAT FOUR as title.

---

[52]Random House files.

Beat Four was only incidentally the villain and was not the hero; it was no concerted assault by Beat Four on humanity.

Secondly, every county is divided into what corresponds to beats in Mississippi and other states too; it would be like renaming Grand Hotel Floor Ten.

BEAT FOUR doesn't strike my ear in this case, anymore than Range Four or Township Four would. COUNTY would come nearer fitting.

I wish we could think of a pleasanter word than JUGGLERY. But lacking any short word for substitution, swap, exchange, sleight-of-hand, I think INTRUDER IN THE DUST is best. I am not bound to it, but I dont think Beat Four is right at all. As it is, it means nothing. Then if you let the story give it a significance, you foist the wrong significance on it. Beat Four did no more than all the rest of the county would have in those circumstances.[53]

Faulkner had made his final comment in the title, having given more attention to it than we would suspect he would, a writer who favored short, seemingly unpoetic titles.

On May 5, 1948, Ober received a letter giving permission for the *Sewanee Review* to use "A Courtship."[54] In this letter, Faulkner mentioned to Ober that he had written Haas concerning the selling of the new novel to a magazine. In reply, Ober wrote to Faulkner, "Bob Haas has talked to me at some length about your newest novel, and I agree with him that the wisest thing to do is to get it published in book form this autumn. I am sure you would have to do a good deal of rewriting on it before any magazine editor could make up his mind whether he could use it, and this might result in a lot of work without any reward and also would be a good deal of delay, so that the book couldn't be published for another year. I really don't think the chances of a magazine sale would be good enough to advise

---

[53]Random House files.

[54]Ober files.

you to go to all this trouble."[55]　As a result of these letters, the novel was never serialized as such, though it did appear twice in different forms, once as an abridgment in the December 1948 issue of *Omnibook* and then as an example of fiction in *Prose for Comparison* (Norton Publishers, 1956) under the title "Jefferson, Mississippi."

With the setting copy sent in to Random House, Faulkner still had to deal with the novel in one form or another. Blotner notes that from the time Faulkner had been with Hal Smith, there had been no written agreement about who should negotiate the sale of Faulkner's novels and stories to the film studios. Although Ober had dealt with the movie studios on other matters, Random House handled movie sales, a perogative they received from Smith and Haas. In a letter apparently written in mid-May, Faulkner wrote to Cerf concerning the movie rights to *Intruder:* "re my wire: I think Warner should have first shot at buying the book. I dont know if you are up to date about my status, but Bob and Harold Ober know, as all communication was through Ober. Warner agreed to hold no claim on what I did while on leave, but my relations have been amicable with them, about getting time away when I insisted, no great fuss about it. And since they did not become stuffy about relinquishing claim to movie rights on what I do while off their pay, I would like to give them the refusal, then let Cagney [Productions] see it. What do you think? I suggest you talk to Ober about it before you talk to Cagney's people."[56]　In typical fashion, Faulkner was starting a contractual process that would get him into trouble for a short time.

During this time, the typescripts were going through the usual editorial process and there were two pages of suggested editorial emendations and two pages of reply by Faulkner, which will be discussed later. Saxe Commins did not work on this manuscript since he was busy with other work. Instead, Albert Erskine, who recently came to Random House from Reynal and

---

[55]*Ibid.*

[56]Random House files.

Hitchcock, edited the setting copy. Erskine, originally from Memphis, had studied at Louisiana State University and edited the *Southern Review;* he was a careful reader of the text and as he told me did not burden Faulkner with minutiae, but tried to achieve a uniformity in the text that Faulkner sometimes overlooked (see Appendices B and C).

The records of Harold Ober reveal that Ober received an excerpt of *Intruder* concerning Lucas Beauchamp from the publisher on May 12th. This material presumably consisted of pages from the typescript of the novel, as the piece was retyped and the original returned to Random House on May 14th. The Random House records show that the composition order for the printer was made on May 28th. According to James Meriwether, the Ober files contain a twenty-six page carbon typescript of this material and constitutes with minor differences the first two chapters of the novel.[57]   On the verso of the last page of the setting copy [605], there is noted "Received June 1, 1948." This is the date that the printers probably received the setting copy after it had been edited and started setting it up in type. On the verso of [158] of the setting copy is the date "June 18, 1948," possibly the date when the printer finished setting the type. These two dates, plus the letter to Russell, are the important dates in determining where the original draft and the setting copy were at any one point of time.

One June 21st, Miss Anne Louise Davis, Ober's secretary, wrote a memo to Ober saying that Knox Burger of *Collier's* called about the Faulkner novel that Random House is publishing.[58]   Burger had seen parts of the typescript and thought *Collier's* might be interested in publishing it and wondered if he could see the novel. Miss Davis told Burger that there was only one copy of the novel and that the galleys would not be ready until the 29th. Burger asked about the possibility of Random House deferring the publication should *Collier's* not be able to

---

[57]Information supplied by Professor James B. Meriwether. See also my discussion of page [198].

[58]Ober files.

publish it by September.

After writing *Intruder,* Faulkner had some leisure time. On June 26th, Professor Carvel Collins came to see Oxford, Mississippi and Ole Miss in preparation for a seminar at Harvard University on Faulkner's works. Miss Margaret Parker, a friend of Professor Harry Campbell who was a former colleague of Collins, took Collins to visit the Faulkners at Rowan Oak. They had a pleasant chat, skirting most the time literary topics, and the next day, Collins, Miss Parker, and Lamar Stephens, a friend of Faulkner's stepson, Malcolm, went to Ripley to take pictures of scenes connected with the Faulkner family and legend.

The galleys for *Intruder* were received on July 7, 1948.[59] Four days later, Random House sold the movie rights of *Intruder* to M-G-M for $50,000, with Faulkner receiving $40,000 of this. The rest being Random House's commission. Faulkner decided to take $10,000 of this money immediately and receive $10,000 each year for the next three years in order to spread out the tax payments on this income. Ironically, Faulkner began to know a sense of financial security, this time from a place that had often robbed him of emotional and creative security: Hollywood.

When Erskine was editing the typescript setting copy, he showed it with Haas' permission to Miss Carol Brandt, the Eastern story editor of M-G-M. When the galleys were sent out for bids, Miss Brandt phoned Cerf and bid $50,000 for the movie rights. Cerf accepted her offer. Miss Brandt had seen the typescript before any of the other movie companies had a chance to and therefore could make such an immediate bid.

In mid-July, Faulkner wrote to Cerf requesting a change in the galleys which he had not previously made: "In the chapter when Miss H. and the two boys reach the country church that night and throw the flashlight on the tombstone." The tombstone should read:

---

[59]For more information concerning the galleys of *Intruder,* cf. James B. Meriwether's "Short Fiction of Faulkner" in *Proof I* (Columbia: University of South Carolina Press, 1971), p. 320.

AMANDA WORKITT

wife of

N. B. Forrest Gowrie

(date)   (date)
birth   death

Faulkner continued the letter by telling Cerf that he was pleased about the negotiations for *Intruder*. He wanted Warner to be notified that the novel was finished and for sale to interested parties: "Since this was done, I'm satisfied and immensely pleased over your stout effort with the other party [probably a reference to M-G-M]." The sale of *Intruder* to M-G-M, however, did not go unnoticed by the other companies who began to complain that they did not have sufficient time to place their bids with Random House.

Elsa Neuberger of the New York office of Vangard Films wrote to Ivan von Auw at Random House on July 13th saying that her firm was disappointed the "William Faulkner novel, which I had understood you were handling, was not submitted to this office before its purchase by Metro [M-G-M]."[60] The next day, Jacob Wilk of Warner Brothers wrote a telegram to Cerf: "AMAZED AT THE REPORT THAT YOU AND FAULKNER HAVE CLOSED DEAL JULY 11 WITH METRO FOR "INTRUDER IN THE DUST" AFTER YOUR MAY 11TH ASSURANCE TO DON MOORE THAT WARNERS SHOULD HAVE FIRST REFUSAL. WOULD LIKE IMMEDIATE REPLY BECAUSE YOU KNOW OBER SUBMITTED GALLEYS TO US JULY 8TH. STUDIO HAS NOT YET HAD AN OPPORTUNITY TO MAKE DECISION."[61] That same day, Ober wrote to Faulkner:

I am delighted for you over the MGM sale of your novel. This

---

[60]Ober files.

[61]*Ibid.*

will give you freedom to finish your long novel.

I had lunch yesterday with Wilk of Warner Brothers, and he told me that he understood they were offering you a new service contract. He said he would give me the details about it in a day or two. I should think that with the MGM sale, you wouldn't have to think about going to Hollywood for a long, long time. If they should send the new agreement down to you, I am sure you will not sign it without letting me look it over. If they send it to me, I will let you know about it.

As I understand your situation with Warners, it is that you don't have to go back to Hollywood ever to work if you don't want to, but if you do want to work there you will have to work for Warners, as they could probably prevent you from working for any other studio.

The Saturday Evening Post is now reading INTRUDER IN THE DUST. I have been trying for a long while to get a copy of this book for the Post, but saw it for the first time only last week, when I got a set of proofs. As you know, Bob Haas has been abroad for a couple of months; if he had been there, I think I would have been able to get a copy of the novel. I hope there is still time for the Post to use it, if they decide they want it. I have never had a chance myself to read the novel, as Random House sent the one copy off to the printers immediately, and the one set of proofs I got last week I had to hand over to the Post the moment they came in. I hope to get another set shortly, and then I am going to sit down and read it.[62]

Sometime in late July, two attempts were made to place an exerpt of *Intruder* for sale in a magazine. The records do not reveal the number of galleys involved nor what part of the book the galleys were from. On July 19th, Ober received a reply from Faulkner:

Yours received. Sorry you didn't see mss. I thought you had. I sent it direct to Bob, mainly as some concrete return on their

---

[62]*Ibid.*

advances to me, assuming that you would see it immediately. The letter I had in reply, I think from Bob, said as I recall that it had been decided the chance for magazine sale was so slight that they would go ahead with immediate book printing at once. In fact, I wrote Bob and offered to edit the mss. for a mag., with brief synopsis of what I would delete.

He may be right and there is no chance of sale. I hope so however, so you can share in the spoils, since it was your effort with Warner that gave me the freedom to write it in recess from the other, which I will not get back at.

Will see you this fall I think. I want to come up and consult you and Bob both about what to do with this money so my friends and kinfolks dont or cant borrow and spent it.[63]

While Faulkner was thinking about going to New York, the last of the complaints about the sale of the movie rights of *Intruder* was heard. On July 22nd, someone with the initials "pw" sent a memo to Ober and von Auw saying that Universal Studios had just found out about the sale of *Intruder* to M-G-M and they were upset that Random House had sold the rights.[64] It seems that Universal had originally called Random House to ask about the rights and were told that Ober Associates (actually, as noted before, Random House handled Faulkner's movie rights) were handling the rights for this movie. Somewhere in the confusion, they missed out on making a bid at the proper time.

On August 14th, Haas received a letter from Faulkner: "No, I wasn't sick. I was spending most of the time on water. Govt. built a big flood control dam in local river. Here, we have a big pond 11 miles long. A retired army man and 2 friends built a houseboat, 44 x 14, lugger engine. I am his only help in sailing it, I supervised the launching and since have been busy helping them learn to sail a biggish craft, set out two cans to moor between, marked channels, etc., getting her shaken down." His

---

[63]*Ibid.*

[64]*Ibid.*

excursions on Sardis were interrupted only briefly. Because of some technical errors in signing the movie contract for *Intruder,* Faulkner was obliged to sign the contract again on August 16th. When Manny Harper received the second contract, Faulkner wrote:

> Us country folk in Miss. dont know very much about these long fine-print contracts. We just pass our word and have done.
>
> So my notary may have mixed things up too much. Maybe you can get enough clean pages by shuffling them about, and let me have the buggered up one.
>
> Or maybe they will be all right. In any case, here they are. I signed where you indicated anyway, though Miss [Ruby] McCoy's notarising may have gone astray here and there.
>
> I think we all did mighty well on this book. I have not read the contract, since your legal staff has checked it and I couldn't make head nor tail of it anyway; too much verbiage for me.[65]

In mid-September, Faulkner turned his attention to the dedication of *Intruder.* He wrote to Haas: "I have been more or less out of circulation for the last two weeks. So I didn't get your word about a dedication. I dont have one and anyway you did quite right to go ahead since you didn't hear. This is just to say I didn't ignore it." On September 15, Faulkner went to New Orleans with W. W. Joor, an Oxford accountant, to discuss the 1944 income tax bill with government representatives. It must have been a relief coming home and knowing that the tax bill had been reduced by $1000. On September 27, Faulkner could breathe another sigh of relief: *Intruder* was published. Millgate notes "*Intruder in the Dust* was the first novel of Faulkner's to have appeared since *Go Down, Moses,* more than six years earlier; it seemed to speak out with a new directness and explicitness upon a burning issue of the day, and it sold more copies (about 18,000 in the first year) than any of his previous books had done. *Intruder in the Dust,* indeed, completed what

---

[65]Random House files.

The Portable Faulkner had begun, the re-establishment of Faulkner as a literary nobility."[66] Random House continued to feel proud of one of their famous authors and in September decided to continue with a stipend of $500 monthly to Faulkner as an advance on his fable. He had received $7000 since the sale of *Intruder* and $1000 for reprinting portions of this novel. He needed a vacation and had the finances to take one.

During the summer of 1948, Malcolm Cowley had done some research on Hemingway's life in preparation for an article in *Life*. Robert Coughlan wanted Cowley to follow the Hemingway article with one on Faulkner. Likewise in late September, Hamilton Basso had been asked by *The New Yorker* to write a personality sketch of Faulkner. After contacting Faulkner about this he received a letter from Faulkner saying that while he was welcome to come to Oxford, but he would prefer that he not have his private life written up in an article. This feeling of privacy had always been a dominant trait in Faulkner's personality and now as he was becoming better known throughout the nation and the world, he would take more precautions not to have this privacy invaded by reporters or curiosity seekers. He would always welcome old friends as he did during this time. Mrs. Helen Baird Lyman and her two sons, Guy and Jim, visited the Faulkners and received an inscribed copy of *Intruder*.

In two letters to Haas, on September 18th and 28th, he mentioned his plans about visiting New York for a while and working some more on the volume of collected short stories. He asked Haas to send again a list of short story titles: "Please send me a copy of this list. I would like to mull it over, try to give this volume an integrated form of its own, like the Moses book if possible, or at least These 13." Faulkner had not put aside his interest in the fable. "The big mss. is coming, but slow at present. I will probably not get seriously at it until winter and the bad weather. With four years ahead free of money worries, that is having to borrow from you as I did for 3 years, I will get a lot done on it; I may get hot and finish it next year. I got thrown for a slight loss last month with an ulcer which still

---

[66]*Achievement of William Faulkner*, p. 47.

bothers me a little. But it is getting better and next month I hope to feel like coming up for a week or so; then I will get back at the big mss. in earnest." In a lighter vein, Faulkner had to decide where he would stay once in New York. "Malcolm Cowley was kind enough to offer the Harvard Club, but being an old Yale man (vide the two days I spent at the Yale Club on your cuff in 1935) this might be lese majesty, unless it may be considered post graduate work." Faulkner spent three more weeks at Rowan Oak before his memorable visit to New York.[67]

Faulkner arrived in LaGuardia Airport on Monday, October 18, 1948, and took a taxi to the Algonquin Hotel, a favorite for the litterateurs of the day. Cerf had said he would meet Faulkner at the airport, but Faulkner did not want to interrupt the Cerfs who were entertaining Sinclair Lewis. The next day Faulkner visited the Random House offices on Madison Avenue, an impressive brownstone built in the 1880's by Henry Villard behind St. Patrick's Cathedral. He was greeted by Cerf, Klopfer, Commins, Erskine and others of the Random House staff. That night the Haases gave a dinner party for Malcom and Muriel Cowley, Don and Pat Klopfer, Bennett and Phyllis Cerf, Harrison "Hal" Smith, and Eric "Jim" Devine. On October 20th, he had some of the usual engagements in the morning, then lunch at "21" with Klopfer, and in the afternoon an interview with Ralph Thompson of the New York *Times.* During this trip to New York City two interviews were published.

The first few paragraphs from the "On the Books" section of the New York *Herald Tribune Weekly Book Review* for October 31st carried the following interview with John K. Hutchens:

> Up from Oxford, Miss., on this first visit in ten years to New York, William Faulkner preferred—as on other visits—not to talk

---

[67]Random House microfilm archives. On September 22nd, an agreement was signed with Chatto and Windus for the British Empire rights (except Canada) for *Intruder.* Also, on September 29th, Bennett Cerf agreed to let *Omnibook* publish a 25,000-word abridgment of *Intruder* for $2,000.

about his writing. Small, graying, still very shy, he sat the other day in the mansion of his publisher, Random House, and said: 'I think of myself as a farmer, not a writer.' But finally he did say something about his writing. He said that for several years he has been at work on a 'big book' that will need five or six years more, the longest, single effort of his career thus far. "I call it,' said Mr. Faulkner, 'a fable based on the story of the Crucifixion and the Resurrection,' and that would be all for the moment, please, about that.

In the eight years between his last novel and his current one, *Intruder in the Dust,* he hasn't done much writing, he said—only the fable-in-progress and his new book. Not many short stories, because 'I never wrote a short story I liked.' He didn't like 'The Bear'? Yes, but he didn't call that a short story. A short story is 3,000 words or less. Anything more is, well, a piece of writing.

Not much reading, either, except of 'the old books,' to which he goes back regularly: *Don Quixote, Moby Dick, The Nigger of the Narcissus* and Dickens; and he carries a one-volume Shakespeare wherever he goes, though he doesn't travel much. ('Too many people,' he said.) In the last fifteen years he has not read a book by a contemporary.

He would rather talk of the life around him in Oxford, though 'this is a bad time.' He guesses the Dixiecrats will carry Mississippi this Tuesday, and 'I'd be a Dixiecrat myself if they hadn't hollered "nigger." I'm a States' Rights man. Hodding Carter's a good man, and he's right when he says the solution of the Negro problem belongs to the South.' He paused a moment and added, with mild irony: 'There isn't a Southerner alive who doesn't curse the day the first Northern ship captain landed a Negro slave in this country.'

He once avoided reviews of his books, but now he reads them, and he appreciates the high estimate most critics have of him. He especially liked the *Portable Faulkner* which Malcolm Cowley edited, though he regretted it, in a way.

'I planned to get out a book like that myself some day, when I was all written out,' he said.

The interview with Ralph Thompson appeared in the New York

Times on November 7th as follows:

There are, according to a recent issue of a literary quarterly, 'images of linear discreteness' in William Faulkner's fiction. Also 'images of curve.'

Mr. Faulkner is a shy man. This sort of lingo makes him shyer still. In town the other day from his home in Oxford, Miss., he did his best to be accommodating, but clearly preferred to talk about almost anything except curves and linear discreteness. No, he hadn't seen the piece in the quarterly. No, he didn't much care about reading such pieces. Long silence. 'Look,' he said at last, 'I'm just a writer. Not a literary man.'

Small, sharp-nosed, gray-haired, he shifted uncomfortably in his chair. 'I write about people. Maybe all sorts of symbols and images get in—I don't know. When a good carpenter builds something, he puts the nails where they belong. Maybe they make a fancy pattern when he's through, but that's not why he put them in that way.

'I'm just a writer. I wrote about the Civil War because I'd heard about it all my life. I knew where every battle was fought. As a boy I saw General Longstreet once. I marched up to him and said, "General, what happened to you at Gettysburg?" The old man about blew his top.

'I write about the people around Oxford. I know them, and they know me. They don't much care what I write. "Why, look here," they say. "Bill Faulkner's gone and got his picture in the New York paper. It says here he's written a book." So they come around and try to borrow money, figuring I've made a million dollars. Or else they look twice and figure I couldn't make a thousand.

'I got to be a writer pretty much by chance. After the first war I was down in New Orleans, bumming around. Met Sherwood Anderson. I thought he led a good life—worked a few hours during the day, and sat around evenings talking and drinking. So I went off and wrote a novel myself: *Soldiers' Pay*. When it was done, Sherwood said, "Bill, if you promise you won't make me read it, I'll tell Horace Liveright to bring it out."

'Sure enough, Liveright did. In those days I was a free man. Had one pair of pants, one pair of shoes, and an old trenchcoat with a pocket big enough for a whisky bottle. Now I get stacks of letters asking what I eat for breakfast and what about curves and linear discreteness. Suppose I ought to answer them, but I don't. Got my own work to do, and haven't got a secretary.'[68]

Both interviews reveal the laconic charm Faulkner had with those reporters who did not press him too hard. The interviews, however, do not reveal the emotional pressures Faulkner must have been experiencing.

When Ruth Ford, an old friend of the Faulkner family (she had dated Dean Swift Falkner), called on October 19th to invite Faulkner to a party, his voice did not sound quite right to her. By the 22nd, she learned that Faulkner had missed a number of appointments and was not answering the phone at all. Was Faulkner sick? It was soon apparent that he had been drinking for three days and eating little if anything. With Haas and a few friends, Cowley made arrangements to take him to Fieldstone Sanitarium on 250th Street. Ruth Ford and Harvey Breit visited Faulkner the next day and he pleaded that they help him get released. Finally they decided a visit to the Cowley's in Sherman, Connecticut, might provide the quiet rest Faulkner needed. On October 23rd, Cowley drove to New York and with Breit and Ruth Ford he took Faulkner out of the city and back to his house in Sherman. Breit and Ruth Ford went to the outskirts of New York City and then returned.

Under Cowley's care, Faulkner began to recuperate and gradually confided in Cowley and talked about himself and his life in the South. Cowley, in turn, wrote summaries of his discussions with Faulkner in his notebook. During this visit, Cowley and Faulkner discussed the arrangement of the *Collected Stories* and concluded that the arrangement should be by subject

---

[68]The allusion in the first paragraph is to Richard Chase's article "The Stone and the Crucifixion: Faulkner's *Light in August*," *Kenyon Review*, 10 (Autumn 1948), 539-51. The *Times* story (not in Meriwether's account) mentions that 2,500 volumes of obscene works were seized in Philadelphia recently and the booksellers were indicted on criminal charges.

matter: "Then he told me about his new novel, of which he has written 500 pages. It is about Christ in the French army, a corporal with a squad of 12 men—and a general who is Antichrist and takes him up on a hill and offers him the world. Symbolic and unreal, except for 300 wild pages about a three-legged racehorse in Tennessee. Mary Magdalene and the other two Marys. There is a strange mutiny in which the soldiers on both sides simply refuse to fight. The corporal's body is chosen for that of the Unknown Soldier. Christ (or his disciple) lives again in the crowd."[69] They discussed a wide range of topics: the title, *A Fable*, and how Faulkner would have preferred rebus of a cross, but his publishers argued against this; about working for Warner Brothers where he thought "The Southerner," done in collaboration with Jean Renoir, was his best picture; about Caroline Barr, the black woman who cared for him and his family for many years. They took a drive across the foothills of the Taconic Range into the Harlem Valley.

On October 26, 1948, Cowley noted that Faulkner had returned to New York by train. Symbolically the book Faulkner had as he caught the train was one he borrowed from Cowley, Charles Jackson's *The Lost Weekend.* He brought the book back with him to Oxford. When Faulkner arrived in New York, Breit took Faulkner, at Ruth Ford's suggestion, to the planetarium and at 7 P.M. they went to Ruth's apartment for dinner. In his notebook, Cowley tried to highlight Faulkner's visit. After a brief autobiographical sketch, he mentioned, "We talked about *Intruder in the Dust,* though without mentioning my review; I assumed that he hadn't read it. Still, what he said about Gavin Stevens may have been an indirect answer to my interpretation of the novel. Stevens, he explained, was not speaking for the author, but for the best type of liberal Southerners; that is how they feel about the Negroes. 'If the race problems were just left to the children,' Faulkner told me, 'they'd be solved soon enough. It's the grown-ups and especially the women who keep the prejudice alive.' "[70] In addition, Fraulkner explained to

---

[69]*Faulkner-Cowley File*, p. 105.

[70]*Ibid.*, pp. 110-111.

Cowley that in Mississippi the counties are divided into "beats" which in the midwest correspond to townships. Whenever there are many voters in a beat, the roads get more attention. For example, behind Faulkner's farm, an old plantation is broken up into little freeholdings owned by Negroes and since there isn't a vote for a few miles between the highway and river, there isn't a road either. Faulkner's ambition, as he explained it, "is to put everything into one sentence—not only the present but the whole past on which it depends and which keeps overtaking the present, second by second." Perhaps he had *Intruder* in mind when he said, "There are some kinds of writing that you have to do very fast, like riding a bicycle on a tightrope." Faulkner was able to explain to Cowley all that the reporters had wanted to know, but which he could not explain in a public forum.

By Monday, November 1, 1948, Faulkner was busy at work in Oxford trying to think of a suitable forward for the *Collected Stories;* the best he could do was to paraphrase one by Henryk Sienkiewicz: "This book written in. . .travail (he may have said even agony and sacrifice) for the uplifting of men's hearts." As Cowley noted, *Pan Michael,* the book Faulkner was referring to, has no forward, but the last sentence reads, "Here ends this series of books, written in the course of a number of years and with no little toil, for the strengthening of men's hearts."[71] Cowley thought this was the genesis of the Nobel Prize speech. John Faulkner connects *Intruder* with this speech: "When Bill received word he had won the Nobel Prize, I fully believed he was about written out. He had said years ago that if that happened, he'd turn to writing mystery stories. One thing about them, he said, was that once you found a formula that worked, you could keep on using it over and over, by simply changing names and places. That's what he was fooling around with, I think, in *Intruder in the Dust,* in which an innocent man is saved from a mob and the guilty party caught by comparing the fatal bullet with the weapons belonging to two other suspects."[72]

---

[71]Henryk Sienkiewicz, *Pan Michael,* trans. Samuel Bincon (Philadelphia: Henry Altemors, 1898), p. 529.

[72]*My Brother Bill* (New York: Trident Press, 1963), p. 240.

Faulkner subscribed to Sienkiewicz's literary philosophy and then in his letter to Cowley outlined the order of the short stories and indicated he would do the forward.

Though Cowley kept one ear on the presidential election, he was also attentive to what Faulkner was saying too. He liked Faulkner's arrangement of the stories, though Faulkner did not take his advice on this arrangement. On November 11th, Faulkner wrote to Haas that he was working on the big manuscript and was preparing for another hunting trip. When he returned from this trip, he told a student, Miss Doyle Halford of Mississippi College, that he was writing a story concerning a lawyer who solved a case and prevented a murder. On Wednesday, November 24th, the New York *Times* reported that John Steinbeck, Mark Van Doren, Leon Kroll (an artist and designer), and Faulkner, were elected members of the American Academy of Arts and Letters:

> The academy is limited to fifty members selected from the 250 members of the National Institute of Arts and Letters, who must be citizens, either native or naturalized, 'qualified by notable achievement in the fields of art, literature and music,' and dedicated to the furtherance of those arts.

> Mr. Faulkner lives in Oxford, Miss., and was educated at the University of Mississippi. His best known novels are "Absalom, Absalom," [sic] "Sanctuary," and "As I Lay Dying." He recently published "Intruder in the Dust." In 1939 he won first prize in the O. Henry Memorial Award.

Faulkner later explained that the telegraph must have been misplaced and he did not formally acknowledge his membership until December 31, 1948. On November 29th, Ober wrote to Faulkner thanking him for his visit of New York and, in what must have appeared as a mystery to him, congratulating him on his election to the Academy.[73] Also in late November, Howard Horton of M-G-M visited the Faulkners and walked around Oxford imagining room for a hundred people M-G-M might bring

---

[73] Ober files.

in to film *Intruder* the following April. The University agreed to house at least that number. This must have pleased Director Clarence Brown who wanted to film on location.

As he planned the volume of collected stories, it must have become evident that the Gavin Stevens' stories could be collected, too, into a single volume. Probably on Wednesday, December 1st, Faulkner wrote to Commins and asked him to talk to Bennett and Haas about "what I seem to be hottest on now, would like first, is another volume." He explained what he meant. "I am thinking of a 'Gavin Stevens' volume, more or less detective stories. I have four or five short pieces, averaging 20 pages, in which Stevens solves or prevents crime to protect the weak, right injustice, or punish evil. There is one more which no one has bought. The reason is, it is a novel which I tried to compress into short story length. It is a love story, in which Stevens prevents a crime (murder) not for justice but to gain (he is now fifty plus) the childhood sweetheart which he had lost 20 years ago. It will probably run about 150 pages, which should make a volume as big as *INTRUDER*." Faulkner anticipated a fall 1949 publication date. On December 8th, Commins replied and gave Faulkner the encouragement he needed. Since he had a choice of which books he would like to have reprinted, Faulkner preferred *Absalom, Absalom!*. Not only was he planning three new volumes, but he now could name the books he would like reprinted.

Towards the end of December, Faulkner wrote to Haas: "Tell Saxe I am working on the Gavin Stevens book at present, rewriting the long story, novella of which he knows." On December 30th, he wrote to Random House: "Yours at hand. Since the estimated tax is not due until Jan 15th, I am all right. As soon after Jan 1st as practicable, will you send me $4,000.00. This will leave $6,000.00 of the next MGM payment or $500.00 per month. 12 months. I thought of you and Miss Merle, Xmas, had a drink to you both *in absentia,* and will do the same tomorrow night."[74] Since Faulkner planned on receiving the remaining $6,000 in monthly installments as they had agreed on, this

---

[74]Random House files.

would mean that he would not be pressured into writing his fable, in addition to assembling the other two volumes.

Faulkner also began to reflect some more on his privacy now that he was back at Rowan Oak. On January 5th, 1949, he wrote Cowley about not trying to do the *Life* article:

> I have waited two weeks, and am still no nearer getting into the dentist's chair. About 10 years ago I had no little difficulty in convincing Life (or somebody) that I didn't want a piece about me in their mag., and two years ago it took six months and a considerable correspondence and telegrams to convince Vogue that I would have no part of their same project.
>
> I still dont want it, I mean, me as a private individual, my past, my family, my house. I would prefer nothing about the books, but they are in the public domain and I was paid for that right. The only plan I can accept is one giving me the privilege of editing the result. Which means I will want to blue pencil everything which even intimates that something breathing and moving sat behind the typewriter which produced the books.
>
> I imagine this wont go down with LIFE. I imagine the last thing on earth they will pay their good money for is a piece about somebody's mere output even though art, since I imagine they dont care two whoops in the bad place about art but only about what they would call 'personalities.' But I am still trying to think of some workable approach so you can collect on it. I haven't done it yet, since I cant know what or how much you can do keeping me out; that is how much material suitable to Life will be left.
>
> This is a damned bastardly clumsy letter. I'm trying to say No, but in a ten-page polysyllable since conscience, heart, liking and what dregs of gratitude I might possess forbid that simple rapid word. Write me again, lets see if we cant work out something Life will take.[75]

The January 10, 1949 issue of *Life* featured the article on

---

[75]*Faulkner-Cowley File*, pp. 121-122.

Hemingway. Over four years later (October 5 and 12, 1953), *Life* carried a series on Faulkner. Though he tried very hard, Faulkner would never remain a totally private individual.

As Faulkner was looking ahead with the three books he had in mind, he was not finished with *Intruder* however. He wanted to add something to one of Gavin's speeches. Critics of this novel often mention that Gavin's long and abstract remarks about the role of the Negro in the South and the fate of civil rights have rendered the novel less effective than it might have been. Faulkner maintained that when Gavin was "a county attorney, an amateur Sherlock Holmes, then he was at home, but he got out of that. He got into a real world in which people anguished and suffered, not simply did things which they shouldn't do. And he wasn't as prepared to cope with people who were following their own bent, not for profit but simply because they had to. That is, he knew a good deal less about people than he knew about the law and the ways of evidence and drawing the right conclusions from what he saw with his legal mind. When he had to deal with people, he was an amateur, he was—at times he had a good deal less judgment than his nephew did."[76] As Olga Vickery observed, Gavin continually puts a cushion of words between himself and the world of people, events, and human experiences.[77] He deals with the past in such a way as almost to sterilize its power; he needs the help of an old woman and two young boys to dramatize his philosophical beliefs.

In the latter part of *Intruder*, Gavin refers to Lucas Beauchamp, now considered innocent of murder, and the other Negroes in the South as "Sambo," a term not used pejoratively in this situation. Gavin believes that the Southerners and the New Englanders are the only homogeneous groups in America, though most of the New England homogeneity has been lost. The Negro, too, has a mode of homogeneity which Gavin praises.

---

[76] *Faulkner in the University*, p. 140.

[77] Olga Vickery, "Gavin Stevens: From Rhetoric to Dialectic," *Faulkner Studies*, 2 (Spring 1953), 2.

Sambo has survived certain historical periods when liberty was surrendered to a demagogue and he may even survive the time when freedom is allowed to exist. In Gavin's view, the South must continue to band together against the federal government which has gradually absorbed the personal liberty of its citizens.

About four months after the publication of *Intruder*, Faulkner considered adding new material, expanding Gavin's theory of Negro homogeneity. In an unsigned letter on Random House stationery dated January 10, 1949 and marked "COPY" in red letters Faulkner is asked about the possibility of changing the story titles in *Go Down, Moses, The Hamlet*, and *The Wild Palms*, and about the possibility of changing the story titles in *Go Down, Moses* to numbers in order to express better the unity of the book as a novel.[78] The third paragraph of this letter contains the following (I have altered the spelling and punctuation when necessary): "Are there, by any chance, any other corrections you would like made in any of the three books? I know you'll realize they are plated, but if you want slight changes, just say so and we'll fix." On the reverse side of this letter Faulkner typed:

> Mystic trace of Norman, so that in five hundred years or perhaps less than that all America can paraphrase the tag line of a book by another Mississipian about 20 years ago, in which a fictitious Canadian said to a fictitious Mississippian in a dormitory room in a not too authentic Harvard: 'I who regard you will have also sprung from the loins of African kings". . . .'

In a letter to Haas sent from Oxford, Mississippi, on "Wednesday" January 26, 1949, Faulkner apologized for misplacing Haas's recent correspondence.[79] In this letter Faulkner indicated his concern about the title of *Go Down, Moses* and concluded with a short paragraph about some new material for *Intruder in the Dust:*

---

[78]This is found in Series VIII, Item 18 of the Faulkner Collection, Alderman Library.

[79]Blotner's files.

I did not receive the copy of the MOSES jacket. MOSES is indeed a novel. I would not eliminate the story or the section titles. Do you think it necessary to number these stories like chapters? Why not reprint exactly, but change the title from GO DOWN, MOSES and other stories, to simply: GO DOWN, MOSES, with whatever change is necessary in the jacket description. We did THE UNVANQUISHED in this manner, without either confusion or anticipation of such; and, for that matter. THE WILD PALMS had two completely unrelated stories in it. Yet nobody thought it should be titled THE WILD PALMS and another story. Indeed, if you will permit me to say so at this late date, nobody but Random House seemed to labor under the impression that GO DOWN MOSES should be titled 'and other stories.' I remember the shock (mild) I got when I saw the printed title page. I say reprint it, call it simply GO DOWN MOSES, which was the way I set it in to you 8 years ago.

No, don't know of any changes in the three sets of plates. But if we ever reprint INTRUDER, I left something out of it which I would like very much to put in. A single page, or 3 to make the smooth insert, will do it. I remembered it last year only after the book was in press.

At this point, it looks like Faulkner had not made up his mind as to the exact wording of the new material since he could expand it from one page to three if he wanted to.

In a letter dated January 31st, Haas thanked Faulkner for the inscribed copy of *Intruder in the Dust* which Faulkner was sending from Oxford.[80]   Haas agreed to change the title page of *Go Down, Moses* to meet Faulkner's wishes, though Faulkner himself was a bit ambiguous about the title; in the January 26th letter he is not clear whether he wants a comma in the title or not. In his final paragraphy, Haas wrote: "As for the omission in *Intruder,* if you'll send me the material you have in mind, we'll try to get it into reprints, should there be any." In early February, Faulkner replied to Haas's letter and sent him the new material (again, I have corrected the spelling slightly):

---

[80] *Ibid.*

William Faulkner INTRUDER IN THE DUST
7 Feb. 1949
Dear Bob:

Here is the insert for INTRUDER re our recent correspondence.

Page 156 [of the 1948 edition] as set down through end of the paragraph, Stevens' speech ending: '. . . .hide from one another behind a loud lipservice to a flag.'

(INSERT—NEW MATTER)

'But what will happen?' he said. 'What will we do and he do, both of us, all of us. What will become of him—Sambo?'

'I just told you,' his uncle said. 'He will disappear. There are not enough of him to resist, to repel, to hold intact his integrity even if he wished to remain a Negro. In time he would have got equity and justice without even asking for it. But by insisting on social equality, what he is actually demanding is racial extinction. Three hundred years ago he didn't exist in America; five hundred years from now he will have vanished and will be no more. Oh, he will still exist now and then as isolate and insulate phenomena, incorrigible, tieless, anachronic and paradox; archaeological and geological expeditions will stumble on him occasionally by individuals and even intact nests in caves in remote Tennessee and Carolina mountain fastnesses or Mississippi and Alabama and Louisiana swamps or, generations ago lost and unrecorded, in the mapless back areas of Detroit or Los Angeles tenement districts; travellers passing through the rotundas of the Croydon or Le Bourget or La Guardia airports or the supra transfer stations of space ships will gape at him intact

[Page Two]

with banjo and hound and screenless mudchinked cabin and naked pickaninnies playing with empty snuff-bottles in the dust, even to the washpot in the backyard and his bandana-turbaned mate bending over it, as the Union Pacific railroad used to establish tepecs of authentically costumed Blackfoot and Shoshone Indians in the lobby of the Commodore Hotel. But as a race he will be no more; his blood will exist only in the dusty files of genealogical societies for the members of what will then be the Daughters of the Founding Fathers or the Lost Causes to wrangle and brag over as the Briton does over his mystic trace of Norman, so that in five hundred years or perhaps even less than that, all America can paraphrase the tag line of a book a novel of about twenty years ago by another Mississippian, a mild retiring little man over yonder at Oxford, in which a fictitious Canadian said to a fictitious self-lacerated Southerner in a dormitory room in a not too authentic Harvard: "I who regard you will have also sprung from the loins of African kings".'

(RESUME: P 156)

Now they were there and not too long behind the sheriff. For though the car etc etc CONTINUED[81]

In this section which Faulkner wanted inserted into the second printing of *Intruder,* three points are worth considering: Gavin's elaboration on the fusion of the white and Negro races, the thematic link Faulkner establishes between *Intruder in the Dust* and *Absalom, Absalom!,* and the reference to himself as the mild, retiring, little man from Oxford. The "confederation" of the white and Negro races would mean that the Negroes, and presumably the whites too, would disappear as races, though small enclaves of Negroes would exist for tourists and archeologists to see from time to time. Thus Faulkner has raised the issue of racial intermarriage to a national concern and not just a regional one. In *Absalom, Absalom!,* when Miss Rosa Coldfield and Quentin Compson visit Sutpen's house in September 1910, they see Jim Bond, the last of the Sutpen dynasty, who repre-

---

[81]This is found in Series 1A, Item 14C of the Faulkner Collection, Alderman Library. The first page is 21 cm. x 28 cm. on onion skin. There are two pages of the second page: the original on bond paper (21.5 cm. x 27.8 cm.); a carbon of the above on onion skin (21 cm. x 28 cm.). For a brief explanation of this material, see my article "New Material for Faulkner's *Intruder in the Dust,*" in *A Faulkner Miscellany,* ed. James B. Meriwether (Jackson: University Press of Mississippi, 1974), pp. 107-112. The material that Faulkner wanted included in the second printing of *Intruder* is reproduced at the front of this present book.

sents the degenerate conclusion of the fusion of the two races. Bond appears almost the opposite of what Gavin envisions when he proclaims "that only from homogeneity comes anything of a people or for a people of durable and lasting value. . . ."[82]   Yet the Canadian, Shreve McCannon, thinks that the Jim Bonds of this world will capture the western hemisphere and will eventually be fully assimilated into their environment.   In a few thousand years, Shreve fancifully projects that he himself "will also have sprung from the loins of African kings."[83]   These two novels contain certain common elements (murder, mystery, miscegenation, youthful narrators) and it would seem that Faulkner, by connecting these two novels with a reference to himself, would like his readers to explore these relationships, a suggestion he rarely gives in his fiction. After this, at least in his correspondence and interviews, Faulkner gave little public notice to *Intruder.*

On February 2, 1949, Clarence Brown and four assistants came to look at possible film locations. Brown pleaded his case before the Civic Leaders' luncheon and received their enthusiastic support and forty merchants from Oxford signed a statement in the *Eagle* applauding the filming of *Intruder* in their home town. On February 3rd, the paper carried a statement by Brown: "As a Southerner, I believe this motion picture can be a great accomplishment towards nationwide better understanding of the true relationship between the races in the South and of the gradualism that is solving this very old problem. Just as Mr. Faulkner's book is the finest thing ever written about that theme." As the townsfolk of Oxford became more and more excited about the filming of *Intruder,* William Faulkner seemed to want to withdraw into himself. On February 11th, he replied to Cowley's suggestion that the focus of the *Life* article should be put on Yoknapatawpha County and not

---

[82]William Faulkner, *Intruder in the Dust* (New York: Random House, 1948), p. 154.

[83]William Faulkner, *Absalom, Absalom!* (New York: Random House, 1936), p. 278.

on Faulkner personally.[84]   Faulkner said he was sure the *Life* article on Hemingway was appropriate (he hadn't read it), and he would "protest to the last: no photographs, no recorded documents. It is my ambition to be, as a private individual, abolished and voided from history, leaving it markless, no refuse save the printed books. . . ." He wanted his epitaph to be simply, "He made the books and he died"—dramatic words which seem to signal the end of the *Intruder* period of Faulkner's life.

---

[84]*Faulkner-Cowley File,* p. 126.

II

THE ORIGINAL DRAFT

The Alderman Library of the University of Virginia at Charlottesville contains most, if not all, of the material needed for a textual study of *Intruder in the Dust.* For an exhibit on Faulkner's works at Princeton University, from May 10-August 30, 1957, Professor James B. Meriwether compiled a list of the manuscripts and typescripts of *Intruder* and included this list in his *The Literary Career of William Faulkner,* published in 1961. Meriwether lists the following 617 pages:

a. Manuscript, 8 pp. One of these is a version of the beginning of the novel. The other seven are of miscellaneous passages of dialogue between characters of the book, as if in dramatic form.

b. Typescript, 284 pp. Many manuscript corrections. There are pages, including carbons, of several different versions, none of them complete.

c. Typescript setting copy, 317 pp., plus 8 pp. front matter. Many manuscript corrections. The text is complete, and is numbered from .1 through 281, with the following thirty-six insertions: 15a, 16a, 18a, 21a, 21b, 28a, 29a, 39a, 87a, 93a, 136a, 143a, 178a, 179a, 220a, 224a, 234a, 234b, 234d, 238a, 243a, 243b, 244a, 247a, 257a, 257b, 257c, 259a, 264a, 266a, 269a, 270a, 276a. [P. 218, between pp. 217 and 220, is numbered 218-219.]

The manuscripts, typescripts and galley proofs of *Intruder,* were formally presented to the University of Virginia on June 11, 1959 where they now reside.

In a compilation of the Faulkner Collection entitled *"Man Working." 1919-1962: William Faulkner: A Catalogue of the William Faulkner Collections at the University of Virginia,* published in 1968, the compiler, Mr. Linton R. Massey, repeats the information in Meriwether's book concerning *Intruder* without any modifications. At present, according to my calculations, there are 609 pages of manuscript, typescript, and miscellaneous pages in the *Intruder* box in the Alderman Library, not 617 pages as Meriwether counted. My breakdown of this material is as follows:

> 11 pp. front matter
> 139 pp. of the original draft of *Intruder*
> 321 pp. of the setting copy of *Intruder*
> 138 pp. of miscellaneous pages
> _____
> 609 Total

How then to account for the eight-page discrepancy between my counting and Meriwether's? The problem is complicated by the fact that a complete inventory of the *Intruder* material was not always on file in the Alderman Library. Meriwether says there are 317 pages of typescript setting copy; the first page of this setting copy, however, is stamped with the job number "2 40972" which means that, if each page were counted individually, there are really 316 pages of setting copy since the first page is numbered, in effect, page two.

On July 1, 1959, a copy of Princeton's original inventory of *Intruder* with notes penciled by a student assistant arrived at the Alderman Library. The list contained the following information:

> 317 pp. of typescript setting copy
> 253 pp. of miscellaneous typescript of earlier versions
> 7 pp. of manuscript

The student assistant noted, too, "folder 4 pp" and Miss Anne Freudenberg, associate curator of the manuscript department of the Alderman Library, put a question mark after this note. Subsequently, Miss Freudenberg altered the Princeton list: she noted there were 317 pages "plus 8 pp. front material." She changed 253 pages of miscellaneous pages to "284 pp." and noted that there were seven pages of manuscript plus "autograph ms., first page, 1 page." Her total, if added up, is 617 pages.

However, she must have counted each of the pages, as I have done, and realized that there were 616 pages in all at that time, thus confirming Meriwether's count (as modified by me).

On January 4, 1960, a second list of the *Intruder* material was made; it is the same as the one found in Meriwether's *Literary Career.* Later, on August 12, 1971, a researcher removed two pages of miscellaneous typescript from the *Intruder* box since this researcher thought they were pages belonging to *Knight's Gambit* and *A Fable;* unfortunately no record was made of the page numbers of these two pages. On September 1, 1971, I removed one page ("120-2-43") and placed it in box sixteen of *A Fable.* Again on April 3, 1973, I removed one page ("23") and placed it in box fifteen of *A Fable;* this page had been placed in the *Intruder* box in August 1963, because some unidentified person thought it belonged there. Since this page had been placed in the *Intruder* box in 1963, Meriwether did not count it and since it has been replaced in its proper box, one can dismiss it.

Since Meriwether overcounted by one page, there is a seven-page discrepancy and since four of these pages were removed by a researcher and myself, there is really only a three-page discrepancy between Meriwether's count and mine. A note, dated June 22, 1959, initialed by Miss Freudenberg, reads: "3 miscellaneous typescript sheets with revisions removed before listing from this folder and combined with the rest of the miscellaneous typescript." On February 17, 1973, Miss Freudenberg told me that she was unable to remember writing this note, though she was certain it was in her handwriting. It looks like Miss Freudenberg merely moved three pages from one folder in the *Intruder* box to another folder. To account for the missing three pages, one must assume that either they have been removed from the *Intruder* box without anyone noting their removal, which is a distinct possibility, or they are somehow connected with Miss Freudenberg's note. It is possible that Miss Freudenberg counted the 616 pages first and then shifted the three pages from one folder to another and then eventually put them in another box altogether. She does not rule out this possibility. Given the incomplete running inventory of the *Intruder* material, I doubt if this three-page discrepancy can ever be fully solved.

The 609 manuscript, typescript, and miscellaneous pages of the *Intruder* material are described (both recto and verso) in Appendix A. The eleven pages of front matter include the following:

1. A piece of soiled parchment (23.1 cm. x 29.6 cm.). On the lower right hand corner of the page is stamped in red ink the job-number "40972." According to another red stamp, this page was received about 8:45 A.M., June 1, 1948. The parchment is folded in half and in the upper left quadrant is the heading "Chapter One," written by hand in pencil. Under the chapter heading is a dotted line followed by twenty-five penciled lines going half way across the top of the page. In pencil, the first paragraph, indicated by the first of the twenty-five lines, begins with the words "FRENCH-MAN'S BEND." It should be noted that this is an unusual paragraph beginning for anything connected with *Intruder*. In the upper right quadrant are three lines with the following information:

   a. Intruder in Dust [sic]
   b. 24 Bask ital
   c. Number 262 in Haddon Book—p. 727. [This book manufactured by the Haddon Craftsmen, Inc., Scranton, Pennsylvania.]

2. A rectangular piece of parchment (42.1 cm. x 34.5 cm.) with two rectangles drawn inside in pencil. In the upper right side within the drawn rectangle is penciled "Intruder in the Dust." A marginal note indicated that this lettering should be "Set same as Chapter Head/HALF-TITLE." This parchment is numbered "318 40972" and was received about 8:45 A.M. on July 12, 1948. The format of this page occurs twice in the first edition, before and after the title page.

3. A rectangular parchment (26.2 cm. x 20.2 cm.) with a piece of white paper inside. The edges of the parchment are taped back and the white paper inside is to highlight the lettering on the parchment. This is a dummy of the title page and there is an indication that it should be done in two colors. On the left side is the heading "Books by William Faulkner" with fifteen spaces underneath for book titles. On the right side is:

Intruder

in   the

Dust

by

William Faulkner

[colophon]   Random House

New York

This parchment is stamped "319 40972." Both the "I" in *Intruder* and the "D" in *Dust* are in blue ink in the first edition. On the reverse side are numbers indicating the type size for the lettering on the title page; some of these numbers are unclear:

48 pt.   18 number 1

18 pt. number 2 [?]   11/13 [?]

24 pt.

12

4. One page of manuscript (21.4 cm. x 27.7 cm. on Hammermill Bond) in Faulkner's hand. This page, written in blue ink, closely resembles page three of the first edition. On the left side of the page in pencil are the following notations:

Sunday morning

Spring

Early May

5-11. The next seven pages, all on Requisition Bond (21.4 cm. x 27.8 cm.), are Faulkner's own corrections for the film script of *Intruder*. In an interview I had with Mr. Ben Maddow, the screenwriter for *Intruder,* in Hollywood, California, on August 21, 1972, Mr. Maddow told me that he never met Faulkner, nor as far as he knew did Faulkner ever work on the screenplay for *Intruder.* Maddow loaned me a copy of the screenplay and when I compared it with the seven pages of screenplay in Faulkner's writing at the Alderman Library, I am quite certain that what Faulkner did was to get a copy of the screenplay from one of the actors or from Clarence Brown, the film's director, and then sit down and change a few scenes he did not like in the original. Most of *Intruder* was filmed on location in Oxford, Mississippi. Faulkner had been writing screenplays for a number of years and would have felt quite at home modifying the screenplay of *Intruder.* A number of the scenes in the seven-page Faulkner script merely say "OK" which means he did not want to make any changes with them; with others, however, he changed them slightly. He changed the last scene considerably to make it less sentimental. The scene numbers in the Faulkner script correspond to those of the Maddow script exactly, and since Maddow did not borrow from Faulkner, it must have been that Faulkner read Maddow's script at some point and made his own personal corrections. The scenes that Faulkner modified are numbers 249-263 and numbers 442-444.

5. This page, written in blue ink in Faulkner's hand as are the remaining six pages, is numbered "65," a reference to page sixty-five of Maddow's script. In this page, Faulkner remained close to Maddow's script, but abbreviated the dialogue and made it more succinct. The verso, written in pencil, has additional Gavin-Chick dialogue similar to that on page forty-one of the Maddow script.

6. This page is numbered "66." On the verso are pages thirty-eight and thirty-nine of the script.

7. This page is number "67," and is a new version of the above page.

8. This page is numbered "67."

9. This page is numbered "68."

10. This page is numbered "69." For scenes number 262 and number 263 on this page Faulkner wrote "OK."

11. This page is numbered "113" and corresponds to the last page in the Maddow script. Faulkner attempted to take away the message of the movie that was in the Maddow version by making the ending less explicit.

In approaching the *Intruder* manuscripts and typescripts, I originally had no specific methodology in mind, though I had profited immensely from the articles, dissertations, and books by Professors Blotner, Bowers, Fadiman, Meriwether, Millgate, Polk, and Thorpe, in addition to a number of conversations with Professor Stephen Dennis. Each of these scholars has raised important issues concerning textual studies. It is quite valid to say that these particular scholars, most of whom have dealt with Faulkner's manuscripts, have their own textual methodology. Eventually, I decided not to follow in an *a priori* fashion any specific methodology recommended by these scholars; rather, I hoped to familiarize myself completely with the *Intruder* typescripts and let the methodology emerge from this material.

Initially, I found two separate groupings in the *Intruder* box: the complete setting copy (321 pp.) and assorted miscellaneous typescript. For many weeks, I went through the miscellaneous typescript until I gradually realized that among these papers was the original draft of *Intruder* (139 pp.). The remaining 138 pages were all discarded pages which at one time had been part of the setting copy. In studying the imaginative genesis of this novel, I have tried to look closely at the typescript pages in the chronological order that Faulkner wrote them. My intention is to give a thorough evaluation of the composition and significance of this novel. I have paid particular attention to the material deleted by Faulkner, material, not available to the average reader, since this often illuminates the text as we have it.

A major difficulty in approaching these particular typescripts, one that is characteristic of most of the later Faulkner novels as far as I can tell, is that the task of finding continuity from one page to another is greatly complicated by the fact that Faulkner often used the same piece of paper two or three different times, sometimes without the logical sequence one would hope for. Until an adequate computer program is written, anyone hoping to work with these later Faulkner manuscripts and typescripts should contemplate spending tedious weeks of rearranging pages in order to discover the correct writing sequences. Here, however, is where the reward is, in understanding the subtlety of Faulkner's imagination at work.

Chapter One of the Original Draft

According to his own statements, Faulkner wrote the original draft of *Intruder* between January 15, 1948 and February 22, 1948. In the original draft, Faulkner typed more or less in order; in the setting copy, however, he agonized over various sections of the novel, often shifting pages around in complicated patterns. I have regularized some of Faulkner's spelling and deleted some of the words and phrases he crossed off; my intent, however, has been to remain faithful to what Faulkner actually thought and wrote. As mentioned previously, the numbers in brackets refer to the typescript pages of *Intruder* as explained in Appendix A.

There are twenty-two pages or parts of pages used in this first chapter of the original draft with only a moderate amount of revision. Faulkner began on [12(V)] by giving some of the facts which would begin a typical murder mystery. He indicates it was about noon when an unnamed sheriff brought Lucas Beauchamp to town, turned him over to the jailor, and then went to his office in the courthouse and put a .41 caliber Colt pistol, presumably Lucas', into the desk drawer. After typing out Lucas' full name, in the second line, Faulkner crossed it off and Lucas became an anonymous character, at least initially. The narrator, who is not omniscient, (see page [21] where the narrator has to rely on information supplied by someone else) states that the whole town and county had known that a Negro killed a white bachelor sawmill-hand and stock-trader by the name of Jake Montgomery (later changed to Vinson Gowrie).

Faulkner thus began this first chapter of the original draft with Jake Montgomery being murdered. Why he later changed the victim from Jake Montgomery to Vinson Gowrie would go beyond the evidence in the text and would become a matter of speculation. It should be remembered, however, that Jake Montgomery is eventually murdered in a later revision of the original draft. One possible clue to Lucas' guilt at this point is, as far as the community is concerned, that the gun he had possessed was old and the type one would expect him to use. Faulkner concluded the initial introduction to the story by saying that the killing of a white man by a Negro was nothing more than a temporary interruption in the sheriff's daily schedule. Lucas is mentioned by name once in this first paragraph in a sentence after the one where his name was crossed off. While Faulkner delayed identifying Lucas, it is clear that he was not trying to hide his identity.

Faulkner then turned this first page over and started the story again completely on [12]. He repeated the basic story line in the first sentence of this second attempt with some variations: at noon, the unnamed sheriff brings Lucas Beauchamp (this time his name is not crossed off) to jail, though the town and county had known since the night before that he had killed a white man (this time unnamed). This first sentence had originally been two sentences; the phrase "The boy was there" had been part of this sentence but it was crossed off and retyped as the first sentence in the second paragraph. This phrase was again modified in the second paragraph as Faulkner deleted the two words "The boy" and substituted the word "He," that is, someone who is pictured as standing "under the shed in front of the blacksmith's across from the jail" out of view, should this person's uncle walk from his office to the courthouse. Thus, there is a slight suggestion that the unnamed uncle might go to the courthouse and make arrangements to defend Lucas. In these first two paragraphs, then, Faulkner has mentioned five characters: the sheriff, Lucas Beauchamp, a murdered white man, a boy ("He"), and the boy's uncle. More and more, the focus of the first chapter is on this boy who is not given a name until page [53].

The third paragraph of [12] beginning "Because he knew Lucas Beauchamp too—" heightens the suggestion, with the word "too," that the uncle knew Lucas and might be disposed to help him. Aside from Carothers Edmonds on whose place Lucas lived seventeen miles from town, the unnamed boy knew Lucas better than anyone else because he had eaten in Lucas' house. With this information, Faulkner set the scene for a flashback; after typing "It was in the early winter two years ago. . .," the "two" is crossed off and "four" is substituted. The phrase "he had been only twelve then" was subsequently added by Faulkner. The information that the boy was only twelve had been typed in as an afterthought at this point, then deleted, and probably written in again when Faulkner reread the text. It does not change the chronology of the story however. We learn in the flashback that the uncle had been County Attorney for years and was an old friend of Carothers Edmonds who had come to see him on county business. While at supper, Edmonds invited the boy to go home with him the following day and go rabbit hunting. From this first page of typescript, it seems that Faulkner knew the direction his story would take, though he had to resolve specific details, such as chronology, as he went along.

On the bottom of [12] the uncle, Gavin, now named, tells Edmonds that his nephew has a friend ("boy") who would accompany his nephew. Since there are three boys in this section of the novel, I will refer to the unnamed boy as "the nephew" until the time Faulkner actually identifies him. Twice on the next page [13], Faulkner spelled the nephew's friend's name "Aleck Zander" and then changed the "Z" to an "S." With this short prelude to the flashback, a simple narration follows. The son of one of Edmonds' tenants came to take the unnamed nephew and Aleck Sander hunting. At one point, they crossed a footlog and, like a girl, the nephew slipped into the water. Faulkner reworked this scene on [13] by crossing off lines and inserting revisions. He added that there was ice on the creek and that the nephew was carrying a gun. Faulkner went back and inserted this new material because in the first version he had written that the nephew, once he had fallen into the water, dove to find his gun (originally the reader had not known the nephew had a gun). Thus, the various insertions and corrections are for the sake of continuity and clarity, rather than for Faulkner to set a mood or polish his style.

When Faulkner revised the above scene on [13], he noted in the margin "the pot-licker dog" which he later integrated into the setting copy. After the nephew retrieved the gun and held it up, Edmonds' boy took it. Aleck Sander held out a pole but the nephew climbed the bank without it. When the nephew looked up, he saw a Negro, Lucas Beauchamp, for the first time. Once he reached this part of the text, Faulkner went back and revised the narrative slightly, often repeating words and phrases he deleted. In the revision, the nephew sees Lucas as through a camera lens: "he saw the pair of feet and then the legs planted and motionless on the bank" [13]. It is as if Faulkner were having the nephew approach an important statue placed high on a pedestal. Lucas is viewed enigmatically, just "a face inside a Negro's skin" [13]. When Edmonds' boy addresses Lucas by name ("Mr. Lucas"), the nephew knows Lucas' identity and realizes Lucas' relationship to Edmonds' great-grandfather, as both son and slave. Lucas, called "the man" at this point "with nothing whatever in his face" [14], tells the nephew to come to his house and for Edmonds' boy, Joe, to tote the nephew's gun.

The next paragraph begins with a telling phrase: "So he [i.e., the nephew] followed, the man" [14]; later, however, Faulkner crossed off "the man." Initially the inference was that the newphew would follow Lucas almost in a quasi-biblical way, as one might follow a prophetic leader, a suggestion that is later repeated on [15]. The four then march single file: Lucas, the nephew, Joe, and Aleck Sander coming last. On their way, they pass by Edmonds' gate and the narrator suggests that the nephew should have taken the road to Edmonds' house, but for some inexplicable reason he does not; Lucas does not look back to see whether Gavin's nephew had gone through the gate or not. Lucas has some magnetic, intangible power over the nephew, though there is no suggestion of anything sinister about it.

The fourth page of the original draft continues on [12 (V)]. As the small procession approaches the house where Lucas lives, the landscape is described as a reflection of Lucas' personality: "a hill with an air solitary independent and intractible [sic]" [12 (V)]. Faulkner continually misspelled "intractable" (cf. [15], [17], [25], [32], [47], [50], [121], [162]). When the nephew approaches Lucas' cabin, he remembers the rest of the legend about Lucas, how Edmonds' father deeded to his Negro first cousin and heirs ten acres of land "an oblong of earth set forever in the middle of the two-thousand acre plantation like a postage stamp in the center of an envelope" [12 (V)], a phrase that seems to repeat the often quoted "postage stamp of native soil" phrase. The nephew imagines what it would be like here even in summer with no grass or weeds and women sweeping the dust each morning. Then in a neo-Homeric simile, the prints of chicken feet become like "a terrain in miniature out of the age of the great lizards. . ." [15]. Thus, this property takes on a mythic dimension. Faulkner then repeats a phrase he had used earlier and had modified: "he followed the man" [15] as the nephew walks behind Lucas towards the cabin. There is something special about Lucas' house and Faulkner is careful not to hurry through the murder mystery part of the story without allowing the fulness of his imagination to reveal the significance of this environment.

At this point, Faulkner's writing slows down and becomes more involved; it is almost as if he had a chance to exercise some of his famous linguistic virtuosity as he takes sixteen lines to depict the walk up to the cabin and the cabin itself:

> . . .and he followed the man up not a walk because its surface was the same dirt as the yard but it ran straight as two plumblines, bordered on each side by a row of tin cans and shards of stoneware jugs, empty bottles set into the earth, to the paintless gallery along whose edge sat more cans but larger ones—empty gallon-sized cans which once contained molasses and worn-out pails and one five-gallon can with its top cut off and half of what had once been someone's (without doubt Edmonds') kitchen hot water tank sliced long ways like a banana—out of which last summer flowers had grown and from which the dead stalks and the dried and brittle tendrils still drooped or stood, and behind them the house, the cabin, paintless too, not so much paintless as independent of and intractable to paint so that the house was not only the one possible continuation of the stern untended road but was as the carved ailanthus leaves are the Greek column's capital. [15]

The four enter the house and the nephew notices the "vast shadowy tester bed under a bright quilt" [15], a Grand Rapids dresser, and a chimney with smoldering ends of wood in it. In time, he notices too an elderly, doll-sized black woman, a figure reminiscent of Maud Butler Falkner's picture of "Callie" Barr, whose head is bound in immaculate white cloth. As Joe builds up the fire and Aleck Sander undresses, "the man" tells the nephew to strip off his clothes. He does so and sits enveloped in a quilt and the odor of Negroes, "that smell not really of a race nor actually of poverty but of a condition: an idea: a belief: an acceptance, a passive acceptance of the idea that they were not supposed to have facilities with which to bathe proper-ly. . ." [16]. The nephew is familiar with this smell and does not consciously avert to it because he had eaten the food Paralee (Aleck Sander's mother) served and knew the smell. The nephew sits "stark naked" in Lucas' house with Lucas standing over him as he had down at the creek, almost in a protective sense like a godfather after a baptismal initiation.

After this, Faulkner began to look closer at his characters. Lucas is pictured as having a gold watch-chain looped into his upper pocket, and owning a beaver hat like the boy's grand-father had, and having a nose high on the bridge "and even hooked" [17]—in all, a face that was "neither black nor white, not at all rapacious and not even scornful: just intolerant, in-tractable and composed" [17]. Once the nephew had dressed, he ate what was to have been Lucas' dinner, a typical meal of collard greens, a slice of side meat, and biscuits. At the end of [17], the nephew goes back to the bedroom and sees from there "the old woman was sitting again in the chair in the hearth corner, the man still stood with his back to the fire: and he drew the half dollar from his pocket and the old woman would have taken it but the man said:" [17]-[18]. The last part of this sentence is crossed off on [18] and then Faulkner repeats a word from [17.26], the word: "kitchens." Faulkner had come to what would develop into one of the key scenes in the novel: the nephew trying to pay Lucas for his hospitality.

After typing "kitchens" Faulkner stopped, skipped a few lines down the page, and like a screen writer typed out a the-matic statement about the novel:

> These characters and incidents are fictional, imaginative, and—
> some will say—impossible. In which case let them be accepted
> not as the puppet-play of a whodunit but as the protagonist-
> pattern of a belief that not government first but the white man of
> the South owes a responsibility to the Negro, not because of his
> past since a man or a race if it be any good can survive his past
> without having to escape from it (and the fact that the Negro has

survived his in the way he has is his proof) but because of his present condition, whether the Negro wishes to accept it or not. [18]

After the above declaration, Faulkner retyped "kitchens" on [19], then crossed it off, and picked up from [17.21] indicating that a glass of buttermilk was part of the dinner. Faulkner suggests that there might be a note of tragedy in this dinner scene. After eating, the narrator says that the nephew thought it might have been "the food which had thrown him off but he knew better, his initial error, misjudgment, had been there all the time" [19], as if Faulkner, already thinking in terms of Greek myth, were trying to point to some *hamartia.*

As has been noted, the end of [17] would have been the nephew giving Lucas money, but Faulkner crossed off this section and did not pick it up again until the middle of [19]. When the nephew offers Lucas the half-dollar (one coin) and feels "the blood in his face he stood before him [i.e., Lucas] exactly as he might have stood before his grandfather," Faulkner suggests that Lucas is somehow a grandfather figure to the nephew (Lucas and the grandfather both had beaver hats, too). Lucas merely dismisses the nephew by telling him to go and shoot his rabbit and keep out of the creek. At this stage, Faulkner did not play up the drama of this scene by having Lucas throw the coin on the floor; that came with the rewriting for the setting copy. It is clear that for the most part Faulkner had little doubt about the general story line (Chapters Nine and Ten of setting copy are notable exceptions). Once started it looked like Faulkner could compose at his typewriter with facility as the description on [15] suggests. Faulkner, however, was never sure when he wanted to terminate any particular chapter. Even in the setting copy Faulkner had difficulty with his "sense of an ending"; yet in all fairness, his chapter endings conclude with a dramatic climax, capped by a bit of dialogue, usually understated. The only exception is the end of Chapter Seven in the setting copy when the protagonists dig up the empty coffin. Even here, it does end with a "whispering pattering sound" [166]. In the setting copy but not the original draft, Faulkner concluded his first chapter with Lucas telling Joe and Aleck Sander to give the money back to the nephew and by ordering the nephew and Aleck Sander to be on their way and go hunting.

The two boys then go out chasing rabbits. Aleck Sander tells the nephew to shoot a fleeing rabbit. The nephew does not shoot; instead he takes out the half-dollar coin and flings it into the creek water as if he could psychologically wash it clean or drown it. The nephew realizes that Lucas had beaten him by being host at old Carothers McCaslin's plantation, not accepting payment, "and acting as a white landholder would." The nephew also realizes in a very personal way what the men of the county had known for a long time: they have to get Lucas to admit he is a "nigger" [20]. Only then they will accept him. Likewise, during the next six months the nephew learns a lot about Lucas: "He didn't hear it: he learned it" [20], how Lucas often addressed white people as other white people did. This bit of knowledge is continued by an example in the second flashback of the story.

One Saturday afternoon, three years before, at a cross-roads store, four miles from Edmonds' place, a crowd of towns-folk were "loafing about" as usual [21]. Noticeable were three white men from the lumber mill who had been drinking. Lucas came into the store wearing his black broadcloth suit and watch chain (no toothpick is noted here in the text) and according to the rumor something happened ("the tale didn't say what") [21]. One of the men verbally attacks Lucas. Lucas responds: "I aint a Edmonds. I dont belong to these new folks. I belong to the old lot. I'm a McCaslin." [21]. Lucas thus identifies himself as part of the old aristocracy and says that those who accuse him do not have Edmonds blood themselves. Finally Lucas is ordered out as one of the white men attempts to strike him with a plow handle. The proprietor shouts at him, "Get out of here, you fool!" [22]; yet, Faulkner knew, as he had expressed himself in letters previous to writing the novel, that Lucas, though foolish at times, had much wisdom. This vignette captures, in brief, the attitude Lucas has about himself and the attitude others have towards him.

In a quick transition, the narrator picks up the story by reflecting on the nephew's attitude towards the half-dollar. The nephew tried gradually to assume some independence and responsibility by helping his uncle at the office because of a "blind and absolute attachment for his bachelor uncle. . ." [22]. The narrator compares the nephew to another young boy who

lifts his calf over the fence once each week and "years passed
and they were a grown man and a bull, still being lifted each
day over the fence" [22]. During the first week of December,
the boy bought snuff for Lucas' wife and four cigars for Lucas
as a form of payment for the dinner he had eaten at Lucas'
house. He gave them to Edmonds to deliver to Lucas on Christmas, all the time thinking that Lucas should consider himself a
"nigger" first and then everything would be all right [23]. In
February, the boy started saving money again, without any reason being stated by the author, until by May he had enough to
buy and send to Molly, Lucas' wife, an imitation silk dress. At
this point, the nephew's emotions changed: he felt not rage,
but shame. Summer came and he was going on thirteen. Then
in September he received some homemade sorghum molasses
from Lucas delivered by a white boy. Though the narrative
seems simple enough at this point, Faulkner will later explain
the hidden complications surrounding these gifts. It is in the retelling of certain episodes that Faulkner, almost by a process of
discovery himself, reveals the tenuity of the relationships he has
established.

On [14 (V)] Faulkner indicated that now that Lucas had re-
paid his debt to the nephew, the nephew had to start all over a-
gain to gain the upper hand. The nephew could not return the
molasses, partly because he was ashamed to ride a small Shetland
pony that far. Whatever would set the nephew free, a motif
Faulkner also stressed in a short story taken from the typescripts
of the setting copy (cf. [198ⱼ) of this novel, was at this moment
beyond his ken and "he could only wait for it if it came and if it
didn't, do without it. . ." [14 (V)]. The narrative breaks off on
[14 (V)]. Faulkner probably realized that the nephew would
be put into an ambivalent situation of now being able to out-
maneuver Lucas immediately and therefore the story would
lack a sense of linear development.

Faulkner began again and returned back to the present.
He mentioned that Molly was dead and because the daughter
had moved away, Lucas lived alone. In discussing the murder,
the narrator states that Lucas was brought in at 9 A.M.
In addition, the nephew had heard talk that morning in the
barbershop when he entered town; this dialogue about
lynching Lucas on [26] is roughly the same as that on [234]-

[235] (page 40 of the first edition) with only a few words changed. It seems as if, at this point at least, Faulkner felt that he had captured the voices of the townsfolk and did not need to improve on them. He was sure what the townsfolk would say; he knew their every word.

The nephew left the shop after this dialogue: "He had seen Lucas three times more in the four years, on the Square in town and not always on Saturdays, like a prosperous or at least independent white planter or landowner, as though he refused, declined to accept that much of the pattern not only of Negro but of country Negro behavior. . ." [26]-[27]. The first time that they met again the nephew thanked Lucas for the molasses and Lucas answered "They turned out good this year" [27]. The second time the nephew saw Lucas, who did not have the toothpick in his mouth, Lucas looked straight ahead and did not recognize the nephew. The nephew thought *"He doesn't even remember me"* [27] until amost the next year when his uncle told him that Molly had recently died, thus explaining Lucas' air of indifference. "You dont have to not be a nigger in order to grieve" [27]-[28]. The nephew waited around the Square continuously until one day he realized that Lucas only came to town to pay his taxes. Then in January on a bright cold afternoon he saw Lucas for the third time, coming out of the courthouse and coming directly toward him, "then Lucas looked up and looked straight into his eyes for perhaps a half minute almost and then away and came straight on and then stepped slightly aside to pass him and went on. . ." [28]. Thus the nephew thought that his relationship with Lucas was all over.

In a crossed-off section, Faulkner next had the nephew think about going home and getting his horse. In the rewriting, Faulkner hinted at what will happen: "The store, the crossroads settlement where they said the constable was holding Lucas was fifteen miles from town, on a gravel road not too good but the sheriff should certainly go there and be back with his prisoner in two hours" [29]-[30]. Faulkner then continued with a theme that is characteristic of much of his writing: man, or in this case, a boy, in motion. "Before that time he would go home and get his horse: not to sit nursing his hands in a back upstairs room at home waiting for it to be over but to be moving, having to concentrate on motion, on the motion of the horse and on watching where it put its feet. . ." [30]. He hoped to ride in one direction for twelve hours and witness Lucas' execution and then ride back. At 10:30 A.M. on Sunday, he went down the street toward the blacksmith's, opposite the jail. As the men and women pass by until the street is empty, the boy thinks, "*What the hell am I doing here? So he can look back at me not just from the edge of death but out of a gout* [sic] *of blazing gasoline and not remember me either*" [30]-[31]. The nephew radically questions his relationship with Lucas, a relationship that is at the heart of this novel.

Suddenly the empty street becomes full of men. Then the nephew sees the car with a deputy driving. When Lucas emerges from the car, his hat falls to the ground. "He began to bend stiffly to retrieve it but already the sheriff in one vast deliberate yet curiously supple stoop had already picked it up and handed it to him and erect now he took it and pushed out the crumpled crown and creased it again and set it again on his head at the old half swaggering rake and now for the first time he looked at them, erect in the black suit a little crumpled too from whatever night he had spent (there was a long smear of dust down one side of his leg as though he had been lying on an unswept floor), his head tilted back a little looking at them without fear: just calm intractable and composed. . ." [31]-[32]. Lucas looks at the nephew and in a shock of recognition the nephew admits that he was wrong about Lucas. Lucas then tells the nephew to get his uncle. The chapter ends with the sheriff speaking to the mob, "I told you once to get out of here. I aint going to tell you again." [33]. This same sentence concludes Chapter Two of the first edition. Thus the scene begins and ends at or near noon on Sunday with Lucas arriving at the jail, giving the first chapter of the original draft a sense of completeness. The focus of this first chapter has been to establish the allegation that Lucas has killed a white man and to the present the main outlines of the Lucas-Chick (though he has not revealed Chick's name yet) relationship.

Chapter Two of the Original Draft

Faulkner began the second chapter of the original draft

with what is now the second paragraph of the third chapter of the first edition: "There were no bells now" [34]. There are twenty-six pages or parts of pages in this second chapter. Except for a few pages ([34], [50], [54], [55], [58]), the pages in this chapter were typed without much revision. Faulkner began this second chapter, by creating a mood similar to the prologue to James Agee's *A Death in the Family*, with Gavin and his nephew out walking on the evening of that Sunday night in May. In describing one of the townsfolk, Mr. Lilley, Faulkner expanded his original introduction: "But tonight they passed only one man and he was [the following words are crossed-off] not walking, but standing just inside a gate, himself darker than a shadow and certainly stiller—proprietor of a small side street grocery store whose customers were mostly Negroes, whom they had not even seen until they were right on him though he had already recognized them or anyway his uncle. . ." [34]. In revising this sentence on [35], Faulkner typed in a section about Mr. Lilley owning a grocery store, then crossed off this section, added another part concerning the uncle explaining to the nephew about hearing owls and roosters and living close to the people: "Where you were born and raised and lived all your life where you cant hear anything but owls at night and roosters at dawn. . .you like to live where you can hear and smell people. . ." [35] and then went back and for the third time put in the section about the grocery store. Gavin's short dialogue and his explanation of Mr. Lilley's behavior [36]-[37] are almost word-for-word like pages 48-49 of the first edition.

Mr. Lilley, a representative white Southerner, lives by two standards: he likes Negroes, but if one steps out of line, then lynching might be the appropriate course of action. Gavin thinks that he knows what Mr. Lilley wants: "All he requires is that they act like niggers" [36]. In this section concerning Mr. Lilley, Faulkner did not revise it much; [36]-[41] is close to pages 48-54 of the first edition. Mr. Lilley expects violent action to be taken against Lucas since Lucas allegedly committed a violent crime by killing a white man. Mr. Lilley never directly explains his philosophy; it is interpreted for us by Gavin. When Gavin and his nephew reach the Square, it is empty and the silence is broken only by a car hurriedly circling the courthouse and heading towards the jail. Then almost like a lens zooming in, Gavin explains how courthouses were "the true records of a county's history, since not only the cryptic forgotten initials and words and even phrases of defiance and indictment scratched into the walls but the very bricks and stones themselves held not in solution but in suspension intact and biding and potent and indestructible, the agonies and shames and griefs with which hearts long since unmarked and unremembered dust had strained and perhaps burst. . ." [37]. Thus Lucas' house and the courthouse are described in some detail, both with a sense of history and sympathy.

Faulkner also tells the story of an unnamed girl who scratched her name in a jail window in 1864. In a foreshadowing of Gavin's later theory concerning Lucas, the narrator presents Gavin's interpretation of this story of the young girl with the diamond ring, beginning with "and his uncle who had everything an explanation not of facts but long since beyond dry facts into something far more moving because it was truth: the truth which moved the heart. . ." [38]. At the end of the prologue to Act III of the first edition of *Requiem for a Nun*, Faulkner again made mention of this story of Cecilia Farmer, now given a name, who scratched on the window her cryptic self-proclamation: "*Listen, stranger; this was myself: this was I*" (p. 262). According to this version, Cecilia scratched her name on the window on April 16, 1861. She is described in *Requiem for a Nun* as a passive individual who has become an important part of the community's history precisely because she left her name for all to see:

> . . .a frail anemic girl with narrow workless hands lacking even the strength to milk a cow. . .the frail blonde girl not only incapable of (or at least excused from) helping her mother cook, but even of drying the dishes after her mother (or father perhaps) washed them,—musing, not even waiting for anyone or anything, as far as the town knew, not even pensive, as far as the town knew: just musing amid her blonde hair in the window facing the country town street, day after day and month after month and—as the town remembers it—year after year for what must have been three or four of them. . . . (p. 229)

In both novels, the story ends the same with the unnamed lieutenant returning to claim this young and fragile girl. It is not so much that Faulkner is manipulating the past by recounting this story, and thereby juxtaposing the romantic nostalgia connected with Cecilia to the harsh realism of Lucas' situation, but rather he is allowing the weight of Jefferson's past to find its proper expression in a description of the town.

Continuing the mood of Cecilia Farmer's story, Faulkner relates that at 8 P.M. it is quiet and only Will Legate, whose last name signified perhaps a person at a gate, guards the entrance to the jail. Soon Mr. Tubbs, the jailer ("a snuffy untidy pot bellied man" [40]) appears and warns Legate that a gun might not be enough to stop a mob. Tubbs then leads Gavin and his nephew up to see Lucas. Tubbs does not want Lucas to remain in the jail because Tubbs' wife and two children might be injured in some way:

> 'Yes,' the jailer said. Then he turned and went on, drawing from his pocket a bunch of keys. There was a barred steel door, quite modern, a little shocking, at the top of the stairs. The jailer unlocked it and swung it back but already *they had passed out of the world of man, men,* [emphasis mine] people who worked and had homes and raised families and tried to make a little more money than they perhaps deserved, by fair means of course or at least by legal, to spend a little on fun and still save some against old age because even as the steel grille which was only a skeleton of a door and a barrier swung back there seemed to rush out and down at him the lost breath of all human degradation and shame—a smell of creosote and excrement and stale vomit and incorrigibility and defiance and repudiation like something palpable against the thrusting limbs as they mounted the last steps into a corridor which was actually the main room. . . . [42]

This section was later expanded in the setting copy, where greater emphasis was put on the value of the heavy oak door at the top of the stairs. Pages [43]-[50] are similar to pages 57-65 of the first edition. In the setting copy, Faulkner also relates the story of an architect who stayed overnight in the jail. As I have noted, the act of entering this jail cell in both the original draft and the setting copy is like passing out of the world of ordinary men. Faulkner is gradually preparing his reader for some philosophical reflections on civil rights, reflections that originate when Gavin meets Lucas in Lucas' jail cell. This might explain the emphasis put on the act of entering this particular cell.

Tubbs, Gavin, and his nephew walk to the cell area and look in on five Negro prisoners who are feigning sleep. When they enter Lucas' cell, they see his coat and hat before seeing him. The nephew thinks that the mob already has taken Lucas. The nephew's interior monologue reveals an immediate response to Lucas' predicament and helps to interpret the action of the story and the sympathies involved. Lucas is sleeping in the lower bunk. At this point the nephew, like his uncle, considers Lucas guilty: "*Only a nigger could kill a man, let alone shoot him in the back, and then sleep like a baby as soon as he found something flat enough to lie down on. . .*" [44]. Lucas responds to Gavin's greeting with an air of unconcern; he gets up from the bunk stiffly, not anxious, "but doing it as if he had the rest of a natural life in which to be checked each time he moved by the old familiar catch" [44]. This crucial meeting does not get off to a propitious start.

Lucas asks Gavin, a county lawyer, to take his case and he will pay him. Gavin replies that he does not defend murderers. The nephew then remembers an old lady, a spinster, perhaps an oblique reference to Miss Habersham, who played cards with neighborhood children years before and who, like Lucas, would play the wrong cards at the wrong times. The stakes, however, soon become more like those in a poker game [46]. Gavin refuses the job and demands that Lucas tell him what happened at the store. Lucas begins by saying, "they was two folks, partners in a sawmill; leastways they was buying the lumber as the sawmill cut it—" [47]. When Lucas continues the story, he tells how the two men, Vinson Gowrie and another man, were storing lumber in order to sell it: "Only the other man was hauling it off at night, coming in at night with a truck and picking up a load, and hauling it over to Glasgow [no mention of Hollymount] and selling it and putting the money in his pocket" [48]. The nephew remembers "Ephriam" [sic], Paralee's father, who used to walk at night, too. Faulkner constantly misspelled Ephraim's name. Gavin then accuses Lucas of interfering with two white men, one of whom was stealing lumber. In a marginal note, Gavin asks Lucas what he expects. His answer, not included in the setting copy, is cleverly sardonic: " 'Nothing,' Lucas said. 'No more than I do now' " [49]. Gavin is not at all convinced by Lucas' story. At best, Gavin will have Sheriff Hampton move Lucas to Mottstown until the court can convene in June. In the setting copy, Lucas is asked the identity of the other man with Vinson Gowrie in the sawmill operation. He refuses to tell Gavin. Likewise, this short exchange is not in the original draft. Before leaving Gavin asks Lucas if he wants him to stay all night with him in the cell. Lucas shrewdly replies that he does not want Gavin talking at him until morning.

The manuscript writing at the bottom of [50] concerns Lucas' wish to have some tobacco, the means by which Chick can return to see Lucas, an afterthought which Faulkner later included here. The uncle and nephew leave and go through the cell door. The act of exiting is as impressive as the act of entering:

> They passed through it, his uncle letting him go first then drawing the flimsy similitude of bars after him and removing the padlock from the staple and slipping the hasp over it then hooking the padlock through the hasp and snapping it to again. Then his uncle turned and he was about to follow when he didn't know what it was, no sound heard: he just stopped while his uncle's feet echoes on down the corridor and turned and looked back into the cell. Lucas was standing now in the center of the floor beneath the light, looking through the flimsy mesh at him with such urgency that he believed for a second that Lucas had spoken, called his name. But he had not, he was making no sound: just looking at him with that mute and incredible urgency so that his uncle's footsteps echoed on past the turn of the corridor and were already dying away toward the stairs before he moved, turned and hurried after him. [50]-[51]

Faulkner modified the above section considerably in the setting copy, as will be seen later, by having the act of closing the door have a cosmological significance "like that ultimate cosmolined doom itself" [271].

The nephew gets tobacco for Lucas and confronts Lucas with it thinking, "*If he will just remind me of that goddam plate of collards and sidemeat I ate four years ago. Or maybe he'll tell me I'm all he's got to help him. Then I'll be free*" [53]. But Lucas does not mention any of this, thus keeping the nephew in his power. Lucas asks the nephew to go out to the cemetery and help him and for his efforts he will be paid [52].

There is no mention about riding Highboy out of Jefferson. There follows a simple directive:

> 'Go out there and look at him,' Lucas said.
> 'Go out where and look at who?' he said,
> harsh impatient and inattentive. Then he understood. He said: 'Me?' [53]

Faulkner realized the importance of this confrontation and later expanded this part of the Lucas-nephew dialogue in the setting copy:

> 'Go out where and look at who?' he said. But he understood all right. It seemed to him that he had known all the time what it would be; he thought with a kind of relief *So that's all it is* even while his automatic voice was screeching with outrage disbelief: 'Me? *Me*?' It was like something you have dreaded and feared and dodged for years until it seemed like all your life, then despite everything it happened to you and all it was was just pain, all it did was hurt and so it was all over, all finished, all right.

Faulkner puts the nephew in the middle of the spotlight and from now on the nephew will assume more and more personal responsibility.

For the first time, the nephew's name is given on [53]: Charles Mallison (no "junior" is added as in the setting copy). On [54] Charles (hereafter referred to as "Chick" since it seems clear that Faulkner preferred this nickname) repeatedly asks Lucas why he should go out to the cemetery. Faulkner crossed off some of this repetition and added in the margin that Chick should take the first right-hand turn up into the hills just beyond the "9 mile branch bridge" and that he can be there in half an hour in his uncle's automobile. He also added in the margin that the Gowries bury in Mount Hope Chapel. The deleted section at the bottom of [54] is repeated on the top of the next page; here, too, Chick tells Lucas that it would be necessary to bring in the dead body to town for examination. Faulkner crossed off this idea and started again with an inserted page. In the inserted version [56], the emphasis is on the fact that Lucas' .41 caliber Colt could not have killed Vinson. Lucas does not answer what Vinson was shot with and he says he would never tell about the gun to any white man even if he were being dragged from jail, but he would tell a child. Thus the narrator makes a distinction between a white man and a child, inferring, perhaps, the Matthaean tenet that only those who are childlike will inherit the kingdom. This episode leads quite naturally into the story of Ephraim who, like Lucas, walked at night [56].

It seems that both Chick's mother and her former girlfriend had inexpensive rings and that Chick's mother lost hers and subsequently searched for it. For a half-dollar (note this sum since it is the same amount that Chick threw into the creek) Ephraim would locate the ring. A week later, Ephraim said the ring was under the hog trough at Chick's grandfather's farm. Apparently Mrs. Downs, an old white woman, could find things if consulted. Chick was surprised that Ephraim did not spontaneously tell his mother where the ring was during the preceding week. Ephraim, like Lucas later on, then informs Chick that the minds of young folks and women "aint cluttered" [57]. Ephraim would have told Chick's mother, but she needed his form of assistance. Eventually, Chick's mother and father (without Gavin's help) went out and found the ring under the trough. The original draft differs little from the setting copy, except that the specific locale of Sweetbriar is added in the setting copy. In this revision on [58], the narrator adds deliberately that Lucas' problem is not the same as an "obscure valueless little ring."

On [280] Faulkner modified the seventeen miles which Lucas had requested Chick to go to nine, a modification not found on [58]. At the bottom of [58] Faulkner wrote in pencil: "They [i.e., Lucas' eyes] were not even urgent now and he [i.e., Chick] thought quietly: *He's not only beat me but he knows it.*" At this point Lucas again has the advantage. The final page of this original draft of the second chapter [59] ends on the note that Chick will have to dig up Vinson's dead body and get it to town where an expert can check the bullet. As Chick leaves, Lucas characteristically adds, "I'll try to wait." Faulkner ends the second chapter in a jail cell and thus did not accomplish the marginal note on [34] to "*get through to daylight.*" In this chapter, Faulkner has introduced two respected men in the Jefferson community: Gavin Stevens and Mr. Lilley. Neither of them believes that Lucas is innocent; this only heightens the Lucas-Chick relationship which is gradually assuming the nature of a trusting friendship. At the close of this chapter, Chick is on his own to assist Lucas and he has no specific guidelines to follow since he has been put into such a unique situation. In the Ephraim story, Faulkner has suggested that young people and women do not have cluttered minds, a belief that is dramatically portrayed in the next chapter.

Chapter Three of the Original Draft

Again, Faulkner noted on [60] his intention to move to daylight. Chapter Three of the original draft eventually became Chapter Four of the setting copy. There are twenty-five pages or parts of pages used in this chapter. The time on page [60] is after 8 P.M., Sunday evening, when Chick arrives home and knows he has less than four hours left to get permission to go to Mount Hope Church (not Caledonia) and dig up Vinson Gowrie's body and return. The phrase "in lieu of permission from the Gowries, which for any reason whatever, worst of all to save a nigger from being burned over a bonfire, the President of the United States himself let alone a country sheriff would never get" is added by Faulkner in pencil on [60]. Also on [60], Faulkner typed, "The door was closed; he could hear the murmur of the farmer's voice beyond it. . . ." Later, in the setting copy, the farmer's voice became a "man's voice," thus suggesting that originally a farmer might have come to see Gavin that evening, though Faulkner later explains on [62] that the man's voice belongs to Chick's uncle.

When Chick walks into the room, he sees not a farmer, but a woman, Miss Habersham, whom we are told, lives alone in a paintless, columned colonial house on the edge of the town. Faulkner then mentioned Miss Habersham's business of selling and delivering vegetables and chickens [61]. Faulkner crossed off this material and started this page over again on [62]. In the revision, Faulkner went back and included some information about Dr. Habersham, thus giving some of Miss Habersham's family background. Throughout all of this, Faulkner was undecided about Miss Habersham's age. She is sixty in the original draft [76]. Later, on [76] and [79], she is seventy or near seventy. In the setting copy [284], she is sixty, though the first edition (page 76) mentions that she is near seventy. Whatever, Miss Habersham has the wisdom of the ancients combined with the spry generosity and curiosity of a much younger woman.

When Chick interrupts the conversation between Miss Habersham and his uncle on [64], the narrator states, "Nor did he [i.e., Chick] need to look at Miss Habersham again. He knew what had nudged at him now, why Miss Habersham was here. He didn't have to remember it, into his attention: a flash: then dismissed, not even needing to remember how or when or who had told him: old Molly, Lucas' wife, had been the daughter of one of the Habersham slaves, she and Miss Habersham were the same age, born in the same week, both had suckled at Molly's mother's breast and had grown up together, slept in the same room almost until Lucas and Molly were married; into his mind then gone, blotted away beneath the urgency" [64]. Thus Faulkner originally hinted that Miss Habersham was seeing Gavin about Lucas' plight because of her relationship to Molly. Faulkner then decided to delete this matter (he would use it later) and substitute the text he had written out by hand on [61] and [62] concerning Chick rushing into Gavin's room. In the revision of this section, the reader has no real notion why Miss Habersham is visiting Gavin.

Faulkner next added in pencil on [64] a suggestion or clue, perhaps to whet the appetite of murder mystery fans: "He [i.e., Lucas] probably even told you what he actually shot at. Was it rabbit? or maybe a tin can or even a mark on a tree just to see if the bullets would still shoot?" Then Chick asks that his uncle go out and dig up Gowrie's body; in the setting copy, this is changed to a question concerning Sheriff Hampton going out and digging up the body. When Chick finally emerges from Gavin's room [70 (V)], he smells his father's cigar and stands "in a cold almost unbearable fury not at his uncle but at Lucas: and then he realized, discovered it was not even at Lucas but at himself and now he knew that he was lost; he had realized fifteen minutes ago as he stood holding to his side." Faulkner went back and crossed off these lines; if not, Chick would have been stymied and perhaps incapable of carrying out his intention of helping Lucas. Apparently Faulkner did not want this inner disgust on Chick's part to be a factor in motivating him to help

Lucas; a complicated generation-gap motif might obscure the simple lines of the mystery story.

Since it is impossible to obtain a car, Chick muses that he will have to take a horse. In an imaginary dialogue with Lucas, Chick hears Luas say: *"Of course you gonter do it you way. I aint gonter critixise* [sic]. *After all, it aint you them Gowries is fixing to set on fire"* [69 (V)]. In a revision of this entire section, Chick emerges from his uncle's office "thinking with the frantic niggling preoccupation of a man in a burning house trying to pick up a broken string of beads" [66]. He mentally plans on going back to the jail when the smell of his father's cigar reaches him. Faulkner is using material he had briefly sketched out before. Chick soon remembers that Lucas had already told him the location and distance to Gowrie's gravesite. In a flip way, he imagines that he will ask his father for the keys to the family car: *"Let me have the keys, Pop. I want to run out to the country and dig up a grave. . ."* [66]. Then, too, he thinks of Miss Habersham. In pencil, Faulkner added, "not her: he never thought of her again. He just remembered the truck in front of the house" [66]. Chick thinks that the Gowrie who catches him robbing a grave might as well catch him stealing a car. Immediately after this Faulkner typed: "Then he remembered: that the reason he was going out there tonight was that not even Sheriff Hampton and his uncle were absolutely convinced that the Gowries and their kin and friends would not try to take Lucas out of the jail tonight and if they were all in town tonight there wouldn't be anybody to catch him digging up the grave" [66]-[67]. Later in the setting copy [297]-[298], Faulkner supplied Chick's reflections on going out to the graveyard:

> He could see himself reaching the church, the graveyard without effort nor even any great elapse of time; he could see himself singlehanded even having the body up and out still with no effort, no pant and strain of muscles and lungs nor laceration of the shrinking sensibilities. It was only then that the whole wrecked and tumbling midnight which peer and pant though he would he couldn't see past and beyond, would come crashing down on him. So (moving: he had not stopped since the first second's fraction while he closed the office door) he flung himself bodily with one heave into a kind of deadly reasonableness of enraged calculation,

a calm sagacious and desperate rationality not of pros and cons because there were no pros: the reason he was going out there. . . . [297]-[298]

Thus in the rewriting Faulkner provided a deeper insight into Chick's psyche as he contemplates helping Lucas.

Chick takes on the burden of doing the job by himself in spite of all the odds ("there were no pros"). On [67], Faulkner omitted something that he mentions in the setting copy; Chick really cannot do it all by himself, that he needs Aleck Sander to help him with Vinson Gowrie's body. It would take three times as long to dig up the body by himself. On [297] of the setting copy, Chick reflects on the situation by imagining confetti "quitting abandoning emerging from scattering with one sweep that confetti-swirl of raging facetiae"; his reflections end, again imagining confetti "and suddenly he found himself escaped back into the confetti exactly as you put off having to step finally into the cold water" [300], thus forming an *inclusio* in this revised text. Chick thinks of the excuses he could tell Lucas, such as having no horse or being locked in the house. In the original draft Chick then crosses the yard to Paralee's dark cabin, but in the setting copy [300]-[301] Faulkner added drama to each step of Chick's decision. The new material concerns the fact that Chick was wrong and "here was the irrevocable moment after which there would be no return; he could stop here and never pass it, let the wreckage of midnight crash harmless and impotent against these walls because they were strong, they would endure; they were home, taller than wreckage, stronger than fear. . . ." Chick continues walking; there is no turning back and each step forward is evaluated in his mind. It is these moments of evaluation that Faulkner concentrated on during the second draft of the novel.

Chick finally asks Aleck Sander to help him dig up Vinson Gowrie's body. Then he and Aleck Sander go to get Highboy and Chick turns and thinks:

At first he thought it was his uncle coming rapidly along the flank of the house from the front, simply because he could not imagine anyone else suspecting, anticipating what he might be about, then he believed it was his mother because he had completely forgotten that Miss Habersham existed even after she was near enough for him to distinguish the shape of the hat and his impulse was to step quickly and quietly around the corner of the garage from where he could reach the lot fence unseen and climb it and meet Aleck Sander with the horse at the stable and go out the pasture gate but it was too late, she had seen him too and Miss Habersham's voice spoke his name as she came rapidly up and stopped facing him. . . . [71]

After almost sixty pages of this draft of the novel, Faulkner has established the major personal relationships in this novel.

In the revision of this section, Faulkner made the scene more specific. He changed "anyone" to his "uncle" [303] and inserted the idea that Gávin had dismissed the idea immediately that Chick would go out and dig up Vinson's body. In the original draft [71], Faulkner wrote that Chick had forgotten about Miss Habersham's existence. He deleted this notion in the rewriting. Then as if writing a screenplay, Faulkner wrote that Miss Habersham spoke his name and in the revision [304] included the name "Charles" for dramatic effect. Then Faulkner reintroduced the information he had previously deleted on [64] : Miss Habersham and Molly were very close and had grown up like sisters [71]-[72]. In the margin of [71] Faulkner included a phrase that was dropped in the setting copy: " 'What did he tell you?' she said in the same tense rapid murmur." Then Faulkner inserted these words in blue ink: "yet with something else too: an urgency almost matching whatever had been in Lucas' eyes that drew him even through the back of his head to ponder [?] and stop and look back." In this way, Faulkner created a type of identification between Lucas and Miss Habersham which would give Chick the courage to start his mission. In addition, Miss Habersham might also represent or embody the social and moral attitudes of Lucas and carry them with her on their journey out to the graveyard, so that in a sense Lucas would be present out there, too. But Faulkner never used this material; perhaps it was forcing the issue and trying to find relationships that were not genuine or adequately prepared for.

Once Chick pleads that he is not sure what is happening ("I just dont know. I still dont know" [72]), Miss Habersham looks at Chick and speaks to him using the same tone and pitch as he used, "the two of them not conspiratorial but rather like two people who have already accepted irrevocably a threat which they are not at all certain they can cope with: only that they will resist it" [72]. Then Faulkner deleted these words, inserted a few sentences, and retyped these words on the next page [73], substituting "threat" with "gambit," a word that was probably on his mind since he was working on the Gavin stories in *Knight's Gambit*.

On [74] Faulkner established the basic line of thought he later expanded in the second draft. Here Chick tells Miss Habersham what Lucas started to tell Gavin in the jail before he shut up. In the setting copy, Faulkner expanded this section into a longer dialogue between Miss Habersham and Chick. Faulkner has Miss Habersham repeat what Gavin told Chick in his study, that Lucas would say it was not his pistol [306]. What they have to do, according to the revision, is "look at him [i.e., Vinson Gowrie's body]" and transport the corpse to town for a bullet expert to make a judgment. In the original draft, Chick, assuming some of the philosophical habits of Gavin, imagines that for the second time in one day he heard the truth repeated and paraphrased: "because it was truth and there was not a great deal of truth because being truth it was universal, it had to be universal to be truth and it didn't take a great deal of it to keep something running no bigger than one earth and anybody could know it if they only paused, only stopped, only waited" [74]. As with other philosophical passages, Faulkner revised this one in the setting copy: "it was in the first place because the deliberate violent blotting out obliteration of a human life was itself so simple and so final that the verbiage which surrounded it enclosed it insulated it intact into the chronicle of man had of necessity to be simple and uncomplex too, repetitive, almost monotonous even; and in the second place, vaster than that, adumbrating that, because what Miss Habersham paraphrased was simple truth, not even fact and so there was not needed a great deal of diversification and originality to express it because truth was universal. . ." [307]. A passage like this indicates that the philosophical truth that Faulkner was attempting to deal with was simple, though his method of describing it is stylistically complex, and more importantly that Chick has a knowledge of philosophical truth which later will be counterbalanced by Gavin's long monologues.

It is important to note that Chick is the first one to give some form of philosophical reflection, thus confirming to some extent his contention that truth is simple.

The next ten pages [75]-[84] were written with almost no marginal notes, except for one, which will be discussed later, on [81]. The conversation about preparing for the trip out to the cemetery [75]-[76] required little modification in the setting copy [308]-[310]; the only significant change is that in the re-writing for the setting copy Faulkner added some detail about saddling Highboy. On [311]-[312] of the setting copy, Faulk-ner inserted a paragraph not in the original draft, a recollection of the famous hunters of Yoknapatawpha: Major de Spain, Chick's grandfather's cousin, old General Compson, Uncle Ike McCaslin, who was Carother's Edmonds' great-uncle and was still alive at ninety, Boon Hogganbeck, Sam Fathers, and Major de Spain's one-eyed mule Alice "who wasn't afraid even of the smell of bear and he thought if you really were the sum of your ancestry it was too bad the ancestors who had evoluted him into a secret resurrector of country graveyards hadn't thought to equip him with a descendant of that unspookable one-eyed mule to transport his subjects on" [311]-[312]. This is the first time that Faulkner has included a link with the historical past in his revisions, giving the impression of Chick being the summation of all the best hunters in the county's past. This impression is undercut by Chick's desire to have a mule in the line of Alice to carry dead bodies for him, thus providing a humorous note in what could be a lugubrious situation.

There follows a description of the trip out to the cemetery, which includes a short sequence about Miss Habersham, Chick, and Aleck Sander passing a number of Negro cabins [78]. In the second draft of this sequence, Faulkner added most of pages [315] and [317]. The new material included a section concern-ing Chick's philosophical evaluation of their mission: "before he could leap and spring and smother and blot it from thinking not because he couldn't really believe they possibly could and not because you dont dare think whole even to yourself the entirety of a dear hope or wish let alone a desperate one else you yourself have doomed it because thinking it into words even only to himself was like the struck match which doesn't dispel the dark but only exposes its terror—one weak flash and glare revealing for a second the empty road's the dark and empty land's irrevocable immitigable negation" [315]. Chick has a problem of trying to foresee the whole of the future and by doing so either hexes it or dooms it to failure. He does not want to expose the evil he senses to the light of clarity. On [78], after commenting that Aleck Sander has wisely put the truck off to the side of the road and led the horse down for a drink, Faulkner noted in the margin, "quicksand: horse wont drink. A. S. 'Smell quicksand'." The idea of quicksand is only mentioned once in this chapter and that in a marginal note. Faulkner is trying to blend a sense of philosophical reflection with the elements of a murder story and to his credit at this point neither dimension has been given undue emphasis.

In revising the trip to the cemetery, Faulkner included a section showing how the blacks who stayed in their homes during these anxious days were acting as they were expected to act. Here the narrator comments on the Negroes in the cabins in a way that foreshadows much of what Gavin says later. The Negroes were "not crouching cringing shrinking, not in anger and not quite in fear: just waiting, biding since theirs was an armament which the white man could not match for—if he but knew it—even cope with: patience; just keeping out of sight and out of the way. . ." [318]. Chick is described too as a provincial Mississippian, "a child who when the sun set this same day had appeared to be—and even himself believed, provided he had thought about it at all—himself to be still a swaddled unwitting infant in the long tradition of his native land—or for that matter a witless foetus itself struggling—if he was aware that there had been any throcs—blind and insentient and not even yet awaked in the simple painless convulsion of emergence. . ." [318]. The actual journey from the road to the graveyard was interrupted only by someone leading a mule or horse down from the graveyard. This interruption complicates the story and adds a new twist, one, however, Lucas had prepared the reader for by mentioning that Vinson Gowrie had an unknown partner. The actual digging is a classic graveyard scene and could easily be made into a frightening movie scene, as Clarence Brown later did in a very stylized manner, culminating in finding Jake Montgomery's body, not Vinson Gowrie's. Faulkner did not revise this episode in the setting copy except for a few minor additions and emendations.

On [81], Faulkner typed a passage about Chick being re-vivified by the smell of the pine trees; Faulkner suggested that breathing was like tasting wine: "he imagined: he had never tasted it. He could have—the sip from the communion cup ['in the banded hands' is typed in, but does not fit the context] didn't count because it was just a sip, sour consecrated and sharp; a significance, a symbol which not downward to the stomach but upward or outward into wherever [and then in a marginal note] dwelt the knowledge between good and evil and the choice and the repudiation and the acceptance of Jesus Christ. . . ." In the later revision of this passage, Faulkner omitted this revery concerning the acceptance or repudiation of Jesus Christ [322]. Another modification is the insertion in the setting copy [323] that the mountains Chick saw were similar to the ones in "Carolina and before that in Scotland where his ancestors had come from." On [82] the gravestone reads "Amanda Gowrie. 1882 [a "9" is subsequently placed over the "8"] — [1916] 1922 [with a "6" imposed subsequently over the last "2"]." Faulkner later wanted to change some of this information. Faulkner was also ambivalent about Jake Montgomery's hometown. On [84], Montgomery is listed as being from three places: Glasgow, Hollymount, and Hollyvale with Glasgow and Hollymount eventually being crossed off. In the setting copy, however, he is from Crossman County. The conclusion of this chapter then introduces a classic complication of the murder mystery genre: a body-switch. Though Faulkner has mentioned that Vinson Gowrie had a business partner, he has not established a reason for a double murder. From here on, part of the story will be to reveal the situation and motives surrounding the death of both Vinson Gowrie and Jake Montgomery. Thus, at the end of the third chapter of the original draft, two men have been murdered, a fact brought to light by an old woman and two boys in a lonely cemetery outside of Jefferson.

Chapter Four of the Original Draft

Faulkner began this fourth chapter (later changed to "V") with the material that appears on page 107 of the first edition concerning Sheriff Hampton's service record. There are twenty-five pages or parts of pages in this chapter. On the top of [85]

Faulkner made some emendations in manuscript in blue ink; the words that can be deciphered are (though I am mostly guessing): "His mother when he left the house: a wail not of disappointment but of denial, repudiation of the fact that he really could button his own clothing." In pencil Faulkner also wrote what looks like a note to himself: "They had had to fill the grave up again." Another emendation in blue ink on the top of the page resembles the first paragraph of page 107 of the first edition where women and children "can stand anything, can accept any fact, can accept any fact [fifteen undecipherable worlds follow] like a bribe" [85]. These manuscript notations in pen and pencil indicate that at this stage Faulkner had more to expand when he revised this chapter. From here the narrative continues by explaining that there was still some time left until daylight when his uncle stopped the car at the sheriff's gate. In the setting copy, Faulkner transposed these two sections and Gavin pulls up to Hampton's gate and then the information about the sheriff's service record is given [330]-[331].

After this, in the original draft, Faulkner indicated Miss Habersham was tired because of the "anticlimax which hadn't even been decent anticlimax but a shock and an amazement coming before they had even had time to draw the first breath of vindication and relief" [85]. He deleted this phrase and continued on the top of [88] by having Miss Habersham merely exclaim "Pah" in exasperation. Then skipping to [87], Gavin mentions that Hampton is a country man and that Mrs. Hampton is away in Memphis with their daughter. And so Gavin enters Hampton's house without knocking. Faulkner crossed off this material on [88] and [87]. On [89 (V)] the sheriff responds to Gavin, "You wouldn't come here at four oclock in the morning with a tale like that if it wasn't so," though nowhere in the text has Gavin told Hampton the story of the exhumation of Montgomery's body.

In order to achieve the right collocation of words, Faulkner three times describes Hampton moving around the stove to get an iron skillet. In a crossed-off section at the bottom of [89 (V)], Gavin again speaks to Hampton: "They saw him coming down the hill with Gowrie's body in front of him on the mule, and you dont ride around the country even at night any longer than you have to with a murdered corpse on your saddle. [Then, in pencil, 'So he probably didn't go in (?) with it'.] Suppose he was watching them while they were digging up Jake Montgomery. If he was, how long do you think he can afford to let Lucas sit there. . . ." But this was advancing the story line too quickly, so Faulkner went back to the beginning of the chapter and revised this section. In going back, Faulkner inserted [86], repeating the information about Mrs. Hampton and her daughter being away and added in the margin, "She comes in at a decent hour about 8 oclock and washes the dishes," referring to Hampton's cook. Then follows a description of Hampton's house and himself. In the revision of this sequence on [88], Faulkner has Gavin actually tell the sheriff the story of digging up Vinson Gowrie's body, thus making sense out of Hampton's quip that they would not come to his house unless the story were true.

At this point, Faulkner's narrative becomes a bit rough. On [88], Gavin tells the sheriff that he has to drive sixty miles to Harrisburg to the "Distruct Attorney" [sic] to petition for an exhumation, though the sheriff is hesitant about implicating the three grave diggers. On [89], Jim Halladay's name is spelled as "Holladay." In a crossed-off passage on [90 (V)], Chick remembers other times when Negroes had communicated with his own mother without really understanding what they had communicated, as when Miss Habersham looked penetratingly at Aleck Sander as he suggested that it might have been a horse, not a mule, that came down the hill at night. After this, the sheriff goes across the hall [90 (V)]. In a crossed-off marginal note, Miss Habersham asks if they have to go to Harrisburg. Apparently the answer is "no," though it is difficult to decipher Faulkner's writing. Miss Habersham then starts breakfast and when the sheriff returns from finishing dressing, he asks how many eggs they want. The boys will eat two and the grown-ups one each. Faulkner crossed off this section about the eggs, probably because he again felt the story was continuing too rapidly. In revising it, Faulkner went back to [89] and this time abbreviated the glance Miss Habersham gives Aleck Sander. The focus of the story is therefore restored to Lucas and his needs; with the sheriff she agrees that the person who needs help and secrecy is not in the room with them.

On [90] Faulkner retyped this short piece of dialogue, with little change, more to clean up the appearance of the page.

Next Faulkner copied the material on [93 (V)] that he had previously written on [85] and again raises the problem of whether they will all have to go to Harrisburg or not. Gavin replies [93 (V)] that Mr. Hampton says "no" and that Hampton is running the show. They must wait until daylight, however, before they can do anything. When Miss Habersham replies, "We didn't," Gavin says, "But Mr. Hampton's not a lady and two sixteen-year-old boys. . . . He's just a man, a country sheriff. He's got to break the law in his own fashion just as you and Charles and Aleck Sander did in yours" [93 (V)]. Faulkner did not continue with this line of development; it is difficult to speculate why Faulkner would stop this section and start over. He might have thought that the sheriff was going to follow the law as best he could and Faulkner did not want to give the impression that any of his heroes, including the sheriff, were lawbreakers.

After this, on [94 (V)], the sheriff returns quickly and questions Aleck Sander as to why he went out to dig up a white man's body. On [95], Aleck Sander says that no one made him do it; it just more or less happened. With this, the sheriff asks how many eggs they can eat. Faulkner then proceeded to cross off [93 (V)], [94 (V)], and the top of [95]. For the fourth time, Faulkner retreated a bit in his narrative and started over. He went back to [90] and picked up at the point where Hampton leaves the room to finish dressing. Miss Habersham then asks, "Cant he telephone to Harrisburg and have the District Attorney telephone back to Judge Maycox?" [91]. Miss Habersham continues to assume the initiative in the discussion and makes suggestions such as the above; she becomes more aggressive than Gavin does, who in the earlier version had told her to let Hampton handle the whole matter. Aleck Sander then informs her that Hampton is calling Harrisburg. When Miss Habersham replies this time to Gavin's suggestion that they wait for daylight, Chick looks at Miss Habersham and begins to think that a lady should not have to do this and that he would have to do it by himself, though really it was only when Miss Habersham came along that he was sure in his own mind that he would actually go through with it. In transferring the crossed-off dialogue on [95] to [94], Faulkner slows down the action by having the sheriff note, "It'll be daylight in fifteen minutes and folks dont start lynchings in daylight. They might finish one by daylight if they had a little trouble or bad luck with it. . ." [94]. This

chapter caused Faulkner considerable anxiety as he pulled sheets
of paper from his typewriter and began all over again.

On [88 (V)], Faulkner typed a short sequence concerning
Chick asking for a glass of milk while Aleck Sander is asleep.
Aleck Sander wakes up suddenly and says, "All we thought
about was just to take a ride into the country and dig up a dead
man. But that aint hardly started it." This bit of sudden wide-
eyed dialogue is out of character, especially from a black boy
waking from a deep sleep. Faulkner wrote this scene over again,
this time portraying Chick as being very sleepy and more or less
overhearing the conversation that is going on. This revision foreshadows the technique that Faulkner uses later on, of having
Chick relive a number of events in a dream-like state. As Chick
wakes up, he hears Legate and the sheriff discuss Jake Montgomery. On [96], Faulkner omits the information that is found
on [340] of the setting copy, namely that Jake Montgomery and
Vinson Gowrie were involved in some type of lumber business
deal. The sheriff would like to take Miss Habersham home. He
is also aware that the two boys should go to school. Gavin, on
the other hand, suggests that Miss Habersham go to town and
protect the jail entrance. Chick begins to think philosophically
about man's need to kill and invent a motive afterwards. The
word "man" on [97.18] is in upper case, though it is in lower
case in the setting copy [342]. This is the first time that Faulkner has used this Germanic form in the novel, a practice he uses
more frequently later on.

On [343], Faulkner inserted a new section: Miss Habersham
looks at Gavin and Chick thinks about Gavin's visit to Lucas
the night before. Unlike the passage on [72]-[73] where Miss
Habersham also looks at Chick, Faulkner depicted Gavin looking
at Miss Habersham not as the meeting of two souls, but more as
"looking into each other's physical eyes instead of bending each
upon the other that absolute concentration of all the senses in
the sum of which mere clumsy fallible perception weighed little
more than the ability to read Sanskrit would. . . ." The act of
looking at one another shows on an intuitive level that there is
greater rapport between Chick and Miss Habersham than between Gavin and Miss Habersham. Before she will go to the jail,
however, Miss Habersham would like to pick up some mending at
home first. In the original draft, Faulkner did not indicate the

end of this chapter and the beginning of the next. The text merely continues on. In the setting copy [344], the text also continues, though in revising the setting copy, Faulkner started a new chapter (Chapter Six) at the conclusion of this scene.

After being driven home, Miss Habersham goes into her house and gives orders to Molly's brother, her handyman. In the setting copy [346]-[348], excluding [347.18-26], Faulkner inserted a panoramic view describing the ride from Miss Habersham's house to the Square, a lyric passage trying to give both an historical and contemporary sense of what this part of town is like. Such a passage lengthens the narrative and involves the whole history of the town in this murder situation, including children, colored maids, and wives "in sandals and pants and painted toenails puffed lipstick-stained cigarettes over shopping bags in the chain groceries and drugstores" [347]. The attitudes of these women are obviously juxtaposed to the machinations of an old spinster and two boys who have been out to a country cemetery digging up a corpse.

In the original draft, Miss Habersham and Gavin get out of the car after a short drive and walk up to the jail. The small contingent soon returns to Chick's house and Gavin insists Chick go to school, then Gavin changes his mind and thinks Chick should go to bed [99]-[100]. Chick's mother shows her concern by objecting to Chick drinking coffee since she did not want him to start this until he is eighteen. She also tells Gavin to go and speak to Paralee who has been worried about Aleck Sander. In the original draft, Faulkner omits pages 122-126 of the first edition [349]-[356], at least as he conceived the progress of the story at this point. The omitted section concerns Gavin reading Chick's mind: Chick thinks he will have to confront his mother sooner or later about going to school. At one point Chick tells Gavin, "You're just my uncle" and Gavin replies that he is worse than that: "I'm just a man" [350]. Gavin finally agrees to talk to Paralee since "motherhood doesn't seem to have any pigment in its skin" [350].

After this (in the setting copy only) Chick launches into a long dream-like revery about a football game in which he goes to Mottstown to play an away game. His mother hires a car and attends the game also. Chick is hurt in the game and returns

home to his house in Jefferson with his mother and some team-
mates in the hired car. Being another step removed from childhood, Chick reflects on his mother's face, "the familiar face
wearing the familiar expression of amazement and protest and
anxiety and invincible repudiation which it had worn all his
life each time he had done anything removing him one more step
from infancy, from childhood. . ." [354]. Faulkner had originally put this description of Chick's mother's face after his
mother finally insisted Chick drink the coffee. Thus on [101]
in original draft, Faulkner begins with the above quote about
Mrs. Mallison's face and then follows with an abbreviated version
of the football game at Mottstown, which does not have the same
overtones of a dream-sequence as the setting copy has. In the
original draft, it is a straightforward account that he went to
Mottstown to play on Saturday afternoon and "bottom-most
beneath the piled mass of both teams, the ball clutched to his
chest, on the chalked goal-line, he heard the one voice above all
the others shrill bloodthirsty and triumphant and when he was
picked up at last and the wind thumped back into him, he saw
her foremost among the crowd. . ." [101]. After this, when
asked about the situation, Gavin replies "It took an old woman
and two children for that, to believe truth for no other reason
that it was truth, worthy of pity and belief" [102]. In revising
this statement, Faulkner made it a bit more specific, pointing to
the Lucas-Chick relationship. "It took an old woman and two
children for that, to believe truth for no other reason than that
it was truth, told by an old man in a fix deserving pity and belief, to someone capable of the pity even when none of them
really believed him" [356].

The setting copy [357] continues with the discussion about
coffee but in the original draft Faulkner omitted the section
about Chick drinking coffee since he had already mentioned this
briefly on [100]. Chick's mother then continues in the original
draft by saying that she would not let Miss Habersham sit all by
herself at the jail [102]. Chick's father then insists that Chick
go to school and his mother retorts that missing one day won't
hurt him. After this, Gavin asks whether Chick knows how to
drive Miss Habersham's truck. Then in a crossed-off section
[102], Chick drives the truck behind his uncle's car and watches
his mother and uncle stop and go into the jail. Miss Habersham
takes out a cardboard box of sewing and knitting and puts it

beside her. Faulkner would later use this section and rework it in the final version. It should be noted that [102 (V)] is an attempt to rewrite this section in the setting copy; therefore this verso is not part of the original draft.

On [103] Gavin tells Aleck Sander and Chick that there won't be any school for them that day: "Nor any white school either for that matter, if you hadn't listened to Lucas or Miss Habersham, which I didn't, or whatever it was that enabled Mr. Hampton to tell the mayor when he telephoned him this morning, to tell Professor Henry to go ahead and earn the salary the town was paying him." Faulkner omitted this reference to Professor Henry in the setting copy. Then on [103] Faulkner continues the narrative. Gavin explains that there wont be any school today either for the whites or blacks. Then about 8 A.M. on Monday, (in effect omitting pages 129-133 of the first edition), Chick drives the truck back to the jail following his uncle's car. In the setting copy, Faulkner added a retelling of the exhumation episode [358]-[366], giving a deeper glimpse into the mentality of the three gravediggers. In the rewriting, the coffee wakes Chick up and he feels the "pseudo-scornful humorous impugnment of his and Aleck Sander's courage which blinked not, even as much at a rifled grave in the dark as it did at Miss Habersham's will,—in fact the whole heavyhanded aspersion of the whole thing by reducing it to the terms of a kind of kindergarten witch hunt. . ." [363]. The retelling of this episode in the setting copy keeps the reader's mind on the essential outline of the grave-digging event and relates the events of Monday morning back to those of Sunday night.

On [103], Faulkner continued with the description of the townsfolk and ended on [104] with a description of town marshall. The last few sentences on [104] concern Miss Habersham sitting in the jail knitting, a section that Faulkner had previously used but discarded. Most of the material on pages 136-138 of the first edition was omitted from the original draft: this material [370]-[373] is another of Chick's reveries concerning the crowds that gathered about the Square. It is like the preliminary settling down before a play involving a courtroom scene with Lucas as the chief actor. The townsfolk had "come not to see what they called justice done nor even retribution exacted but to see that Beat Four should not fail its white man's high

estate" [372]. The new material contains the type of opaque
writing often associated with Faulkner. It should be pointed out,
however, that this was a second level of writing for Faulkner and
was not part of the original design:

> . . .then he remembered again the faces myriad yet curiously
> identical in their lack of individual identity, their complete re-
> linquishment of individual identity into one We not even impa-
> tient, not even hurryable, almost gala in its complete obliviousness
> of its own menace, not to be stampeded by a hundred running
> children: and then in the same flash the obverse: not to be halted
> or deflected by a hundred times a hundred of them, and having
> realized its sheer hopelessness when it was still only an intention
> and then its physical imponderability when it entered accomplish-
> ment he now recognised the enormity of what he had blindly
> meddled with. . . . [372]

Faulkner worked some more on this material. On [104], he
sketched a picture of Miss Habersham sitting in the jail and on
[106 (V)] Mrs. Mallison joined her. The sheriff joins them too
and asks where the other detective is, the one who can see in the
dark, meaning Aleck Sander. Faulkner then decided not to use
[106 (V)] and on [105] typed out the same scene again changing some of the parts around slightly, but not enough to make
much difference dramatically. Rather than ending with Chick's
mother darning one of Chick's socks as he had done on [106
(V)], Faulkner ends by asking where Aleck Sander is. Again,
Faulkner crossed off the dialogue about where Aleck Sander is
on the bottom of [105] since he would use it on [108], as he
assembled various characters to get ready to go out to the cemetery. Before leaving town for the cemetery, however, Faulkner
has the sheriff and Gavin converse for four pages [106]-[109]
(this material is similar to that found in pages 139-143 of the
first edition) about the townsfolk who have assembled about the
Square. Faulkner is careful not to rush from one scene to another in his haste to solve the murder mystery, but rather to let
all the people who are part of any one scene, such as this one,
express themselves as fully as the story would allow. The only
important new information for the murder mystery plot is that
Lucas has been transferred to Hampton's house without the
townsfolk knowing it. Thus the two women are in less danger
at the jail than one might suppose. On the bottom of [109],

Faulkner crossed off the last three lines in order to bring the chapter to a close. Thus, the chapter ends with Gavin's statement about getting out to the cemetery and back as soon as possible.

Chapter Five of the Original Draft

Faulkner continued this chapter from the previous one with the word "ineffable" linking the two pages [109] and [111]. He stopped typing half-way down [111] and then went back and crossed off this section so he could have the chapter end evenly on [109]. There are twenty-two pages or parts of pages in this chapter, which was originally labeled "V," but changed to "VII." It resembles Chapter Seven of the first edition. According to the crossed-off section on [111], Chick is trying to fight off sleep, "realizing now how he had believed that as soon as he and his uncle and Miss Habersham reached the sheriff's house, that would be all of it. . . ." In writing this, it might have seemed to Faulkner that he had not given sufficient emphasis to the fact that Chick is recalling a prior desire on his part. In rewriting this section on [110], Faulkner is careful to delineate more carefully Chick's thought processes: "remembering how he—and without doubt Miss Habersham and Aleck Sander too—had believed that as soon as they and his uncle entered the sheriff's house. . . ." Since Faulkner is putting Chick into a deeper state of exhaustion, he is careful to give directional signals at the beginning before Chick lapses into a complicated stream-of-consciousness dream sequence.

Faulkner was not satisfied with rushing the plot. On [114 (V)], Faulkner realized that he had written hurriedly about the route to the cemetery, so he stopped and began again. On [111 (V)], he continued for a few sentences about Gavin driving fast and the sheriff driving faster. Then he crossed this off and went back to [110.16] and picked it up from the quote about "the whole night's nightmare of doubt and indecision and sleeplessness and strain and fatigue and shock and amazement." At this point Chick becomes wide awake and Faulkner repeated the phrase concerning the white man's view of the situation as they gather in the Square, "the whole white part of the county already there patient and biding and neither to be dispersed nor hurried since the county was theirs and hence the town which the county supported by sufferance, theirs the murdered white man and the bereavement of his vacating and the forfeit life of the black protagonist of the grief, theirs the right not to mere justice but to vengeance too to allot or withhold" [111 (V) (bottom)] and [116 (V) (top)]. At this point, Faulkner is trying to portray the larger Jefferson community and its reaction to Vinson Gowrie's death.

The troubles and anxiety which Miss Habersham and the two boys felt did not vanish once they had gone to the sheriff's house [111]. Instead they were forced to consider the townsfolk, or rather the faces of the townsfolk, once they arrived into town, "the faces and voices not taunting and not even jeering: just perspicuant jocular and without pity" [111]. The crowd is not defined and seems only to have a corporate personality. Then, going out of town, Chick is as wide awake as his uncle [111] and once on the way out of town, he could see people heading towards town, now about 9 A.M. [112]. Again the country folk were going to town "to crowd and jam and block its streets too if they saw fit patient and biding the unpitying, neither to be hurried nor dispersed nor denied since theirs was the murdered and the murderer too: the white man and the bereavement of his vacating and the forfeit life of begrievement's [sic] and fury's black protagonist; theirs the right not just to mere justice but to vengeance too to allot or withhold" [112]. The trip out to the cemetery was fast because Gavin was driving faster than Chick ever remembered him driving before.

Now being daylight, "morning's bland ineffable May" [112], Chick enjoyed the freshness of the view where dogwoods were "standing like nuns in the cloistral patches and bands of greening woods and the pink and white of peach and pear trees and the pinkwhite of the first apples in the orchards which last night he had only smelled" [112], thus expanding some of the observations he presented on [116 (V)]. At the bottom of [112], Faulkner noted that here fields "empty, vacant of any movement or [and then crossed off the following: "any life where this morning, at this hour there should have been in each field a figure, a group, ritualistic and formal animal plow and man, ritualistic and formal, monotonous, repetitive and identical as milestones and tying the town to the county's ultimate rim as milestones would—animal plow and man tremendous with effort yet at the same time vacant of motion like groups of wrestling statuary set against the immensity of the land. . ."] [112] and [114]. Though Faulkner crossed off most of the above passage, it does give an indication of how he was composing at the typewriter at this time, of repeating a phrase or an image until the richness of it appeared. On [114], he continued with this complex image of the empty field after trying to reformulate it on the bottom of [113] too. Faulkner noted that it is the second Monday in May and further down this page, Gavin states that "Today is the ["sixt" is indicated] ninth of May. This county's got half of [82] forty-two thousand acres to plant yet." This would probably make the year 1938, as Monday, May 9th, can only occur in 1910, 1921, 1927, 1932, or 1938. It looks like Faulkner had second thoughts and did not continue with the word "sixth" or "sixteenth." He was trying to be accurate not only with seasonal description, but also with calendar dates.

On [114], Faulkner originally noted that the car was five miles from town on its way to the cemetery and then in order to speed up the action, he changed it to eight miles. It remained eight miles in the first edition. Again, Faulkner depicted Chick as looking into someone's eyes, this time the eyes of a black man as he passes by him in the car: "the face black and passionate with effort, tense concentrated and composed. . ." [114]. As Chick looked back through the window, he feels a sense of admiration for "the man and the mule and the wooden plow which coupled them furious solitary and leaning terrifically against the earth" [115]. With the exception of Gavin's soliloquy, the rest of this chapter of the original draft is almost verbatim the same as the setting copy text, that is [120]-[127] is almost identical to [396]-[407], or pages 156-166 or the first edition. In the original draft, Faulkner spelled Fraser as "Frazier" [115]. Armstead was originally spelled "Armstid" [116]. The name Bookwright on page 149 of the first edition was not included in the original list of names on [116]. It is Gavin's speech that Faulkner later revised and expanded, as might be expected. Gavin's speech about Sambo begins on [116] and includes all the material on [386] (page 149 of the first edition) except the following parenthesis:

> Which incidently—the premise that man really wants peace and
> freedom—is the trouble with our relations with Europe right
> now, whose people not only dont know what peace is but—ex-
> cept for Anglo-Saxons—actively fear and distrust personal liberty;
> we are hoping without really any hope that our atom bomb will
> be enough to defend an idea as obsolete as Noah's [Ark].
> [386]

The reference to the atom bomb in 1938 is anachronistic, but a
detail that would not have bothered Faulkner who sometimes
forgot the names of some of his own imaginary characters.

Gavin introduces his philosophical beliefs by maintaining
that not all white people can endure slavery and no person can
stand freedom. Mankind has handed over his rights to
demagogues in the past to destroy his own freedom himself. As
the car ride continues, Charles thinks not only about the horse
or the mule they had seen but also that his uncle will have to
slow down when they reach the turnoff up to the cemetery. On
[117] Faulkner crossed off the phrase "but at least there wasn't
any question about what that was even though only Aleck
Sander seemed to have known until they got back to town
and his uncle told them." This was getting ahead of the story; at
this point they did not know what the rider had on the horse or
mule though Aleck Sander guessed it was a mule. So far, the
sheriff's posse had not dug up Vinson Gowrie's grave to see Jake
Montgomery's body; they only have Miss Habersham's and the
boys' word that a body-switch has taken place.

The lower half of page 152 and the first paragraph of
page 153 of the first edition ([389]-[390]) concerning Chick's
fantasy about building a wall and looking at countless rows of
faces were not part of the original draft. When the narrator picks
up with Gavin's speech again, it is a truncated version of what
is in the setting copy. It reads essentially like this:

> 'It's because alone among all Americans we in the South are a
> homogeneous people. I mean the only homogeneous people of any
> size. The New Englander is homogeneous but there are not enough
> of him just as there are not enough of the Swiss, who are not a
> people so much as a neat, clean, quite solvent business. We are
> defending not actually our politics or beliefs or even our way of

life but simply our homogeneity from a federal government to which in simple desperation the rest of the country had had to surrender voluntarily more and more of its personal and private liberty in order to exist as a nation': not even realising he had spoken alone but still believing his uncle had merely once more read his mind, when his uncle said: 'Of course we defend it. We dont know why it is valuable. That out from that comes anything of durable value.—literature, art, a national character worth anything in a crisis. What? What's that?' and then continued, not even waiting for him to answer: 'That's why we must resist them: not to preserve ourselves nor even to preserve them but to preserve the very thing which three generations ago we lost a bloody war so that it remains intact. In time this sort of thing wont happen. It shouldn't now and it never should have. Yet it does and it will again. But some day it wont anymore, it will be finished; Lucas Beauchamp can shoot a white man in the back with the same impunity to lynchropes and gasoline bonfires as another white man. In time Lucas Beauchamp will vote as when and where white men vote and send his children to the same school with white men's children and travel as white men travel. But it wont be tomorrow. Yet people in the North believed it can be compelled into tomorrow by the simple ratification by votes of a printed statute on a Congressional page. They have forgotten that, although a long quarter-century ago Lucas Beauchamp's freedom was made an article in our constitution and Lucas Beauchamp's master was not merely beaten to his knees but trampled for ten years into the dust to make him swallow it, yet only three short generations later they are faced again with the necessity of passing legislation in Congress to set Lucas Beauchamp free.' [119]-[120]

The rest of the text beginning, "Now they were there and not too long behind the sheriff. . ." as found on [120], [396], and page 156 of the first edition continues and follows the first edition very closely except that at one point Mr. Gowrie is called "Mrs. Gowrie" [128], "Henry" is listed [129] as the eldest Gowrie boy, not Forrest, and one of the "McCaslin" [130] boys, not one of the McCallum boys, had traded his gun to Crawford Gowrie.

In the first draft of the long paragraph quoted above, Gavin develops his argument, not in any formal way, since the body of his speech does not coherently express the ideas which he wished to impress on Chick. Though the Americans in the South are the only homogeneous people of any size [119], Gavin fails to specify what is the central ingredient of this homogeneity, nor does he define the boundaries of the South. New England is homogeneous like the South, but there are not enough people there to give it the character he is after. And the South is defending its homogeneity, which is somehow related to its politics, beliefs, and *modus vivendi,* from the government which has absorbed both personal and private liberty. Apparently the Swiss are not an homogenous group since they are too efficient and too small a nation. If anything the basis of this homogeneity is something in the Southern character which is related at the same time to the large population in the South. The Southerners defend this homogeneity though they are not sure why it is valuable.

From this homogeneity comes literature, art, and a national character. It is difficult to see his jump from a regional characteristic to a national character, and even if he had meant "natural" [119] (the word in the original is difficult to decipher and I base my reading on assistance from the setting copy), it still would not explain the case, since presumably the New Englanders and the Swiss have natural characters, too. Also, the Southern Americans must resist the government in order to preserve the "very thing" [119] which they had lost in the Civil War. What exactly they had lost (or for that matter gained) is again left ambiguous. While a warlike situation would not happen in the present, Gavin knows that it is part of human nature and that it will occur again [119]. A time will hopefully come in the future when all of this strife and conflict will be over and then Lucas and a white man will receive equal justice should either break the law. This is an enormous psychological and logical jump to make, since Gavin has not previously discussed the civil rights of the black man in the South. In Gavin's mind surrendering personal and private liberties to the federal government is related to the injustice that the Negro has suffered in the South.

For a lawyer, Gavin does not show the sophistication he should in distinguishing what types of freedom an individual or state or section of the country surrenders to the federal government in order to achieve peace and unity throughout the country. Gavin does not argue the case adequately, partly because the premise of homogeneity is not a legal premise but a sociological one. In time, in the future tomorrow, Lucas, ("Sambo"), now a metonym for all blacks in the South (it seems that Gavin has not thought of other minority groups in the country), will have the same legal and educational rights as his white counterpart. The Northerners who think this can come about by a legal fiat are making a mistake. Gavin concludes with a nonsequitur which seems to argue against what he is suggesting; that is, defending the homogeneity of the South. He maintains that a "long quarter-century ago" [120] Lucas' freedom was constitutionally assured. If the novel takes place in 1938, then indeed it was a long quarter-century before then. Then three short generations later, the Northerners again are faced with the necessity to pass legislation setting the Negro free. Gavin seems to oppose this Congressional act freeing the Negro when he has all along maintained that Lucas and the other blacks will some day have their freedom.

It is quite apparent that Gavin wants change, but only gradually though he does not rationally support the benefits of gradualism. His argument is to resist the federal government from taking over the liberty and private freedoms of Southerners, at the same time he is ambivalent about when and how the Negro should have and enjoy his constitutional freedom as an equal American. On [116], Gavin had prefaced these remarks by saying that not all white people can endure slavery and no person can stand freedom. This type of ambiguity is frustrating, because it is evasive and simply not true; some men can stand freedom. Man, according to Gavin, has in the past handed over his freedom to a demagogue or, if there is no demagogue, he destroys his freedom so quickly that it resembles neighbors stamping out a grass fire [116]. Only the Negro ("Sambo") has survived the demagogue and he may even endure the destruction of freedom altogether. At this point, Gavin has praise for the Negro. But when he resumes with his speech about homogeneity, he seems to have shelved this praise of the Negro in order to focus on gradualism.

In revising this speech by Gavin, Faulkner modified it as he went along. At times the modifications are subordinate ideas that do not advance the argument though they do give it some

historical interest. After maintaining that "no man can stand
freedom" [386], Faulkner parenthetically added that America's
difficulty with Europe "right now" (1938) is based on the premise that "man really wants peace and freedom." Europeans do
not know what peace is and fear and distrust personal liberty;
Gavin's only exception are the Anglo-Saxons. As mentioned
before, he concludes this parenthesis by saying "we are hoping
without really any hope that our atom bomb will be enough to
defend an idea as obsolete as Noah's [Ark]" [386]. What is
most lacking in these apodictic remarks is any sense of historical
accuracy of facts or evidence. Gavin puts the blame on the
Europeans who fear personal liberty, as if this statement is to
give credence that no man can stand freedom; it looks like he
is supporting his case with an example. His example in no way
hits the mark. As a concept, Noah's Ark has great validity when
put into it's theological context; it was a means by which God
saved his people. While Gavin might not think these people have
been saved, theologically they were, and a rainbow became a
sign of their convenant with their Creator. Gavin believes that
freedom has not worked, but he has given us so far only hints
at what he expects of free men in a free society. By saying,
freedom is as obsolete as Noah's Ark is to beg the question, as he
has not shown any connection between the protasis and the
apodosis.

Faulkner revised the body of the argument in the setting
copy. When speaking of homogeneity, Gavin expands the
notion from that of the South to the United States in general
[390], though he reserves judgment about the black man "Sambo" for a while. The New Englander (implying a contrast between New England and some other parts of the United States)
is "too of course back inland from the coastal spew of Europe"
[390] (page 153 of the first edition) which is hardly the case.
New England is as directly open to the spew of Europe as any
part of the United States, though there is a vast ocean separating
the two areas. If one grants that Gavin is talking about the inner
reaches of New England, then his case might have some merit.
To describe this as "quarantined unrootable into the rootless
ephemeral cities" [390] is to exaggerate the conditions beyond
recognition. Gavin is trying too hard to caricature the industrial
Northeast. Thus he can dismiss this region and establish that he
is not really resisting "progress and enlightenment" [391].

Gavin maintains in the revised version, "we" (he has not at this point isolated the South as he premised his remarks by speaking about the United States) are trying to preserve "our homogeneity from a federal government. . ." [391]. The South (though at this point Gavin is still vague about what he means by the South) will continue to defend this homogeneity; in the setting copy he retains the comment about not knowing the values of this homogeneity though when trying to define "we" he is a bit more precise: "We," that is, "I mean all of us. . ." [391], meaning presumably, at least, those living in Yoknapatawpha County. Gavin expects an eye-for-an-eye biblical type of retribution; a black man will have to die to compensate for Vinson Gowrie's death and the entire county expects this to be done in Gavin's view. Gavin then expands what had formerly been a marginal note on [119] into a summary statement of his position: "Only a few of us know that only from homogeneity comes anything of a people or for a people of durable and lasting value—the literature, the art, the science, that *minimum* [emphasis mine] of government and police which is the meaning of freedom and liberty and perhaps most valuable of all a national character worth anything in a crisis—that crisis we shall face someday when we meet an enemy with as many men as we have and as much material as we have and—who knows?—who can even brag and boast as we brag and boast" [391]-[392]. Thus Gavin has restated what is normally considered a classic Southern position, that a "minimum of government and police" and a "national character" [391] worth anything in a crisis are part of this Southern homogeneity. But his terms are so vague that they really do not substantiate his beliefs; they merely indicate where they lay.

The South fought a bloody war in order to maintain the freedom of the Negro and what Gavin wants to defend is "the privilege of setting him free ourselves" [392]. Presumably the North has done this, but from a sociological and psychological point of view, the South must do this, too. Thus Gavin is coming closer, still on an abstract level, to formulating a clearer thesis than he did in his first draft. Racial crises will happen in the future but they will one day come to an end: "the shame will still be there of course but then the whole chronicle of man's immortality is in the suffering he has endured, his struggle toward the stars in the stepping-stones of his expiations" [392].

In these romantically lyric phrases, Gavin balances them with Lucas' concrete situation, to achieve a strophe-antistrophe type of argument. Gavin still retains the "long quarter-century" [392] and "three short generations later" [393] time scheme which does not clarify what he means; it merely allows the rhetoric to obfuscate the historical sequence of events.

After repeating the belief that he had expressed in the original draft that the Northerners cannot compel freedom by a Congressional proclamation, Faulkner added in the revised version a new conclusion to Gavin's speech. Like the Southerner, the Negro is homogeneous too, though he is not seeking the best that is part of his racial heritage; rather he is imitating inferior white modes of behavior [393]-[394]. Yet Gavin praises the Negro because "he had patience even when he didn't have hope, the long view even when there was nothing to see at the end of it, not even just the will but the desire to endure because he loved the old few simple things which no one wanted to take from him. . ." [394]. Gavin now shifts levels and the "we" becomes the white Southerners and the black Southerners. The blacks and whites in the South should confederate and "swap him the rest of the economic and political and cultural privileges which are his right, for the reversion of his capacity to wait and endure and survive" [395]. Together they would prevail and dominate the United States. Not even the greedy in America nor the shallow superpatriots would be able to threaten this coalition of black and white Southerners who would demonstrate the best qualities of a national character. The conclusion to Gavin's speech foreshadows the notion of "prevailing" that Faulkner restated in his Nobel Prize Speech of 1950. It is a far more fitting climax to Gavin's speech than his first attempt.

Faulkner originally finished Gavin's speech on [120] and picked up the narrative again; the car containing Gavin and his nephew draws up behind the sheriff's car. On the bottom of [120] Faulkner had some difficulty picking up after Gavin's speech, in describing the church and the churchyard. Though not painted, the church is not in disrepair nor shabby looking. In revising his description on [121], Faulkner smoothed out the previous description without changing his basic attitude towards the church, though he did lengthen his description of it by a catalogue of adjectives, "solitary but not forlorn, intractable and independent, asking nothing of any, making compromise with none. . ." [121]. The sheriff's two Negroes carried the pick and shovel. As Faulkner described the cemetery, he seemed to faulter with his expression. In a crossed-off section on [121], Faulkner described the cemetery as a fenced-in square of earth less large "than garden plots he had seen and dotted without order with slabs of cheap gray granite of the same gray color as the paintless church as if they had been hewed out of its flanks with axes and it had not been decay or time which compelled into the church's walls the raw new patching but the exigencies of mortality. . . ." In revising this section on [122] Faulkner speculated what the cemetery would look like in September, full of sagegrass, ragweed, and beggarlice. The tombstones stood out like bookmarks resembling the church in color.

As the posse prepares to dig up Vinson Gowrie's grave, which they thought contained the body of Jake Montgomery, the sheriff asks why the three original gravediggers had not put back the flowers on the grave. Chick's recollections are vague; he thought he had asked Aleck Sander to put the flowers back [123] or perhaps it was Miss Habersham reminding him to put the flowers back. Thus, Faulkner provides a small clue that the grave has been tampered with again. As they began to dig, Mr. Gowrie appears from behind the church, followed by his two sons riding double on a big mule, followed by two Trigg fox-hounds. Faulkner noted in pencil that it was Gowrie's "left" sleeve [123] that was folded up and the cuff pinned to the shoulder. Also, Faulkner wrote in pencil, "I got your message" [124] before Nub Gowrie asked the sheriff what was happening. Faulkner never used these words in the setting copy, nor did he use the crossed-off marginal note in blue ink: "I got word from a Nigra at breakfast this morning that some kind of biby sheelying [?] was going on up here. But he ran. I couldn't fetch him or I'd whupped the rest of it out of him. What are *you* going to do?" [124]. The sheriff insists he will open the grave. Gowrie takes out his gun and the sheriff grabs the two Negroes so that he is between them and Gowrie. The Negroes want to flee but both Gowrie and the sheriff persuade them that running around in convict pants is asking for trouble. Finally, the sheriff tells Gowrie his boy is not in the grave.

The narrator next paraphrases two early monologues: the

sheriff had told Gavin before that he would not be telling him about the exhumation unless it were true; likewise, Mr. Gowrie is thinking, according to the narrator who is explaining Chick's thoughts, that the sheriff would not be telling him about Vinson not being in the grave unless it were true [125]. In addition, Chick thinks of his own previous feelings towards Lucas when he discovered that Lucas was grieving for his dead wife; now he realizes that Mr. Gowrie is grieving for Vinson [126]. In a crossed-off section on the bottom of [125], before Chick realizes that Gowrie is grieving, Gowrie asks the sheriff to tell him the name of the person who proved that Vinson was not in the grave. Gowrie then orders his sons to come and start digging, but the sheriff interrupts and says, "We'll do it" [125]. Faulkner deleted this bit of dialogue and on [126] elaborated on the grief Chick had seen, once in an "old nigger who had just happened to outlive his old nigger wife" [126] and now in a "violent foul-mouthed ungodly old man" [126] who had lost a lawless and idle son. Thus at this point, there is some identity between Mr. Gowrie and Lucas, not in their philosophy, but on an affective level, since both grieve because they have lost someone dear to them, regardless of how society viewed the deceased.

Faulkner typed out on [126] the dialogue between the sheriff and Gowrie about revealing the name of the one who could prove Vinson is not in the grave. The sheriff tells Gowrie that Jake Montgomery is in the grave. Again Faulkner went back and crossed off this material, some of it for the second time. On [127], Faulkner composed the upper part of this page, by typing and then crossing off phrases and typing some more. At first, Faulkner had typed that when the sheriff told Gowrie that the grave was not empty, Gowrie stared at the sheriff who stared back and "afterward he realized that his was when he should have understood comprehended not only why the old man and his two sons happened to ride out of the woods behind the church almost as soon as he and the sheriff and his uncle reached the grave but. . ." [127], but then he went back and deleted this section and in place of "should have understood" wrote "believed he knew," adding "not perhaps why Lucas had ever reached town alive because there had been no Gowries present at his capture except the dead one, but at least how the old man and two of his sons happened to ride out of the woods behind the church almost as soon as he and the sheriff and his

uncle reached the grave and why Lucas was breathing yet"
[127]. Here is a critical point in the original draft of the novel;
the sheriff intuited "how" the Gowries came to be at the cemetery just when the sheriff and his posse would arrive. Faulkner
does not elaborate on this, perhaps because those at the cemetery
have not dug up the grave, yet somebody who knew both the
mystery of the body-switch in the grave and the Gowrie family
is directly involved in the murder.

On [125], Faulkner had originally written, " 'Why, I just
hope you wont tell me the name of the feller that proved my boy
aint there, Shurf. I just hope you wont' and then turned shouting to the two younger men who had moved, still sitting on the
mule outside the fence: 'Here, boys—' ". On [126], Faulkner
expanded this section, altering the last part to "the two younger
men who had not moved, not even to get down from the mule
outside the fence. . . ." In a third version of this material in the
original draft, Faulkner wrote, "The old man turned, immediate,
not hurriedly nor even quickly but just easily as if his spare small
fleshless frame offered neither resistance to the air nor weight
to the motive muscles, and shouted toward the fence beyond
which the two younger men still sat the mule, not even having
moved yet to get down: 'Here, boys' " [127]. In the setting
copy, this section was typed as follows: "The old man turned,
immediate, not hurriedly and even quickly but just easily as if
his spare small fleshless frame offered neither resistance to the
air nor weight to the motive muscles, and shouted toward the
fence where the two younger men still sat the mule identical as
two clothing store dummies and as immobile, not even having
begun yet to descend until the old man shouted: 'Here, boys' "
[403]. In this last version, Faulkner added to the previous
version the description of the twins as being like clothing store
dummies. As with previous examples, Faulkner composed this
final version by slowly adding on to the previous versions and
trying to let the force of the situation emerge with all its in-
herent power. It was not so much his imagination working in
quantum leaps as working in a circular fashion going back over
the previous material and building up the total scene gradually.

Eventually Nub Gowrie insists that he and his boys will
dig up the grave. Faulkner typed out and then crossed off the
following, perhaps because it expressed a certain degree of

doubt which at this point might have been inappropriate for Gowrie to have: "We dont want no Nigras digging in our boy's grave whether he's. . ." [128]. However the sheriff says that the exhumation of Montgomery's body is his business. Gowrie draws his gun and threatens the two black men and the sheriff orders them back to the car. The two black convicts go around the twins now "identical as two clothespins on a line" [129] and return to the two cars. The twins start digging the grave and Faulkner identifies each of the Gowrie boys by name.

In describing Crawford Gowrie, Faulkner pictures him as an army deserter who lived in the hills near Jefferson for almost eighteen months. Ironically, Gavin noted that Crawford defended his freedom with a captured German automatic pistol which one of the McCaslin [130] (later changed to McCallum [406]) boys had taken from a captured "German office" [sic] [130]. Henry is originally mentioned as the oldest Gowrie son [129], but later Faulkner wrote that Forrest was the oldest [189]. When Crawford returned home, he worked "a little timber and cattle" and even "a little land" [130]. With this Faulkner has given the necessary clue: Crawford Gowrie was involved in lumber. But because this clue is submerged in a good deal of information about all the Gowrie boys it is likely to go unnoticed until a second reading. Besides, at this point, the sheriff and his posse still have to prove to the Gowries that Vinson is not in the grave, but Jake Montgomery. As Faulkner described the twins digging up the coffin on the last page of this chapter [131], he seemed to have known what he wanted to write as he changed it very little in the setting copy [407]. He did try to soften down the last sentence in the original draft; he had written that a "Thin cascade of dirt flowed down into it with a whispering rattling sound. He changed "cascade" to "trickle" and "rattling" to "pattering" perhaps because of a marginal note in blue ink next to this last sentence which seems to suggest "blood stain [plus two words that are undecipherable]." This is one of those chapters that Faulkner could bring to a conclusion without having to cut down a longer section and revise. Faulkner has presented a number of important clues: 1) Vinson and someone else were involved in sawmill operation. The unknown party was robbing the stacked lumber at night and hauling it to Glasgow and selling it; 2) Lucas maintains Vinson was not killed with his gun; 3) Lucas was in custody when Vinson's body was exhumed and when Montgomery was killed and later exhumed, too: 4) Crawford Gowrie had been involved in timber business and owned a captured German pistol. With these clues, Faulkner could easily bring the mystery to a close, at least in his own mind.

Chapter Six of the Original Draft

The chapter was originally labeled "VI," but altered to "VIII." It is similar to Chapter Eight in the first edition. In this chapter Faulkner was back with his country people; the episodes and dialogue seemed to come easy. There are twelve pages or parts of pages used in this chapter. This chapter required almost no rewriting for the final version and must have given Faulkner a degree of confidence because he saw at this point the direction the novel was headed and would not have to write more than a few pages once he had finished with this chapter. Another indication that Faulkner thought his work was coming along fine is that he used no versos in this chapter and there are few penciled-in corrections. This is the smoothest chapter he has written so far, at least from the point of view of composition.

Most of the revisions are to provide a greater sense of continuity rather than to give philosophical depth or a new dimension to the novel. For instance, after trying to figure out where one would bury a body before dawn without a shovel, Gavin thinks "In sand" [135]. In the revision, Faulkner added three sentences: "In the bed of the branch. Didn't they tell you at three oclock this morning that they saw him going there with it? What are we waiting for?" [412] (page 170 of the first edition). Yet in revising his descripton of Nub Gowrie as originally found on [135], which went as far as Gowrie buttoning his shirt, Faulkner noted, Gowrie "took the pistol from the armpit and thrust it back inside the shirt then buttoned the shirt again then turned even faster quicker than the two sons half his age, already in front of everybody when he hopped back over the fence and went to the mare and caught reins and pommel all in one hand, already swinging up. . ." [412]. Occasionally there would be mistyped or misspelled words such as "crasjhing" [135] for "crashing" or "hall" [136] for "hill." "Sword" on [141] is changed to "scythe" [420] (page 177 of the first edition) and "blank depthless milklike" is added before "sand" on [420]. On [142], Faulkner typed that "the old man. . .wiped at the dead face rapidly." In the final version, he typed on [422] that he "wiped the [dead face] or at the dead face" when it looks like the word "or" belongs to the two crossed-off words. Thus I believe the "the or" should be deleted (page 178 of the first edition). This is an example of where a precise reading of the setting copy is needed in order to bring about as accurate a text of the novel as possible.

On [136], the sheriff confirms that the body was brought down the hill on a mule. In the revised version Gavin says he hopes it is not a black mule with a rope burn, "Not even a murderer is that crassly and arrogantly extrovert" [414]. The sheriff adds that is why such criminals are dangerous and should be locked up. On the botton of [136], Faulkner had originally included a dialogue between the sheriff and Gavin concerning the two trips the murderer made. This dialogue was crossed off and Faulkner included the same information on [137] in a monologue that the sheriff seems to carry on with himself. Also on [137], Faulkner made a short insertion about the mule carrying a burden he was not meant to carry. On [140], the sheriff asks one of the Gowrie twins where the quicksand is. The second twin responds it's "Under the highway bridge" where it has always been. In the revision of this section, Chick replies before the second Gowrie twin can: " 'It's by the bridge:' then—he didn't know why: and then that didn't matter either —'It wasn't Aleck Sander that time. It was Highboy' " [418]. The sheriff in the setting copy asks "which one was Highboy?", but his question is never answered [419]. All of these revisions are minor and do not alter in any significant way the original conception of this chapter.

This sixth chapter begins with the words, "And he would remember it. . ." [132], that is, Chick would remember the five of them standing over the empty coffin. This act of memory has been a stylistic device that Faulkner has prepared his reader for and one he used with great effect earlier in *Absalom, Absalom!* when Quentin and Shreve are talking. On [132], Faulkner's typing is sloppy and there are mistyped words, "steike" for "strike," "sild" for "slid," "troysers" for "trousers." The hunt then begins using the two Twigg hounds to search for Vinson Gowrie. On [133], Nub Gowrie tells the sheriff, "You're the one that seems to know all about this, that sent me out to my breakfast table at six oclock this morning to meet you here. Now you get started," thus using the marginal note Faulkner had written on [124] in a slightly different form. It is the sheriff who had Gowrie come to the graveyard, not Crawford.

The sheriff then reconstructs the scene and again from a mystery point of view, the action which had been acted out, is now filled in from a speculative point of view. Those present pretend it is 11 P.M. on Sunday night. What would the murderer do? Gavin suggests the murderer would put the body back into the earth [133]. It is presupposed by Gavin that Lucas would be able to persuade someone to come out and look at the body which had to be moved so that the bullet could not be verified. Gavin's speculations are abstract and do not visually help in understanding the situation: "Especially when he still had time to come back and do it all over again, alone, by himself, no hand but his on the shovel—And think of that too: the need, the terrible need, not just to have it all to do again but to have to do it again for the reason that he had. . ." [134]. The murderer had exhumed Vinson Gowrie's body, buried Jake Montgomery's in its place, and transported Gowrie's body down for another burial. The three saw the murderer transport the body, and then they went up and discovered Montgomery's body. As they dug up the grave with Montgomery's body in it, the murderer returned, spied on them, and later exhumed Montgomery's body, too. At this point Gavin does not ask why Montgomery's body was buried there to begin with. The murderer must have suspected that someone would try and dig up Gowrie's body. Should they find Montgomery's body too, the murderer would be leaving evidence that he killed another man, thus indicating that Lucas is innocent and that it was not just a matter of mischevious grave-robbers stealing Gowrie's body. Nub Gowrie tells Chick: "Show us exactly where you were when you saw the mule pass" [135]. Everyone then goes off in search of Vinson Gowrie's new gravesite. The sheriff, finding some mule prints, agrees that Aleck Sander was right the first time [136].

On the bottom of [136], Faulkner wrote twelve lines and

then crossed them off; he repeated this material on the following page. It concerned the movements of the murderer up to the graveyard and back. In this first try, Faulkner did not resolve the movements of the murderer. In the second try, the sheriff tried to offer an explanation why the murderer would not come back to the original gravesite. "The first time he didn't have time" [137] and he went straight up the hill and heard something, perhaps Aleck Sander whistling. Then they found where the murderer had tied the mule to a sapling and carried something since his footprints were deeper than usual. Towards the bottom of [137], Faulkner added in blue ink: "he thought of that too: the anguish, the desperation, the urgency," which eventually became in the setting copy: "his prints also deeper than any man no matter how heavy should have made and he thought of that too: the anguish, the desperation, the urgency in the black dark and the briers and the dizzy irrevocable fleeing on seconds, carrying a burden man was not intended to carry. . ." [415].

As they discover a new gravesite, Nub Gowrie bounds down and creates a state of pandemonium. The grave turns out to be Montgomery's, buried when the murderer was in a hurry. Faulkner fills in the details of early Monday morning; except for changing the time from three o'clock, the rest of the corrections are minor stylistic ones: "after two oclock when he and Aleck Sander, even two of them working with furious speed, had got the grave filled back up again so that by the time the murderer, not only alone but who had already moved the six feet of dirt and put it back once since the sun set yesterday, had the second body out and the grave filled again it must have been daylight, later than daylight, the sun itself watching him while he rode for the second time down the road and across to the branch, morning itself watching him while he hacked furiously from the shelving bank just enough dirt to hide it. . ." [139]. Gradually Faulkner is establishing the chronology of events for the reader, more supplying it since no one here is trying to guess it any more.

The sheriff then tells Gowrie that he thinks the murderer was foolish because he acted in a hurry. The sheriff asks where the quicksand is [139]. One of the twins informs them that it is under the bridge. Unfortunately Faulkner does not explain how it was easier to bury Montgomery in a shallow grave than in the quicksand under the bridge; the opposite would seem more true.

Again Nub Gowrie whirls around and runs for the bank. Eventually he lands in the quicksand and stands on Vinson's body. Unlike Chick, Vinson is buried in quicksand rather than falling into a river and coming out alive. Vinson's body is pulled out feet first with "smacking plop" sounds [141]. Gavin extends a handkerchief and Gowrie wipes "at the dead face rapidly" [142]. Thus the sheriff is able now to tell Nub Gowrie that Lucas did not kill Vinson, that Montgomery was at Vinson's funeral on Sunday, and during the funeral Lucas was in jail [143]. Gowrie responds that he is not concerned about Montgomery, that he does not care whether Lucas killed Montgomery or not. But the sheriff replies that he is talking about Lucas not killing Vinson. Finally Gowrie has enough courage to ask what type of gun killed his son. The sheriff replies that it was a German Luger automatic like the one Buddy McCallum brought home from France in 1919. The sheriff gives no real evidence for this claim, though Gowrie seems to accept this as if he realizes its truth deep down in his heart. Before Gowrie orders his sons to load Vinson's body on the mule, Faulkner added in pencil the feeling he wanted to achieve as Nub Gowrie speaks to his sons "peremptory and loud, not brookless of opposition or argument, simply incapable of conceiving it" [143].

Faulkner ended this chapter at the very bottom of page [143]; it is impossible to say whether he intended to end it here or not as the next page [144] is labeled in pencil "IX," not "VII" as would be expected if he were typing the chapter heads consecutively. It looks like the "IX" in pencil was added while writing the setting copy and the division of the chapter was made then, not while writing the original draft. In any case, the murder is almost solved and the only thing left to do is to obtain a confession from Crawford, have Lucas explain the situation a bit more fully from his point of view, and establish the relationship between Vinson, Crawford, Montgomery, and Lucas. Faulkner has led us to suspect that Crawford killed both Vinson and Montgomery, though we have no absolute evidence for this.

The Last Chapter of the Original Draft

This short last chapter of the original draft was labeled

as "IX" in pencil. There are seven pages or parts of pages in this chapter and at best is a compilation of assorted pages whose interlocking arrangement is difficult to follow. The energy has obviously gone out of Faulkner's intention of finishing the first draft, and he must have seen at this point the direction he would take in the second version. This chapter begins with the phrase "He would remember" [144] which occurs in the final version on page 211 of the first edition [506], part way into Chapter Ten. These words are similar to the previous chapter in the original draft on [132] where the chapter begins "and he would remember it. . . ." In effect, then, Faulkner did not originally conceive of all the material in Chapter Nine of the setting copy in this original draft.

Faulkner begins with Chick's recollection of standing with his uncle beside the sheriff's car in the alley beside the jail. The two watch Lucas and the sheriff emerge from the jail and go to a car. His uncle says that they should take someone with them since he did not want Lucas to go with so little protection. Faulkner does not give any indication where the sheriff is taking Lucas or for what purpose. We do know in a crossed-off section of [144] however that it is past 10 P.M. on Monday evening and that the first movie show had already started. Usually the cars and trucks would be going home this time of evening, but not tonight. Faulkner wrote that at 11 A.M. that morning [144] and then he changed it to 2 P.M. that afternoon [144], and then on [146] and [145] kept it two o'clock that afternoon, in his uncle's car just behind the sheriff's, Chick had seen a mass of people crowding the Square. After typing [144], Faulkner continued on [147] linking the two pages by the phrase "it seemed to him that the people—all men now and not just countrymen but town men too. . . ." Faulkner then crossed this page off and inserted [150] which picked up Gavin's comment from [144], "I dont like this. Take somebody with you" [150], repeating much of what is on [144]. Page [150] is continued on [146 (V)] which was crossed off and then Faulkner picked up the phrase "sleep-ward tomorrow-ward" from the middle of [150].

Faulkner then went back to [144] at the bottom and picked up the crossed-off line (third from the bottom) "last were dispersing" and tried to continue with this line twice, once on [145] and then on [146]. He labeled page [146] as "119-A" and inserted it before [147]. In all of this Faulkner is not really advancing the story or making major modifications; it is more a matter of shifting phrases around in a haphazard fashion. Faulkner then concluded the chapter with two more attempts on [148] and [149], both of which begin with a line he had crossed off in the middle of [147], "waiting to recognize the sheriff's car. . . ."

On [148] Faulkner had typed a section about the towns-folk:

> . . .waiting to recognize or for that matter look at the sheriff's car, flow and stream like the set of a tide in one single converging direction, across the mouth of the street where it entered the Square and across the Square itself and even into the alley behind his uncle's car so that even before the sheriff drove into the closed loading ramp behind the undertaker's where the coroner would be waiting [for them] the whole street was blocked with them, the faces massed pressed against the plate glass window beyond which there was nothing to see but in a maroon earthenware pot against a sunfaded purple curtain one shabby palm, he and his uncle walking now since it was impossible to move their car, up the narrow passage beside the undertaker's walking into the bleak faces no longer jocular now, the faces making way for them to pass. . . .
> [148]

This material was crossed off by Faulkner and discarded; it is found on [144] and [464] of the setting copy as part of the beginning of Chapter Nine of the first edition, especially pages 181 and 183.

When Faulkner repeated this material on [149] he added that Gavin told Chick "I'm going to take you home so you can get some sleep." The final words of this final chapter of the first draft are "This morning they were merely coping with a must-not. Now they are faced with a shall-not. . . ." [149]; this phrase was probably the catalyst that prompted Faulkner to think that he had much more to give to Gavin and his philosophy about Sambo and the South. Faulkner ended his original draft of the novel with an attempt to describe the townsfolk viewing the sheriff bringing Jake Montgomery's body to the undertaker's and with one voice speaking for all those gathered that "Jake Montgomery was at the funeral. And Hope had that nigger locked up in jail" [149]. Thus Faulkner had developed the mystery up to the point where the townsfolk knew that neither Montgomery nor Lucas had killed Vinson Gowrie. Once this knowledge became public, it was a matter of bringing all the evidence together and tying up the case. In a sense this was probably Faulkner's intention and he must have felt confident enough with the story at this point that he could begin again and conclude the story with one major revision. In fact though, the last few chapters of the setting copy took considerable rewriting.

Faulkner concluded this unfinished chapter by having Chick remember the events of Monday night as the sheriff brought Lucas from the jail and put him in the car. Gavin objects to such an action by the sheriff; it is past 10 P.M. and the sheriff and Lucas would be vulnerable to an attack especially as their departure might be seen by townsfolk. But few people were on the street now; it is empty in contrast to 2 P.M. that afternoon when a large group of countrymen, merchants, clerks and mechanics were on their way back from lunch, many of whom were in the street when the sheriff brought Lucas in at noon. When Gavin's car followed the sheriff's which pulled into the loading ramp by the undertaker's back door, the mass of people crowded close around. The emphasis in these final pages is on the crowd and Faulkner tries to capture their moods and movement. They flow like a river and have impersonal faces which in the setting copy [463] will become one corporate "face." The people "flow and stream like the set of a tide" across "the mouth of the street" [148]. When the crowd sees the sheriff's car pull up to the undertaker's, they ask Gavin who it is. He tells them it is Jake Montgomery and they realize too that Jake was at Vinson's funeral and Lucas was in jail during that time. With this the crowd departs "ebbing as tideturn slacks and ebbs" [149] and Gavin's concern is to get Charles home so he can sleep [149]. As he concluded the final pages of the first draft, Faulkner was impatient with his material. Clearly, he might better start over and let what by now was a familiar story to him take definite shape.

III

THE SETTING COPY

In a letter to Haas on February 22, 1948, Faulkner mentioned that he had finished the first draft of *Intruder* and was rewriting it. He had no definite timetable in mind for finishing the second draft; he said he would just work at it. In a little over six weeks, by April 9th, he was working on the last chapter of the second draft and by April 23rd, Haas received word that he should expect to receive the finished manuscript in the mail within a few days. Faulkner wasted no time in finishing this novel as he typed methodically from chapter to chapter.

The preliminary material of the setting copy consists of the following five pages all on Management Bond paper (21.3 cm. x 27.6 cm.), a Hammermill product:

[151]   [320 40972]   The title "Intruder in the Dust" is written in blue ink in a hand other than Faulkner's. In the margin, it is noted in pencil that the type size is to be 24 point Baskerville italic.

[152]   [321 40972]   This is the "bastard page" with "Intruder in the Dust" written in blue ink in a hand other than Faulkner's. A note indicates that the same type size as used on [151] will be used here too.

[153]   [322 40972]   A list of Faulkner's previous books is to go on this page. The book titles themselves will be in 11/13 point Baskerville type. The heading "Books by William Faulkner" will be set in two centered lines in 18 point Baskerville italic type.

[154]   [323 40972]   This is the title page. The "I" and "D" will be in 60 point Ultra Bodini caps and the rest of the lettering

in the title will be in 48 point lower case Baskerville. The word "by" will be in 18 point Baskerville italic; the words "William Faulkner" in 24 point Baskerville; and the words "Random House/New York" in 11/13 point Baskerville.

[155]   [324 40972] This is the copyright page. The type size will be 9 point Baskerville with the words "First Printing" flush with the first line of the page of text and "Manufactured in United States of America" flush with the last line of the page of text.

All the other pages in the setting copy are on Hammermill Bond (21.6 cm. x 27.9 cm.).

Faulkner typed the second draft of *Intruder in the Dust* with the intention that it be used as the setting copy. He took great care to keep the pages in order and made legible corrections as was not often the case in the original draft. He also took great care in crossing off certain sections with bold horizontal and vertical strokes in either blue or red ink. Though a few carbon pages exist in the setting copy, as noted in Appendix A, I do not believe Faulkner actually made a complete carbon copy of the entire setting copy. Inserting sheets of carbon paper and making corrections on the carbon paper would have slowed down enormously the process of composing and it does not seem as if Faulkner felt a great need to have an extra complete copy at home should the setting copy get lost in the mail. He never mentioned this problem in his correspondence with Random House.

In analyzing the setting copy, I will explain how it differs from the first draft in order to appreciate the second level of Faulkner's imagination at work. Except for the last few chapters where Faulkner did not have the original draft to use as a basis, the setting copy is not unduly complicated. As with the analysis of the first draft, I will indicate Faulkner's method of composition, not only by focusing on the final version that Faulkner sent to New York, but also by discussing the importance of the 138 pages of miscellaneous text that were rejected. As I did previously, I will incorporate key sections from these discarded pages into this book. The following textual evaluation of *Intruder* should give the scholar who prepares a definitive edition some of the necessary background to begin his job. Thus, I hope that this textual evaluation will ultimately have a practical value of assisting in the production of an accurate edition of *Intruder.*

Chapter One of the Setting Copy

In the setting copy, Faulkner was careful to achieve a text that read smoothly and contained only those calculated ambiguities he considered part of this mystery novel. The first chapter of the setting copy is not significantly different from that of the original draft. There are twenty-one pages or parts of pages used in this chapter. In manuscript in blue ink, Faulkner noted on [156] that the sheriff reached town with Lucas about noon on Sunday morning, a fact already determined in the original draft. Faulkner is careful not to give Lucas' full name in the first sentence of the first chapter, even to the point of changing a reference to him ("he") back to just his first name. As he had done in the original draft, however, Faulkner retained the indefinite reference to Chick ("He") in the first sentence of the second paragraph.

Faulkner clarified the time scheme in this part of the setting copy. He revealed that Gavin's purpose (though Gavin is only identified at this point as the "uncle") for going to the post office might be to get the 11 A.M. mail, though it does seem strange that Gavin would be concerned about mail on Sunday. Faulkner also decided that Chick had eaten at Lucas' house four years before, when he was twelve. This removes the note of ambiguity in the chronology that had been part of the first draft. Likewise, Faulkner clarifies some chronology concerning Gavin's background. Originally he had typed that Carothers Edmonds had gone to the State University together with Gavin before "his uncle had gone to Harvard and then to Heidelberg." This phrase was crossed off and changed so that Gavin attended the State University after he had been at Harvard and Heidelberg [156].

Faulkner also made some oblique connections between Chick and Vinson Gowrie. In the setting copy, Faulkner noted that Chick and Aleck Sander and Edmonds went to Edmonds' house and on their way they passed the Nine Mile branch. With hindsight, the reader realizes that both Chick and Vinson Gowrie wind up in the same creek. The relationship is made even stronger when Faulkner typed that the empty carcasses ("of hogs" which he later deleted) would be "immobilised by the heels" [157], an image similar to the one used later on of Vinson Gowrie being plucked from the quicksand by his heels. In addition, the "potlicker dog" which Faulkner had mentioned in a marginal note in the original draft is now said to have an affinity with rabbits like "Negroes had with mules" [158]; Aleck Sander knew that it was a mule not a horse that the murderer used to bring Vinson Gowrie's body down from the cemetery.

This early part of the novel reveals something about Faulkner's method of revision. As the three boys go out hunting rabbits, each is carrying something. Chick has a gun and the two other boys have one tapstick each [158], though in a crossed-off section on [158] Edmonds' boy had two tapsticks to begin with. As Faulkner typed this page concerning the activity of the three boys [158], he came to the bottom of the page and crossed off two lines in blue ink, then repeated the information on [159] beginning with the word "happened." Thus, Faulkner made his corrections as he wrote and did not write a whole chapter and then go back and retype certain sections. He tried to achieve an accurate and final form of expression as he composed each page.

Faulkner had ended the last chapter of the original draft by focusing on the faces of the mob as they witnessed Jake Montgomery's body being brought into the undertakers. Now in the first chapter of the setting copy, he also focuses on Lucas' face, a technique he had tried in a limited way in the original draft. Chick first hears Lucas speak [159], a change from the original draft. When he looks up, he sees "—a face which in his estimation might have been under fifty or even under forty except for the hat and the eyes, and inside a Negro's skin but that was all even to a boy of twelve shaking with cold and still panting from shock and exertion because what looked out of it had no pigment at all, not even the white man's lack of it, not arrogant, not even scornful; just intractable and composed" [160]. By concentrating on Lucas' face here, Faulkner has achieved a moral perspective in addition to a physical description. Lucas as a moral person has no distinctive pigmentation, not that he is like a white man, but that he cannot be characterized by the features and attributes that a Southern writer would be expected to use in a description of a black man. It is this touch, one that is often overlooked in analyzing this book, that adds to the philosophical quality of the novel in a way that Gavin's speeches cannot.

After this description of Lucas, Faulkner followed his original draft closely, not word for word, but more item by item, or event by event. There are slight variations worth noting. Chick, for example, is able to figure out why he does not turn up the road to Edmonds' house when following Lucas to Lucas' house, something he had not done in the original draft. The real reason is that he could not contradict Lucas any more than he could do so to his grandfather [161]; a pseudo reason is that Edmonds might send him home. As the four enter Lucas' house in single file, Faulkner gives a more ample description of the house, beginning with a dim hall, not a bedroom as in the original draft [15]. Also in the setting copy, Chick notes that he recognizes the smell where Negroes live; he is sure about this in much the same way he is sure that "all people named Mollison [sic] are Methodists. . ." [163]. So far, this is the first indication the reader has of any part of Chick's name.

In the description of Lucas' house, Faulkner continued to make some changes. He mentions a kerosene lamp, a colored lithograph, and a chrome portrait of two people. The house is a bit warmer and more cheerful than in the original conception; a "halfburned backlog glowed" [164], not just the smoldering ends of logs. In the setting copy [164], Chick tries to remember what his uncle had told him, until he forgets having been told anything at all. As Chick is enveloped in the quilt and the smell of the house, Faulkner prepares the reader for some unspecified future event: ". . .it was still an hour yet before the thing would happen and it would be four years more before he would realize the extent of its ramifications and what it had done to him and he would be a man grown before he would realize, admit that he had to accept it" [166]. In describing Lucas by the mantel, Faulkner notes that not only did he have a beaver hat like Chick's grandfather, but he had a gold toothpick like his grandfather, an item mentioned in the first draft but not where this section initially occurred.

Faulkner takes his time in bulding up the eating scene in Lucas' house. He first of all has Chick announce that he will have dinner at Mr. Edmonds' house [167], only to have Lucas reply that his wife has already dished out his portion. Faulkner did not vary the menu from the first to the second draft. When Chick finished, he got up from the table, took out a half-dollar [168], presumably one coin as in the original draft, and walked into the other room (a bedroom in the original [19]), and noticed the details of a group portrait containing Lucas and his wife. It should be noted that Lucas is looking out of the picture as "out of a seer's crystal ball" [169]. In the setting copy, Molly speaks about the picture and Lucas comments that Molly does not like the picture because they made her take off her headrag [169]. On [171], Chick remembers what he had forgotten on [164], that this woman was Molly whose death would later cause Lucas to withdraw into his own private world.

Eventually Chick puts the half-dollar back into his pocket and fingers a quarter and two nickels [171]. Chick talks to Molly and he says that his uncle, Gavin, knows her and Molly, in turn, replies that she knows Mrs. Mallison, who used to be Miss Maggie Witten. Chick extends the coins to Molly who would have taken them, but does not. Lucas asks what the money is for [171] and Chick puts the coins back into his pocket. Subsequently the three boys run from the house [173] and Lucas orders them to stay out of the creek. Faulkner then continued on [173] with the material that is at the beginning of the second chapter. It is clear that as he wrote the setting copy, Faulkner had not made up his mind where he would end the first chapter; the original draft did not indicate a distinction between the first and second chapters at this point either. Faulkner continued typing up to the point where Aleck Sander wanted Chick to shoot a rabbit that had run out in front of them. Chick then takes four coins from his pocket and throws them into the creek.

Then Faulkner revised the ending. He typed on [179] the exact same words he had typed on [171] and as he would later type on [172]: ". . .she had hair. . . ." Page [170] is almost a duplicate of the material on [171], though here Chick scoops out a dime and two nickels from his pocket rather than fingering a quarter and two nickels as previously indicated. Also, on [170] Chick's grandmother's maiden name is "Whitten," not the name "Witten" his mother was supposed to have had [171]. The conclusion to [170] is the order of Lucas to the three boys to go and shoot rabbits and stay out of the creek, the ending as is found in the first edition.

In retyping this material for the third time on [172], Chick puts the half-dollar back into his pocket and scoops out a dime and two nickels. Also Molly says that she knows Chick's mother, the former Miss Maggie Dandridge, but Chick corrects her and says that was his grandmother. His mother was a Stevens. The last scene of this version reverberates with Lucas' voice when, after Chick turns his hand upside down and scatters the seventy cents on the floor, Lucas tells the boys to go and shoot their rabbit and stay out of the creek [175], a warning which unfortunately Vinson Gowrie did not heed. On [510 (V)], Faulkner typed a five-line draft of [175] in which he noted the coins had "an almost infinitesmal" motion as they fell to the floor. Faulkner's most important change, therefore, is to give the chapter a sharper form by having the boys warned to stay out of the creek. Not only has Lucas been a generous host, but he has communicated to the boys a sense of personal power and authority.

Chapter Two of the Setting Copy

Because the original first page of the second chapter of the setting copy [174] (following the discarded [170]) was not numbered, I am certain Faulkner had not decided in advance where to end the first chapter of the setting copy. It was when writing [176] that he labeled this page "II." There are seventy-six pages or parts of pages used in this chapter. Pages [176]-[177] repeat what Faulkner had written on [174] with only very slight stylistic changes. The only noticeable change from the original draft is that the ante has been raised from fifty cents [20] to seventy cents [177]. As Faulkner continued writing the second chapter, he followed substantially the original draft, giving all the time a certain fulness to his writing, such as including a list of items in the crossroads store: sodapop, tobacco, cigarettes, and pipes [178]. When Lucas enters the store, he has his gold toothpick [179], something not in the original.

Faulkner in the setting copy is able to show how Lucas, by casually eating a gingersnap, is above the charges and epithets leveled at him. Also, by sucking his teeth, Lucas shows a disdainful attitude which further infuriates the white men. Faulkner ends this scene with Lucas leaving the store, ironically being ordered out as Chick had been ordered out of Lucas' house.

In the original version of the man attacking Lucas with a plow handle on [181], which Faulkner later crossed off, Faulkner had used two sentences to describe this action; in revising it on [180], he made it into one sentence, with the result that the scene is a more fluid piece of writing, reflecting the uninterrupted quality of the altercation itself. On [181], Faulkner repeated a phrase he had used originally on [22]: "Because there was the half-dollar." In the setting copy, Faulkner had previously changed the amount and therefore he now explains that by half-dollar he actually means seventy cents, a sum which now in Chick's mind is all out of proportion to its actual worth. The half-dollar becomes the hard round symbol of his anguish; he would like to block it out of his mind, to eclipse it with his life, to restore the manhood both to himself and his race, to put up a fighting battle. This congeries of feelings motivates Chick to achieve some type of financial responsibility by helping his uncle at his law office. Chick simulates responsibility and gives an intimation of his willingness to assume an adult role in public. It is interesting to note that on [182] in telling the story of the boy and the calf, Faulkner added "He deserted his calf," a phrase not found in the original story. If Chick were to grow up, he would have to strike out on his own and not follow a formula that did not allow for spontaneous growth. Since Faulkner begins the episode of Chick earning money to buy Christmas presents for Lucas and Molly with the phrase "Because there was the half-dollar," it is obvious that he is uniting in some meaningful way the boy-calf story with Chick's desire to pay back Lucas. Both episodes express a sense of individual responsibility; the first does not succeed and the second is undetermined at present.

In the crossed-off section on [183], Faulkner gives the same chronological information about Chick's age as he did on [23], that is, the summer after Chick had given the presents to Edmonds to deliver to Lucas, Chick was going on thirteen. On

[202 (V)], when Mrs. Mallison mentioned that the molasses had been delivered by a white boy, the narrator then added (later crossed-off): "And that was almost all. He was thirteen and fourteen; one day he was fifteen and suddenly he realised that it was over, that in effect he had seen Lucas for the last time. He has seen him three times more in the three years, on the Square in town. . . ." At this point, Faulkner was getting ahead of himself, so he returned to his original draft [24] and noted that that event was four years ago and Molly was dead. Then on [186], he copied his material over again, repeating the information about the white boy bringing the molasses, then typing out the material he had crossed off on [202 (V)], still repeating that Chick would never see Lucas again. It seems that in this part Faulkner wanted a permanent separation between Chick and Lucas to take place, almost as if he never really envisioned the last scene of the book where the two actually meet in some type of mutual recognition. Here Chick is pictured as carrying into manhood a sense of anguish, not for revenge, but for "re-equalization, reaffirmation of his masculinity and his race" [186].

At the end of [186], Faulkner again typed the information about that event being four years ago and Molly was dead. Then Faulkner went back and crossed off the lower half of [183] and continued on [188 (bottom)] which provided continuity between the gifts to Lucas, which led up to the return gift of the molasses. The middle section of [188] is the original draft of [184]-[185] about Chick and Lucas being even, and Chick realizing that, in fact, he was losing because he could not take the molasses back to Lucas, partly because he was ashamed to ride a pony that far to Lucas' house. In another try on [199 (V)], Faulkner again went back to get this sequence in order; he repeated the information about the molasses and the white boy, then about it being four years ago and Molly being dead, and then picking up directly from the original draft on [24], he explained how yesterday Lucas returned to the same store where he had troubled a white man before, this time to kill a white man. The next-to-last line on [199 (V)] begins with the words, "a Negro," relating how the Gowries were the last people in the world to let a Negro kill one of the members of their family. Faulkner then spent three pages ([229], [191], [193]), each beginning with "a Negro," trying to fill out this section about the Gowries and their feelings towards black men.

On [229], the narrator speculates that the reason Lucas shot a white man was that the only man who would have stopped him, Carothers Edmonds, was in a New Orleans hospital after having an operation to remove gallstones. In the second try on [191], he omitted any reference to Edmonds, but suggested that a Negro such as Lucas was "a foreign outlander;" the emphasis here is on the Gowries being not only a clan, but a race and a species who inhabit Beat Four, where police officers seldom went and Negroes never. On the final try on [193], Faulkner numbered the page "23," thus having it follow [199 (V)] which he had numbered "22," both of which he would discard. On [193], Faulkner mentioned Edmonds again, repeating the information about the hospital, and then speculating that no man really could come between Lucas and what he wanted to do. Page [200 (V)] is another copy of [199 (V)] and [186].

When Faulkner came to the section on [200 (V)] about Chick seeking a reaffirmation of his masculinity, he continued with this section on the top of [189], which then, in turn, led into another version about Molly being dead and Lucas living alone. He added that Lucas only came into town on Saturdays usually a year apart, for the purpose of paying taxes, though he does not mention it here. Page [201 (V)] continues the thought of [189] (though leaving the reason still vague):

> . . .he saw him then was not that Lucas' presence had happened to coincide with his passage through the Square but that he had coincided with Lucas' solitary annual visits—but on weekdays like the white men who were not farmers but planters who wore neckties and vests like merchants and doctors and lawyers themselves, as if he refused, declined to accept even that little of the pattern not only of Negro but of country Negro behavior, always in worn brushed obviously once-expensive black broadcloth suit of the portrait picture on the gold easel and the raked fine hat and the boiled white shirt of his own grandfather's time and the tieless collar and the heavy watch-chain and the gold tooth pick like the one his own grandfather had carried in his upper vest pocket [text stops] . . . . [201 (V)]

Page [194] is the final version of [189] and here Faulkner gives the suggestion that Lucas' visits were "annual and necessary" [194].

After recounting meeting Lucas the first time in the second winter, information not in the original draft, Lucas tells Chick that the molasses turned out good, a response exactly like Chick's grandfather might have given [195]. The second time Chick saw Lucas was just after Molly had died and Lucas walked right passsed Chick. In retrospect Chick understood that Lucas was grieving for his dead wife and his attitude was therefore understandable. Finally, on [196], the reason for Lucas' visits to town is revealed: to pay his land taxes. Faulkner builds up to the third time Chick sees Lucas. This time Lucas sees Chick, but does not formally acknowledge him, except to bypass him, and then walk on. Chick feels enormously relieved because now there will be no communication between them apparently, and now Lucas can be remembered as a "ghost" [197], not a real flesh-and-blood black man who orders black boys to pick up coins, soon to become not even a ghost but a breath or whisper like the taste of sheep sorrel "eaten by the boy in his dead child-hood" [197].

In describing an imaginary meeting between Lucas and Chick as old men, Faulkner used the image "inesthetisable nerve-ends." Albert Erskine of Random House noted that "inesthetisable doesn't mean anything (unless it be 'incapable of being made sentient'); meaning, I think, calls for inanesthetis-able." The correction was adopted in the first edition. Likewise, in the imaginary dialogue between Chick and Lucas, Lucas "turned around and it was Lucas saying I was the man. . ." [198]; Erskine wanted a colon inserted after "saying;" while Faulkner apparently approved this changed, it was not made in the first edition. After this bit of dialogue, Chick again repeats this great feeling of freedom and the narrator says "He was free" [198]. In a marginal note, partly erased, it states, "End of suggested story." The note does not appear to be in Faulkner's handwriting; it probably indicates the end of the story "Lucas Beauchamp" which Meriwether said was sent out for publication before the completion of the setting copy.* The last part of the original draft to be included in the setting copy up to this point

---

*For a fuller treatment of the significance of this short story, see my article "Faulkner's Hidden Story in *Intruder in the Dust*," *Delta* (Université Paul Valéry: Montpellier, France) 3 (November 1976) 63-81.

was the fact of Molly's death and Lucas living alone. The ending to this short story segment then is not part of the original conception of the story as found in this part of the original draft. What Faulkner had actually done was to transpose a later part of the original draft [28] to this section of the setting copy. The event of meeting Lucas three times is in the original draft, but it occurs, after the dialogue in the barbershop which becomes a later scene in the setting copy. Artistically, it would be appropriate to end the short story where he did, because the emphasis would be on Lucas as a captured man who, though an alleged murderer, has freed a white boy from any obligation to him.

On [198], when Faulkner started typing again after finishing this short story, the narrator returns to the present time (Saturday afternoon); he picks up from the original draft on [24] right after Molly's death. Chick hears that Lucas had killed Vinson Gowrie; originally, however, Faulkner had typed, as in the original draft, "a white man." Faulkner then fills in the chronology by noting that word had come to the sheriff about 3 P.M. on Saturday, though the sheriff was out of town. In a crossed-off section on [198], Chick heads home, but turns back and goes to his uncle's office where Gavin is sitting with his feet on the desk and smoking a pipe. It might have been that Faulkner wanted to change the story around and have Chick and Gavin meet for a serious talk alone before bringing up the possibility of a Lucas-Gavin meeting. Whatever, Faulkner crossed this section off and made five successive attempts ([199], [203], [204], [206], [540 (V)]) to pick up from the phrase "judgment would have chosen":

> . . .judgment would have chosen—or for that matter anyone of any color to shoot anybody named Gowrie before or behind either, last of all this one: youngest of a family of six brothers and a ramification of cousins and inlaws whose total number probably even the old women of the connection could not have stated offhand—a family or farmers and foxhunters and stock- and timber-traders one of whom had already served a year in a federal penitentiary for armed resistance as an army deserter and another term at the state penal farm for making whiskey,—a family who would not even be the last anywhere to let one of their number be killed by anyone but only among the first since they were interlocked and intermarried and interrelated not even into a clan or a tribe

but into a race, a species [text stops] .... [540 (V)]

On [203] Faulkner deleted any mention of Chick going to Gavin's office and rather concentrated on the Gowries, again remaining close to his original draft [24], adding here that they were also "timber-traders." When he came to describe Beat Four, the section where the Gowries lived, "a synonym for independence and violence," the author mentions that Lucas found or followed or waylaid his victim, no one was sure which [203].

Again Faulkner modified his views about Beat Four on [226] explaining that few people went there at all, and no Negroes at any time. On [225], Faulkner went back and incorporated on this page all the material from the two previous pages ([203] and [226]). This section recounts the alleged murder; it mentions in a crossed-off section that the only reason Lucas was not lynched on the spot was that no Gowries were around. This was later changed to read that the reason was that the son of the store owner and the constable held the crowd off until the constable could take custody of Lucas. Faulkner then retained this notion of Beat Four as a "synonym of independence and violence," originally used on [25], for a later section [223], since it did not easily fit into what he wanted to do here. On [206], he again mentioned that Chick went up to Gavin's office, as mentioned earlier and crossed-off on [198], this time giving some dialogue between the two. When Chick asks why Lucas is in trouble, Gavin replies, "Does it matter?" and then even answers himself: "Not now. Not to Lucas nor anybody else of his color out there" [206]. The real question for Gavin is why Lucas of all people had to shoot a Gowrie. Then on [227], Faulkner again went back to his description of Beat Four, this time linking this material to the mid-1920's when people, as he put it, knew where Cicero, Illinois was and who lived there and what they did without knowing or caring where Chicago was or in what state it was located in. He followed this with thoughts on violence and independence though now "not so much for violence as for independence." Thematically it should be noted in terms of Gavin's later speeches about homogeneity, that here, at least, the Gowries are a "race, a species—a homogeneity which before this had made their hill stronghold good against the county and the federal government too so that, as a local wit said once, the only stranger ever to enter it with impunity was God and He only. . .by daylight and on Sunday. . ." [227].

When Faulkner started again on [204], he began to stretch out the story and get further away from the original draft at this point. His inclination earlier had been to get into the story of Lucas' alleged murder of Vinson, something already mentioned [198], a page he considered good copy at this point. He would not get to the part of the story of Lucas going into the woods where a gun shot was heard until thirteen pages later in the setting copy [224]. At this point, then, his original draft would not be his guide, except in a provisional sense. On [204], the transition is from a brief description of the young men who hung around the poolhall and barbershop to the fact that they were present at the store and helped transport Lucas to the constable's home where the constable waited for the sheriff and Edmonds to come, thus negating that maybe Edmonds was in a New Orleans hospital for an operation. The sheriff is fairly sure that Edmonds is at his house only four miles away. Chick, unlike Lucas, is free and so he retraces his footsteps and goes to Gavin's office. In this version, Chick unlocks the office door, enters the office, and sits at Gavin's table, much like Gavin did and like his grandfather had done before him at the rolltop desk. It looks as if Chick is about to become a third generation lawyer. On [211], in Gavin's office, Chick compares some twists of newspapers here with a vase on Lucas' mantel and recalls Gavin's remarks about time being all that man had. Chick also remembers that Edmonds was in New Orleans for sure. But Chick is not bound to anyone and so he wanders home freely. Since this last version is closest to the setting copy version, it is safe to presume that it was the last written and became the model for [207]-[213].

In this sequence of pages, [199], [200 (V)], [201], and [202] (including [189 (V)]), Faulkner again begins with "judgment would have chosen" and then goes on to mention that the last car load of young men had driven the fifteen miles to the constable's house where Lucas is handcuffed to a bedpost. The insert on [189 (V)] mentions that Edmonds would be there if he had been available and something nagged at Chick as he thought that only Edmonds and the constable would be the two people to defend Lucas. Chick, because he is free, walked to the corner. He thought that if something happened to keep his uncle at the office, then he could walk home with him, so he retraced his steps and went up to the stairs. There is an emphasis on Chick opening the door to the office [199], more like a minor echo of the door of the jail cell which, when opened, gives a cosmological groan. He makes the relationship between the newspaper twists and Lucas' vase and notes that his mother would have known what time the baseball game would be over, even if she had not heard the cheering [200 (V)]. Then remembering that Edmonds was in New Orleans in the hospital, he locks the door and goes out where people could gather to hear the news from Fraser's store.

Using a stream-of-consciousness technique, Faulkner has Chick recall, after seeing the jail, Sheriff Hampton and the in-laws who usually follow a man elected or appointed to office. Then again the refrain "he was free" [201]. Chick thinks how hungry he is and then almost immediately he is at the dinner table eating very little for which his mother reprimands him. She does not want him to go to the movies either. Then Gavin suggests that Chick do an errand for him and they go on to the front gallery. Gavin tells his nephew that it does not matter not "to Lucas nor anybody of his color out there. In fact the true why is not what crisis he faced beyond which life would be no longer bearable unless he shot a white man in the back but why of all people he picked a Gowrie to shoot and of all places Beat Four to do it in. —Go on. But don't be late now. After all a man ought to be kind to his parents now and then" [202]. Chick then thinks that perhaps one of the cars returned to the barbershop. In his mind, Lucas is still chained to the bedpost and perhaps the constable's wife is serving supper.

Chick would have some free time before going to the movies. Before he crossed the courthouse yard, he stopped long enough to hear that the sheriff had finally got the word and notified the town he would return on Sunday morning. On [174 (V)], Faulkner finished this section by noting "the Ingrums and Gowries and Workitts were waiting not until they had buried Vinson tomorrow as much as because it would be Sunday in three hours now and they didn't want to have to hurry, rush, bolt through the business by midnight so as not to break the

Sabbath" [text stops]. . . . Faulkner would use all this material, but not necessarily in the order he had written it here; it would take another draft ([204], [205], [211] etc.) before he was ready to put it into setting copy form. As Faulkner typed out [207], [208], [209], [210] and following, he incorporated the material from the previous drafts of this section, this time, especially on [209], eliminating any unnecessary punctuation and making it all one sentence as it appears in the first edition on pages 28-31.

On [213], Faulkner continued by noting that Sheriff Hampton is big enough or at least a man with enough sense to run the county and fill the vacant jobs with his relatives. Again, Faulkner repeats that Chick is free and that if everything were not finished with Lucas "he knew what he was going to do and there was plenty of time yet for that, tomorrow would be time enough for that. . ." [213]. Thus at this point, it does not look like Chick has any inclination that he would help Lucas as he would have plenty of time on Sunday to do whatever he had in mind. On [214], at the dinner table, Chick's name is mentioned for the first time, when his mother says "Charles!" Page [215] repeats material about Gavin explaining that the "true why" is why Lucas killed a Gowrie and [216] is a clean copy of this material. Again, Faulkner was into totally new material as he incorporated not what was in the original draft but what he had written out in the discarded versions of the setting copy. The sheriff sends word that he will be back on Sunday [217]. He did not have to hurry because he knew how the people in Beat Four would act in a situation like this; they were not the type that would hurry through this situation on Saturday night nor on Sunday.

When Chick reached the corner of the yard, this uncle told him that he had contacted Hampton personally and that Fraser went to Skipworth's house and saw Lucas handcuffed. Chick knows the score as well as Hampton and his uncle: Lucas is safe until the early hours of Monday. Then Faulkner repeats the motif concerning Chick's freedom: "Because he was free: in bed: in the cool. . ." [221]. Originally on [218], Faulkner had written that Hampton was down in "Waterboro Old Town" and then this was changed to "Pittsboro Old Town" and then to "Pitts Old Town" before finally becoming "Peddlers Field

Old Town" on [211]. On [515 (V)], Faulkner typed out a ten-line preliminary shorter version of [219] in which Gavin says "It's all right with me. It's Lucas' business, it's not mine." This was changed to "It's all right with me. Lucas didn't have to work this hard not to be a nigger on my account" [219]. Otherwise, [515 (V)] resembles [219] though shortened somewhat.

On the bottom of [219] Faulkner repeated his idea that the Gowries were "a race, a species, a homogeneity," a phrase which did not get into the setting copy. Pages [218]-[220] are the rough draft of [221]-[223]. On [220], Faulkner picks up material he had earlier discarded, that is, his reference to Beat Four and Chicago, Illinois, and the fact that his uncle could never have pointed out the man who would come between Lucas and what Lucas wanted to do. Faulkner finally on [224] uses his original draft again [24] in recalling the speculation, now regarded as fact, that Lucas went into the woods and shot his victim. Faulkner had reworded this considerably and it contained a number of key elements of the murder story: Lucas was his own man, no one could interfere and save Lucas in any way; Lucas had caused trouble at the same store before and therefore from the community's point of view, his action of murder was consistent with previous behavior; he used an old single action Colt pistol; he was proud enough to walk around with a gold toothpick; the store was a perfect place for an ambush as most everyone from that area passed by on Saturdays. Partly because he had reworked this section so often and partly because of his imaginary bent, Faulkner repeated twice the fact that Lucas "shot him" [224], as he had done on the original page of the original draft [24].

On [231], Faulkner mentions Doyle Fraser's full name and amplifies the description of Skipworth who from the beginning was a "weazened" driedup old man and who was also stone deaf and "not much larger than a halfgrown boy" [231]. Because of his boylike stature, Skipworth might be included as one of the children in Ephraim's story who would listen and save people. Again Faulkner mentions after discussing Lucas' capture, the fact that Chick was free: ". . .but then he was free" [231]. The scene soon shifts to Sunday morning [232] and Chick is thinking over in his mind what he will do. Page [233] is an inserted page adding a few words to the crossed-off section on [234] about the

Sunday being a good day for the bootblacks to shine shoes, draw baths, and run errands for the young men who lived in rented rooms and those who worked hard all week in the poolhall.

After this Faulkner returned to the original draft and copied out almost verbatim on [234]-[235] the dialogue he wrote on [26]. This is the voice of the town speaking and once written Faulkner did not change it; barbershop talk is very predictable and seemed to come easy to Faulkner. In the original draft, Faulkner followed the barbershop conversation with the section about seeing Lucas only three times after the original meeting, then giving the accounts of each meeting. Since he had already used this material in an expanded form in the setting copy, Faulkner gives Chick a new sense of determination at this point in time. The sheriff had left town about 9 A.M. Sunday to get Lucas at the constable's house fifteen miles away. He would be back by noon. Chick wanted to get on Highboy and ride out in the direction of Fraser's store for twelve hours and then return, taking in all thirty-six hours if need be. This expanded section elaborates the cryptic sentence in the original draft: "Before that time he would go home and get his horse: not to sit nursing his hands in a back upstairs room at home waiting for it to be over but to be moving, having to concentrate on motion, on the motion of the horse and on watching where it put its feet—to ride in one undeviable direction for twelve hours which would be midnight tonight then rest the horse until morning then ride the twelve hours back. . ." [30].

Finally Chick walks over to a shed in front of the closed blacksmith's shop out of sight. The full street became empty quickly. Still following the original draft [30], Chick is not afraid to use curse words and ask himself what the hell he is doing there. In the original draft, Chick answered: "*So he can look back at me not just from the edge of death but out of a gout of blazing gasoline and not remember me either?*" [30]-[31]. In the setting copy, Chick answered thus: ". . .not to see Lucas, he had seen Lucas but so that Lucas could see him again if he so wished, to look back at him not just from the edge of mere uniqueless death but from the gasoline-roar of apotheosis" [237]. Then in the setting copy, Faulkner again asserts, "Because he [i.e., Chick] was free. Lucas was no longer his responsibility, he was no longer Lucas' keeper; Lucas himself had discharged him" [237]. Thus in revising the original draft, Faulkner in this section, not only incorporated his refrain about Chick being free, but he pushed the two images to their outermost limits: "edge of mere uniqueless death" and "gasoline-roar of apotheosis."

The last two pages of the original draft [31]-[32] (there are only two lines on [33]) are expanded in the setting copy to three and a half pages ([238], [241], [242], [243]). The street fills up quickly again, mostly with young men whom Chick recognizes. The car driven by a deputy and containing Lucas drives up. Faulkner sticks close to the original draft. On [239], Faulkner originally had Lucas put his hat back on his head at the old angle "inflexible and cavalier," but in revising this page on [241], he omitted this reference, perhaps because of the incongruity of the word "cavalier." When Lucas first emerges from the car Faulkner notes, too, (something he did not write on [239]) that the white people see Lucas for the first time without his hat, the first time they could look on him directly: "And that was the first time he had ever seen Lucas without the hat on and in the same second he realised that with the possible exception of Edmonds there in the street watching him were probably the only white people in the county who had ever seen him uncovered: watching as, still bent over as he had emerged from the car, Lucas began to reach stiffly for the hat" [241]. Chick anxiously tries to figure out what Lucas will do, thinking first that Lucas will look at him, then believing Lucas saw him, and finally concluding that perhaps Lucas never saw anybody because he kept on looking toward him, but not at him.

On [240], a rough draft of [242], Faulkner had not included the section about Chick trying so hard to get a reaction from Lucas. Page [240] describes the smear down Lucas' suit and then presents an evaluation of Lucas' eyes and face. We do not have on [240] Chick's interior dialogue with himself. The sheriff tells the crowd to go back to the barbershop. On [32], Chick admitted he was wrong: "And watching, he saw Lucas look at them [i.e., young men assembled] for another moment with nothing whatever in his face, then turn to follow the sheriff and take perhaps three steps and then stop and turn and now he looked full at him for the first time and he thought, *I was wrong. I was wrong all the time.*" In the setting copy

[242] this sentence is omitted. Instead Chick thinks about saddling Highboy and leaving home. Also in the original draft [32], the sheriff warns the crowd to leave in a "calm heatless voice as though he were speaking to children." In the setting copy [243], the reference to children is dropped and the effect is that the sheriff is a serious person who is in charge of the situation. It also suggests that the crowd are not children, but angry men who want revenge. In this chapter, Faulkner struggled very much to put the murder in a community context by showing the relationship between the Gowries and the police officials. And by the use of a refrain, he reminded his readers that Chick was the person free enough to deal adequately with the various factions in Jefferson. Faulkner would highlight this even more in the next chapter when Chick confronts Lucas in jail.

Chapter Three of the Setting Copy

As Faulkner began the third chapter of the setting copy, he was using the second chapter of the original draft as his model. There are thirty-eight pages or parts of pages used in this chapter. He prefaced this third chapter by speculating that if Chick had gone home after visiting the barbershop in the morning, he could have saddled Highboy and might be fifty miles away by now [244]. Faulkner was working again with this freedom-escape motif that had not been an integral part of the original draft. Page [244] corresponds to page [34] almost word for word; the only change is to smooth out a few expressions. Faulkner had exercised considerable attention on the original draft as the page is fairly well marked up; on the setting copy, he had few modifications. In his discussion of Sunday, Faulkner presents a different type of human interaction, of Chick and Gavin meeting people on the street and recognizing their presence or aura, as if they were shadows in some Greek underworld. Again the street is empty [245]. Faulkner seems to use the street as a focal point for determining the mood of the town and he often introduces a scene by commenting on whether the street is empty or not, or whether there are bells or not.

Faulkner also follows the original draft very closely in presenting Mr. Lilley, changing only a phrase here or there. On

[246], Faulkner added the comment that Chick "remembered his uncle saying once how little of vocabulary man really needed to get comfortably and even efficiently through his life, how not only in the individual but within his whole type and race and kind a few simple clichés served his few simple passions and needs and lusts. . ." [246]. Mr. Lilley referred to Lucas in the original as a "son of a bitch" [36]. This was changed in the setting copy to "nigger" [246], and then changed again on the same page in manuscript to "sonofabitch." On [37], Faulkner typed: "Now they [i.e., Chick and Gavin] could see the Square, empty too—the slender white pencil of the Confederate monument against the looming columned upsoar of the courthouse to the dim quadruple face of the clock lighted each by a single faint almost intransigeant bulb." In the revision on [247], this became: "Now they could see the Square empty too—the amphitheatric lightless stores, the slender white pencil of the Confederate monument against the mass of the courthouse looming in columned upsoar to the dim quadruple face of the clock lighted each by a single faint [a marginal note is indicated here: "Author: bulb? light? /?"] with a quality as intransigeant against those four fixed mechanical shouts of adjuration and warning as the glow of a firefly." In the revision, Faulkner keeps the basic images he described originally, but is able to add on to them, capturing through additional imagery a new softness in tone, reflecting the calm of a Sunday evening in May. Faulkner's description of the jail [248] likewise follows the original draft very closely.

In describing the young girl scratching her name on the jailhouse window, Faulkner [249] again remained faithful to the original [38] where he had noted that the jailer could be what people called a gentleman. In revising this he said that the jailer, innkeeper, farrier, or vegetable peddler were the equal of a lawyer, planter, doctor, or parson; then again on [249] he went back to the original mode of expression, that the jailer was like a lawyer and could be called a gentleman, thus preserving the original indirect approach. In describing the jail, Faulkner kept the structure the same though he reworked some sentences adding that "the Sunday nights which seemed now to belong to a time as dead as Nineveh," a biblical reference not in the original. It seemed too that the notion of Lucas being "intractable" was something Faulkner wanted to keep; on [39],

the "mellow untroubled intractable voices" of the prisoners
shouting down to the passing cooks and nurses became the
"mellow untroubled repentless voices" [250]. In the original
draft Faulkner tended not to make or indicate paragraphs; in the
revision he was careful to put in paragraphs, thus developing
discrete units of thought.

In the original [39], Gavin and Chick mount the stairs to
the jail and though Chick does not know the man protecting the
jail, he knows his name. In the revision [250], Chick recognizes
him and gives Legate's full name, not just his last. When Faulkner describes Legate's gun, he says it was a "worn hand-patina-
ed rifle" [39], which later became "hand-worn rifle" [251].
Faulkner still stays close to the original draft in the Gavin-Legate
dialogue, with one minor addition about Gavin and Chick seeing
a car make a trip around the square to scare the law enforcement
officers, an addition not part of the first version [252] of this
setting copy page [253]. Later, in describing the door which
closed off the top of the stairs in the jail [255], Faulkner expanded this section. In a sense, this particular door prefigures
the cell door Faulkner is to describe later on. This door on the
top of the stairs was one solid handhewn "piece over two inches
thick, locked with a heavy modern padlock in a handwrought
iron bar through two iron slots which like the heavy risette-
shaped hinges were handwrought too, hammered out over a
hundred years ago in the blacksmith shop across the street where
he had stood yesterday. . . ." The setting copy then follows
with a long digression about a stranger driving through a plate
glass window and landing up in jail and offering to buy the door,
or even just the bar, and slots and hinges if possible.

The jail door separated the world of men from the world
of human degradation: "But already they had passed out of
the world of man, men: people who worked and had homes and
raised families and tried to make a little more money than they
perhaps deserved by fair means of course or at least by legal,
to spend a little on fun and still save something against old
age. . ." [256]. Once inside the jail, Faulkner again returned to
the original draft and followed it closely. When the visitors arrived at Lucas' cell, Faulkner originally wrote: ". . .they came
suddenly on a single wooden door caught by a clumsy hasp such
as you might see on a farm crib or smokehouse, and a heavy pad-

lock, and unlocked the padlocked and flipped away the hasp and snapped the padlock back into the empty staple and flung the door open and turned and was gone almost running back down the corridor" [43]. In the margin, it looks like Faulkner has written (barely legible) in pencil: "Jim Crow murderer's cell." In the setting copy [257], Faulkner cut this section down: "Just beyond there was a door in the mesh, not padlocked but just hooked with a hasp and staple such as you might see on a dog-kennel or a corncrib but the jailer passed it." Lucas gets a private cell, though in the setting copy we are told the jailer took all the blankets off the cot.

As they are about to enter the cell, Chick thinks about the meaning of murder, a sequence not in the original draft: ". . .he thought how of all human pursuits murder had the most deadly need of privacy; how man will go to almost any lengths to preserve the solitude in which he evacuates or makes love but he will go to any length for that in which he takes life, even to homicide, yet by no act can he more completely and irrevocably destroy it. . ." [257]-[258]. This time the door to Lucas' cell is "a modern steel barred door" [258]. As Gavin and Chick enter the cell, Faulkner again returns to the original draft. Then like a movie director, Chick focuses on Lucas, a little slower than in the original draft, but with roughly the same sense of ease. The conversation in the cell block is the same in both the original draft and the setting copy. On [260], Gavin says that the district attorney will send Lucas to Parchman; the original draft merely mentions an unspecified penitentiary [45]. Likewise, the Gavin-Lucas conversation is the same in both drafts. On [264], Lucas admits that Vinson Gowrie is only one of the two men involved in the lumber deal whose identity has been made public. Gavin maintains the affair was made public because Gowrie was shot in the back. Faulkner had not included this bit of dialogue in the original draft. Also when Gavin asks who the other man is [265], Lucas does not answer. This suspense prepares the reader to be on the look-out as the murder mystery progresses to search for possible suspects for the murderer of Vinson.

On [265], Lucas says that Vinson Gowrie's partner was taking the lumber and hauling it to Glasgow or Hollymount; it was originally Hollymount, then changed to Hollyvale, and than back to Hollymount. Again in the setting copy, Faulkner remains close to the original draft, at this point, even retyping "Ephriam" [48] the same way on [265]. On [268], Faulkner broke up some of the dialogue he had written in by hand on [49]; Lucas wants to hire Gavin but Gavin insists on telling his version of the murder and concluding that he has little time for what Lucas wants. On [268], Gavin agrees to send some tobacco on the following day as Lucas requested. In the revision on [271], Lucas asks for tobacco and Gavin says he will send it the following day because he does not want to keep Lucas awake any further. On [268] Faulkner typed for the first time, the passage about "the last carborundum-grooved door" which is the same essentially as it is on [271]. Afterwards on [268], Faulkner wrote: ". . .he just stopped while his uncle went on down the corridor, and turned and looked back into the cell and saw Lucas standing now in the middle of the floor beneath the light, looking through the steel bars at him in such a way—something: in his face: his attitude: or perhaps in the vanished motion which had brought or left him standing there—that for a second he believed he had heard Lucas speak, call his name." But Lucas did not speak and though Faulkner kept this passage in the setting copy [271], he changed it and, in my opinion, took some of the drama out of it. Faulkner wrote two preliminary tries on [269] and [270]; in the second, he added some phrases which were deleted on [272]. When Gavin says that buying tobacco can wait for the following morning, Chick replies: " 'Yes,' he said, feeling his uncle watching him, waiting but whether for his uncle to say no or not he didn't know, wondering what he would really do if his uncle said no, then not even wondering about that anymore but just waiting" [270]. By the time Faulkner reached [273] he had almost doubled the number of pages of the original draft: page [52] (page 39 of the original draft) resembles page [273] (page 73 of the setting copy).

In the original draft [52], Faulkner wrote: "So he [i.e., Chick] didn't say yes or no; he even turned and walked on toward the Square, walking on until the sound of his uncle's feet had died away and even his walking silhouette had disappeared far up the street. Then he turned and came back to the jail and into it with Legate's pleasant weathered face already watching him across the lowered page, thinking *He was not only watching me before I even turned in off the street, he had already recognized me:* and again the jailer came quickly out the door in the side wall, his expression already giving way to the one of harried outrage." On [283], Faulkner modified this section by having Gavin's silhouette change to a white gleam because of his linen suit. Faulkner then repeated the freedom-escape motif about where Chick could be if he had ridden Highboy early that morning and escaped not only from town but from all involvement with "nigger murderers." When Chick returns to the jail, "the jailer unlocked the bar across the oak door" [274], not the "authentic steel door" [52] as in the original draft. Though Faulkner crossed off two sections on [274] he did not alter the story line; the corrected sections after the crossed-off lines merely help with the continuity of the story. The main difference between the original draft and the setting copy there is that in the original draft Chick said: *"If he will just remind me of that goddamn plate of collards and sidemeat I ate four years ago. Or maybe he'll tell me I'm all he's got to help him. Then I'll be free. . ."* [53]. In the setting copy, this was modified and the note of freedom was dropped: *"Maybe he will remind me of that goddamn plate of collards and sidemeat or maybe he'll even tell me I'm all he's got, all that's left and that will be enough. . ."* [274]-[275]. As noted in the analysis in the original draft, Faulkner expanded the section [275] when Charles repeats Lucas's words " 'Go out where and look at who?' he said," as found on page 68 of the first edition. At this point, as an individual, as Charles Mallison "junior" [276] as the setting copy has it, Chick is involved in Lucas' alleged murder situation in a personal way.

On [54], Faulkner made considerable changes in order to get this meeting of Lucas and Chick correct. The setting copy [276], however, is a clean page; Faulkner had been able to make the changes on the original draft and did not have to reword it on the setting copy page. On [54], Faulkner made three marginal inserts in pencil which he now incorporated into the setting copy: 1) "You can be there in a half an hour in your uncle's automobile." 2) "You takes the first right hand up into the hills beyond the 9 mile branch bridge." 3) " 'Nine,' Lucas said. 'The Gowries buries at Mount Hope Chapel'—Nine." The chapel was later changed to Caledonia Chapel. In the setting copy, Faulkner noted that Lucas "took hold of two of the bars as a child stands inside a fence" [267], a phrase not in the original.

Otherwise, Faulkner kept to the original material. He scrupu-
lously followed the original draft, changing only "standing there
on his side of the mesh, his hands. . .motionless in the mesh"
[56] to "standing there on his side of the steel door, his hands
light-clasped and motionless around the two bars" [277].
Faulkner also noted that Chick's mother went to school in
Sweetbriar, Virginia [278].

In retelling the story of Ephraim, Faulkner changed it
slightly, modifying the description of Mrs. Downs' house: "an
old white woman who lived in a small filthy house on the edge of
town which smelled like a fox's den" [57] became "an old white
woman who lived alone in a small filthy shoebox of a house that
smelled like a foxden on the edge of town in a settlement of
Negro houses. . ." [278]. On [279] it is Aleck Sander who
tells about Mrs. Downs, not Aleck Sander and Paralee as in the
original draft. Also on [279], Chick "believed at once and so
implicitly that the ring was now found that he dismissed that
phase at once and forever and it was only the thing's secondary
and corollary which moved his interest," a section not in the
original draft. Likewise on [279], Ephraim says a bit more than
in the original draft: "If you ever needs to get anything done
outside the common run, dont waste yo time on the menfolks;
get the womens and children to working at it." It should be
noted that on [279] Faulkner indicated something not in the
original draft, that up until this point Gavin "had no more
trouble than he believing things that all other grown people
doubted for the sole reason that they were unreasonable. . . ."
Thus Gavin is seen briefly as having something of a childlike
quality of acceptance as also indicated in the crossed-off section
of [59] (the original of [279]), a trait not really borne out in
the story at all.

As Faulkner drew to the close of this chapter, he heightened
the drama by expanding the original text. The original text read:

> But this was no obscure valueless little ring exchanged twenty
> years ago between two young girls, it was the death by shameful
> violence of a human being who would die not because he was a
> murderer but because his skin was black; his uncle would have to
> believe now whether the sheriff would or not and he thought in a
> kind of rage: *Believe what?* who (Lucas) had merely requested him

to go seventeen miles in the dark to risk being caught violating the grave of a member of a clan of men already at the pitch to commit the absolute of furious and bloody outrage, without even telling him why. [58]

It should be noted that Faulkner crossed off the line about the doubts Chick had about Lucas' guilt, something not previously articulated and which would not be put so baldly in the setting copy either. On [280], Faulkner changed this section omitting the reference to Gavin and making the dilemma Chick's alone:

Only this was no obscure valueless little ring exchanged twenty years ago between two young girls but the death by shameful violence of a man who would die not because he was a murderer but because his skin was black. Yet this was all Lucas was going to tell him and he knew it was all; he thought in a kind of raging fury: *Believe? Believe what?* because Lucas was not even asking him to believe anything; he was not even asking a favor, making no last desperate plea to his humanity and pity but was even going to pay him provided the price was not too high, to go alone seventeen miles (no, nine: he remembered at least that he had heard that now) in the dark and risk being caught violating the grave of a member of a clan of men already at the pitch to commit the absolute of furious and bloody outrage, without even telling him why.

Note the emphasis on belief in a person, perhaps the key premise in Chick's philosophy.

On the last page of this chapter [281], Chick thinks (not in the original draft): "*He's not only beat me, he never for one second had any doubt of it.*" Also Chick says that he does not see how he can get out to the graveyard, dig up the body, get back to town before midnight if that is not already too late (also not in the original draft). Lucas answers cryptically, "I'll try to wait." Thus the original ending and the lead-up to it follow the original draft closely. Faulkner wanted the Chick-Lucas encounter to reflect accurately their two distinct personalities. He spent time on this chapter of the setting copy to achieve this.

Chapter Four of the Setting Copy

Faulkner began this chapter as he did the third chapter of the original draft by mentioning the battered pickup truck in front of the house when Chick reaches home. There are forty-seven pages or parts of pages used in this chapter. In typing out [282], Faulkner followed the draft on [60] fairly closely though he was expanding the text as he had done in the past. On [60], Faulkner had written in pencil: ". . .in lieu of permission from the Gowries which the President of the U.S. himself, let alone a county sheriff, would never get." On [282], Faulkner typed out the following sentence:

> It was now well past eight oclock; it was a good deal more than a possibility that there remained less than four hours for his uncle to go to the sheriff's house and convince him and then find a J.P. or whoever they would have to find and wake and then convince too to open the grave [and-then- get -out-to -Mount Hope church -and -dig- up -the- body- and -get-back -to-town -with- it] (in lieu of permission from the Gowries, which for any reason whatever, worst of all to save a nigger from being burned over a bonfire, the President of the United States himself let alone a county sheriff would never get) and then go out to Mount Hope church and dig up the body and get back to town with it in time.

What is worth noticing here is Faulkner's method of composition at the typewriter. It looks like he typed out [60] first, then when typing out [282], he copied [60] until he got to the phrase "to town with it," then wrote in pencil on [60] the additional phrase beginning "in lieu of permission. . .", then went back to [282] and crossed off the section beginning "and then get out. . .", and finally typed in the addition he had noted on [60]. From this evidence, it looks like the handwritten corrections and insertions in plain pencil on the original draft were made when Faulkner was typing out the setting copy. This would also be supported by the chapter numbers which Faulkner marked in pencil on the later chapters of the original draft; they correspond to the chapter numbers of the setting copy. Page [85] was originally marked "IV" and then changed to "V"; [110] was originally marked "V" and changed to "VII"; [132] was originally marked "VI" and then changed to "VIII"; and [144] only has the marking "IX" in pencil.

Faulkner followed his original draft closely, making slight changes, as on [283] where he notes that it is a Memphis paper that his father was reading; no city had been mentioned previously. The insert attached to [283] is a typed version of #41 on the correction list which Faulkner sent to Erskine (cf. Appendix C). This insertion was not typed by Faulkner, though the typing looks the same except for certain letters such as the "a." On the back on the insertion in red print is the word "MEMORANDUM," probably from Erskine's desk; it should be noted that the manuscript in blue ink "INSERT ON P. 83" is not in Faulkner's hand. The handwriting for the marginal corrections on the setting copy seems to be the same as Erskine's on #39 and #40 of the corrections in the corrections list. Both the original draft and the setting copy are very close at this point, though on [284] Miss Habersham is a spinster of sixty. In the first edition, she is "seventy" and as far as I can tell there is no reason for the change except for a typesetter changing it. On [285], there is an insert ("with the neat small gold watch pinned to the flat unmammary front") typed again, though this time not taped to, on the page itself by Erskine's typewriter. Also on [285] Faulkner added that Miss Habersham's shoes from New York cost thirty and forty dollars a pair, an additional phase not in the original draft.

At the bottom of [285], too, Faulkner added, "—recognized, remembered, even (his attention) nagged at and already dismissed because there wasn't time. . .", a phrase not in the original, though it is important because of the motif of recognition in the story. Here Chick recognizes Miss Habersham and remembers her background, but for the moment dismisses it. Faulkner made five attempts before finally accepting the sixth concerning Chick saying "Good Evening" to Miss Habersham and beginning his conversation with Gavin. Faulkner's main intention in these five tries is to let Gavin know that Chick wants to speak with him. In the second try on [286], (the first try on [292] is like the second), Faulkner crossed off the lines where Gavin comments that Chick took the tobacco up to Lucas, hoping that Lucas' tale was good. This attempt ends with Charles saying, "I've got to speak to you. . . ." In the third try [287], Faulkner included what he had crossed off in the previous try and when Chick tells Gavin he has to speak with him, he begins to tell his feeling, "Suppose it wasn't his pistol that killed him. . . ." But that was as far as he got. In the fourth attempt, Faulkner again went back as he had done on [287] to the comment by Gavin: "So is Miss Habersham." When Chick says here that it might not have been Lucas' pistol that killed Vinson Gowrie, Gavin responded: " 'Of course,' his uncle said, pleasant impenetrable and immediate. 'That's exactly what I would claim if I were him or any other Negro murderer for that matter or any white murderer for the matter of fact. He probably even told you what he actually fired the shot from his own pistol at. Was it a rabbit? or maybe a tin can or a mark on a tree, just to see if the pistol was really loaded, would really go off? But grant it for the moment. Then what? What do you suggest? No: what did Lucas tell you to do?' " [288]. At this point Faulkner was copying what he had probably just written in pencil on the original draft [64]. In the last try [289], Faulkner went back to the "Good evening, Miss Habersham" phrase and this time slowed down the pace of his writing; this try is very close to the setting copy page [290]. Once he had finished with [289], Faulkner went back and polished it up, not changing the content, but merely smoothing out the sentences.

When Faulkner came to the phrase on [290] "And that was all" (the last phrase he had typed on [289]), he departed from the original draft and began to compose at the typewriter. Faulkner then states that Chick could go now and in fact should do so. It might have been better for Chick never to have come into the house, but to have bypassed it and called Aleck Sander. Lucas had told Chick thirty minutes before that speaking to his uncle or any white man would accomplish nothing. Faulkner noted on [291] that two people remained in the room; this was an oversight and changed it to three, as found on page 78 of the first edition. Still composing new material, Faulkner noted that Gavin had probably a dozen of the corncob "pipes in various stages of char, while outside the quiet lamplit room the vast millrace of time roared not toward midnight but hurling midnight toward him in one poised skyblotting yawn of jumbled wreckage and he knew now that the irrevocable moment was not when he had said 'All right' to Lucas through the steel bars of the cell door but when he would step back into the hall and close this one behind him. So he tried again, still calm, not even rapid now, not even urgent: specious explicit and reasonable." On [292], Faulkner expanded the above passage which he had crossed out. In revising this, Faulkner referred to Lucas as the "old kinless friendless opinionated arrogant hardheaded intractable independent (insolent too) Negro," as if Faulkner somehow had to constantly remind the reader of the unusual quality of the Chick-Lucas bond.

On [293], Faulkner used that material he had previously written by hand on [64] and had rejected on [288], about Lucas shooting at a rabbit, or a tin can, or possibly a tree. On the middle of [293] he returned to the original draft [64]; Chick now asks if Sheriff Hampton (not Gavin himself as in the original) could go out and dig up Vinson. On [65], Faulkner had crossed off the line, " '. . .I've told him [i.e., Lucas] what to do.' Now his uncle was speaking to Miss Habersham too. . . ." On [293] he put in its place, "And if I went that far, I'd heap rather tell him I just wanted to exhume it [dig it up] to dig the gold out of its teeth than to tell him the reason was to save a nigger from being lynched." The two words "dig it" were crossed off by Faulkner on the typewriter, but the word "up" was crossed off by Erskine with a blue pencil. Erskine also wrote in the margin "OK?" concerning his correction. Since it is impossible to tell how careful Faulkner was at reading these corrections, this presents an ambiguous textual situation. There are three possibilities: 1) "just wanted to exhume it to dig. . ." (as the text is now); 2) "just wanted to exhume up to dig. . ." (the text as Faulkner typed it minus the Erskine correction); 3) "just wanted to exhume it up to dig. . ." (incorporating the Erskine correction without deleting any words [this is the least like possibility]). As Faulkner continued, he stayed close to the original text, though it is obvious he wanted to revise the section concerning the jail door. On [65] he had written, "Lucas has got the best protection Hampton can possibly give him. As Will Legate said, there are enough people in this county to pass him and Tubbs if they really tried." On [294], this became: "Lucas is locked behind a proof steel door. He's got the best protection Hampton or anybody else in this county can possibly give him. As Will Legate said, there are enough people in this county to pass him and Tubbs and even that door if they really want to."

As Gavin speaks about Lucas' alleged killing, Chick reflects on the notion of vocabulary, something not included in the original draft: ". . .and he marvelled again at the paucity, the

really almost standardised meagreness not of individual vocabularies but of Vocabulary itself, by means of which even man
can live in vast droves and herds even in concrete warrens in
comparative amity. . ." [294]. As Gavin continues talking Chick
realizes that he is speaking to Miss Habersham, too, and "at the
moment he was neither rediscovering her presence in the room
nor even discovering it; he did not even remember that she had
already long since ceased to exist. . ." [294], thus building on
this recognition or lack-of-recognition motif not established that
fully in the original draft.

On the bottom of [295] Faulkner made some changes in
the setting copy by switching two parts of the original draft
around.   On [66], Faulkner first wrote that Chick imagined he
would have to ask Lucas where the grave is, and then he hears
the crackle of the paper on his father's lap, and finally remembers that Lucas had told him where to go.   On [295], Faulkner
had Chick remember that Lucas had told him where to go, and
then he heard the crackling of the paper and smelled his father's
cigar.   Faulkner crossed off the material on [295] and retyped it
on [296], again expanding it a bit as he was used to doing,
though the phrase "realising how Lucas probability doubts"
(cf. page 81:19 of the first edition) is probably not accurate
since there is an asterisk in pencil between "probability" and
"doubts."   Thus it might be more accurately written "probably
doubts."

At this point Faulkner began amplifying the original draft.
On [297], he gave a fuller indication of Chick's mentality:

> Because (quitting abandoning emerging from scattering with one
> sweep that confetti-swirl of ranging facetiae) he realized that he
> had never doubted getting out there and even getting the body
> up.   He could see himself reaching the church, the graveyard
> without effort nor even any great elapse of time; he could see him-
> self single-handed even having the body up and out still with no
> effort, no pant and strain of muscles and lungs nor laceration of
> the shrinking sensibility.   It was only then that the whole wrecked
> and tumbling midnight which peer and pant though he would he
> couldn't see past and beyond, would come crashing down on him.
> So (moving, he had not stopped since the first second's fraction
> while he closed the office door) he flung himself bodily with one

heave into a calm, a sagacious, an even deadly rationality of pro
and con [the last part of this sentence is crossed-off]. [297]

Faulkner then revised the last part of this sentence on [298]
and then returned back to the original draft. On [298], Faulkner noted that fifty or a hundred men and boys could possibly
stumble on Chick and Aleck Sander while digging up the grave;
the original number had been forty or fifty [67].

Faulkner continued with new material on [298]-[299]
highlighting Chick's dilemma: ". . .either to go alone on the
horse in half the time and spend three times the time getting the
body up alone because alone he would not only have to do all
the digging but the watching and listening too, or take Aleck
Sander with him. . . ." The original draft merely noted that
Charles was "doomed and lost" [67], not really offering an option of going alone or taking Aleck Sander. If the Gowrie kin
and friends discovered him, then that would be the end of it all.
In revising the text, Faulkner drops this note of finality which
would not be appropriate for someone working up courage to
perform so difficult a task. It should be noted that Faulkner's
rather favorable account of Highboy's skill might be biographical
as the Faulkners once owned a horse named Highboy. On [105]
Faulkner concluded with the image of the confetti: ". . .and suddenly he found himself escaped back into the confetti exactly
as you put off having to step finally into the cold water. . . ."
Though Faulkner had altered this section in the original draft
(cf. [66] and [69] for similar passages about where the crowd of
men were, either in town or in the county), he follows the original draft as it was finally put together.

As Chick leaves his house, Faulkner again added new material, this time revealing Chick's interior state: ". . .and he was
wrong; not when he had said All right to Lucas through the
steel bars nor when he had stepped back into the hall and closed
the office door behind him, but here was the irrevocable moment
after which there would be no return; he could stop here and
never pass it, let the wreckage of midnight crash harmless and
impotent against these walls because they were strong, they
would endure; they were home, taller than wreckage, stronger
than fear;—not even stopping, not even curious to ask himself
if perhaps he dared not stop, letting the screen door quietly to

behind him [sic] and down the steps into the vast furious vortex
of the soft May night. . ." [300]-[301]. From this point Faulkner returned to the original draft and followed it closely. Again
it seems that the Chick-Aleck Sander dialogue was something
that Faulkner did not have to rewrite; he merely copied the
original draft with slight variations.

When Chick turned back to the house after speaking with
Aleck Sander he heard someone and "at first he thought it was
his uncle coming rapidly around the house from the front, not
because he believed that his uncle might have suspected and anticipated what he was about because he did not, his uncle had
dismissed that too immediately and thoroughly not only from
conception but from possibility too, but because he no longer
remembered anyone else available for it to have been and even
after he saw it was a woman he assumed it was his mother. . ."
[303]-[304]. In the original draft, Faulkner, had noted that
Chick had forgotten about Miss Habersham's existence; here
it is more a lack of recognition or confusion of her with his
mother. Faulkner then continued from the original draft with
the question "What did he tell you?" [304]. Then in identifying the relationship between Miss Habersham and Molly, Faulkner changed the text; in the original draft [71] he had written:
"old Molly, Lucas' wife, had been the daughter of one of old
Doctor Habersham's slaves son's, young Doctor's, Miss Habersham's father's, slaves, she and Miss Habersham the same
age. . . ." On [304], he wrote: "old Molly, Lucas' wife, who had
been the daughter of one of old Doctor Habersham's, Miss
Habersham's grandfather's, slaves, she and Miss Habersham the
same age. . .", thus keeping the same type of collocation of
words, though substituting new words to clarify the point.
Often Faulkner did not change the rhythm of his sentences in
rewriting them.

On [305], Faulkner again departed from the original draft
[72]. Chick now says, "I'm just going out there. . ." and though
Faulkner does not finish the sentence in the setting copy, Miss
Habersham merely murmurs "Of course. . .", while Chick thinks
he should "cry, protest, ejaculate, and bring the whole house
down on him" [305]. Miss Habersham understood far more
than Chick ever expected; they are "like two people who have
irrevocably accepted a gambit they are not at all certain they can

cope with. . ." [306]. Then Faulkner develops the character of Miss Habersham on [306] with some new material; she questions Chick and ascertains that Lucas did not say whose gun killed Vinson or even whether he was the one to fire it or not. He merely said it was not his gun. In true detective story fashion, Miss Habersham explores the possibilities of the murder case. She concludes: "Now what? To find out if it wasn't his pistol—find out whatever it was he meant? Go out there and [do] what?" [306]. This time Chick responds to Miss Habersham's questions in a precise way. He wants to go out, dig up the body, bring it in, and have an expert check the bullet hole in Gowrie, a far more explicit answer than he gave on [74] where he merely said, "To prove it."

Page [307] contains one long paragraph expanding a short section on [74], trying to achieve a definition or approximation of truth. Miss Habersham makes a basic distinction in this new material on [307] between Lucas as a Negro and Gavin as a man, with the result that Lucas would not speak openly with Gavin. From this initial distinction, a key one in terms of the psychological nuances of the novel, Chick makes two observations. As he had mentioned before with reference to Gavin [294] (Chick marvelling at the paucity and the "standardised meagreness not of individual vocabularies but of Vocabulary itself"), Chick does not now believe it was not really a paucity or meagreness of vocabulary, because the deliberate killing of human life is so final in itself, and that the words used to describe it and incorporate it into the chronicle of mankind had to be simple too. Secondly, Miss Habersham spoke simple truth and there was no need to use metaphors and circumlocutions to express it because truth is a universal phenomenon. With this introduction to universal truth, Faulkner then went back and leaned on what he had written in the original draft. It did not take a lot of truth to keep the world going and anybody could know the truth, even a child and an old woman who were not concerned with evidence. Such a smooth transition from a double observation by Chick on Miss Habersham's comment, which incorporated some older material from the original draft, and accomplished with almost no false starts, reveals a remarkable creative achievement.

On [308], concerning the Miss Habersham-Chick dialogue,

Faulkner returned to the original draft again [75] and added occasional phrases. On [309], he wrote: "He [i.e., Chick] unsnapped the tie-rope from the bit-ring before he remembered and remembered [sic: cf. page 91:5 of the first edition] and snapped it back and rove [sic] the other end through its knot around the wall-ring and looped it and the reins up over Highboy's head and led him out of the hallway and got up." The original on [76] is as follows: "He unsnapped the tierope from the bitring and threw the reins over Highboy's head and led him out of the hall and checked him and got up." Faulkner also expanded and gave a sense of drama to the mounting of the horse by the two boys, almost as if he were weighing every action and trying to describe it with a greater sense of action and urgency. Likewise, Faulkner carefully prepares the reader for the trip to the cemetery. On [76] he wrote that Aleck Sander saw the pickup truck: "Then Aleck Sander saw it." In revising this on [310], he wrote: "But Aleck Sander actually saw it: who seemed able to see in the dark almost like an animal." Throughout this section, the revisions mostly provide a sense of continuity of action, rather than supplying new material. As one character, for example, makes a comment, Faulkner tries in the revision in the setting copy to give the corresponding action. Both the original copy and the setting copy have the same sentence "She's gonter take the truck" [76] and [310], though only the setting copy gives the subsequent action: ". . .and not even dropping the pick and shovel but flinging them clattering and clanging against the gate and slipping down himself and just in time because now Highboy stood erect on his hind feet until he struck him hard between the ears with the looped tie-rope."

On [311] Faulkner departs from the original draft for a minor apostrophe to a mule, something he had done previously in *The Hamlet*. Chick remembered his grandfather (again note the grandfather reference) that the deer, and bear, and wild turkey were hunted within twelve miles of Jefferson and that Major de Spain, whom Faulkner noted in a manuscript insertion, "had been his grandfather's cousin," old General Compson, Uncle Ike McCaslin, still alive at ninety, who was Carothers Edmonds' great-uncle, Boon Hogganbeck, and Sam Fathers, and the one-eyed mule, named Alice, were the members of the hunting party. Chick wishes for a descendent of Old Alice to transport his subjects on, an ironic commentary on the hunting practices of the inhabitants of Yoknapatawpha County. On [321], Faulkner returned to the original draft again by noting that Highboy was still edgy and that it was a cool evening. Faulkner stuck close to the original draft describing the trip out to the cemetery, though he did change the time sequence with certain words he crossed off: ". . .five miles from town and [~~now~~] he would cross (probably [~~which~~] Miss Habersham and Aleck Sander in the truck probably already had [~~had-long-since done~~]). . . ." In this way, Faulkner integrated character development with a heightened sense of chronology.

On [77], Faulkner noted that it took two boys of age sixteen and "an old white spinster [~~going on~~] seventy" to do the two things that would most upset Beat Four: violate a grave of one of its citizens and save a Negro murderer from its vengeance. On [313], Miss Habersham is given the age of seventy without any qualification. Again at this point Faulkner sticks close to the original copy. On [78], Faulkner had written: ". . .the dark land stretched away. He had not even passed Negroes. . . ." In revising this on [313]-[314], most of which he rejected, Chick feels himself rooted in the countryside:

> . . .the dark land stretched away into the darkness strong with the smell of plowed earth; (from time to time he road breasted through as through motionless skeins of smoke and scent of flowering orchards) so maybe they were making better time than even he had hoped and before he could stop it he had thought *Maybe we will after all:* —before he could leap spring smother and blot it from thinking, not because he couldn't really believe they possibly could, not because you don't dare think whole even to yourself the entirety of a dear hope or wish let alone a desperate one else you yourself have doomed it, but because the dark empty land itself already offered him immitigable portent: he had not seen one Negro. . . .

On [315], Faulkner again revised the above text, expanding it even more thirteen lines, until he wrote on [315] he "had not passed one Negro since leaving town. . . ."

He then continued to expand this section for the rest of [315]-[316]. On [317] Faulkner copied over much of what he had written on [315]-[316]. The short ten-line description of the Negroes on [78] was expanded to approximately two and a half pages of typescript, ([313 (bottom)], [315], [317], [318] [cf. pages 95:4-97:10 of the first edition]), not counting the deleted portions. When Faulkner mentions on [318] that High-boy tightened and even began to drive a little, he is returning back to the original draft [78]. In the margin of [78], Faulkner had written in blue ink: "quicksand: horse wont drink. A.S. — 'smell quicksand'," and on [319], Aleck Sander makes the comment that Highboy smells quicksand, something not initially typed on the original draft. Faulkner expanded the section of getting Highboy up into the hills, though again only to give the text a more graceful reading. The conversation going up the hill is basically the same as in the setting copy with only a few phrases altered. In the original [80], Aleck Sander says: "What was that he was toting in front of him?"; in the revised copy setting copy: "What was that he was toting on the saddle in front of him?" [322].

On [322], following the penciled marginal notes on [81], Faulkner added that the sip of consecrated wine is "the deathless blood of our Lord not to be tasted, moving not downward toward the stomach but upward and outward into the Allknowl-edge between good and evil and the choice and the repudiation and the acceptance forever. . . ." This taste is very much associated in his mind with the smell of pine trees. The reference to the mountains seemed to be an afterthought: ". . .in similitude of the actual mountains in Carolina and before that in Scotland where his ancestors had come from but he hadn't seen yet. . ." [323]. In the setting copy too [323], Chick notes to himself when they come to the fresh grave, *"I'm going to make a heap more mistakes but dont let this be one of them."* When Faulkner came to the headstone of Amanda Gowrie, on [324], he added her dates, 1892-1926, then changed them to 1878-1926. Originally it had been 1882-1916, then 1892-1922, then changed to 1892-1926 on [82].

Both the original draft and the setting copy mention that it was nearing 11 P.M. and Faulkner stayed close to the original draft at this point, though he added: "Aleck Sander was right: the thing to do was to go back to the truck and drive away, back to town and through town and on, not to stop, not even to have time to think for having to keep on driving, steering, keeping the truck going in order to keep on moving, never to come back; but then they had never had time, they had known that before they ever left Jefferson and he thought for an instant how if Aleck Sander really had meant it when he said he would not come and if he would have come alone in that case and then (quickly) he wouldn't think about that at all. . ." [324]-[325]. As Faulkner followed the original draft, he added in the setting copy [128] that Aleck Sander had a keen sense which helped him to realize that Highboy had smelled quicksand at the branch (not mentioned in the original draft) and that he had discovered, a minute before either Miss Habersham or Chick, a horse or a mule. Also, both drafts on [83] and [325] note that Miss Habersham was seen motionless in silhouette against the sky. Later he was to describe Gavin as being silhouetted, too, in a passage that took many tries. On [327], after following the original draft closely, Faulkner typed: ". . .he's some kind of a shoestring timber-buyer over in Crossman County." On [84], he had typed Glasgow, then Hollymount, and finally Hollyvale. In the setting copy, he only typed Crossman County. With this emendation, he had finished the fourth chapter.

This chapter accentuates the murder mystery dimension of this novel; it begins with the meeting of Chick and Miss Habersham and ends with the two of them, plus Aleck Sander, digging up a corpse in the middle of the night. The initial meeting of the two protagonists was important to Faulkner and he reworked it considerably. He also expanded the section concerning the ride out to the cemetery which, in this case, relates the story not only to the value of the countryside but to the blacks who live in it. Once he revealed that Montgomery's body was in the grave and not Vinson Gowrie's, Faulkner had reached a plateau; most of the rest of the novel would consist in explaining Montgomery's death, particularly as it concerned Lucas.

Chapter Five of the Setting Copy

By the time Faulkner came to Chapter Five in the setting copy, he numbered the first page of this chapter as page "120." There are seventeen pages or parts of pages used in this chapter. Chapter Four in original draft, the basis of this setting copy

chapter, is numbered page "65" at this point. The beginning of
the original draft chapter [85] concerns Sheriff Hampton not
being able to succeed himself since he is already in his third
term as sheriff. The setting copy chapter [328] gives a greater
sense of continuity with the previous chapter. Chick and Aleck
Sander fill up the grave and Chick returns home explaining to
his uncle what they had accomplished at the graveyard. Then
Chick reflects on his action in military images, perhaps reflecting Faulkner's work on *A Fable* at this time:

> . . .and he thought again how you could never really beat them
> because of their fluidity which was not just a capacity for mo-
> bility but a willingness to abandon with the substanceless prompti-
> tude of wind or air itself not only position but principle too;
> you didn't have to marshal your forces because you already had
> them: superior artillery, weight, right justice and precedent and
> usage and everything else and made your attack and cleared the
> field, swept all before you—or so you thought until you discovered
> that the enemy had not retreated at all but had already abandoned
> the field and had not merely abandoned the field but had usurped
> your very battlecry in the process; you believed you had captured a
> citadel and instead found you had merely entered an untenable
> position and then found the unimpaired and even unmarked battle
> set up again in your unprotected and unsuspecting rear. . . . [329]

Chick's mother concludes by insisting that he should get some
sleep.

At this point the interior perspective becomes complicated.
Chick hears his uncle talk to him, moves towards his uncle's
car and Miss Habersham's truck, then recalls that later he would
remember to ask his uncle where he had searched for him, and
finally repeats his uncle's words again. In his own way Gavin begins to understand: " 'Out of the mouths of babes and sucklings
and old ladies—' he paraphrased. 'Quite true, as a lot of truth
often is, only a man just dont like to have it flung in his teeth
at three oclock in the morning. And dont forget your mother,
which of course you cant; she has already long since seen to that.
Just remember that they can stand anything, accept any fact
(it's only men who burk at facts) provided they dont have to
face it; can assimilate it with their heads turned away and one
hand extended behind them as the politician accepts the bribe' "

[330]. Thus, in his own way, Gavin underlines the Ephraim motif that had been established back in the third chapter.

With this as prologue to the fifth chapter, Faulkner then returns to the original draft and picks up with his analysis of the sheriff. He repeats the same background information about the sheriff [330] as he did in the original draft. At this point, Faulkner revised the text on the original draft in blue ink and pencil; the pencil revisions are prior because he crossed off lines in pencil and then wrote over them in ink. He followed the original draft closely, occasionally changing a word such as substituting "mama" [331] for "mammy" [86] (cf. page 108.9 in the first edition) in reference to Paralee. On [332] the sheriff has hair mussed "like that of a ten-year-old boy," thus putting him on the side of the old women and the children. Faulkner then copied the original draft almost verbatim, though Jim Halladay [333] is "Holladay" in the original draft [89]. The reason for the staying close to the original draft is, I suspect, that most of the text concerns a dialogue with the sheriff. The three lines crossed-off at the bottom of [336] are a typing mistake: Faulkner as he copied the original draft misread the original draft text because both lines twenty-two and twenty-three begin with "and then" [92]. He jumped to the second one, instead of following the first; this section shows that Faulkner would cross off a few lines in the setting copy and start again in the setting copy rather than drop one line of the original draft.

On [339] and [96], the sheriff asks Legate if he knew Jake Montgomery from over in Crossman County, as found on page 115 of the first edition. On [340], Legate mentions that since Montgomery has been kicked out of Tennessee, he been laying abound his father's farm beyond Glasgow; on [96], the father's farm had been over in Crossman County. Also on [340], Faulkner adds a bit of dialogue in the setting copy which gives more continuity to the murder story:

> 'What was he [i.e., Montgomery] doing around here?' the sheriff said: then Legate:

> 'Buying timber, aint he? Aint him and Vinson Gowrie. . . .' Then Legate said with the barest inflection, *'Was?'* and then with no inflection at all: 'What is he doing?' and he this time, his own

voice indifferent along the soft deep edge of sleep, too indifferent
to bother if it were aloud or not:

'He aint doing anything now.'

Then Faulkner returned again to the original draft.

He changed the phrase on [96] "in one soft high soundless
level wash" to [340] "in one soft high level [wash] golden
wash. . ." [340]. The sheriff's tie changed from a "bright red-
and-orange striped necktie" [96] to a "bright orange-and-yellow
necktie." Beginning on [341] Faulkner began to amplify some
sentences. On [97] he wrote, for example: "A lady without
nothing but a chicken and vegetable farm to run might not have
nothing to do all day." On [341], this became: "A lady without
nothing but a couple thousand chickens to feed and nurse and
water and a vegetable farm hardly five acres big to run, might
not have nothing to do all day." On [343]-[344], Faulkner
added a new section which he wrote parts of twice, once as a preliminary draft on [343], which he crossed out and then rewrote
on [343]-[344]. Gavin and Miss Habersham stare at one another
instead of "bending each upon the other that absolute concentration of all the senses in the sum of which mere clumsy fallible
perception weighed [no] little more than the ability to read
Sanskrit would. . ." [343]-[344]. On [344] Faulkner continued
to follow the original draft very closely as he had throughout this
chapter even to the point of not determining precisely the conclusion of this chapter; however, he decided to end with Gavin
answering Miss Habersham with a "yessum." Faulkner crossed
off the last two and a half lines in red ink and the chapter came
to a predictable close. Since most of this chapter takes place at
the sheriff's house where there was already considerable dialogue
in the original draft, Faulkner did not alter his conception of this
chapter in the setting copy. His major concern had been to establish greater continuity with the fourth chapter.

Chapter Six of the Setting Copy

Faulkner began Chapter Six on [345] in what was originally
the middle of Chapter Four [99], which was later designated as

Chapter Five in the original draft. There are thirty-six pages or parts of pages used in this chapter. This is one of those setting copy chapters that had no clear-cut division in the original version. It begins with Miss Habersham being driven home to the edge of town. In the middle of [346], Faulkner began to compose new material at the typewriter explaining how the big old decaying wooden houses had given way to the encroachment of subdivisions in what twenty-five (Faulkner originally wrote "fifty") years ago had been even too small for a decent front lawn. The young couples with their memberships in the bridge clubs and rotary clubs and who have enough wealth to afford colored maids have taken over the area and formed a new generation of landowners. Still one expected to see a Negro on Monday but this was not the case. Even when Faulkner repeated material from the original draft on [347], he amplified his original text concerning the young Negroes who would not put on their *Harper's Bazaar* uniforms until they were in the houses.

All the while, as Gavin takes Miss Habersham this time to the jail, Chick is growing sleepy and, in the setting copy [348], Faulkner added the phrase: ". . .and he [i.e., Chick] heaved himself bodily again out of the long soft timeless rushing black of sleep to find as usual that no time had passed. . ." On the top of [349] Faulkner retyped a section he had originally typed on [348], amplifying to a minor degree the original draft [100]. On [100] Faulkner had written that Chick had said: "You may have to talk to Paralee too." In the setting copy, Faulkner again began to compose new material in which Chick thinks of his mother, not of Paralee. The simplest thing for Chick to do at this point would be to get in the sheriff's car and stay in it until they were ready to go out to the church. He would have done it if he had not "been so worn out and anti-climaxed and dull for sleep and he knew he couldn't cope with her [i.e., his mother] this time even if he had been completely fresh. . ." [349]. Thus, in the revision of this section in the setting copy Faulkner puts great emphasis on Chick's exhaustion, so much so that it has "doomed him completer now to defeat and rout. . . ." It is interesting to note that Faulkner changed the word "presence" to "attack" when Chick "musing on his uncle's naive and childlike rationalising about school and bed when faced with that fluid and implacable attack because his uncle had read his mind again and again: 'Come on. . .' " [349]. On

[350], Faulkner expanded part of this statement repeating the word "attack" as Gavin looked down at Chick with compassion and "no hope."

Mrs. Mallison does not appear sympathetic, particularly when she would not listen to the reasons the group might advance: ". . .civic duty or simple justice or humanity or to save a life or even the peace of his own immortal soul" [350] would not be enough to keep Chick at home or going to school. After Gavin replies to Chick's statement that he is just his uncle, Gavin retorts, "I'm worse than that. . . I'm just a man." Gavin says that he will speak to Paralee since motherhood does not have any skin pigment, an observation not in the original draft. Originally on [351] Faulkner had written:

> Since she [i.e., Mrs. Mallison] was a woman and a mother too and he had discovered a long time. . .ago that that condition had no pigment in its skin:
>
> 'You're going to have to talk to Paralee too.'
>
> 'Right,' his uncle said, turning again, so briskly and confidently that anyway he realised again that his uncle for all his bachelorhood and hence thirty-five years from woman's dominion was not completely besotted. . . .

Faulkner rejected this version, perhaps because "besotted" might have been too strong a word. The observation had originally been made in connection with Mrs. Mallison about skin pigmentation, not in connection, as the final draft shows, with Paralee.

From this, Chick in a stream-of-consciousness technique, mentally wanders from Gavin's statement about skin pigmentation, to thoughts of a battlefield and defeat, to the high school football team two years ago when he had been chosen for one of the positions to play in an away game because one of the players could not make it ([350] and [352]). In the original draft, the sequence of events included: 1) a request to talk to Paralee; 2) a scene at the dinner table where Chick is sleepy and is drinking coffee much to the displeasure of one of his parents; 3) Mrs. Mallison urging Gavin to speak to Paralee since she too is worried about her son; 4) Chick drinking hot coffee and then splashing cold water on his face; 5) Chick's mother standing and watching him as she had in the past when he did anything that made him less of a child as when he trained his Shetland pony to jump and afterwards when he had received his first powder-shooting gun; 6) a discussion of the football game at Mottstown. The story had been told in outline form in the original draft. In the setting copy, Faulkner elaborated on it more than he had in the past. In trying to seek permission to go to the football game, Chick felt "worried and perplexed with a blending of anger and shame and shame at being angry and ashamed. . ." [352]. In the setting copy also, Chick imagines himself a soldier being wrenched out of his mother's arms to fight a battle for some shameful cause, thus echoing the introduction to this passage about the battle-field. That Friday evening two years before he had a difficult time getting to sleep and on Saturday he "thought better for the team if he had not come since he probably had too much on his mind to be worth anything to it. . ." [253]. This football sequence is almost like portraying Chick preparing for his battle to go out and dig up the grave; here we have a weekend fight with Chick very much the underdog.

On the bottom of [353], Faulkner typed out a section, later expanded on [354], which repeated some of the episodes in the original draft: Chick going to the bathroom and washing his face and thinking about his mother's face "the familiar face wearing the familiar expression of amazement and protest and anxiety and invincible repudiation. . ." [354]; his reflections on the Shetland pony, the powder shooting gun, the day Highboy, a bit rambunctious for such a boy to handle, was delivered; the echo of his mother asking in the car coming home from the game whether his arm hurt or not; and the time when his father discovered that he was jumping Highboy over a watertrough. In the original draft [101], Faulkner mentioned that Paralee must be all right because Gavin had spoken to her and then Chick looked into his father's face and thought that Aleck Sander must have told him too he was not certain it was a mule. In the setting copy, [356] when Faulkner returned to the original draft text with "Dammit, why didn't you tell me last night?", he deleted the reference to the Aleck Sander and the mule.

When Gavin speaks to Mr. Mallison, he explains both in

the original draft and in the setting copy that it took an old woman and two "children" to believe truth for no other reason than it was truth worthy of pity and belief. In the setting copy [356], he added to this statement that the truth was told to someone capable of pity though none of them originally believed them. In an *ad hominem* manner, Gavin asks Chick when he began to believe: was it when Chick saw the coffin opened with his own eyes? Gavin also remarks about himself: "Maybe I'm not too old to learn either." Then with deeper insight, Chick says that he had known all the time, that he never really believed Lucas, and that perhaps the whole thing had not happened at all. With this, and being in a tired mood, his mother brings him coffee and sets it before him and his father complains that Chick is not going to drink coffee until he is eighteen.

Next, those present notice that Mrs. Mallison is dressed to go out, not to the cemetery as they suppose, but to the jail to help Miss Habersham. Chick's father insists both in the original draft [102] and in the setting copy [358] that Chick should go to school. Faulkner then follows the original draft again after deviating from it and altering the sequence of thoughts in Chick's mind as mentioned above. Faulkner deleted in the setting copy the reference to Hampton calling the mayor to tell Professor Henry to keep school open.

Faulkner then composed at the typewriter for six and a half pages ([358]-[363] and [366]-[367]) before he would return to the original draft. Both the beginning of this six-and-a-half page passage and the end of it concern the coffee Chick was drinking: "So he drank the coffee which the soap and water and hard toweling had unfogged him enough to know he didn't like" [358]. . . "But at least he was awake. The coffee had accomplished that anyway" [366] (cf. pages 128-133 of the first edition). The insertion of these pages slows down the action and gives a clearer picture of Chick as a person. Chick admits to himself that he was very scared at the graveyard and Miss Habersham's prodding helped them to go through the motions of digging up the corpse. This section is a retelling of the murder story from another perspective, one after the event and in a Chick-Gavin dialogue framework where the meaning of the action can be evaluated, reformulated, and put into some perspective. The words seem to come easy to Faulkner at this point: " 'Fill it up,' Miss Habersham said. They did, the (five times now) loosened dirt going down much faster than it came up though it seemed forever in the thin starlight filled with the constant sound of the windless pines like one vast abateless hum not of amazement but of attention, watching, curiosity; amoral, detached, not involved and missing nothing" [359]-[360]. This section seems to infer that Miss Habersham is present since the reader hears her voice; in fact it is being recounted by Chick. As they returned to the truck from the graveyard, there is an extra note of suspense added because all three are aware that they might be watched by the murderer. Perhaps the most memorable paragraph [363]-[364] (cf. pages 131-132 of the first edition) is the one in which Chick rides Highboy back down to the road; he let him go until the truck came and overtook them and they were out of the pine area, though the pines and their "miration" could have for a long time informed the inhabitants of Beat Four what had transpired at the cemetery and "so he stopped thinking about it now, all in the same flash in which he had remembered it. . ." [363].

Then in a spirit almost of nonchalance and perhaps disdain, Mr. Mallison says he will have to go to work while the rest play cops-and-robbers, which Chick analyzed as the "pseudo-scornful humorous impugnment of his and Aleck Sander's courage. . ." [363]. Pages [364]-[365] are rough drafts of [366]-[367] and are close to the final version. What is remarkable is that in this material (none of it is in the original draft) Faulkner had Chick compare his father's reactions to the gravedigging and helping Lucas with Gavin's reactions: his father's emotional blow-up revealed him and exposed him as one who looked at his son "from beyond the bridgeless abyss of that begetting not with just pride but with envy too; it was his uncle's abnegant and rhetorical self-lacerating which was the phony one and his father was gnawing the true bitter irremediable bone of all which was dismatchment with time, being born too soon or late to have been himself sixteen and gallop a horse ten miles in the dark to save an old nigger's insolent and friendless neck" [366]. Such a passage highlights the uniqueness of Chick's actions.

On [103], Faulkner noted that while "the street was dotted with children," the flat beds of the "trucks which should have been dense with Negroes but not one today." On [364], Faulkner modified this somewhat and noted that "the street too would be full of children fresh for Monday." Faulkner kept this version on [367], the final setting copy version. As Faulkner wrote this section, he expanded the original draft and the first version of the setting copy. On [365], Faulkner picked up an idea he had deleted in the original draft: ". . .and on the street not one school-bound child although he had heard without any effort to listen enough of his uncle on the telephone to know that his uncle was telling the school superintendent to go on and have school today as usual." On the top of [365] Faulkner had written that Chick "jerked himself, no reflex now, not of sleep but delusion" who thought that the previous night had not happened and that there had been no Saturday at all and re-membering that there had been no children on the school bus but only grown people. In the final version, Faulkner polished this: "Whereupon this time he jerked himself, no reflex now, not even out of sleep but illusion, who had carried hypnosis right out of the house with him even into the bright strong sun of day, even driving the pickup truck which before last night he would not even have recognised yet which since last night had become as inexpugnable a part of his memory and experience and breathing as hiss of shovelled dirt of [sic] the scrape of a metal blade on a pine box would ever be, through a mirage-vacuum in which not simply last night had not happened but there had been no Saturday either. . ." [368].

Faulkner repeated his previous draft that no child was on the street. On [104] he had originally and awkwardly written the following before crossing off some of the words:

> As he drew up behind his uncle's car in front of the jail he could [see] two steady streams of them crossing each other at the end of the street and at each corner where the street entered the Square a crowd, standing, looking as one into the street toward the jail and the space before it and then he saw opposite the jail in front of the blacksmith's where he had stood yesterday another that the throng on the opposite corner stretched all the way up the street until the end of it had passed the blacksmith's where he had stood yesterday and he watched his mother and his uncle get out of the car and go up the short walk and onto the gallery and across it into the jail and then he could see Miss Habersham then he saw standing slightly in front of the crowd. . . .

On [369], Faulkner expanded this scene twice: "As he drove the pickup into the curb behind his uncle's car he could see a mass of people bulging out into the street itself from both corners where the street entered the Square, staring up the street toward the jail and another flow of them already crept up the opposite side of the street until it had reached and even passed the blacksmith's where he had stood trying to be invisible yesterday. . .", and secondly, ". . .behind his uncle's car he could see where visible and sense where not a moil and mass of movement, a steady flow back and forth across the end of the street where it entered the Square and beyond this filling the Square itself a sense a feeling of one dense pulse and hum as when the crowd overflows the carnival midway or the football field. . . ." On [102 (V)] Faulkner typed five lines picking up from [369.5] concerning the crowd looking like one "waiting to enter a football stadium."

On [370], Faulkner wove these various strands together for the final version in the setting copy: ". . .no exodus of men toward the stock pens nor women into the stores so that as he drove the pickup into the curb behind his uncle's car he could see already where visible and sense where not a moil and mass of movement, one dense pulse and hum filling the Square as when the crowd overflows the carnival midway or the football field, flowing into the street and already massed along the side opposite to the jail until the head of it had already passed the blacksmith's where he had stood yesterday trying to be invisible as if they were waiting for a parade to pass. . ." Faulkner then continued to identify the marshal as an Ingrum who now lived in town. For the next two and a half pages [371]-[373], Faulkner again composed new material at the typewriter devoting some time to the townsfolk and their reaction to the event. Now people thronged the Square as if the stores were closed or as if a play were to begin. Then like a veil being lifted from his eyes Chick sees for the first time, not an audience for a play, but one in a courtroom waiting for the officer to begin the trial. They had come to pass judgment not on Lucas Beauchamp, but on Beat Four and to see that Beat Four should not fail in "its white man's high estate" [372].

The crowd for Chick is highly impersonal: their faces were myriad "yet curiously identical in their lack of individual identity, their complete relinquishment of individual identity into one We not even impatient, nor even hurryable, almost gala in its complete obliviousness of its own menace, not to be stampeded by a hundred running children. . ." [372]. Chick sees both sides of the crowd's personality; just as a hundred people could not get them into action, so too a hundred could not stop them once in motion. Faulkner then unites the freedom-escape motif with the desire first to go to sleep and then return when it is all over. But Chick knows this is not the right course because he is responsible for exposing something shameful and shocking, something which might have disappeared "with the fading embers of Lucas' crucifixion" [373]. With this reference to Lucas' crucifixion, Faulkner returns to the original draft, not to Chick's mother and uncle going up to the jail as in the original draft [104], but to Miss Habersham sitting in the jail doorway.

Faulkner keeps the placid scene of Miss Habersham undaunted by the activities of the day and the previous night; the contrast with the gala mood of the crowd is striking. In both the original draft [105] and the setting copy [373], Faulkner mentions that Mrs. Mallison was sitting beside Miss Habersham; however in the setting copy, Faulkner crossed off "his mother" and substituted the word "her" in its place. As Faulkner returned to the conversation of the marshal and the sheriff with the crowd, he repeated the original draft as would be expected. He added occasional touches, such as comparing the crowd to a herd of cattle and calling them "tolerant, good-humored, debonair almost" [376]. At one point, Faulkner gave more attention to the mob: on [109], he had written: "Watching him [i.e., Hampton] and Lucas and Beat Four, to see what would happen. The ones here now are not a mob; they brought their women with them." In the setting copy [378] it became; "Watching him and Beat Four, to see what would happen. These people just came to town to see what either or both of them are going to do." Faulkner continues to follow the original draft to the end and concludes this chapter as if he intended it to end here; there is no carry-over to another page.

In this setting copy chapter, Faulkner concentrated his efforts on three areas; making Chick sufficiently tired, retelling the exhumation story, and giving a more elaborate description of the townsfolk. With Chick so tired, Faulkner is able to

associate various events in Chick's mind and establish their sur-
realistic connection. This is especially true in linking Chick's
feelings about the football game with those of his present situation. In retelling the exhumation story, Faulkner approaches it
from a different perspective and reaffirms its centrality. And by
giving more attention to the townsfolk, Faulkner is able to create
a communal, ironically joyful, environment in which Lucas'
crucifixion takes on greater pathos.

Chapter Seven of the Setting Copy

This chapter, like Chapter Eight, follows the original draft
closely. There are thirty pages or parts of pages used in this
chapter. On [110], Faulkner had written "in the ten miles of
gravel" and on [380]-[381], Faulkner gives a greater sense of
chronological continuity, not found in the original draft, as he
develops the sleep motif: "And when they reached town a little
before three this morning nobody could have persuaded him
that by this time, almost nine oclock, he would not have made
back at least five and a half hours of sleep even if not the full
six. . . ." On [111] Faulkner had noted that one person crossed
the street and went over to the sheriff's car to block it; in the
setting copy [381], many crowded around the sheriff's car.
It looks like the original on [111] was a typing mistake: "one"
instead of "ones" (cf. page 145:10 of the first edition) since
the context of the original suggests a number of people. Also on
[381] Faulkner notes that the faces of the crowd are like those
times when a "busy parent pauses for an instant to check over
and anticipate the intentions of a loved though not too reliable
child." This further emphasizes the fact that those in the car
are children and therefore fit the Ephraim story; this comment
is likewise not in the original.

On [382] Faulkner notes in the setting copy, though not
in the original draft, that the roads around Jefferson were good
all-weather roads because "their taxes and votes of their kin
and connections who could bring pressure on the congressmen
who had the giving away of the funds had built them. . . ." On
[112], Faulkner noted too that the crowd could not be hurried
or denied "since theirs was the murdered and the murderer too:

the white man and the bereavement of his vacating and the forfeit life of begrievement's and fury's black protagonist; theirs the
right not just to mere justice but to vengeance too to allot or
withhold." In revising this on [382] Faulkner wrote: ". . .since
theirs was the murdered and the murderer too; theirs the af-
fronter and the principle affronted: the white man and the bereavement of his vacancy, theirs the right not just to mere justice but vengeance too to allot or withhold."

Faulkner continued to follow his original draft changing
phrases occasionally. On [383] Faulkner repeats page [113]
almost exactly:

> . . .the farmhouses from which no smoke rose because breakfast
> was long over by now and no dinner to be cooked where none
> would be home to eat it, the paintless Negro cabins where on
> Monday morning in the dust of the grassless treeless yards half-
> naked children should have been crawling and scrabbling after
> broken cultivator wheels and wornout automobile tires and empty
> snuff-bottles and tin cans and in the back yards smoke-blackened
> iron pots should have been bubbling over wood fires beside the
> sagging fences of vegetable patches and chickenruns which by
> nightfall would be gaudy with drying overalls and aprons and
> towels and unionsuits: but not this morning, not now. . . .

On [114], he noted that on this second Monday in May there
"should have been a figure, a formal group of ritual almost
mystic significance, monotonous, repetitive and identical as
milestones and tying the town to the county's ultimate rim as
milestones would. . . ." In revising this on [384], he wrote that
there "should have been fixed in monotonous repetition the
land's living symbol—a formal group of ritual almost mystic
significance identical and monotonous as milestones tying the
county-seat to the county's ultimate rim as milestones
would. . . ." Thus, Faulkner discriminated very much in the
rhythm and imagery he would ultimately use.

Also, on [114], Faulkner noted that the group was "five"
miles from town; this was later changed in pencil to "8" which
corresponds with the number on [384], though on [384] he
had originally written two other numbers and then crossed them
off: five and nine. On [114], Chick had not seen a Negro in

thirty-six hours and on [384] this was changed to forty-eight hours. On [114] Faulkner had originally typed that it was the "sixt" day of May, that is, either sixth or sixteenth. Then he typed on [114] it was the ninth of May. After he typed on [114] that there were "forty-two thousand" acres to be planted; this was changed to"82." On [384] he originally typed in "eighty-two thousand" and then wrote in blue "a hundred and forty." Faulkner was trying to find the exact figures for his imaginary world. Also on [386] Faulkner added that they could see the bridge where Aleck Sander had waited for him in the dark and "below which Highboy had smelled quicksand." The smelling of quicksand was not in the original.

Though Faulkner remained close to the original draft, ironically, at times, the setting copy is less clear than the original. On [117], he had typed that the car was almost at the cemetery and "what remained not even to be measured in miles yet measured in quarters though it be, to be compassed at a crawl, the car whining in second speed now. . . ." On [387]-[388], this is cryptically expressed as: "Though that little at a crawl, the car whining in second gear now. . . ." At other times he tried to be more precise. On [388], Faulkner noted that the earth which had bred Chick's bones "and those of this fathers for six generations." Later, on [388], he explained the images of "unfolding" on [117], that it was "like a map" [388]. For the next few pages Faulkner added new phrases, especially as he was approaching Gavin's speech about Sambo. He added on [389], for example, that the distance the United States stretched in all directions was "not merely to where the ultimate headlands frowned back to back upon the waste of the two oceans and the long barrier of Canada but to the uttermost rim of earth itself. . . ." Faulkner was expanding Gavin's philosophical reflections and making them more and more cosmological.

Then from the word "defy" on [389] Faulkner added an entire new section to the setting copy (cf. pages 152.15-153.11 of the first edition). This addition in the setting copy concerns Chick's growth to manhood. Like the corporal in *A Fable,* Chick is confronted with the faces of men who resemble himself. From the top of a wall where the scope of the "teeming never-ravaged land of glittering undefiled cities and unburned towns and unwasted farms so long-secured and opulent" [390], he looks at

the faces of people who were like him, yet there is no real kinship since soon the very language they use would have different
meanings. These faces looking down at him serve as a type of
prelude to Gavin's remarks about the South and Sambo.

On [390] Gavin talks about "we" alone in the United
States and notes parenthetically he is "not speaking of Sambo
right now."   Faulkner adds, too, on [391]: "So we are not
really resisting what the outland calls (and we too) progress
and enlightenment." Later on [391] Faulkner initially calls the
United States, "America," before crossing it off and typing
"United States" (cf. page 153.29-30 of the first edition). On
[391] Faulkner added: "And of course we will continue to defend it [i.e., homogeneity]. We (I mean all of us: Beat Four
will be unable to sleep at night until it has cancelled Lucas Beauchamp (or someone else) against Vinson Gowrie in the same
color of ink, and Beat One and Two and Three and Five who on
heatless principle intend to see that Beat Four makes that cancellation) dont know why it is valuable." Faulkner typed nine
more lines explaining that from homogeneity comes art, literature, science, that minimum of government and police "which is
the meaning of freedom and liberty. . . ." But the most valuable
product of homogeneity is a "national character" which is
proven in a crisis.

On [391], Faulkner has Gavin say that the Southerners
must resist the "North" not an impersonal "them" as in [119].
On [392], Faulkner added two additions to the original draft:
". . .the postulate that Sambo is a human being living in a free
country and hence must be free. That's what we are really defending: the privilege of setting him free ourselves: which we will
have to do for the reason that nobody else can since going on a
century ago now the North tried it and have been admitting for
seventy-five years that they failed. So it will have to be us."
Then Faulkner noted that the shame "will be finished; the shame
will be there of course but the whole chronicle of man's immortality is in the suffering he has endured, his struggle toward
the stars in the stepping-stones of his expiation." On [392]
Faulkner makes the word "tomorrow" [120] more precise by
calling it first "next Tuesday" and then in the following sentence
"next Monday."

Faulkner then added a new paragraph in the setting copy [393]-[395] (cf. pages 155.18-156.23 of the first edition) and rewrote parts of it twice. The focus now is on Lucas as Sambo. Gavin is not referring to the black man who seeks what is mediocre in white society, but the part of the black man that has a better homogeneity than the white man because he has proved it by finding roots in a land not his own, because he had patience and a long view of life and the desire to endure, and because he loved the simple things of life. Originally on [396] Faulkner reached the climax of Gavin's thought when he wrote: "We—he and us—should confederate: he to have more of our freedom of opportunity, we to learn something of his solidarity. Then we in the South would dominate the United States." Faulkner then crossed this out, modified it, and finally on [395] typed: "We—he and us should confederate: swap him the rest of the economic and political and cultural privileges which are his right, for the reversion of his capacity to wait and endure and survive. Then we would prevail; together we would dominate the United States. . . ." Though Gavin never drew up a precise blueprint for this confederation, he nevertheless wanted to indicate possible areas of racial interaction.

Faulkner then went back to his original draft adding short phrases occasionally: 1) he noted that the tombstones were like "toothpicks in a loaf. . ." [397]; 2) he noted that the names and dates on the stone were "as though there had been nothing even their mourners remembered of them than they had lived and they had died. . ." [398]; 3) he added an ambiguous statement that as Chick and his uncle went to where the sheriff and two Negroes stood over the fresh grave "he who had violated it now actually saw for the first time" [398] (this refers to Chick not Crawford since Crawford is not at the scene); 4) he noted that the twins sat on a mule like "two clothing store dummies and as immobile. . ." [403]. Otherwise, Faulkner retyped this chapter as he had composed it in the original draft. Faulkner's major addition to this chapter is the refinement of his ideas concerning the notion of the black man's homogeneity. He is careful above all to balance the black man's weaknesses and strengths.

Chapter Eight of the Setting Copy

This chapter of the setting copy follows the original draft except in a few instances. There are fourteen pages or parts of pages used in this chapter. On [133] the "cold light blue tearshaped" flames became "cold lightblue tearshaped" [409]. On [135], Gavin noted that the body might be buried in the bed of the branch and on [412] Faulkner added, "Didn't they tell you at three oclock this morning that they saw him going there with it? What are we waiting for?" Also on [412] Faulkner added that Nub Gowrie turned faster than the two sons half his age and went to the mare and caught the reins and pommel and swung up quickly. This fills out the picture but does not really add to the story.

On [136] the sheriff said that Aleck Sander was right, that it was a mule the murderer had used. On [414], Faulkner added some lines:

> 'Not a black one with a rope-burn,' his uncle said.
> 'Surely not that. Not even a murderer is that crassly and arrogantly extrovert.'
>
> 'Yes,' the sheriff said. 'That's why they're dangerous, why we must destroy them or lock them up:'

On [415] Faulkner also added that the tracks indicate that the murderer was "carrying a burden man was not intended to carry. . . ." This is not in the original draft. On [418], after Mr. Gowrie has been told that Vinson has possibly been buried in quicksand and he wants to know where the quicksand is, Faulkner added that Chick answered: " 'It's by the bridge:' then—he didn't know why: and then that didn't matter either— 'It wasn't Aleck Sander that time. It was Highboy.' " The other important changes have been noted in the discussion of this chapter as found in the original draft. Faulkner seemed to be saving his creative energy for the next chapter, one that would take considerable time to write.

Chapter Nine of the Setting Copy

This is the most complicated chapter Faulkner wrote. There are one hundred and fifty-four pages or parts of pages used in this chapter. The preliminary material written in manuscript in blue and red ink (as far as I can determine there is no significance in the use of two colors; it was more a matter of which ink was available when Faulkner was composing) begins with, "He would remember: he and his uncle standing besides the sheriff's car in the alley beside the jail and cross the dark yard toward them" [106]. The evening was dark and neither light nor sound reached back to where Chick stood. It was only a little after 10 P.M. on Monday night and the night sky resembled a bride's bouquet under a cupped bowl. Chick remembered the other normal Monday nights "when the loud fury of blood and vengeance and racial solidarity had not roared in from Beat One and Two and Three and Four and Five (and for the matter of that from the purlieus of the Georgian porticoes themselves) to rattle and clash among the old brick and the old trees and the Doric capitals and leave them for one night anyway stricken" [106] (cf. page 213 of the first edition). In this way, page [423] of Chapter Eight (page "207") leads directly into page [106] (page "208").

The following day everything would wake and stir and "another day and it would even fling off hangover [sic]" and shame, and "on Saturday the whole country with one pierceless unanimity of click and pulse and hum would even deny that the moment had ever existed when it could have been mistaken" [106]. But not tonight and although a few movie patrons who came in late would still be passing homeward and "all the young men and girls sitting since that time drinking coca cola and playing nickels into the drug store jukebox, strolling timeless and in no haste since they were going nowhere since the May night itself was their destination and they carried that with them, walked in it. . ." [105]. The last few words of the section are "dispersing nightward sleepward tommorrow-ward about the dark mile-compassing land" [105].

But tonight the Square was deserted and the poolroom and drugstore were both locked up. Only the cafe was open and some said its real purpose "was to keep Willy Ingrum's nocturnal counterpart awake" [105] because he would not stay in the little cubbyhole of an office which had a stove and a telephone. Rather he used the cafe where old ladies could telephone him as the telephone "had been connected to a big burglar alarm bell on the outside wall loud enough for the counterman or a truck driver in the cafe to hear it and tell him it was ringing" [104]. But the phone was silent tonight. Chick heard that his uncle had gone from his house to the jail without passing the cafe where he could have heard the music, had the jukebox been on. Except for punching the clock on the outside of the bank, shutting off the jukebox for twelve hours "had probably been the night marshal's first official act. . ." [104].

Tonight there was no sound nor movement: "It had been empty last night too but not like this and even last night's emptiness had not been the emptiness merely of Sunday night. . ." [104], an emptiness like the deserted and silent terrain in front of a mobilized army, or the quiet like that in a vestibule to a powder magazine or the spillway under a dam [104]. The top half of [103] continues the previous text and is a shortened version of the top of page 214 of the first edition. The upper part of this page ends with "for all purposes Lucas was already dead since he had died then and theirs was merely to preside at his suttee" [103]. The next paragraph on [103] begins:

> But not even that tonight and he remembered: two oclock that afternoon in his uncle's car just behind the truck (it was another pickup; they—the sheriff—had commandeered it with a slatted cattle frame on the bed; one of the Gowrie twins had known where it would be standing in the deserted yard of the house two miles away which had the telephone—and he remembered wondering what it was doing there, how they had got us to town who had left it—and the Gowrie had turned the switch on with a table fork which by the Gowrie's direction he had found in the un-locked kitchen when his uncle went in to telephone the coroner and the Gowrie was driving it) blinking rapidly and steadily not against glare so much as something hot and gritty inside his eyelids like a dust of ground glass. . . . [103]

Faulkner thus started with the material which would eventually begin Chapter Nine, while the previous preliminary material is found in what is eventually Chapter Ten. It should be noticed that the above paragraph is very close to the setting copy and first edition; Faulkner seemed to switch around the scenes considerably but he did not do extensive rewriting once he had put his ideas and story down on paper.

On [102] Faulkner continued by having Chick see the inhabitants of the various beats and the town, too, "the merchants and cotton buyers and the men who were the clerks in the stores and cotton offices and mechanics in the garages and filling stations on the way back from lunch, and the faces he had seen in the barbershop yesterday morning and here in the street at noon yesterday when the sheriff drove up with Lucas, who had no jobs and didn't want any, who even in little lost Mississippi towns like this could live without working: children of this lost fabulous nation which out of all earth could still afford to keep some of its own idle and sweatless—crowding the street in front of the jail from the blacksmith's to the Square: who without even waiting to recognize the sheriff's car or for that matter even looking at it, turned and began to flow away like the flux of a tide, already in motion. . ." [102]. Faulkner then continued the text on the bottom of [364], still remaining close to what would be his final version. He noted that the crowd "in a moment a second now it would overtake and snatch them up in order: his uncle's car then the truck then the sheriff's: like 3 hencoops in front of a broken [undecipherable word] and sweep and fling them on in one inextricable aborted now-worthless jumble onto the unloading ramp behind the undertaker's at the coroner's feet. . ." [364]. Faulkner then continued on [101] and wrote in order pages [100], [99], [98], [97], [96], [95], and ended on [93].

Page [101] begins with the text found on page 181.29 of first edition. The text runs continuously until page 184.11 where on [99] it reads differently. The crowd was streaming into the Square:

> . . .the khaki and denim and the printed cotton streaming into it [i.e., the Square] and across it toward the parked cars and trucks, crowding around them and even halted momentarily while they climbed and crawled into the seats and cabs and beds; already engines were starting up while the crowd still [streamed?] across

the Square toward them and now not one but five or six at once
had backed out from the curb and begun to turn and straighten
out and presently, almost at once in fact he could no longer keep
back of them, four streams of them flowing across the Square into
the 4 streets leading out of town already going fast even across the
Square, the faces in each one for just one moment more looking
not back but just out and just once and not long, not at anything
but just out just once and then no more, vanishing rapidly from
sight in profile and seeming to be themselves moving much faster
than the vehicles which bore them, already out of town long before
the simple undeviable postulate time by space by velocity could
have evicted them. [99]

Faulkner then continued on [98] which follows the setting
copy closely. When he came to the bottom of [97], Faulkner
wrote material he was later to revise and rearrange.

On [97] and [96] Faulkner wrote:

'Go on,' his mother said, 'Make somebody else stop or turn
out:' and he knew they were not going by the jail at all. He said,

'Miss Habersham—'

'You see?' his uncle said to no one: 'That's why no man can
ever really be a woman no matter how hard he tries.'

'How many collisions did you ever see with women driving both
of them?' his mother said.

'All right,' his uncle said. 'That's because one of them's car is
still in the shop where a man ran into it yesterday. —All right.'
his uncle said. 'How do I do it? Just shut my eyes and mash hard
with my right foot?' and perhaps did. Anyway they were in the
stream themselves now, beginning to move even a little fast now
toward home and he said again:

'Miss Habersham—'

'She has her truck,' his uncle said. 'Don't you remember?'

Faulkner then continued on [96] describing Miss Habersham;

again this page and the two following ones are a rougher draft of the setting copy than what we have previously seen in this manuscript segment:

Her house was almost half a mile away; what was wrong with it was that it was on the opposite side of town, on the other side of that unpierceable barrier of rushing almost bumper-locked cars and trucks and so almost as interdict to an old maiden lady in a second-hand vegetable peddler's truck even if she did dig up murdered men's graves at night, as if it had been in the moon or Russia: and suddenly he saw her sitting in the truck with the engine running, gripping the wheel and her foot already pressing the accelerator, independent solitary and forlorn too, erect and slight beneath the exact archaic even moribund hat waiting and watching for a chance to get through it and put the darned clothes away and feed the chickens and eat supper and get some rest too for the first time in going on 36 hours which to seventy must have been worse and longer than 72 or a 100 to sixteen, watching and waiting that dizzying endless profiled blur and no [gap?] nor even a symptom of one: but she was practical and would do the simple practical thing and not long about it either: which would be to go around it and now he watched her the truck in motion now driving along parallel with it in its direction, forlorn and solitary still yet independent still too and only a little nervous perhaps just realizing that she was already driving a littler faster than she was used to, ever had [undecipherable word] and even then not keeping abreast but only beside it because it was going quite fast now: one endless profiled whizz and now she would know that when the gap came perhaps she would not have the skill or strength or speed or quickness of eye or maybe even the simple nerve to bring it all: herself going faster and faster and so intent with not to miss the chance when it came that she wouldn't realise until afterward that she had made a turn going not south now but east and not just her house diminishing rapidly and squarely behind her but Jefferson too because they or it were not moving in just one direction out of town but in all of them on all the main roads leading away from the jail and the undertaker's and Lucas Beauchamp and what was left of Vinson Gowrie and Montgomery like the frantic scattering of waterbugs when you drop a rock into a stagnant pond and she would be more desperate than [undercipherable word] that he was going to laugh or rather that he was already laughing, stopping it only after it had already begun: [undecipherable word] not among the faces this time because the backs of the heads were all toward him: the back of one head not rushing at him but rushing away, fleeing concorded and aghast: until he stopped it.

'Blow the horn' his mother said.

'They ran,' he said. [96], [95], [93].

Faulkner ended this segment on the middle of [93] with Chick proclaiming "They ran."

At this point, Faulkner went back and took [93], which had been page "221," and used it again and wrote some new material and renumbered the page as page "212;" thus the page was numbered three times as "71," as "221," and finally as "212." It is possible to put the revised pages in order, but it is more difficult to see how Faulkner inserted them into the manuscript pages he had previously written. Pages [93], [427], and [469] are in consecutive order and are numbered in ink as pages "212," "213," "214" with [469] leading into [97]. Page [93] at the bottom begins with an image of the children "who should have been in school at this hour—not one country face nor even one true man. . ." Faulkner had typed a version of this material on [99] and in revising this material, he noted that the Square was not empty but it was getting that way. On [427], he noted the dress of the crowd:

> . . .khaki and denim and the printed cotton streaming onto it [i.e., the Square] and across it towed the parked cars and trucks, crowding and clotting about the doors while they crawled and climbed into the seats and cabs and beds: already starters were whining and engines catching and gears scraping and grinding while the people still hurried toward them and now not one but five or six at once backed away from the curb and turned and straightened out and people still running toward them and scrambling in and then he could no longer have kept count of them if he had ever been trying to, standing beside his uncle and watching them stream across the Square and into the four streets leading out of town in the four directions, already going fast even before they were out of the Square, the faces in one last moment more looking not back but out, not at anything: just out just once and that not for long and then no more, vanishing rapidly in profile

and seeming to be travelling themselves faster than the vehicle
which bore them, already by their faces out of town long before
they had from his view [sic].

Faulkner would later modify this too.

Faulkner then continued on [427] by noting that Chick's
mother came walking up past where they were lifting Montgomery's body out of the truck. In a parenthetical comment on
this typescript page, Faulkner noted: ". . .but then his uncle
had told him they could stand anything provided they still retained always the right to refuse to admit it was visible. . . ."
On [469] Mrs. Mallison turned "back into the walkway ahead of
them, walking slender and erect and rigid with her back looking
and her heels clicking and popping on the concrete as they did
on the floor at home and where he and Aleck Sander and his
father and his uncle all four had better walk pretty light, back
past the ramp where only the sheriff's empty car and the empty
truck stood now and on the alley where she was already holding
the car door open when he and his uncle got there; and saw
them again crossing the mouth of the alley too like across a
stage—the cars and trucks, the faces in invincible profile not
amazed and not aghast but in a sort of irrevocable repudiation,
shooting across the alley-mouth [text stops]." Also on [364]
towards the bottom, Faulkner crossed off the phrase "and sweep
and fling;" it would seem logical that he then wrote out the text
in blue ink on [147] beginning with "them in one inextricable
aborted now-worthless jumble. . . ." Another possibility, and the
one I prefer, is that [147] is a revision of [446] since both these
pages begin with the same words. On page 181.25-27 of the first
edition, the text reads in part: ". . .and sweep them on and
flung them at last in one inextricable aborted now-worthless
jumble. . . ." Page [147] is similar to pages 181.26-183.1 of the
first edition without, however, the phrase "hanging suspended
face to face with him just beyond the glass of the back window
yet in the same instant rushing and monstrous down at him so
that he actually started back and had even begun to think *In a
second more it will*."

The latter part of the manuscript writing on [98] has been
crossed-off and one page unnumbered [449] seems to fit here,
again judging from the first edition text on page 185. On [98]

Faulkner had written a version of the theater metaphor as found on page 185 of the first edition and then crossed it off. Page [449] picks up with the phrase, "He said: 'We'll take Miss Haber-sham home first.' " It ends with " 'Go on,' his mother said. 'Make them let you in:' and he knew they were not going by the jail at all [text stops] " (cf. page 186.11-12 of the first edition). Page [123] seems to be a later version of [147] and includes the missing lines of [146] beginning, "suspended face to face just beyond the glass. . . ." Page [123] seems to be a page that follows [102]. Faulkner had obviously not found the rhythms and images that had come to him much easier in the original draft. He was writing new material and he did not have the original draft to rely on; this accounts partially for the constant revision.

Faulkner began the second version of Chapter Nine (labeled "IX") on [38 (V)] with the words "He would remember: he and his uncle standing beside the sheriff's car in the alley beside the jail watching the sheriff and Lucas emerge from the side door and cross the dark yard toward them." The street is dark and there is little sound. The time is only a little after 10 P.M. on Monday and the sky is domed and "cupped as though in a vacuum like the old bride's bouquet" under a glass bell. The town is abandoned and Chick remembers the other normal nights when "the loud fury of blood and vengeance and racial solidari-ty had not roared in from Beat One or Two or Three or Four or Five" or even from behind the Georgian porticoes in town to upset the town's surroundings. On [22 (V)] Faulkner continued by writing that on the following day the town would wake up and gradually get back to business, and by Saturday the whole town would deny that any wrong doing had taken place. Thus, this version parallels the first one on [106].

Then Faulkner returned to the present: "But not yet, not tonight; ten oclock on Monday night and although the first run of film at the picture show would be forty or fifty minutes over now, a few of the patrons who had come in late would still be passing homeward. . ." [22 (V)]. Faulkner again presents a very casual scene of boys and girls "strolling timeless" and walking about with no direction, "since the May night itself was their destination. . . ." A few cars were seen taking people home from the movies or visits with friends and were now "departing at last nightward sleepward tomorrow-ward about the dark mile-compassing land." Then like a variation of the *haec nox est* of the Easter *Exsultet* Faulkner repeats himself: "But not to-night. The Square was empty, deserted. . ." [22 (V)]. The only lighted place was the all-night cafe which stayed open for the long-haul trucks though "some said its real purpose, the true reason for the grant of its license by the town, was to keep Willy Ingrum's nocturnal counterpart awake. . . ." Here the night marshal could be paged though some of the elderly women of the town did not like to page a policewoman in a cafe so the "office telephone had been connected to a burglar alarm bell on the outside wall loud enough for the counterman or a truck driver in the cafe to hear it and tell him it was ringing. . ." [34 (V)]. This sentence, though used before on [104], is not finished here and ends by comparing the cafe to a power plant since both are public institutions. Faulkner was writing material he would later use in the tenth chapter (cf. pages 211-212 of the first edition).

On [549 (V)] Faulkner numbered this page as "208" and labeled it chapter "IX." He began this third attempt of the setting copy with the words "He would remember. . .", that is, the night when Chick and Gavin stood beside the sheriff's car in the alley near the jail watching the sheriff bring Lucas from the side door of the jail. The sheriff tells Lucas to jump in the car. Gavin says, "I dont like this. Take somebody with you." The sheriff responds on [443] that he thought they settled that problem three times that afternoon. No light nor soound penetrated back that far down the alley. It was only a little past 10 P.M. on Monday and the first run of the movie "was forty or fifty minutes over now" and the young people in the drug store would be passing by soon "since their moment and destination was the May night itself. . . ." As Faulkner had written twice before in the setting copy, the trucks and cars would be going too "at last dispersing nightward sleepward tomorrow-ward about the dark mile-compassing land." Faulkner was here using the scene he had typed on the original draft of *Intruder* on [144], [145], [150], and which would eventually be used in the setting copy of Chapter Ten [546]-[547] (cf. page 213 of the first edition).

At the bottom of [443] Faulkner began the second paragraph with "But not now, not tonight; the Square was empty, already deserted; even the drugstore was dark." The Square had been empty the night before, but not like this evening. Even a normal Sunday night was not like this; last night had been Sunday only because the calendar said so. Then Faulkner uses the images of silence [444] : the terrain in front of a mobilized army, the vestibule to a powder magazine, and the spillway under the locks of a dam. There is a sense not of waiting but of "incre-mention" [sic]. Again, Faulkner was repeating material he had used on [104]. The townsfolk were expecting "the moment the time when in volitionless concord they themselves would create the event, preside at and even serve an instant which was not even six or twelve or fifteen hours belated but instead was the attenuation of the one in which the bullet had struck Vinson Gowrie in the back and there had been no time between and Lucas was already dead since he had died then and they would merely preside at his suttee. . . ." Then in a crossed-off section at the bottom of [444] Faulkner began the paragraph which would eventually be the actual first paragraph in Chapter Nine of the setting copy: "But not tonight; two oclock this afternoon in his uncle's car just behind the pickup truck it was commandeered, it had a slatted cattle frame on the bed and one of the Gowrie twins had known where it would be and it was, standing in the yard of an otherwise deserted house two miles away—and he wondered for a moment what it was doing there, how they had got to town today who had left if there and then no more. . . ." The truck contained Montgomery's body [444] ; then on [445] which immediately follows [444] ([544 (V)] resembles the low-er half of [444] and is a brief but expanded version of [444] but does not contain any crossed-off lines), Faulkner continued. Chick saw not just Beat One through Five, but merchants and cotton-buyers and younger men who were clerks and mechanics in the garages. After crossing off the lower half of [444], num-bered page "210," Faulkner inserted [462] numbered "210 A."

Page [462] begins, "But they were gone now, in less than eight hours, in less than one in fact (besides he had slept for al-most seven hours or maybe because he had slept was better): at two oclock in his uncle's car just behind the truck. . . ." Faulkner had originally done a preliminary draft of [462] on [548 (V)] and both versions are substantially the same. He then transferred the material he had crossed off on [444] to [462] in order to provide continuity. From [462] he continued to [445] and typed six pages in order without breaking the continuity ([445], [446], [448], [478], [479], [471], with [447] being a carbon of [446]). Page [445] (cf. page 181 of the first edition) concerns Chick seeing the people from the five beats; many young men in town, the merchants, cotton-buyers, clerks, and mechanics and others who even in "little lost Mississippi towns like this could live without working: children of this last vast fabulous nation which out of all earth could still keep some of its own with no compulsion of them to earn their bread. . . ." The crowd starts to flow like an ebb of a tide. The sheriff turns into the alley beside the jail, then the truck, and finally his uncle's car. The crowd flows into the alley behind them until on [446] they reach in one "inextricable aborted now-worthless jumble" the ramp where the coroner waited.

Then Chick sees not a mass of faces but "one Face not even ravening, not even insatiate: just in motion, insensate, vacant of thought: *'You fools! Don't you see you're too late. . . .'*" Chick looks through the back window at the mosaic of faces, like the picture which emerges from the "juxtaposition of trees and clouds and landscape" or like the severed head of a newspaper photograph of a Chinese or Balkan atrocity. The alley cleared and framed "a section of the street and of the blacksmith shop and all that opposite stretch which only a second ago had been crowded with people yet with nobody in it at all now. . ." ([446] and [448]). On [448] Chick sees a group propping a stretcher up to the truck's open endgate. Gavin turns and says, "Now I'm going to take you home where you can go to sleep before we have to have a doctor to give you a hypodermic." Chick replies to Gavin: "They've gone to the front!" and gets out of the car and goes up the walkway and sees the crowd "one last crash and surge across the Square" through the plate glass and trampling the membership plaque in the national funeraleer association and the "shabby stunted palm in the maroon earthenware pot. . . ." Here Faulkner is writing material that he will retain as part of Chapter Nine.

Then Chick goes out to the street and sees the crowd "there blocking the pavement nose pressed to the plate glass then flick! again and he saw that there were less than a dozen of them and some boys who should have been in school. . . ." ([448] and

[478]). On [478] this crowd is like those who always "gather first when the epileptic falls or the dog is run over;" this was later changed to "old epileptic Uncle Hogeye Mosby from the poorhouse." The mad dog becomes the one Willy Ingrum shot [464]. On [478] Faulkner describes the Square as not empty, "but emptying," and he continues to use the metaphor of moving water with "the ebb the flux swapping legs for wheels and concentric for eccentric, the constant stream which he had watched this morning in reverse faster and faster along the four streets leading out of town. . . ." The only ones left were Chick "and his uncle on the pavement and the sheriff and the coroner and the undertaker and whoeverelse the rules demanded wrestling with their inert anticlimax at the backdoor. . . ." Chick also remembers his mother, too, "come from the jail through the walkway too right past where it was going tediously and clumsily on or he would have seen her. . . ." From a comparison with pages 184-185 of the first edition, it is obvious that the above draft is much simpler, less complicated than the first edition, particularly in Faulkner's description of the chaotic scene of the cars and trucks leaving the Square.

On [479], in response to the question of where the car is, Mrs. Mallison mutters "Nonsense" and "Men" in contempt. In this section Faulkner has not included page 185.17-31 of the first edition; he mainly describes Mrs. Mallison's manner of walking to the car and opening the door. Gavin suggests they take Miss Habersham home first. Once they start Mrs. Mallison says, "You don't have to rehearse for that funeral too, do you?" [479]. They move fast and Gavin remembers he had left the truck at the jail and so they would not have to take Miss Habersham home. Mrs. Mallison again interrupts, " 'Go on,' his mother said. 'Make somebody else stop.' " On [471] Gavin replies, "That's why no man could ever be a woman no matter how hard he tried." Mrs. Mallison asks how many collisions Gavin has seen involving two women drivers. To which Gavin answers, "Maybe it's because one of them's car is still in the garage where a man ran into it yesterday." Faulkner is again rewriting material he had first used on [97] and [96].

Gavin continues driving through traffic. At home, Chick goes to his room: ". . .he could hear it he could hear nothing else even through the drawn shades even through the red jumping behind his closed eyelids, his mother's hand slim and cool but too dry rough on his forehead, the dry hot gritty feel of his head better than the palm but now to escape it, her voice dry and cool too: 'That damned Gavin Stevens. Just let go. Jut let go. . .' " [471].

Faulkner crossed off the lower portion of [471] about "That damned Gavin Stevens" and reworked onto the next few pages ([474], [473], [551 (V)], [476], and [477]) what he had previously crossed off. Page [474] picks up from [471.25] with Chick's attempt to fall asleep and how to "escape anything least of all the one frail narrow hand as inevictable as a birthmark. . ." [474]. It is here that we get an insight into the possible meaning of the title as Chick wanted to go to sleep, to "release into that nothing what little of nothing he had which was all he had which was nothing: dust: who had wanted of course to leave his mark on his time in man, some mark at least on his part of earth. . .to perform something passionate and brave and austere and found it all that remained was dust. . . ." Chick, it would seem, is the intruder and the dust is seen as a condition or environment or feeling that remained after one had done a noble deed.

On [473] Faulkner retyped [474], ending again with the phrase that must have stuck in his mind, that Chick wanted a chance to perform something in "man's enduring chronicle passionate and brave and austere and found it and all that remained was dust [text stops]." On [551 (V)] Faulkner typed a very neat version of [473]. In the next two attempts on [476] and [477] Faulkner deleted this reference to "dust." On [476], a nine-line page, for example, Faulkner wrote Chick wanted "to perform something passionate and brave and austere not just in but into man's enduring chronicle, worthy of a place in it—who knew? perhaps adding even one little jot to the austerity of the chronicle of man's brave passion—in gratitude for the gift of his time in it thirty years ago. . . ." It would seem that Faulkner was thinking of Gavin when he referred to "thirty years ago," a phrase not used in the final version of the setting copy.

On [477] Faulkner typed ten lines:

. . .it could possibly be his amazing lot to save a life from death

but only a death from indignity and shame and saved in fact even
the life and saving it found he had merely swapped the death for
the shame, in amazed and baseless hope believing he had cancelled
indignity with its own shame but found he had received from
shame and indignity with grudging pretermission of a death. . . .

On [480] Faulkner retyped the material from [471] including
the part beginning "That damned Gavin Stevens." The next
three pages ([472], [550 (V)], and [481]) Faulkner typed
the same material three times and finally concluded this sequence
of pages with the phrase "the chronicle of man's brave passion."
These three pages include the previous material he had written on
[474], [473], [476], and [477], though [550 (V)] is more
specific about trying to forget about Lucas and in fact "he had
got good and rid of Lucas Beauchamp forever now only he had
forgotten how to go to sleep. . . ." Thus this sequence ends on
Chick trying to sleep and think about his contribution to man's
enduring chronicle.

Faulkner started the next version on [547 (V)] with the
same material he had used on [549 (V)]: "He would remember. . . ." The scene is familiar and repeats Faulkner's initial
version of this chapter: the memory of standing by the sheriff's
car in the alley near the jail with Gavin when the sheriff and
Lucas emerge. No light nor sound penetrate the alley. It is after
10 P.M. on Monday night and the sky's dark bowl is cupped as
though in a vacuum like an old bride's bouquet under a glass bell.
Tomorrow the town would stir and by the following Saturday,
"the whole county with one pierceless unanimity of click and
pulse and hum would even deny that the moment had ever
existed when it could have been mistaken" [547 (V)]. Then
Faulkner began the next two pages ([456] and [536]) with the
emphasis that there was not much activity that evening. On
[456] Chick remembers "the other the normal Monday nights"
when the citizen from the various beats "or for that matter
from the purlieus of the Georgian porticoes themselves" would
come to town "to rattle and clash among the old brick and the
old trees and the Doric columns and leave for one night anyway
stricken. . ." [456]. Usually on 10 P.M. on Monday there is
some movement in town, people leaving the movies and "strolling timeless and in no haste since they were going nowhere since
the May night itself was their destination and they carried it

with them, walked in it. . ." [456]. Soon, too, the cars and trucks would be "dispersing nightward sleepward tomorrow-ward about the dark mile-compassing land." Again Faulkner was repeating material that would eventually not be included in Chapter Nine. On the bottom of [456] Faulkner again mentions "But not tonight. The Square was empty, deserted" and the only light was in the cafe and some believed its real "purpose was to keep Willy Ingrum's nocturnal counterpart awake. . ." [536]. Faulkner discusses the telephone hook-up and the alarm on the outside wall and ends this fragment by comparing the cafe to a power plant. Faulkner never completed this comparison here.

Probably at this point, Faulkner went back to [444] (numbered page "210") and inserted [458] (numbered "211") and then typed out [459], [460] and inserted [461] between these two pages. Pages [458], [459], [461], and [460] repeat the information "But not tonight: two oclock this afternoon in his uncle's car just behind Montgomery's body in the pickup truck. . ." [458]. As Chick followed in a car behind the truck containing Montgomery's body he speculates on how it had been commandeered by one of the Gowrie twins. On the way into town Chick sees not just the county, but the town too, the younger men, clerks, mechanics, and those "who had no jobs and did not want them, who even in a little lost town like this could live without working: children of this last fabulous nation which out of all earth could still afford to keep some of its own idle and sweatless. . ." [458]. Chick then describes the flowing motion of the crowd and soon they would swept "in one inextricable aborted now-worthless jumble onto the ramp where the coroner was waiting. . ." [459]. Chick screams at the crowd and calls them fools. Looking back through the window he sees "not faces but a Face, not a mass nor even a mosaic of them but one Face not even ravening, not even uninsatiate: just in motion, insensate, vacant of thought or even passion. . ." [459]. After the comparison with a Balkan or Chinese atrocity which he used before, Faulkner mentions that "then flick! and there was only the empty alley behind the car with nobody in it at all. . ." [459]. Pages [461] and [460] contain three versions, each of which focuses on the idea of the crowd going around out front and Gavin telling Chick that he won't be a minute and then they will pick up Mrs. Mallison and take Chick home to give them a shot (on [461] "to give us both a squirt with a needle" and on [460] "to give you a hypodermic"). This ended this segment.

Faulkner then took [458], [460] and inserted [543 (V)] (numbered page "208") before [458]. Page [543 (V)] begins the fifth version of this chapter with "The trunk was another pickup" and related in a now familiar pattern how it had been commandeered. The second paragraph of this page begins, "And two oclock that afternoon in his uncle's car just behind the truck. . . ." Chick sees not only the inhabitants of the various beats, but the town too. This section then leads into an amplification of those in the town on [458] (now numbered "209"). Faulkner then remembered page [459]. In this new sequence, [460] followed [459]. After this he numbered pages [458], [469], [449], etc. Then Faulkner apparently modified the pages again by reverting to the former order and renumbered [458] as "221" and [459] as "212." Faulkner arranged the pages as follows: [449], [450], [451], [452], [453], [454], [455], and then continued to the latter part of the setting copy pages beginning with [482] ff. The original Chapter Ten begins on page "228;" the last page of this sequence ended on page "227" (cf. [502]). Faulkner then discarded [458] and [459] and inserted [425], [426], [427] before [469]; thus the sequence is as follows:

[425] as page "208"
[427] "   "   "209"
[469] "   "   "210-211-212" (this pagination is clear from [431
                                    (V)])
[449] "   "   "2143" [sic]
[450] "   "   "214"
[451] "   "   "215"
[452] "   "   "215" (carbon)
[453] "   "   "216"
[454] "   "   "217"
[455] "   "   "218" and the rest of the setting copy beginning
                                    with [482] ff.

Thus by this time Faulkner was achieving a fairly coherent pattern to this chapter. He began the sixth version with the commandeering of the truck by the Gowries [425]. At 2 P.M. in his uncle's car behind the truck, Chick sees the townsfolk who move fluidly in and across the Square [425]-[426]. This is followed on [426] and [469], pages connected by the phrase "in advance beyond the intervening block," with Chick shouting at the crowd and calling them foolish. Chick is entranced by their faces which look like a photo of a Chinese or Balkan atrocity. Then on [469], pages connected by the phrase "just beyond the glass," which is crossed-out on [469] and repeated on [449], a group lifts the stretcher to the truck's endgate and Chick gets out of the car. The crowd rushes across the Square and breaks the plate glass window. Then on [450] there are less than a dozen of the crowd left and some of them are schoolboys. Faulkner mentions the crowds in connection with Uncle Hogeye Mosby and the mad dog Willy Ingrum shot. The street was emptying and people were leaving in their cars and trucks.

On [451] Faulkner describes the cars leaving the Square. Also Chick's mother comes up to him and asks where the car is. On [453], Mrs. Mallison walks to the car. The crowd moves like a troupe staging the Battle of San Juan Hill. Gavin suggests they take Miss Habersham home first. On [454], Gavin and Mrs. Mallison have a brief argument since he is driving slowly. Mrs. Mallison asks, "How many collisions did you ever see with a woman driving both of them?". Next, on [455], Gavin reminds Mrs. Mallison that Miss Habersham has her truck. Then follows a list of what Miss Habersham intends to do when she gets home. Page [482] begins with the words "diminishing rapidly. . ." (cf. page 188.1 of the first edition). From here this version becomes the final setting copy; once Faulkner went beyond [490] (that is, three pages in the setting copy after [482]), the page numeration follows in order, counting of course, the insertions Faulkner included. Thus it seems reasonable to say that at this point Faulkner had the entire chapter in his mind and most of it down on paper. However, he was not entirely satisfied with it and went back and started a cleaner copy. The manuscript material on [427] page "213," [469] page "214," and [437] page "215" (actually no manuscript writing as such, just the appropriate crossed-off lines), refer to the seventh version of this chapter. The manuscript writing on [427] and [469] "shooting across the alley mouth" [469] then picks up on [437] with the words "so constant and unbroken" and ends on [437]. Faulkner began his seventh version of this chapter with the following sequence of pages:

[424]	as page "208"
[428]	" " "209"
[429]	" " "210"
[20 (V)]	" " "210 A"
[430]	" " "211"
[431]	(carbon)
[432]	" " "211 A"
[433]	" " "212"
[434]	(carbon)
[435]	" " "213"
[436]	(carbon)
[427]	" " This page and [469] have manuscript writing related to [433 (bottom)].
[469]	
[437]	" " "215"
[438]	" " "2145" [sic]
[440]	(no page number)
[439]	" " "216"
[470]	" " "217"

With this draft, Faulkner was coming closer to the final setting copy version of this chapter. Page [424], the first page of this draft, later discarded, became the first page of the final setting copy of Chapter Nine. In this version Faulkner builds on previous versions as if he could almost consciously hold the material in his head until it was down on paper. On [424], he began with the time: 2 P.M. in the commandeered truck (this had been developed most recently on [425]) with dust in his eyes Chick enters town. Faulkner seems to have found the appropriate beginning for this chapter.

After mentioning on [424] that the truck had been commandeered by the sheriff and started by a Gowrie with a fork and that Chick was blinking steadily because of the grit inside his eyelids, Faulkner continues on [428] with Chick seeing not only people from the various beats, but merchants, cottonbuyers, clerks, and mechanics who had no jobs and could live in little lost Mississippi towns without working since they were "children of the last fabulous nation which out of all earth would still afford to keep some of its own idle and sweatless. . . ." These people were opposite the street in front of the jail and without waiting for the sheriff's car to approach, they flowed toward the

Square "like the turn of a tide. . . ." The two cars and the truck turn into the alley leading to the undertaker's loading ramp where the coroner would be waiting for them.

The upper part of [429] concerns the images that the crowd, first of all, had "boiled into the alley behind them" and soon the three vehicles "like three hencoops" would be hurled "in one inextricable aborted now-worthless jumble into the ramp" at the coroner's feet. Though not moving, it seemed to Chick as if he were shouting at the crowd "you fools" while leaning out the window or clinging to the runningboard. At some point, Faulkner discarded these two and a half pages, saving the first two for the final setting copy. He then typed out [35 (V)], [36 (V)], [21 (V)] and joined them to [429] and the following sequence linking "looking back through" [21 (V)] to "the rear window. . ." [429].

There are two paragraphs on [35 (V)]; the first begins, "The truck was another pickup" and repeats the information about commandeering it. The second begins, "At two oclock that afternoon in his uncle's car. . . ." Faulkner also repeats the material about the dust in Chick's eyes, changing only the punctuation from the original. On [36 (V)] Faulkner again repeated the material from [429] and modified a few phrases and made two additions. First, the people from the beats are definitely in town now since Chick saw them "crowding the opposite side of the street facing the jail not" just the county. The faces Chick noticed are familiar, not only the ones he had seen before, but the "others who except for the doctors and lawyers were not just the town but the Town." Finally Faulkner tried to smooth out the text and give it both a sense of familiarity and panorama.

Page [21 (V)] repeats almost exactly the material crossed-off on the top of [429]. The lower half of [429] is similar to page 182.3-15 of the first edition. Page [20 (V)] resembles pages 182.15-183.2 of the first edition. The upper half of [430] contains a draft of [20 (V)]; a notable change is the word "face" to "Face" (cf. page 182.18 of the first edition). The lower half is like page 183.2-12 of the first edition. Page [432] is like page 183.12-33 of the first edition. The upper half of [433] is a draft of that page; the lower half resembles pages 183.33-184.12

of the first edition. In this section, Faulkner would eventually delete the reference to the crowd as "loutish idle half-grown men." And he would add later that Gavin came up the walkway "blinking painfully his painful moistureless eyelids he watched why. . . ." Page [435] resembles pages 184.12-185.5 of the first edition, except that Faulkner would delete a phrase he uses here when describing in complicated syntax the cars and trucks leaving town "already out of town long before the simple incorruptible undeviable postulate time by distance by velocity could have evicted them." Then Faulkner wrote out by hand on [427] and [469] the material he had crossed out on the upper part of [437]. Page [427] resembles pages 184.11-185.8 of the first edition and [469] resembles likewise page 185.8-20. The lower half of [437] is like page 185.20-33 of the first edition.

On [438], Faulkner had not reached the final version yet. After Chick realizes they are not going to the jail at all, Gavin states: "That's why no man can ever really be a woman no matter how hard he tries. . . ." Then Mrs. Mallison asks how many accidents involve women drivers in both cars. Gavin replies about one car "still in the shop where a man ran into it yesterday." Gavin adds, "How do I do it? just shut both eyes and mash hard with my right foot?" Both [440] and [439] are versions of page [438]. Pages [440] and [439] are like pages 186.19-187.11 of the first edition; [439] is the last page in this sequence though the text continues on [470]. Page [439] ends with "worse than a hun-" and [470] begins "watching and waiting [sic]. . . ." Faulkner then linked [470] (page "217") to [482], (page "218-219").

Then Faulkner typed the ninth version of this chapter:

[441] as page "209"
[442] "   "   "210"
[463] "   "   "211"
[464] "   "   "212"
[465] "   "   "213"
[466] "   "   "214"
[467] "   "   "215"
[468] "   "   "216"
[470] "   "   "217" this page is also related to [439] of the previous version.

The above pages became part of the setting copy along with [424] (page "208"), which Faulkner had previously typed and put aside. The above ten pages of setting copy, including [424], are the same as pages 180-188.8 of the first edition.

Faulkner continued with this version:

[482] as page "218-219" (originally followed [455])
[483] " " "220"
[484] " " "221"

Pages [482] and [483] resemble pages 188.8-189.16 of the first edition. Page [484], not part of the final setting copy, begins with Mrs. Mallison insisting that Gavin blow the car horn. Chick then retorts with "they ran," a phrase he repeats twice more on this page. The car does not seem to go anywhere and the group is at the Mallison home almost immediately. Even in his room Chick "could still hear it even through the drawn shades and the red jumping behind his eyelids whenever he closed them, starting up onto one elbow right under his mother's hand to say to his uncle beyond the foot of the bed. . ." [484]. Chick wants Gavin to come back for him and Gavin promises to do so. Mrs. Mallison says, "Will you please get to hell out of here, Gavin?" and then orders Chick, "Lie down."

On [485] (numbered page "222"), Mrs. Mallison touches Chick's head, but he has about as "much chance to escape that one frail narrow inevictable touch as to roll your face out from under a birthmark" [485] Mrs. Mallison then says after Chick's thoughts about her touch, "Just let go." Page [485] continues to correspond to page 192 of the first edition, though in the setting copy [494], Faulkner adds that Chick had all the time in the world for "the next fifteen minutes (or the next fifteen days or fifteen years," making this waiting a timeless preoccupation. Chick was also waiting for Buddy McCallum to say "he traded Crawford Gowrie a German pistol twenty-five or [the following is crossed-off] 'thirty years ago, only he had forgotten how, not only forgotten how to go to sleep but didn't dare, didn't dare relinquish surrender into that nothing what little he still had, which was nothing: who had wanted of course to leave at least his mark on his time in man but no more than, some mark at least on his part of earth but humbly, waiting hoping wanting humbly even nothing (which of course was everything) except [text stops] ' " [485].

Page [531] picks up from the phrase "thirty-years ago" on [485] and continues by saying that a young man of sixteen should not have to endure murder and exhumation feet first, though young people can stand anything. Chick then remembers Gavin "telling about British air and infantry officers of seventeen and eighteen and nineteen (by nineteen-eighteen his uncle said all English officers seemed to be either subalterns of seventeen or one-eyed or one-armed or one-legged colonels of twenty-three. . ." [531]. From here, Faulkner again repeats what is by now an important formula that Chick wanted to leave "some mark at least on his part of the earth but humbly, waiting wanting humbly even not really hoping even nothing (which of course was everything) except on chance one right to perform something passionate and brave and austere not just in but into man's enduring chronicle, worthy of a place in it—who knew? perhaps adding even one little jot to the austerity of the chronicle of man's brave passion—in gratitude for the gift of his time in it, wanting only that and not even with hope, willing to accept the fact that he had missed it forever because he wasn't worthy [text stops] " [531].

On [486] Faulkner retyped [531] and expanded this section. In this version Faulkner again used the formula that Chick did not dare go to sleep "not to remember grief nor pity nor triumph nor the vindication of man nor the deathless aspiration of man but one old man for whom grief was not even a component of his own but merely a phenomenon of his slain son jerking a strange corpse over onto its back just to be sure it was the wrong one and saying abashless and cheery and loud: 'Yep its that damned Montgomery damned if it aint:', and a Face aint' and a Face, all the rest of man not even one but one face, all the rest of faces not even one face but Face; who had wanted to leave his mark. . ." [486]. Faulkner later changed this because he had not settled on his final version; most of the ingredients are there but not the precise structure.

On [487] he wrote (the final version begins on page 193 of the first edition) where Chick is willing to accept the fact that he had missed it forever:

. . .because maybe he wasn't worthy yet found it had it received that gift that chance, his amazing incredible lot to save or certainly help not just a death from shame and indignity but a life from death and in amazed and baseless hope expected to have shamed indignity with its own shameful cancellation but found he had merely received of shame and indignity the grudging pretermission of a sentence so that salvation itself had become debased and befouled by having to be saved from that, courage and austerity themselves betrayed and beshamed by what courage and passion had had to cope with: remembering out of all there might have been to remember with humility not the pride of courage and passion nor of pity nor the pride and austerity of grief, but a Face. . . . [487]

This composite face was the face of those he grew up with:

. . .monstrous unravening omniverous and not even uninsatiate, not frustrated nor even thwarted, not biding nor waiting and not even needing to be patient since yesterday today and tomorrow are indivisible One: who had pretermitted not even death but merely Lucas, Lucas in ten thousand Sambo-avatars to scurry unheeding and not even aware through that orifice like mice through a guillotine until at the One unheeding moment the unheeding unwitting uncaring chopper falls; tomorrow or at the latest tomorrow and to intervene where less man angels fear no white and black child sixteen and an old white spinster on the way to eighty. [487]-[488]

Faulkner still had not achieved the complete subtlety he thought this passage should have.

On [488], Chick says *"They ran"* and "his nerveless unretentive hand spurned the cliff away in one long plunge past the long tideless drowsing fathoms upward and upward slowing among the soft impenetrable fathoms still moving though slowing slowed floating moving his wrists faintly coming the soft warm black infinitude but lighter now still soft drowsing still fathomless. . . ." Faulkner, in this version, keeps the water-movement image he had used earlier to describe the action of the crowd. It should be noted that the above passage (cf. page 196.11-13 of the first edition) was considerably shortened and, in my view weakened, in the final version.

Then begins a passage he would rewrite a number of times and since it was the last non-dialogue prose in this chapter it was perhaps an important section to perfect as Chick is about to come out of his stupor, in a mood similar to the beginning of *The Wishing Tree:* ". . .presently he would open his eyes and in fact he could already breathe, agitating his wrists only enough to float rising still rising then still now not even needing to move even his wrists and opened his eyes and with no haste no hurry let seeing seep them well then bring back; the light was on, his uncle is silhouette against it at the foot of the bed in the complete silence in which there was nothing beyond the drawn shades now but the treefrogs and the insects, the myriad tiny beastsounds of summer night. But there was still no haste, no hurry" [488]. Immediately after this Chick says, "They've gone. . . It's gone" [488].

Then on [499] (numbered page "226"), Faulkner began the last page of the original ending of Chapter Nine, though he was to expand this ending another six pages soon after, numbering [500] and [501] each as page "226." On [499], Gavin notes that the crowd is probably all in bed by now. They arrived home before dark to chop wood for breakfast. Then Chick tells Gavin about his funny dream that "maybe this was too much to expect of people just sixteen years old and then right away I was answering what you told me about the English boys not much older than me leading troops in battle in France in 1918 only there was something else too. . . ." To this Gavin replies, "There are some things we must always be unable to bear. Some things we must never stop refusing to bear no matter how young or how old we are. Injustice and outrage and dishonor and shame. 'That it?' " Chick agrees that was what he had wanted to say and the chapter concludes with Gavin noting that it is only a little after 9 P.M. and there is "Plenty of time to have a shower and eat your supper. They wont start until we get there" [499].

What evidence is there that is this is the final page of the original version of Chapter Nine? First of all, Faulkner added, "They wont start until we get there" as an afterthought to the previous statement about having time to have a shower and eat supper, as the crossed-off punctuation indicates. It is also typical for Faulkner to end with a bit of dialogue that naturally carries the thrust of the story forward. Second, this page is numbered "227" and an original (though not first) page of Chapter Ten is numbered "228" (cf. [539 (V)]. Third, the expanded version of the ending of Chapter Nine ends on [505] which has almost the same ending as [502]. Thus Faulkner first began Chapter Ten on [500 (V)], then again on [539 (V)], and then again on [526] after ending Chapter Nine on [502]. The second ending to Chapter Nine was written after Faulkner's attempts at the original versions of Chapter Ten, because of the page numeration, that is, page "227" [502], "228" [539 (V)]. The second ending of Chapter Nine is "226-D" [505].

Page [500] is mostly a retyped version of [499] though here Chick tries to penetrate even more why the crowd ran: "So their women wouldn't have to chop wood in the dark with the children standing around half asleep holding lanterns" [500]. Gavin retorts by saying that it is more than what Chick thinks. Then Chick explains his dream to Gavin. Faulkner crossed off the material on [500] with a red pencil stroke down the front and began again on [501]. Her Chick gives a further explanation why the crowd ran: "Because they had reached the last point where there was nothing else for them to do but admit they were wrong. So they ran home" [501]. Then Chick explains on [501]-[502] about his dream and Gavin again gives the meaning of the dream: "Some things you must always be unable to bear. Some things you must never stop refusing to bear. Injustice and outrage and dishonor and shame. No matter how young or how old are. That it?" [502]. Notice that Faulkner dropped the personal "we" and substituted "you" which has both a personal aspect, as related to Chick, and an impersonal one, being "you" in general. Faulkner then concluded with Gavin's statement about showering and eating supper.

Faulkner then went back and inserted [503], [504], and [505] between [501] and [502]. Apparently as Faulkner reread this material, he considered [501] as page "226-A"; really it is "226" and then he relettered [503], [504], [505] from A, B, C, to B, C, D. With so much revision at this point, Faulkner's numbering scheme is understandable, though not precise. Because of these pages, a number of duplicate passages occur:

1) [503] repeats " 'No,' his uncle said." This is found also on [501].

2) [504.1] begins with " 'Yes,' his uncle said." This answers " 'You cant say that,' he said." [503]. Both lines are repeated on [504].

3) [505] begins with "of the head against the light" which repeats a similar phrase on the bottom of [504].

In all, I do not think any pages are missing. The difficulty is in figuring out Faulkner's numbering system with its accuracies and inaccuracies.

On [503] Faulkner amplified Gavin's views which are close to those found in the final setting copy version:

> They simply repudiated a shall-not and should not which without any warning to them turned into *must*-not. *Thou shalt not kill,* you see—no accusative, heatless: a simple moral precept; we have accepted it, had it so long, cherished it, fed it, kept it alive, handled it so long that all the corners are now worn smoothly off; we can sleep right in the bed with it; we have even distilled our own anti-dotes for it as the foresighted housewife keeps a solution of mustard or egg-whites in the same cupboard with the rat poison, as familiar as grandpa's face beneath the turban of an Indian prince, as abstract as grandpa's flatulence at the supper table. But *Thou shalt not kill thy mother's other child:* it came right down into the street to walk in broad daylight at your elbow. You see? [503]

Then on [504] Chick objects to Gavin's belief (as stated by Chick) that it is one thing for the Gowries, Workitts, and Ingrums to burn Lucas but another for a Gowrie to kill his brother:

> 'You cant say that,' he [i.e., Chick] said.
>
> 'Yes,' his uncle said. 'And not just for them: for us, for all: Stevens and Mallison and Edmonds and McCaslin too. If we are not to hold to the belief that that point not only must not but *can*not come beyond which Gowrie or Ingrum or Workitt or Stevens or Mallison blood, how hope we will reach that one beyond which Lucas Beauchamp's blood not only must not but

cannot be shed?' [504]

Thus Gavin has increased the complexity of this code enormously, and by going from the moral imperatives of "shall not" to
"must not" to "can not," he has almost reached the limits of
physical responsibility far beyond moral obligation.

On the bottom of [504] Chick says to Gavin, "You're a
lawyer." Then he repeats, "They ran" in a mood "completely
final, even with pride, not even triumphant, not even contemptu-
ous, not even listening to ethical and moral ratiocination who
had already declined to be reminded of time. . . ." Chick relates
how he dreamed away the people from the beats: ". . .let them
stay in bed or milking cows before dark or chopping wood before
dark or after by lanterns or not lanterns either. . ." [504]. Then
Faulkner uses the familiar phrase "not even moving yet, watching
looking at his uncle's face or at least where the face would be
inside of silhouette of his head against the light [text stops]. . ."
[504]. After [504], Faulkner typed on [520 (V)] a version
similar to what he had crossed off on [504]. Then on [505]
Faulkner repeated what he had typed on [502] about Chick's
dream and how he used Gavin's story about the English boys
leading the troops in 1918.

Again on [505] Gavin repeated his advice beginning, "Some
things you must always be unable to bear," adding this time it is
done not "for kudos nor cash: your picture in the paper nor
money in the bank. . . ." Chick agrees with Gavin's interpretation of his dream: " 'That was it,' he said." This page, as on
[502], ends with Gavin's reply about there being time for a
shower and supper. On [505] Faulkner deleted with red ink the
last five lines and ends with Chick agreeing, " 'that was it,' he
said." Thus this chapter ended for the second time on page
"226-D."

Page [546 (V)] repeats much of the material on [502]
verbatim. Likewise this page ends with Gavin's recommendation
for a shower and time for supper and it concludes: "They wont
leave until we get there." After typing [483], Faulkner typed
[490] imagining that Miss Haberhsam had to get around an arrogant *"insufferable old nigger who got the whole county upset
trying to pretend he had murdered a white man. . . ."* Faulkner

continued on [490] by noting after Chick's mother directed Gavin to blow the horn, that he, Chick "was not laughing at all, he was crying. . . ." On [489] Faulkner went back and revised the upper part of [490], expanding this section about Chick crying: ". . .he discovered that it not not laughing at all or anyway not just laughing, that is the sound it was making was about the same as laughing but there was more of it and it felt harder, seemed to be having more trouble getting out and the harder it felt and sounded the less and less he could seem to remember what he must have been laughing at and his face was suddenly wet not with a flow but a kind of burst and spring of water. . . ." Faulkner then returned to [490]. There is a staccato effect with Chick saying "They ran" and Mrs. Mallison saying "Pull out, damn you." On [491] Gavin repeats the question Faulkner had used and discarded before: "How many collisions did you ever see with women driving both of them?" On [491] Faulkner crossed off·a sentence of Chick's: "They saved their conscience at least ten cents by not having to buy him a package of tobacco to show they had forgiven him," and used it later on [493].

Faulkner continued typing on [492]. Chick goes up to his room and tells Gavin that he will be ready in fifteen minutes and Gavin promises that he won't go without calling him first. Then Mrs. Mallison orders Chick to lie down and she touches him with her "narrow slim cool palm. . . ." Then on [475] and [17 (V)] Faulkner made two attempts at finishing this scene with Chick and his mother before typing a final version on [493]. On [475] Chick imagines the faces of the crowd as "not faces this time because their backs were toward him, the composite one back of a Head defenseless and unarmed yet terrible in its concorded unanimity not rushing at him but away." On [17 (V)] Faulkner revised this: ". . .and it was not even a face this time because their backs were toward him, it was the back of one head, the composite one back of one Head one fragile mushfilled bulb indefensible as an egg yet terrible in concorded unanimity rushing not at him but away." Faulkner accepted this second version and retyped it on [493] as part of the setting copy.

Faulkner then continued on [17 (V)], smoothing out the copy on [475]: Chick wants very much to get to sleep and "had all the time in the world for the next fifteen minutes only he had forgotten how: or maybe that was it and he didn't dare relinquish into nothing what little he had left: which was nothing: no grief to be remembered nor pity nor even any awareness of shame, no vindication of the deathless aspiration of man by man to man through the catharsis of pity and shame but instead only an old man for whom grief was not even a component of his own but merely a temporary phenomenon of his dead son jerking a strange corpse over onto its back not to appease its one mute indicting cry nor for pity but for justice but just to be sure he had the wrong one. . ." ([17 (V)] and [171 (V)]). After Nub Gowrie recognizes Montgomery, Chick reflects that he never expected Lucas to be swept out of his cell "on a tide of expiation" [171 (V)] and hailed in a public place such as at the base of the Confederate monument or on the balcony of the post office building. He did not expect similar praise for himself, Aleck Sander, or Miss Habersham since part of the value of their work was its anonymous nature.

Then on [171 (V)] and [16 (V)], Faulkner again repeats his pet phrase about "waiting wanting humbly even, not really hoping even," in an anonymous way "to perform something passionate and brave and austere not just in but into man's enduring chronicle worthy of a place in it—and who knew? perhaps adding even one anonymous jot to the austerity of the chronicle's brave passion—" [171 (V)]. Chick had not expected a life saved from death nor even a death saved from shame "nor even the suspension of a sentence but merely the grudging pretermission of a date. . ." [16 (V)]. Faulkner then lists the various abstract combinations Chick had not expected: not indignity shamed with its own shameful cancellation, nor sublimation and humility with humility and pride to be remembered, nor the pride of courage and passion, nor of pity nor the pride and austerity of grief but austerity itself debased by what it had gained, a sense of courage and passion befouled by what they had to cope with, that is, a Face, "the composite Face of his native kind. . ." [16 (V)]. Faulkner had been leading up to this image and he does not develop it except to say the face was of his own people "with whom it had been his joy and pride [text stops] ."

Faulkner then retyped this section on [493] and [495].

On [494] he inserted a page expanding this material; he focuses this time on Crawford Gowrie because there was nothing anybody could do until Crawford decided to give himself up. There would not even be time for a bullet expert to come from Memphis to look at Vinson, because old Nub was going to have his murdered son reburied soon. Faulkner was reminded of Crawford because he was composing Chick's memories of old Nub. As Faulkner continued on [495] he typed without making mistakes or having to correct misspelled words. Faulkner repeated a phrase that must have been fixated in his mind:

> [Chick] wanted of course to leave his mark too on his time in man but only that, no more than that, some mark on his part in earth but humbly, waiting wanting humbly even, not really hoping even, nothing (which of course was everything) except his own one anonymous chance too to perform something passionate and brave and austere not just in but into man's enduring chronicle worthy of a place in it (who knew? perhaps adding even one anonymous jot to the austerity of the chronicle's brave passion) in gratitude for the gift of his time in it wanting only that and not ever with hope really. . . . [495]

Faulkner then continued on [496] typing carefully as he probably realized that these last few pages were to become part of the final setting copy. On [496] he tried to summarize what Chick had experienced:

> . . .not a life saved from death nor even a death saved from shame and indignity nor even the suspension of a sentence but merely the grudging pretermission of a date; not indignity shamed with its own shameful cancellation, not sublimation and humility with humility and pride remembered nor the pride of courage and passion nor of pity nor the pride and austerity and grief, but austerity itself debased by what it had gained, courage and passion befouled by what they had had to cope with. . . .

After mentioning the composite face of his native land, Faulkner again refers to "a Face monstrous unravening omnivorous and not even unsatiate, not frustrated nor even thwarted, not biding nor waiting and not even needing to be patient since yesterday today and tomorrow are indivisible: One: who had pretermitted not even a death but merely Lucas, Lucas in ten thousand

Sambo-avatars to scurry unheeding and not even aware through that orifice like mice through the slot of a guillotine. . . ." With Shakespearean overtones, Faulkner suggested enigmatically that "tomorrow or at least tomorrow or at most tomorrow" would be an intervention which angels fear, yet where two children and an old woman have gone. Faulkner ends this page by having Chick repeat *"They ran"* and suggesting that the reason why the crowd left was so they would not have to send Lucas a can of tobacco and say aloud they were wrong.

Pages [19 (V)], [173 (V)], [497], and [498] each begin with versions of the phrase *"say aloud that they were wrong."* Each of these pages except [173 (V)] is numbered "226-A." Page [173 (V)] contains the following:

> *says out loud that they were wrong* and his unretentive hand spurned the cliff away in one long plunge up and past the long tideless drowsing fathoms and he opened his eyes, not moving yet [cf. [12 (V)] also], looking at his uncle in silhouette against the light beyond the footboard in the complete silence now in which there were only tree-frogs and the bugs, nothing anywhere of urgency for another two or three seconds; only the myriad tiny beastsounds of summer night.
>
> 'They've gone,' he said.
>
> 'What?' his uncle said. 'Oh. Yes. They're probably all in bed by now. They got home in time to milk before dark and [text stops].

Likewise [497] begins with Chick's hand spurning "the cliff away in one long plunge past the long tideless drowsing fathoms up and up" until he opened his eyes and saw Gavin in silhouette against the footboard. Gavin then suggests the crowd is probably all in bed since they had to milk before dark and chop wood for the following day's breakfast. Chick then says he understands why they went home and repeats Gavin's views. But Gavin quickly adds "It was more than that—" Then Chick concludes, "The reached the point where there was nothing for them to do but admit they were wrong. So they ran home."

On [174 (V)] Faulkner typed out this experimental paragraph which according to page 197 of the first edition seems to fit here. It is an isolated paragraph and therefore could have been typed at any time:

> But still he didn't move. He should and in a moment now he would; the urgency was still there or his part in it, the need for himself to be moving not to finish the business because so far as he could tell neither Hampton or his uncle either knew how but just to hold his or their own, not to lose ground like people having to run on a treadmill not to be swept backward out of sight.

On [19 (V)] Faulkner revised the draft of [497], expanding it and adding new phrases in blue ink. In this draft Gavin tells Chick that it is only 9:30 P.M. and he has plenty of time to shower and eat supper, because "They" won't leave before they get there. Chick wants to know what Mr. Hampton plans to do. Gavin tells him, "This is Hampton's scheme. But after all, there's not much else he can do. All he has, is that Lucas says Vinson Gowrie wasn't shot with his pistol, and the only way to prove that is to find the bullet in Vinson's body. And even if he could get Vinson away from old Nub again he still wouldn't have the Luger pistol [text stops]." On [498] Faulkner incorporated the handwritten lines on [19 (V)] but did not make any major changes. The section ends with Chick unbuttoning his shirt and taking off his belt ready to get into the shower.

Page [512 (V)] continues the text of [498] and Chick says the reason the crowd went home was to chop wood without having to use lanterns. But Gavin says it is more than than and Chick replies: "They reached the point where there was nothing left for them to do but admit they were wrong. So they ran home" [512 (V)]. Faulkner then went back to [496] and picked up from the phrase, "a Face monstrous unravening omnivorous and not even uninsatiate, not frustrated nor even patient since yesterday" and then continued on [506] "today and tomorrow are Is. . . ." Pages [506]-[513] correspond to pages 194.17-201.4 of the first edition. These eight pages of setting copy are rather clean pages devoid of many corrections. Page [524] contains a five-line version of [508] with little variation except to change "who didn't run, flee" to "who ran, fled" [508]. Also this material is followed by nine lines of manuscript which resembles the material on [508]. On [508] Faulkner typed the section he had worked on for a considerable time:

> [Chick] spurned the cliff in one long plunge up and up and slowing
> into it already hearing it, only the most faintly oscillant now hear-
> ing it listening to it, not moving yet nor even opening his eyes as
> he lay for a moment longer listening to it, then opened them and
> then his uncle stood silhouetted against the light beyond the foot-
> board in the utter complete that absolute silence now with nothing
> in it now but the breathing of darkness and the tree-frogs and bugs:
> no fleeing nor repudiation nor for this moment more even urgency
> anywhere in the room or outside it either above or below or be-
> fore or behind the tiny myriad beast-sounds and the vast systole
> and diastole of summer night.

Faulkner then followed this with Gavin's remark that the crowd
is probably home in bed since they had to milk and chop wood
before the following day's breakfast.

On the bottom of [520] Chick tells Gavin, "So they ran
to keep from having to lynch Crawford Gowrie." Faulkner
originally continued this page on [534] by having Gavin tell
Chick to turn the equation right side up: "They repudiated
him. Not his act: him. If they had lynched him they would
have taken only his life. What they did was more: they deprived
him to the extent of their capacity of his citizenship in man."
Chick replies they, especially Gavin and Hampton, were left to
clean up the vomit, something dogs do not even do. Gavin insists that he is talking about the Stevens and Mallison families
too. To this Chick replies: "Because somebody had to finish
it, somebody with a strong enough stomach to mop a floor.
Did they think to tell you how to do it? or were they too busy
being—being. . . ." Gavin answers, "Righteous?" [534]. Then
Faulkner continued with the last two pages of the setting copy
of this chapter. Pages [519]-[520] correspond to pages 205.3-
206.14 of the first edition.

Faulkner then went back and inserted a number of pages.
He began with [514] where the crowd was waiting for Beat
Four to lynch Lucas: "But not all of them together because there
is a simple numerical point at which a mob cancels and abolishes
itself, maybe because it has finally got too big for darkness,
the cave it was spawned in is no longer big enough to conceal

it from light and so at last whether it will or not it has to look at itself, or maybe because the amount of blood in one human body is no longer enough, as one peanut might titillate one elephant but not two or ten." There is the suggestion, too, that perhaps man is absorbed into a larger phenomenon where he realizes his quest towards humanity and the one serene universal light. Gavin disagrees with Chick who says that man is always right: "He tries to be if they who use him for their power and aggrandizement let him alone. Pity and justice and conscience too—that belief in more than the divinity of individual man: in the divinity of his continuity as Man: think how easy it would [text stops] " [515 (V)]. Faulkner revised this section on [533] intending it should lead into [535] which he had previously written.

On [533] Faulkner deleted the reference to man's divinity. Instead he returned to thoughts on mob psychology:

> Think how easy it would have been for them to attend to Craw-ford Gowrie: no mob moving fast in darkness watching constantly over its own shoulder but one indivisible public opinion: that peanut vanishing beneath a trampling herd of elephants with hard-ly one to know it was ever there since the main purpose of a mob is that the red hand which actually snapped the thread may vanish into an inviolable confraternity of namelessness: where in this case that one would have to more reason to lie awake at night than a paid public hangman. They didn't want to destroy Crawford. [533]

If they had lynched him, Gavin argues they would have only taken away his life; what they did was more devastating because they deprived him of his citizenship as a man. Faulkner conclud-ed this page with a repetition of Gavin and Hampton having to clean up the imagined vomit. Faulkner put this page aside. He reworked this material on [515], adding [516], [517] (setting copy pages), thus including what is now pages 202.1-204.11 of the first edition. Thus, the last few pages of this section of the setting copy are inserts. With this Faulkner had finished Chapter Nine and was ready to begin the next chapter, sections of which he had already written.

Chapter Ten of the Setting Copy

On [500 (V)] Faulkner began typing his first version of
Chapter Ten. There are ninety pages or parts of pages used in
this chapter. He only typed eight lines before he discarded this
page: "But time or not he didn't waste it, not even eating, not
even pausing to compute how many days since he had had a
meal remembering in the same breath so to speak that it had not
been one yet since he had eaten a good breakfast even though
already more than half asleep at the sheriff's at four this morning, and one last wail from his mother (and it had been even
longer than four this morning since he had heard one of the too
[sic], thinking [text stops]." Faulkner began again on [539
(V)], this time numbering the page as "228" which follows presumably the last page of the original draft of Chapter Nine,
page "227." On [539 (V)], Faulkner again begins with the act
of eating: "Or perhaps it was the eating; the man didn't necessarily eat his way through his life but by the act of eating did he
enter the world, not through the world but into it, burrowing
into the world's teeming solidarity like a moth into wool by the
physical act of chewing and swallowing. . . ." Faulkner then
continued this image of man advancing into history, but also
making history a part of himself and man's memory "the whole
history of man or maybe even relinquishing abandoning eating it
into to be annealed, the proud vain-glorious minuscule which he
called his memory and his self and his I-Am into that vast teeming solidarity of the world from beneath which the ephemeral
rock would cool and spin away to dust not even remarked nor
remembered since there was no yesterday and tomorrow didn't
even exist. . . ."

Gavin continues by insisting that all reality is in the present
and that "Yesterday wont be over until tomorrow and tomorrow
happened ten thousand years ago" [523] (cf. page 194 of the
first edition for this material). Gavin then uses a central image of
the novel, that of a fourteen year old who can recall that instant
about 2 P.M. in July 1863 when Pickett stood ready with hat and
sword looking up the hill waiting for Longstreet to give the word.
Faulkner followed this immediately with the image or someone
in 1492 thinking he had reached the absolute limit and "to turn
back now and make home or sail irrevocably on and either find
land or plunge over the world's roaring edge" [523]. Faulkner

was writing material that eventually would be part of Chapter Nine (cf. pages 193-194 of the first edition). Faulkner began the next paragraph on this page by mentioning that only an ascetic living in a cave on acorns and spring water was capable of vainglory and pride. This led into a reference concerning Chick trying to recall how many days it had been since he had last eaten. On [553 (V)], he remembers he had eaten breakfast at the sheriff's at 4 A.M. that morning. Then the text stops abruptly.

Then on [526] Faulkner began again (cf. page 196 of the first edition for this material): "Without moving yet nor even opening his eyes" Chick in bed listens to the tree-frogs and bugs. Faulkner retyped this section (there are twelve lines on the page) and ended with "no fleeing nor repudiation nor even urgency for a moment yet either above or below or before or behind the dar's [sic] vast diastole. . ." [526]. This is the earliest version of this section, mainly because Chick's eyes are closed, and not opened as in later versions. On [525 (V)], Faulkner typed another version; there are only seven lines on this page ending with "no fleeing nor repudiation or for this moment more even urgency: only the myriad tiny beast-sounds and the night's vast diastole." In this version too, Chick's eyes are closed.

Again on [528], Faulkner began what could be considered his fifth version of Chapter Ten and like the previous two tries this page is unnumbered. So far, Faulkner only numbered one try [539 (V)] since it followed the initial conclusion of Chapter Nine of the setting copy. As he began the several versions after [539 (V)], he did not number them because he had not typed a completed page yet. On [528] he began with a familiar phrase and then mentions Gavin in the room, an addition to the previous attempts: "Without moving yet nor even opening his eyes, he lay listening to it. Then he opened them, his uncle standing in silhouette against the light beyond the footboard. . . ." Faulkner then repeated the image of the tree-frogs and bugs. He concluded this ten-line section by saying that Chick was becoming more awake. In another try on [526 (V)], he began "Still not moving yet, at least he opened his eyes. . . ." In this version of five lines. Gavin is still in silhouette beyond the footboard and only the tree-frogs and bugs break the silence. There is no mention of repudiation or urgency. Then in another attempt (this time there are nine lines of text) on [528 (V)] Chick opens his eyes, and Gavin is still in silhouette. Faulkner crossed off the reference to tree-frogs and bugs, and then included dialogue between Gavin and Chick. Gavin tells Chick it is 9:30 P.M. and that there is plenty of time for a shower and to eat supper too in response to Chick's question, "Is it time?"

Then on [521 (V)], Faulkner began another attempt, this time numbering the page "230," perhaps forgetting that it should be "229." He incorporated the previous elements mentioned above: Chick opening his eyes, Gavin in silhouette, the tree-frogs and bugs, and the lack of urgency anywhere. This time, however, the dialogue between Gavin and Chick is different. Chick mentions "They've gone" to which Gavin replies, "Oh. Yes, they're probably all in bed by now. They got home in time to milk and even chop wood before dark for tomorrow's breakfast too." Chick's last comment on this page is "They ran." Then Faulkner tried again on [530], an attempt that is close to the one on [521 (V)] though there are some manuscript changes. I believe [530] occurs after [521 (V)] because the comment "They've gone" is changed to "It's gone," the version that is used on page 196 of the first edition. Likewise, [530] is numbered page "230."

On [538 (V)] Faulkner continued with the text of [530] (both pages are partly crossed-off with plain pencil) and ended this eleven-line page with the partial sentence: "So he [i.e., Chick] moved then he said: 'Time:' not only repeating the cue-word but even hearing it for the first time, already swinging his legs over [text stops]." Faulkner's next try on [525] incorporates the manuscript corrections on [530.5]; the phrase "nothing [anywhere] now" is changed to "nothing at all in it anywhere now" [525.5]. In this version on [525] and [532] Faulkner indicated that the urgency came back:

> . . .or rather it was still there, had never for one second vacated even from behind the bizarre phantasmagoriae whose ragtag and bobends still befogged him, with or among which he realised now he had wasted nearer fifteen hours than fifteen minutes; it still remained constant and flagless at least his part in it, the need to be moving not to finish with Lucas Beauchamp and Crawford Gowrie because as far as he knew neither Hampton nor his uncle either

knew what they were going to do next but just hold their own in it. . . .

Faulkner then used the images of the treadmill in endless motion and a hobo trapped between the rails beneath a passing train to convey Chick's need to be moving, but not to be caught in useless activity. Likewise, this material would be used in Chapter Nine.

Then on [532] Faulkner picks up Chick's comment "It's gone" and Gavin's reply about them probably all being in bed. Then Chick presses the point: "They ran," he insists. "They reached a point where there was nothing left for them to do but to admit they were wrong. So they ran home." Then on [514 (V)] Faulkner retyped half of page [532] beginning with the words, "Safe only as long as he didn't move." This second typing makes no advances over the first and the page ends after twelve lines of typing. Faulkner then went back and wrote eleven pages of rough draft, some of these rough drafts using pages of the original draft; each of these pages of the rough draft begins with the phrase "Without moving." It should be noted that there are two versions of this rough draft on [23] and the second version is as follows: "Perhaps eating had something to do with it, not even pausing while he tried with no particular curiosity or interest to compute how many days since he had sat down to a table to eat and then in the same chew as it were remember that it had not been one yet since even [text stops]." This is the way the Tenth Chapter begins on page 207 of the first edition.

Faulkner began the final version of Chapter Ten of the setting copy on [530 (V)], which he numbered "238" with the phrase he had used previously on [23] "Perhaps eating had something to do with it. . . ." This page [530 (V)] was written after Faulkner completed Chapter Nine [520] (page "237") and is a preliminary draft of [521]; both pages are fairly close to one another textually. The act of eating triggers off a recollection by Chick of Gavin's belief that by eating man enters the world, like a moth ingesting part of his world around him. From [530 (V)] Faulkner continued on the top of [538] until he crossed it off and began over again on [521] and [537]. The draft on [521], [537], and [538] reflects accurately the original pages [530 (V)] and [538], though Faulkner changed a phrase on [538], "so maybe only an ascetic living in a cave on acorns and spring water was really capable of vainglory and pride" to "maybe you had to live in a cave of acorns and spring water in rapt impregnable contemplation of your vainglory and righteousness and pride in order to keep to that high intolerant pitch of its worship which brooked no compromise" [537].

On [538] and [539] Faulkner continued with the text as it is found in the first edition. He was composing at the typewriter, making no manuscript corrections, just crossing off words and phrases he was not satisfied with. On [540], the phrase "One people One heart One land" became on [541] "one shame if shame must be, one expiation since expiation must surely be but above all one unalterable durable impregnable one: one people one heart one land." Faulkner continued on [541] with the Gavin-Chick dialogue. On [542], Gavin says: "This is the third degree, what do you call it?—" Chick originally answered "First class," but then it was changed to "Eagle scout." On [542] Faulkner crossed off the sentence about Gavin and Chick standing in the alley watching Lucas and the sheriff emerge from jail; he put it at the end of the page and then continued on the top of [546] where he mentioned how the inhabitants of the various beats came into town on normal Monday nights "to rattle and clash among the old bricks and the old trees and the Doric capitals and leave them for one night anyway stricken. . . ." Faulkner then described the scene at 10 P.M. on Monday night when people would be coming out of the movie soon and stroll about. Faulkner now began using material he had written earlier on pages such as [104], [105], [106], [38 (V)], [456] and [536].

He continued this text on [548] mentioning how the true reason for the cafe being open was to keep "Willy Ingrum's nocturnal counterpart awake." The text also mentions that some of the old ladies did not like to page a policeman at the cafe so the office telephone was connected to the burgler alarm bell. Chick thought, too, on [548] and [536 (V)], how shutting off the jukebox for twelve hours had probably been the night marshal's first official act except punching every hour the time clock on the outside wall at the bank's back door since the mad dog scare last August. Then on [536 (V)] Faulkner repeated a phrase beginning "tomorrow-ward about the dark mile-com-passing land. . ." which he had previously crossed off on [546]. About a third of the way down [536 (V)] Faulkner stopped typing the text he was working on.

Originally [543] which was numbered "243-A" and then became "243-B" was placed before [548]. The text picked up with the phrase "the cafe which stayed open all night" [543.23]. At this point, Faulkner's textual progression is not too evident. He discarded [548] and typed in its place [544]-[545], the bottom of [544] and the top of [545] concerned with the light in Gavin's office. Faulkner finally concluded that the lights in Gavin's office were liable to burn anytime Gavin or the janitor forgot to turn them off. Page [545] ends with the reference to the mad-dog scare of late August. This section was shifted about four times before Faulkner finally arrived at the sequence he wanted:

[542]   Chick remembers standing by Gavin in the alley watching Lucas and the sheriff emerge from jail.

[543]   The Square was empty at 10 P.M.

[543]-[544] Gavin asks where Chick is going. Chick goes into the Square and comments on the cafe and Willy Ingrum's nocturnal counterpart.

[544]-[545] Chick observes the light in Gavin's office and specu-lates about it.

[545]   He compares the cafe and the power plant and discusses the night marshal's first official act.

[546]   There follows a discussion of the other normal Monday nights when people would be getting out of the movies and strolling about. It should be pointed out that [145] contains a nine-line version, almost verbatim, of [546].

[547]   Faulkner continued typing and on this page he returns to the events of the previous Sunday evening as if to evoke all possible meaning from these time periods. That par-ticular Sunday was extraordinarily quiet and Faulkner

> uses the comparisons of a quiet battlefield or the vestibule
> of a powder magazine or the spillway under the locks of a
> dam. This material is found in the first edition. Faulkner
> speculates on the attitude of the following Saturday and
> how the people would have forgotten everything by then
> [549].

Chick knows the town is not abandoned; it is just that the townsfolk have withdrawn to do what they should without interfering.

As Chick begins his revery on [549] Faulkner wrote: ". . .his uncle while he stood barefoot on the rug with both edges of the unbuttoned shirt arrested in his hands. . . ." Then follows the interior monologue beginning with *"to defend Lucas nor even the union of the United States. . . ."* Faulkner then crossed off five lines of this revery and on [550] picked up from [549]: ". . .in his hands thirty minutes ago and when they were mounting the last pitch of hill toward the church eleven hours ago and on what must have been a thousand other times since he had got big enough to listen and to understand and to remember. . . ." Faulkner then began the revery as he had started it before on [549]. The revery is typed with few errors or corrections and follows the first edition as found beginning on page 215. Faulkner has given the readers Gavin's views as filtered through Chick.

On [553] Faulkner bogged down a bit as he compared the Southerner to a Russian who must be either a Communist or dead. Originally on [553] he wrote:

> . . .*only we must do it and we alone since only we can in Lucas's
> equality is to be anything more its own prisoner behind a barri-
> cade of federal policemen and when you say without help or inter-
> ference or even (thank you) advice since only we can if Lucas's
> equality is to be anything more than its own prisoner inside a cor-
> don of federal police and when you say Lucas must not wait for
> that tomorrow because that tomorrow will never come because
> you not only cant you wont then we can only repeat Then you
> shall not, a people divided at a time when history is still telling us
> that the anteroom to dissolution is division and you say At least
> we perish in the name of humanity and we say When all is stricken*

> *but the nominative pronoun and that verb what price Lucas's*
> *humanity then* [text stops].

Faulkner then crossed off this section and recomposed it on [552]-[553], adding references this time to 1861-1865, John Brown, Robert E. Lee, and housebreaking a dog (cf. pages 216.27-217.14 of the first edition).

Faulkner then continued on [554] crossing off only one minor word. On [555] Faulkner was still typing with ease as the page is clean and smooth except for a minor correction which he tried to work out on [554 (V)]; it concerns the sheriff telling Gavin that no matter how many times one counts Crawford Gowrie, he is still a Gowrie. Faulkner deleted this sentence on [554 (V)]: "I thought we settled this three times this afternoon" when the sheriff speaks to Gavin. Both [556] and [557] follow the first edition closely. Faulkner originally typed [557], [558], and [583 (V)] in order. On [558] and [583 (V)], this dialogue between the sheriff and Gavin occurs:

> 'What would you do if you was Crawford Gowrie?'
>
> 'Blow my brains out,' his uncle said.
>
> 'All right. What next? say you were sensible enough (if a man unsensible enough to commit murder can ever again be sensible enough to believe he can get back into his old tracks) to get clean out of the country and stay out, what would you do first, want to do first before you left for good never to come back, if your name was Gowrie and your blood and thinking, and acting had been Gowrie all your life [text stops].

In revising this mateial on [559]-[560], Faulkner took a new approach and dropped Gavin's flip (but accurate) speculation about suicide. On [173 (V)], Faulkner typed eight lines of dialogue explaining that "tonight Mr. Hampton is going to take Lucas over to the Hollymount jail tonight to testify tomorrow at an inquest on Jake Montgomery [text stops]." Faulkner did not alter this information on [560]. In the revision Faulkner has the sheriff explain how he too sent a message to Crawford, by excusing Willy Ingrum and telling him that Lucas was to be taken to Hollymount to testify at Montgomery's inquest. They were to leave that evening and take the Whiteleaf cut-off.

Pages [560]-[561] were final setting copy pages used for the first edition. Faulkner discarded [562] and deleted also the lower portion of [561] and retyped this material on [563] (cf. pages 222.27-223.20 of the first edition). He rephrased some minor parts and for the remainder of this section did not make noticeable changes. At this point Faulkner was retyping, rather than recomposing. On [564], Gavin continues to speculate on Lucas' part in observing the criminal activity. He believes that Lucas knew who was moving the lumber (not much lumber each night):

> . . .not quite enough to make anybody suspicious since the crew was being paid by the day and Crawford was field boss or representative since Vinson was busy with his other irons, but what he was doing with it, maybe he learned even as far as Jake Montgomery though Lucas's knowing about Jake made no difference except that by getting himself murdered and into Vinson's grave Jake probably saved Lucas's life. So this afternoon when we had something at last heavy enough to talk to Lucas with I went to Hampton's house to the kitchen and there was Hampton's cook sitting on one side of the kitchen and Lucas on the other eating greens and cornbread not out of a plate but out of the gallon pot and I said,
>
> 'And you let him catch you. So he sent you word to meet him in the woods behind Fraser's store and he would have something for you and so you went to collect the money, get rich—' and he said,
>
> 'No. He come to my house. Only I wouldn't take the money. I told him what to do. I would give him until tomorrow—that was Friday—to make up whatever explanation he wanted to about that lumber to Vinson and Mr. Workitt just so he give them their share of the money, I would go and tell Mr. Workitt he better—'
>
> 'Say that again,' I said, 'Slow.'
>
> 'Tell Mr. Workitt he better start counting his boards.'

Faulkner then crossed off all the above and started to rewrite it first on [569], where he typed six lines before discarding this page, and then on [565]-[567] (cf. pages 224.1-226.5 of the first edition), typing at one point the same phrase twice which Erskine later called his attention to and which Faulkner subsequently corrected.

At this point, Faulkner started using unusual punctuation (' " " '), as found on pages 225-228 of the first edition. On [565]-[566] Gavin asks a key question to the murder mystery, a question not found in the first edition: "Why did Crawford have to kill Vinson in order to obliterate the witness of his thieving?" Faulkner continued typing pages [568] and [570] which were incorporated into the first edition. On [570] and [572] Faulkner wrote that Lucas was told to wait for a receipt from Mr. Workitt about the missing lumber. Lucas never had any suspicions about Crawford: "No. He cussed me so natural." Then on [572] Faulkner tells about Gavin describing Vinson coming to meet Lucas. Lucas then remembered how Vinson "buckled up" and fell forward and then Lucas remembers the shot.

Gavin comments that Crawford Gowrie has been most on his mind, a child of misfortune if ever there was one, he thinks. Miss Habersham then did something, but since she did not disrupt his speaking, he continued on [577 (V)] about Crawford being drafted in 1918, deserting from the army one hour before his discharge, serving time at Leavenworth and Parchman, and finally being caught for stealing lumber from his brother. Faulkner stopped this section about Crawford on [577 (V)] and went back to [569 (V)] and began another attempt at Lucas' speech "He cussed me so natural." In this version, Gavin speculates about what Crawford told Vinson: "I've got that nigger you caught watching that truck is out there in the woods waiting for you. Go talk to him if you still think it was mine." Then on [571] Faulkner typed out another version, this time cutting down the material to "All right. I've got him."

Faulkner then continued on [573], which became the second version of [572]. Page [574] follows [572] though the latter part of [573] was crossed off and eventually [574] was discarded. On [573] Gavin explains again that he was thinking most of Crawford, not Lucas, and then again Miss Habersham does something though no one was sure what. On [574] Crawford becomes "no mere misfortune's supreme and only child." Gavin then repeats the facts of Crawford's life and concludes by noting that Crawford was "snared" not by the "outrage of his dead" but by an old Negro who went out walking one night. Miss Habersham comments that Crawford put Vinson in quicksand. Gavin replies on [574], "Ghastly, wasn't it,—by the simple expedient of that old Negro man's penchant for insomnambulism and then having got away with that through a plan so simple and water-tight as to be what Chick here would call a natural [text stops]." On [575] Faulkner retyped the above passages from [573 (bottom)] and [574], omitting however any references to Crawford's life in the army. Though Faulkner had Crawford's background on his mind while he wrote this section, he did not use this material, perhaps because it would repeat much of what he had already told about Crawford in Chapter Seven.

Faulkner typed the next three pages in order ([576]-[578]) (cf. pages 228.32-231.24 of the first edition). Note that the last word on [576] is "rea-" and this links up with "son" on [577.3]. These three pages resemble the first edition closely. On [579] Faulkner inserted six lines that he had crossed off on [580], changing "a relation" to "your brother or husband or uncle or cousin or grandmother" [580] to "brother or husband or uncle or cousin or mother-in-law. . ." [579]. On [580] Gavin notes that Crawford will show up at Whiteleaf bottom because Willy Ingrum cannot keep a secret and that Crawford, like an amateur gambler, will play a long shot. On [581], the original ending to this chapter, Gavin picks up some material he had previously used on [538 (V)], that is, asking a rhetorical question about what one would do in Crawford's shoes given the fact that he has Gowrie blood in him, especially when one realizes that the prime witness was near at hand and being driven through a lonely creek-bottom. Gavin says he trusts Sheriff Hampton. Miss Habersham counters by saying her trust is in Lucas.

Miss Habersham then agrees that it would be nice to have some coffee while they wait for the news. Faulkner changed the ending somewhat by discarding [581] and inserting in its place [582]-[584]. In recomposing this material Faulkner added

considerable material, though he retained the original conclusion
about having coffee while they wait. On [582] Faulkner noted
there was only one of the original ten bullets in Crawford's
Luger.   On [581] Crawford originally had five bullets left.
Gavin tries to give comfort by saying that the sheriff is armed,
too, though he probably won't use the arm though he used it in
the 1920's when two ladies argued, one demanding that the
sheriff destroy a still belonging to the other's husband. Hampton
went out, following the woman's instructions and found the
still, tended by a Negro. He waited with the Negro for the
owner to return. While there, he had some moonshine and
branch water. As Hampton was sleeping, someone put a pillow
under his head and a quilt over him. Then the unnamed parties
removed the still and Hampton took the quilt and pillow to
Varner's store to be returned to the owner. In this way, Hampton offended neither party. He went after the illegal moon-
shiners as one lady directed and he let the other lady's husband
escape. And he had a good drink too! As a conclusion to this
chapter, this story suggests indirectly that neither Lucas nor
Crawford, like the two ladies, will be subject to any rash moves
by Hampton and that, somehow, each will decide his own fate.

Chapter Eleven of the Setting Copy

Faulkner typed this chapter fairly easily only rejecting
three pages. There are twenty-two pages or parts of pages used
in this chapter. Faulkner began by calling attention to the function of the different days; Monday is stock-auction and trade
day and Saturday is automobile and radio day [585]. Each day
had its own routine. On Monday it was a matter of business and
routine. On Saturday, all the inhabitants from the various beats
came in to shop and buy wedding licenses. It was a jostle of
activity with cars going round and round the Square. On [586],
Faulkner crossed off some lines about the crowds looking at the
neat yards and flowerbeds; then in revising this section he noted
that the townsfolk had come to line their gardens as dense as
sardines or bananas. Then on [587] Faulkner noted that this
is a "Saturday among Saturdays" and that the sidewalks were
"dense and massed and slow with people black and white," a
passage which highlights the integration of the races, something

that had not been true the previous week.

On [587] Faulkner wrote that both races came to town on this Saturday to give balance to "that other Saturday only seven days ago of which they had been despoiled by an old Negro man who had got himself into a position where they had had to believe he had murdered a white man, and the busy almost ubiquitous glint and gleam of Willy Ingrum's cap-badge but above all the motion and noise, the radios and the automobiles. . . ." Faulkner continued this sentence until it reached the point of comparing an amplifier with a "siege gun bolted to the top of an automobile. . ." [587]. On [588], Faulkner went back and revised the lower half of [587] interposing after the phrase about the townsfolk believing that Lucas had murdered a white man, a reference to the previous Saturday, Sunday, and Monday which were now forgotten and one to Crawford's suicide and the astonishment of the visitors that a man in jail could acquire a Luger to shoot himself. At this point, Faulkner is psychologically preparing his readers for the end of the novel.

Everyone, too, seems to be in some proper place: Vinson and Crawford Gowrie buried near their mother; Jake Montgomery buried in Crossman County; Miss Habersham sitting in her own hall mending stockings; Aleck Sander in the Square wearing a flashy Saturday shirt and a pair of zoot pants; and Chick in Gavin's office "watching the dense unhurried unhurryable throng. . . ." The only one missing is Lucas who will momentarily appear. After giving everyone a place, the narrator then resumes with the mention of Willy Ingrum's cap-badge and includes the material deleted on [587]. The perspective is definitely Chick's because on [589] Chick could not actually see the Square, "only the dense impenetrable mass of tops and hoods moving in double line. . . ." Faulkner originally noted that the line was so "slow unified in what movement that you could have cross the Square walking on them—"; then, after Albert Erskine had questioned whether "what" should be written as "that" or not, Faulkner changed the phrase using blue ink and a wide-tipped fountain pen to "slow dowelled into one interlocked mosaic so infinitesmal of motion as to be scarcely worthy of the word that you could have crossed the Square walking on them."

Faulkner praised Highboy or any gaited horse which could

have carried a person out of town. He then juxtaposes his praise for Highboy and gaited horses by having Gavin comment on the love of the average American for his car. On [591] Gavin originally began his observations with "The automobile has become the American sex symbol. We cannot really enjoy anything unless we go up an alley for it" [591]. In revising this on [590], Gavin begins in a more temperate manner: "The American really loves nothing but his automobile. . . ." The text then follows that found in the first edition. On [592], Chick notes that Lucas is on his way up and on [593] Gavin notes that Lucas has come to gloat, adding "he's a gentleman; he wont remind me to my face that I was wrong; he's just going to ask me how much he owes me as his lawyer." In focusing on Lucas, Faulkner had difficulty describing Lucas' clothes. First he is tieless in a black suit, then he is tieless and collarless with an old-timed white waistcoat under his black coat and then in a marginal note Erskine added Faulkner's emendation, "and the worn gold loop of the watchchain—" [593].

Lucas has not changed throughout the ordeal. His face is the same as it was four years before when Chick first saw him as he emerged from the icy creek. The dialogue with Lucas was easy for Faulkner to compose [593]-[595]. When Chick returns from helping Lucas obtain some flowers for Miss Habersham, Gavin lights his pipe and explains that Chick, Aleck Sander, Miss Habersham, and Sheriff Hampton have done what nobody expected nor wanted them to do. Faulkner wrote a draft of this speech on the bottom of [595] and then revised it on the top of [596], though on [596] he added "and they would have been right, actually. Lucas' life is of no more importance, just like yours and mine." Faulkner deleted this and then in a slightly different version included it on [598 (V)]: "Lucas' intrinsic life, the breathing and sleeping and eating, is of no importance, just as yours and mine are not; in fact this earth. . . ." Faulkner then typed this material over again on [596], [598 (V)], [597], [599], and [598] in that order. In the final version on [598] Faulkner wrote: "Lucas' life the breathing and eating and sleeping is of no importance just as yours and mine are not but his unchallengeable right to it in peace and security and in fact this earth. . . ." Pages [599]-[600] continue this sentence, one of those long philosophical sentences that Faulkner worked on to get just right. He said that the earth would be more comfortable with fewer Beauchamps, Stevenses, and Mallisons if it were possible to efface memories:

> . . .that inevictable immortal memory awareness of having once been alive which exists forever still ten thousand years afterward in ten thousand recollections of injustice and suffering, too many of us not because of the room we take up but because we are willing to sell liberty short at any tawdry price for the sake of what we call our own which is a constitutional statutory license to pursue each his private postulate of happiness and contentment regardless of grief and cost even to the crucifixion of someone whose nose or pigment we dont like and even those can be coped with provided that few of others who believe that a human life is valuable simply because it has a right to keep on breathing no matter what pigment its lungs distend or nose inhales the air and are willing to defend that right at any price. . . . [599]-[600]

The rest of the sentence follows the first edition as found on page 244.

The last two pages of the setting copy [604] and [605] were originally typed on [602] and [603]. The original version is very close to the final, though a few changes were made, mostly to make Lucas' actions more deliberate. Page [602] originally has Lucas draw out a worn (though Faulkner crossed off this word after typing it) dollar bill; in revising this on [604], it becomes a "worn bill" and finally "not much larger than a shriveled olive."

Faulkner had trouble working out the amount of money Lucas paid Gavin. On [602] Gavin originally moved the coins "perhaps an inch each;" this was changed on [604] as found on the last two lines of page 245 of the first edition to "about half an inch." On [602], Lucas originally gave Gavin the following:

$1.00 (bill)
  .50 (half-dollar)
  .40 (four dimes)
  .10 (two nickels)

Lucas then picked up the following and put it in his purse:

```
$  .20 (two dimes)
   .05 (nickel)
```

Lucas then replaced this with 25 cents (quarter).

In all, then, Lucas gave Gavin the following:

```
$1.00 (bill)
  .50 (half-dollar)
  .25 (quarter)
  .20 (two dimes)
  .05 (nickel)
```

On [604]-[605], this payment process is drawn out and Lucas handles more coins. The scene becomes more childlike, or perhaps even childish. Lucas finally gives Gavin the following:

```
$1.00 (bill)
  .50 (half-dollar)
  .40 (four dimes)
  .10 (two nickels)
```

Lucas then picks up the following and puts it into his purse:

```
$  .20 (two dimes)
   .05 (nickel)
```

Lucas replaces these coins with 25 cents (quarter). Then he adds three more coins bringing the total to $2.25:

```
$  .20 (two dimes)
   .05 (nickel)
```

Then he takes up 50 cents (half-dollar) making the total at this point to $1.75. Gavin remarks on [604], "That ain't but six bits," meaning 75 cents plus $1.00. Then Lucas takes up 25 cents and puts down 50 cents in pennies, giving a grand total of $2.00. Both the original draft and the setting copy end the same way, with Lucas saying, "My receipt." It is fitting that Faulkner ended with Lucas asking for a receipt since the initial conflict between Chick and Lucas started when Chick tried to pay Lucas for his dinner at Lucas' house.

IV

AN EVALUATION

The critical approaches to *Intruder* have varied over the years, though most essays have focused on Gavin's philosophical response to Lucas' dire situation. The best criticism to date, in my opinion, has been written by Cleanth Brooks, Elizabeth Hardwick, Clifford Lewis, Andrew Lytle, Michael Millgate, Aaron Steinberg, John Tagliabue, and Olga Vickery. Except for the chapter on *Intruder* in Steinberg's dissertation, which takes an unusual psychological approach to the novel, there have been few extended critiques dealing with such elements as possible sources, themes, character development, the murder-mystery plot, and the civil rights motif.[1] Most critics, with the exception of Michael Millgate, have not looked at the typescripts of *Intruder*. As with most works by Faulkner, it should be noted that no criticism can ever be entirely thorough or complete, because the ripples begun in a study of one novel expand into waves until one finds himself drifting into a discussion of the entire Faulkner canon—a never-ending adventure to say the least.

The source of *Intruder*, if indeed there is one and only one, is difficult to establish. As previously mentioned, Faulkner told a friend, Eric Devine, that he had enjoyed a whodunit in which two graves are dug up. On the supposition that this whodunit is still in the Faulkner library at Rowan Oak, I reviewed each of the books listed in *William Faulkner's Library—A Catalogue* with Professor Blotner. Certain books we knew could not have possibly been the source for this novel. The ones that were doubtful,

---

[1]For a general critique of *Intruder*, cf. my analysis "*Intruder in the Dust*: A Re-Evaluation," in *Faulkner: The Unappeased Imagination*, ed. Glenn O. Carey (Troy, New York: Whitston Publishing Co., 1979).

I read. In addition, I made a private catalogue in the summer of 1972 of one hundred and twenty murder mysteries and related books published before 1948 that were located on the first and second floors at Rowan Oak, though I have no way of knowing who owned these books or when they were purchased. As far as I can judge, only one story listed in *William Faulkner's Library* and also found on the shelves at Rowan Oak stands an outside chance of possibly influencing the writing of *Intruder.*

In *Come in at the Door* (1934), by William Campbell (*alias* March), the story concerns young Chester Hurry, a white boy, who lives with his father, Robert, a man with a legal background. During his early years, Chester is tutored by Baptiste (Simon Laroque Baptiste), a Frenchman thought to have some black blood in him. Eventually, the black housekeeper, Mitty, gets a false confession from Chester that Baptiste had assaulted him in some way. Using her magical powers, Mitty creates a strange situation in which Baptiste dies and, after this, Chester is taken away to live with some relatives. He attends school, marries, and tries to forget his father who by now is living with Mitty and having children by her. When Robert Hurry dies, Chester returns home to arrange for his funeral. After the ceremony, Chester goes for a walk and recollects the death of Baptiste who had been hung because he murdered a dwarf. Chester feels enormous guilt about his role in bringing about Baptiste's death, though he never explicitly says he is the sole guilty party. At the end of the novel, Chester seems restored to a balance mental state.

What is worth noticing in this story is that a white boy is concerned with the death of an older man who is partially black. Like Gavin Stevens, the young man's father has a legal background and seems more interested in rehearsing legal arguments than in solving family difficulties. A black woman (not a white woman as in the case of Miss Habersham) is involved in the death of this black man, though here in a sinister way. Two characters in Campbell's book, Thompson and Russell Hodge, plan on building a large sawmill that will usurp a good deal of land, a situation not unlike that involving Vinson and Crawford Gowrie. Unlike *Intruder,* the black man in *Come in at the Door* is hung and the white boy, when older, has guilt feelings about it. It would be misleading to claim that Campbell's novel is the source for *Intruder,* but there is a possibility that it might have been one of the murder mysteries that Faulkner stored in his imaginary lumber room.

Two famous authors readily come to mind when thinking about sources for *Intruder:* Mark Twain and Charles Dickens. In 1955, at Nagano, Japan, Faulkner maintained that "Twain was the first that grew up in the belief that there is an American literature and he found himself producing it. So I call him the father of American literature, though he is not the first one."[2] Earlier in the spring of 1947, at Ole Miss, Faulkner said that people will read *Huck Finn* for a long time, though he did not particularly like the structure of Twain's work: "His work is too loose. We'll assume that a novel has set rules. His work is a mass of stuff—just a series of events."[3] Both Irving Howe and Michael Millgate have called attention to Faulkner's debt to Twain. Howe believes that *Intruder* can profitably be read as a modern version of the Huck Finn-Nigger Jim story.[4] In order to survive, however, Lucas has been transformed by Faulkner into a crotchety old man. Chick's ambivalent feelings towards Lucas, wishing that he would act like a Negro and then helping him because he is alone and without friends, is like Huck's feeling that if not turning in Jim would cause him to go to hell, then it is worth the price because of their friendship. Millgate sees a relationship between the graveyard scene in *Intruder* and the one in *Tom Sawyer;* he notes that Faulkner has little hesitation in juxtaposing comedy and horror.[5] While *Huck Finn* has the basic relationship of black man-white boy as found in *Intruder,* Twain has not developed the social tension that Faulkner has. Also, Twain's work does not incorporate the philosophical attitude that is central to the vision of *Intruder.*

---

[2]*Lion in the Garden,* eds. James B. Meriwether and Michael Millgate (New York: Random House, 1968), p. 137.

[3]*Ibid.,* p. 56.

[4]Irving Howe, *William Faulkner* (New York: Vintage, 1962), p. 101.

[5]Michael Millgate, *The Achievement of William Faulkner* (New York: Random House, 1966), p. 218.

Faulkner had a great fondness for Dickens and admitted that he read in and out of Dickens' works some every year.[6] In a discussion of the Snopeses, he saw a relationship between his work and Dickens':

> . . .there's probably no tribe of Snopeses in Mississippi or any-where else outside of my own apocrypha. They were simply an invention of mine to tell a story of man in his struggle. That I was not trying to say, This is the sort of folks we raise in my part of Mississippi, at all. That they were simply over-emphasized, burlesqued if you like, which is what Mr. Dickens spent a lot of his time doing, for a valid to him and to me reason, which was to tell a story in an amusing, dramatic, tragic, or comical way.[7]

While Andrew Lytle sees a relationship between *Intruder* and *Bleak House,* the more important comparison is between *Intruder* and *Great Expectations.*[8] Joseph Gold has explored this relationship and believes that the influence is not as direct as one might expect. Though both writers had an unmistakable faith in the basic goodness of man revealed under duress, "Faulkner found in Dickens a rejection of political solutions, and a rejection of formal religious solutions to the human dilemma. He found these replaced by an intense and humane individualism that measures all value in human terms. . . ."[9] Dickens tended to celebrate all opposition to tyranny and abstraction, and he moved naturally to individual psychology as the root of the problem. On the other hand, both Dickens and Faulkner share an immense vision of life focusing on the complex forces within social structures.

---

[6]*Lion in the Garden,* p. 111.

[7]*Faulkner in the University,* eds. Frederick Gwynn and Joseph Blotner (New York: Vintage, 1959), p. 282.

[8]Andrew Lytle, *The Hero With the Private Parts* (Baton Rouge: Louisiana State University Press, 1966), p. 130.

[9]Joseph Gold, "Dickens and Faulkner: The Uses of Influence," *Dalhousie Review,* 49 (Spring 1969), 70.

Though both writers use children to a great extent and have a deep sense of *locus,* it is difficult to establish connections between *Intruder* and *Great Expectations* except in a general way. Both Chick and Pip have short names, though Chick's is a nickname for Charles and Pip represents a child's attempt to say Philip Pirrip. Each boy meets a suspected criminal who makes demands on the boy, and the boy, in turn, responds by freeing the alleged criminal. Abel Magwitch, however, bears little resemblance to Lucas Beauchamp; the basic difference being They belong to different races. Yet, both men help these boys enormously. Pip's reaction to Magwitch (Provis) as he helps him try to escape from England has much the same tonal quality as when Chick sees Lucas in jail:

> For now my repugnance to him had all melted away, and in the hunted wounded shackled creature who held my hand in his, I only saw a man who had meant to be my benefactor, and who had felt affectionately, gratefully, and generously, towards me with great constancy through a series of years.[10]

Lucas gives Chick an education in civil rights and Magwitch gives money to Pip so he can further his education in London.

Both novels also contain characters named Molly and Joe. The greatest similarity in names, however, is between Miss Habersham in *Intruder* and Miss Havisham in *Great Expectations.* Miss Havisham, however, is not a warm, loving person; she has been jilted and wishes to train her young ward, Estella, to hurt any man who falls in love with her. In fact, she is more like Miss Emily Grierson in Faulkner's "A Rose for Emily" than like Miss Habersham. Faulkner might have made the identification of Miss Habersham with her counterpart in Dickens' novel because he wanted to call attention to his own portrayal of the young man-old woman relationship. Beyond this, one would wrench the context of both novels in order to find similarities.

Another possible source (or sources) might be any of the

---

[10]Charles Dickens, *Great Expectations* (New York: Odyssey Press, 1965), p. 441.

murders that occurred in or around Oxford during the first half of this century. As with the novels previously mentioned, this area of source-study is also tenuous, but it does give a sense of the historical and cultural background of Faulkner's day. In a letter to me dated February 28, 1974, Professor Blotner notes a situation that reflects the *Intruder* story: "About 1935-36, on Woodson's Ridge, in Beat Two, Ike Roberts' brother, a timber man, was killed by a Negro (had gone to his house) who was brought in. Word got out that he would be let off. Jailer Dave Pritchard led a mob which lynched the Negro. It was later found out that two drunken men did it." The Oxford *Eagle* reported in its September 19, 1935 issue that a black man named Elwood Higginbotham was the confessed murderer of Glen Roberts. Higginbotham "was hanged by a mob of about 75 men just north of Tree-Way, on the old Russell road, about 9 o'clock Tuesday night." The jury was still deliberating when the hanging took place. The paper noted that Jailer Pritchard and his three deputies were unable to reason with the determined white men.

One of the most dramatic murders of Northern Mississippi happened in 1908 when young Billy Faulkner was entering the fifth grade. Nelse Patton, a Negro trusty from the Oxford jail, delivered a message on September 8, 1908, to Mrs. Mattie McMillan whose husband was in jail. Patton slashed Mrs. McMillan's throat and afterwards two boys, the sons of Linburn Cullen and brothers of Hal Cullen, one of Faulkner's friends, wounded Patton. Patton was taken to jail and murdered while in jail, with the apparent approval of W. V. Sullivan, a former United States Senator. This event must have made a tremendous impression on the young boys of Oxford as they talked to the Cullen brothers and learned the details of Patton's capture and death.[11]

During the late 1930's, Oxford witnessed a number of murders involving black men. On December 10, 1936, the *Eagle* carried a story about Wilfred Jenkins who killed Lawrence

---

[11]Cf. Joseph Blotner's *Faulkner: A Biography* (New York: Random House, 1974), I, 122 ff. for a further account of this story.

Marlor. Both of these men, like Nub Gowrie, had only one arm. Sheriff Buddy Jones brought Jenkins to the Oxford jail and soon afterwards removed him to a neighboring county jail, a strategy that was contemplated and partially used in *Intruder*. Between January, 1937 and March, 1937, there were three stories in the paper involving Negroes who had been attacked. On February 3, 1938, the *Eagle* reported that Jesse Tatum committed suicide while at Parchman. It should be remembered that Crawford Gowrie commits suicide while in the Jefferson jail in *Intruder*. The July 31, 1941 issue of the *Eagle* carried a headline noteworthy because of the name of the man involved: "Vinson Held to Grand Jury; Hearing Reveals Enmity That Led to Shooting." The story concerns Adam Vinson who was bound over to await the action of the Grand Jury because he was accused of killing a Beat Two farmer on July 20th. Vinson refused bail and Judge J. W. T. Falkner represented the defense. The trial dragged on until September, 1942, when Vinson was found guilty and received five years on manslaughter charges. It could be that Faulkner saw some relationship between this man and Vinson Gowrie. While none of these newspaper accounts provides sufficient evidence to claim any one particular story as a source, there are interesting details worth noticing, details that might at one time or another have caught Faulkner's eye.

Another possible influence in the writing of *Intruder* might have been a film script that Faulkner wrote in 1943. "Battle Cry," an allegorical film, has, as one of its characters, a Negro by the name of America who is wounded in the war.[12] A young man from the South by the name of Akers cares for America. The young man inspires the soldiers to defend the house they inhabit from a German attack. In this film, Faulkner, as in *Intruder*, wrote about a young man from the South helping a Negro who represents the ideals of his homeland. As is true with this film script, as well as *Intruder* and other works of fiction by Faulkner, such as *The Reivers* which has a white boy-black man relationship or the racehorse episode in *A Fable* which

---

[12]For a more detailed studio synopsis of this film, cf. George Sidney's dissertation "Faulkner in Hollywood: A Study of His Career as a Scenarist" (New Mexico, 1959), pp. 190-192.

will be discussed shortly, it is possible to see similar patterns emerge which serve as touchstones in appreciating an important segment of Faulkner's imaginative world.

In Faulkner's previous stories and novels, there are certain elements which seem to find further expressions in *Intruder,* as if Faulkner were reaching into the past to develop situations or character traits he had written about before. For example, Joseph Mahon, an Episcopal minister and father of Donald in *Soldiers' Pay,* has many of the abstract qualities of thought one finds in Gavin, particularly when Reverend Mahon speaks of youth:

> Had I the arranging of this world I should establish a certain point, say at about the age of thirty, upon reaching which a man would be automatically relegated to a plane where his mind would no longer be troubled with the futile recollection of temptations he had resisted and of beauty he had failed to garner to himself. It is jealousy, I think, which makes us wish to prevent young people doing the things we had not the courage or the opportunity ourselves to accomplish once, and have not the power to do now.[13]

This emphasis on youth and living is likewise echoed in *Mosquitoes* where much of the discussion, whether it be art, politics, or religion, centers on the dichotomy between young and old. Fairchild maintains, for example, that when "youth goes out of you, you get out of it. Out of life, I mean. Up to that time you just live; after that, you are aware of living and living becomes a conscious process."[14] Language is a key to life as Fairchild knows, though some like Mark Frost can disguise their uncreative lives by sheltering themselves behind language and never put words into action, a trait which Chick Mallison does not particularly have as he questions the meaning and value of

---

[13]William Faulkner, *Soldiers' Pay* (New York: Boni and Liveright, 1926), p. 59.

[14]William Faulkner, *Mosquitoes* (New York: Boni and Liveright, 1927), p. 231.

building up a vocabulary.

In *Sartoris*, Aunt Jenny DuPre, a prototype of Miss Habersham, would rather recount Bayard's raid on the enemy camp and his attempt to steal anchovies, than participate in any exciting adventures. In much the same way old Simon Strother, the black servant, is a prototype, this time of Lucas. Yet Simon is eventually found dead in a Negro cabin because of his involvement with Meloney Harris and her hairdressing enterprise. He does not even stand up to Caspey, his belligerent, liberated son and give him direction the way Lucas does to Chick after the meal at Lucas' house. Lucas has far more depth and reserve than Simon, perhaps because he is aware of his genealogy; also, Lucas and Miss Habersham have a sense of the future and trust in man's ability to cope with present difficulties and triumph, qualities lacking in their counterparts in *Sartoris.*

Faulkner used the young man as narrator in a number of short stories and seemed to enjoy the *Bildungsroman* motif. "Divorce in Naples," "That Will be Fine," and "Uncle Willy" all have young men who play important narrative roles. In "Shall Not Perish," the young Grier boy narrates the story and when Mrs. Grier tries to console Major de Spain on the loss of his son, her words seem like a prelude to some of Chick Mallison's thoughts: " 'All men are capable of shame,' Mother said. 'Just as all men are capable of courage and honor and sacrifice. And grief too. It will take time, but they will learn it. It will take more grief than yours and mine, and there will be more. But it will be enough.' "[15]   Likewise in "My Grandmother Millard and General Bedford Forrest and the Battle of Harrykin Creek," young Bayard Sartoris tells the story of General Forrest and Granny Millard arranging a marriage between Lieutenant Backhouse and Melisandre by dreaming up a battle that never occurred in which Backhouse is supposedly killed. Like *Intruder,* two boys and an old woman go out digging, this time to hide treasure. At one point, Granny Millard gives a black man his freedom as Miss Habersham does Lucas. Granny, too, believes

---

[15]William Faulkner, *Collected Stories of William Faulkner* (New York: Random House, 1940), p. 108.

in the wisdom of youth: "Then she even pushed the spectacles up into her front hair and looked at me. 'That's the first sensible thing I've heard said on this place since eleven o'clock this morning,' she said. 'It's so sensible and simple that I reckon only a child could have thought of it'."[16]   In these stories, Faulkner knew a young man is open to suspense, wonder, and discovery; he is susceptible to the advice of his elders as filtered and evaluated through his own experiences. As such, he would make a good storyteller, at least in potential.

Three of the characters in *Intruder* had been previously developed by Faulkner in short stories. In "The Fire and the Hearth," Lucas Beauchamp, at sixty-seven years old, maintains a somewhat comic posture though the constant references to his relationship with the McCaslin family give the story of a unique sense of historicity. In this story, Lucas appears before a magistrate twice, once to settle the problem of his involvement in producing bootleg liquor and another time to admit that he does not want to divorce Molly. Both times Lucas is able to win his case, but not because of any rational argumentation. Throughout both parts of this story, Lucas has a sense of his identity: he tells Zack Edmonds when going to Edmonds' house to take Molly home after she has helped nurse Roth Edmonds, "I'm a nigger. . . . But I'm a man too. I'm more than just a man. The same thing made my pappy that made your grandmaw."[17]   It is precisely the attitude revealed in this self-evaluation that Faulkner is able to give greater significance to in *Intruder*, where Lucas does not have to plead his case before Gavin. He has confidence in himself and this will sustain him in a crisis. A number of other black men in Faulkner's short stories reflect Lucas' situation in *Intruder*. In "A Bear Hunt," Old Man Ash, a Negro servant of Major de Spain, encourages some Indians to scare Luke Hogganbeck because Luke had burned a celluloid collar belonging to Ash. It turns out that Ash had told the Indians that Luke was a revenue agent. The story concludes

---

[16]*Ibid.*, p. 682.

[17]William Faulkner, *Go Down, Moses and Other Stories* (New York: Random House, 1942), p. 47.

with Ash saying that he paid fifty cents for the collar and wished he could buy another like it. As with *Intruder,* this story ends with a Negro talking about money. In "Centaur in Brass" Tom-Tom, a Negro about sixty years old, and his friend Turl are involved in a scheme to steal brass. Flem Snopes, a white man, pits Tom-Tom against Turl. In the end, Snopes is punished by not being able to acquire the brass for profit, and because of his shrewdness, Tom-Tom, like Lucas, has survived a potentially dangerous situation.

While Faulkner had written only one major story about Lucas before writing *Intruder,* he spent considerable time developing the characters of Chick and Gavin. It should be remembered that although *Knight's Gambit* was published a year after *Intruder,* all the stories in it were written before 1948. Four of the six stories in this collection are either told by Chick or narrated from his point of view. The first story, "Smoke," is a murder mystery involving the legal assistance of Gavin. Like *Intruder,* it has a pair of twins, Young Anse and Virginius Holland, whose father attempts to dig up his wife's grave. In a similar fashion in "Hand Upon the Waters," two brothers are involved in a murder situation. In "Smoke," however, the father is discovered dead; apparently he died by falling off a horse that had been severely beaten. In validating the father's will, Judge Dukinfield takes his time. He is portrayed as a man wiser than Gavin: "The very fact that the validating of what was a simple enough document appeared to be taking him an overlong time, was to us but fresh proof that Judge Dukinfield was the one man among us who believed that justice is fifty per cent legal knowledge and fifty per cent unhaste and confidence in himself and God."[18] After the judge is mysteriously shot, Gavin links his death to the death of the father, old Anse.

Though this story contains certain elements of a mystery story that are not entirely convincing, namely the discovery of the Granby-Virge will and the revelation of borrowing money for tax purposes, there are philosophical passages, like those

---

[18]William Faulkner, *Knight's Gambit* (New York: Random House, 1949), p. 11.

found in *Intruder,* that give the story a certain depth, as when the narrator says it is "not realities, circumstances, that astonish us; it is concussion of what we should have known, if we had only not been so busy believing what we discover later we had taken for the truth for no other reason than that we happened to be believing it at the moment."[19]   Likewise in "Knight's Gambit," Chick, as narrator, penetrates into the various levels of Gavin's personality with a perspicacity beyond his years:

> What surprised him was his uncle: that glib and talkative man who talked so much and so glibly, particularly about things which had absolutely no concern with him, that his was indeed a split personality: the one, the lawyer, the county attorney who walked and breathed and displaced air; the other, the garrulous facile voice so garrulous and facile that it seemed to have no connection with reality at all and presently hearing it was like listening not even to fiction but to literature.[20]

In these stories, Chick must evaluate constantly Gavin's performance against the ratiocination his uncle professes, and above all, he must come to terms with outlanders who venture into the community and somehow disrupt it. These stories provide a novitiate for Chick, a time to reflect; ultimately he must act on his own, or at least apart from Gavin, as he eventually does in *Intruder.*

One story in *Knight's Gambit,* "Monk," originally published in 1937, reveals in a rather explicit way the type of preparation Chick had for the *Intruder* situation. Monk, a moronic creature, has been put in jail and Chick perceives that Monk will eventually die by hanging. In some ways, Monk is like Lucas. Monk's background, however, is not like the Negroes of Jefferson; it resembles more that of the Gowries:

> He came—emerged: where he was born there or not, no one knew— from the pine hill country in the eastern part of our county: a

---

[19]*Ibid.,* p. 25.

[20]*Ibid.,* p. 141.

country which twenty-five years ago (Monk was about twenty-five) was without roads almost where even the sheriff of the county did not go—a country impenetrable and almost uncultivated and populated by a clannish people who owed allegiance to no one and no thing and whom outsiders never saw until a few years back when good roads and automobiles penetrated the green fastnesses where the denizens with their corrupt Scotch-Irish names intermarried and made whiskey and shot at all strangers from behind log barns and snake fences.[21]

When Monk's grandmother dies and is buried, Monk tries to exhume her corpse. Afterwards, he goes to live with Fraser for ten years. During the course of events, Monk kills a man in front of two witnesses and is taken to jail. Like Lucas, he seems incapable of showing fear or despair in the face of death. In the courtroom, Monk cannot remember the actual murder and so he is sent to prison for life. Only Gavin takes an interest in the case.

It turns out that one of the dead man's two companions had actually fired the shot and put the pistol in Monk's hand. Gavin obtains a pardon from the court and presents it to Monk who refuses to accept it since he enjoys prison life. Later Gavin reads in a Memphis paper that Monk had killed the prison warden in cold blood. As Monk is about to be hung for his crime, he repeats a phrase about sinning against God and man and how he is going out into a free world to farm. Gavin is able to learn that Bill Terrel taught Monk this phrase; Gavin proves that Terrel had persuaded Monk to kill the warden.

It happened that Terrel said that the first man Monk allegedly killed had seduced Terrel's daughter and that his son had consequently killed the man. Terrel was merely trying to avert suspicion from his son. Gavin threatens Terrel by telling him that if he ever gets into trouble again he would help to put him back behind bars. Characteristically, the freedom Gavin offers is a very limited freedom. As with Lucas in *Intruder*, Gavin is convinced that Terrel is guilty, though at the moment he does

---

[21]*Ibid.*, pp. 40-41.

not have sufficient evidence to prove this. And so Terrel goes free in spite of Gavin's deep wishes. Chick is able to witness Gavin's way of handling Monk and Terrel and see that while his uncle is a forthright lawyer, he does not produce the necessary evidence in this particular case. Thus, Gavin does not really insure Monk a place in society and he fails to bring about a just sentence for Terrel, though one cannot blame Gavin completely because of the extenuating circumstances. But Gavin's approach towards law and the obligations which are his as a lawyer would furnish Chick with sufficient background to act on his own should a similar situation occur.

Before writing *Intruder,* Faulkner had been working on *A Fable* and some of the themes and situations of that novel seem to have influenced him in his composition of *Intruder.* Faulkner continually reiterated his belief in the redemptive values which man could achieve in this world. Behind Faulkner's belief that man is indestructible because of his simple will to freedom lies a vision of man that can only be partially expressed in a Yoknapatawpha setting. *A Fable* is not a thesis on the value of freedom, nor has Faulkner imposed his notions of freedom on a military story; rather he has created a myth, an allegory, a sacred drama where the natural and supernatural fuse into an incarnational humanity replete with tensions, conflicts, and pressures. Faulkner does not conceive of freedom as the absence of external restrictions in an individual's drive for self-determination. The opposite is true: freedom is realized only by struggling to overcome restrictions encountered daily in experience. Ultimately, freedom in *A Fable,* as it is in *Intruder,* is delineated as a response, as the ability to commit oneself to people and human values.

The Corporal, the protagonist of *A Fable,* a person whose life and actions initiate responses in the other characters, shows that freedom is truly a response to communal (if not universal) norms and not just to whimsy; he must give an account for his actions to himself, to his twelve disciples, to the military hierarchy, and to the French people, in a manner which reflects his birthright as a son of man and as a son of the divine. The Corporal's adversary, the Marshal who is also his father, represents a person who feels obliged to defend the military establishment; he is incapable of giving an adequate response to the war situation because he refused to traffic with moral complexity. Neither the Corporal nor the Marshal, it should be noted, was born with the complete freedom he desired. Both made moral decisions according to the dictates of their consciences. Both died for what they considered the good of France.

One section of the novel, about sixty pages in the first edition, involves a story that is directly related to *Intruder*, because Faulkner had been working on it immediately before starting *Intruder*. This section takes place in the spring of 1916 when the runner joins the battalion, and the whole brigade goes from Flanders down to the region around Amiens to get some rest and replacements. The commander informs the runner that a Negro, the Reverend Tobe Sutterfield, is trying to find him and the runner responds by saying he does not recognize Sutterfield's name. Afterwards the runner rejoins the rest of the battalion and when he enters the barracks, he notices a private giving money to some other soldiers and noting the transaction in his small book.

This scene with the private and soldiers is repeated every day after the morning parade and gradually more and more soldiers become involved. On payday, the soldiers give the money back to the private. One day a uniformed driver, a French staff-captain, a British staff-captain, a thin Negro youth, a middle-aged American woman, another French official, and finally "an old Negro in a worn brushed top-hat, with the serene and noble face of an idealised Roman consul" arrive.[22] The private and the Negro confer and the runner realizes that the financial transactions involve an insurance plan whereby the soldiers collect money if they are still alive after a battle. But why did the old Negro come to this locale? From official documents the runner learns about an association called *Les Amis Myriades et Anonymes à la France de Tout le Monde* and joins this insurance plan to find out about these visitors, particularly the old Negro.

----

[22]William Faulkner, *A Fable* (New York: Random House, 1954), p. 143. All future references to this novel will be to this edition.

On April 8, 1917, the runner goes to Paris where he had
previously lived for three years. He enters the headquarters
of *Les Amis* and finds Sutterfield, known as Monsieur Tooley-
man, who begins to relate the story of Mistairy (Mister Harry).
The scene shifts back to 1912, two years before the war, when a
three-year-old horse owned by an Argentinian "prince" was
brought to America by a groom who turns out to be the sentry,
"the man with the ledger and the moneybelt" (p. 157). During
these two years the groom became a different man, without a
past or griefs. The groom and the horse have "an affinity," almost a heart-to-heart relationship. It is only when the groom is
present that the horse would behave; in effect "the man had it
set free" (p. 152). This note of freedom reflects to some degree
the larger theme involving the Corporal and the Marshal.

Soon after the horse's arrival in South America, a United
States oil baron had bought the horse and shipped it to New
Orleans where the old Negro, being a preacher-groom, met it
and worked for the owner. Two days after the horse's arrival,
the old Negro, the groom, and the horse plunged through a weakened trestle. For sixteen of the groom's twenty-two months
in the States, five groups, including state police and private
detectives, pursued the old Negro, the groom, a twelve-year-old
black boy, and the horse from Illinois to the Gulf of Mexico and
between Kansas and Alabama where the horse, now three-legged,
was winning back-country quarter-races. The horse was "not
a theft, but a passion, an immolation, and apotheosis," resembling "the immortal pageant-piece of the tender legend which
was the crowning glory of man's own legend beginning when his
first paired children lost well the world and from which paired
prototypes they still challenged paradise, still paired and still
immortal against the chronicle's grimed and bloodstained
pages. . ." (p. 153). They had hoped to remain undiscovered
after they rescued the horse, but a newsflash from Weatherford,
Texas, alerted the authorities to the horse's existence.

A deputy from Texas pursues the group and soon realizes
he could not catch the Negro and the horse. The deputy is
perplexed; he submits his resignation to the horse's owner in
New York and offers to buy the horse and stop the search. As
an ex-deputy he again joins the search and offers rewards for
the capture of the horse. Like Gavin, the ex-deputy is an edu-

cated man, though he had failed at Harvard and then wasted two years at Oxford. The ex-deputy realizes that the horse and the three keepers are "doomed" because of the greed of those seeking the reward. He even thinks of "confounding corruption with corruption" by putting his own money up against the reward money.

After fifteen months of pursuit, the ex-deputy finally sees the horse just after the English groom, subsequently put in jail, had shot the horse in the forehead. The ex-deputy then goes to New Orleans and sends back a lawyer who faces a mob, a situation similar to one in *Intruder:*

> 'A mob,' the lawyer said, with a sort of unction almost. 'It's a long time since I have coped with a mob.'
>
> 'No no,' the client [groom] said quickly. 'They are just watching, waiting for something, I didn't have time to find out what.' (p. 163)

Eventually the groom is released from jail and the two Negroes disappear, too, along with the body of the horse. The Masons, out of a spirit of brotherhood, help the groom to obtain his release:

> 'The old Negro has got the rest of it [money] in the tail of that frockcoat,' the ex-deputy said.—truth, love, sacrifice, and something else even more important than they: some bond between or from man to his brother man stronger than even the golden shackles which coopered precariously his ramshackled earth—.' (p. 165)

The ex-deputy tells the lawyer that he does not want to capture the three crooks. On the fourth day after his release, an investigator from the Departement of Justice enters the scene and leaves with a man from the sheriff's bonding company. The lawyer fantasizes, as does the ex-deputy, that this situation is a pageant, and even more, "the affirmation of a creed, a belief, the declaration of an undying faith, the postulation of an invincible way of life. . ." (p. 167). He sees this cause as fundamentally an American one and would try to show that all along it was not impossible that the thieves were actually returning the horse, not running away with it.

On the seventh day (the days in a number of Faulkner's works reflect either Holy Week or the biblical days of creation), the old Negro returns to the jail kitchen. When the turnkey brings the Negro to the courtroom with the lawyer, the towns-folk follow and there "the lawyer watched Man pouring steadily into the tabernacle, the shrine itself. . ." (p. 176). The lawyer eventually calls a recess and the Negro and the turnkey go into the judge's chambers. The lawyer says: "You've got to get him to a jail somewhere where they can hold him long enough for you to put a charge on him that the law will accept" (p. 176). The lawyer then orders over the turnkey's objection that the Negro be taken to Blankton, a larger town. Likewise, in *Intruder*, Lucas is taken to Hollymount in a ruse to capture Crawford Gowrie.

The crowd leaves the courtroom and goes outside where the old Negro is being taken to Blankton. The Negro reveals they never actually had much money because they believed gambling is sinful. Finally, when the scene returns back to Paris, the runner mocks the old Negro's society as a place to believe and hope:

> 'Because man can bear anything, provided he has something left, a little something left: his integrity as a creature tough and enduring enough not only to hope but not even to believe in it and not even to miss its lack; to be tough and to endure until the flash, crash, whatever it will be, when he will no longer be anything and none of it will matter any more, even the fact that he was tough and, until then, did endure.' (p. 203)

The Negro replies:

> 'Evil is a part of man, evil and sin and cowardice, the same as repentance and being brave. You got to believe in all of them, or believe in none of them. Believe that man is capable of all of them, or he aint capable of none.' (p. 203)

The runner, like Chick Mallison, thanks the Negro for helping him learn to believe.

Thus, before starting *Intruder* in January 1948, Faulkner had finished the horse race episode the previous November. In this episode, he dealt with an old Negro and two younger males, one white and one black. These three individuals have saved a horse and given it a chance to run uninhibited in small country races. From the viewpoint of the horse's owner, however, the three have stolen the horse and therefore are outlaws. The three-legged horse seems to represent a state of imperfect freedom; were he in the hands of the rightful owner, he would probably be put to stud or shot. Yet, the horse always wins and is given constant care and attention by his three attendants. A deputy pursues the old Negro and his companions in an effort to see that justice, however predetermined, is done, even if he has to spend his own money to bring it about. Though the groom sacrifices the horse rather than betray it, all escape any real form of punishment or imprisonment.

At the end of this section of *A Fable,* Sutterfield is able to explain the totality of his experience in terms of sin, evil, cowardice, repentance, bravery, and belief in mankind, a philosophy which Lucas would acknowledge in his own way. He gives a sense of coherency not only to the part of his life involving the horse, but also to the realities and risks of warfare in France. Likewise, Chick and Alex Sander, each at some point in *Intruder,* are thought to be engaged in illegal activities as they try to give existence to a limping freedom in Jefferson. Like the deputy in *A Fable,* Gavin does not fully understand the significance of the events involved and would rather speculate and fantasize than meet the elusive realities before him. While Gavin does not obstruct justice and freedom in *Intruder,* he does little to promote it either.

It was part of Faulkner's genius that he could write a novel and use whatever events or stories he knew or had read about and transform them into something new and dramatic. It seems clear with *Intruder,* at least, that Faulkner did not rely on one particular work or event to use as the imaginative basis of this novel. As he often said, he let the situation develop; the characters control the plot once it is under way. Yet from his outside reading, his knowledge of the murders in Lafayette County, and his own previous stories and novels, he picked or borrowed characters, situations, relationships, patterns, and themes which he could use as he pleased. As he mentioned in his February 7, 1949 letter to Haas, he wanted to add material to *Intruder* and show an explicit relationship between *Intruder* and *Absalom, Absalom!.* Thus, source-study plays a limited part in a total appreciation of this novel, but it does show the expansive quality of Faulkner's imagination as he brought his creative powers together in composing this novel.

As his letters to Haas also indicate, Faulkner had difficulty choosing a title for this mood. A number of his short stories refer to black men, pursuit, capture, and the meaning of dust. In "Red Leaves," Issetibbeha has a Negro body servant from Guinea. When Issetibbeha dies, the Negro must be captured and killed before the Chief can be buried. Eventually the Negro is chased until he is found. In "Dry September" the event is more drastic. A Negro, Will Mayes, is lynched because it is rumored he had assaulted Miss Minnie Cooper. The whites, except for Hawkshaw, perpetuate the myth that a Southern white woman would not lie about a Negro raping her. Towards the conclusion of the story, Hawkshaw jumps from a moving car and Faulkner relates this action to dust: "They went on; the dust swallowed them; the glare and the sound died away. The dust of them hung for a while; but soon the eternal dust absorbed it again."[23] A similar reference occurs in "The Hound" when Ernest Cotton kills Jack Houston. Like Crawford Gowrie, Cotton had chosen the place of execution well, near Varner's store (not Fraser's as in *Intruder*). When Cotton returns to the tree stump which contains Houston's body, he is afraid Houston's dog will disrupt it. He then takes the body and hurls it into the mist over the river bank. Finally, the sheriff captures Cotton and takes him to the county seat fourteen miles away. The scene ends with a sentence that could have been written for *Intruder:* "When they were within three or four miles of town, they began to pass wagons and cars going home from market day in town, the wagon teams plodding homeward in their own inescapable dust."[24] It is al-

---

[23]*Collected Stories*, p. 180.

[24]William Faulkner, *Doctor Martino and Other Stories* (New York: Harrison Smith and Robert Haas, 1934), p. 68.

most as if nature can assimilate the various forms of violence in three stories and not be thwarted in the process.

Faulkner was determined to use the phrase "in the dust" in the title of this novel. He considered a number of words to place before this phrase: impostor, malfeasance, substitution, malaprop, malpractice, trouble, intruder. It is clear that he did not have a title in mind before writing the novel and that the word "dust" is the operative word in the title. As a young man, Faulkner had apparently studied Conrad Aiken's long poem published in 1920, *The House of Dust: A Symphony,* as he refers to Aiken at least twice, once in 1921 when he mentioned this poem in the Ole Miss newspaper *The Mississippian,* and later in a piece for the New Orleans *Double Dealer* in 1925 when he wrote that "Conrad Aiken's minor music still echoes in my heart."[25] This poem does not directly parallel the plot of

---

[25]Conrad Aiken, *The House of Dust: A Symphony* (Boston: The Four Seas Company, 1920): "Verse Old and Nascent: A Pilgrimage" (*The Double Dealer,* April 1925); *The Mississippian* (16 February 1921). The following section from Aiken's poem will give some idea of its content and tone:

> We are like searchers in a house of darkness,
> A house of dust; we creep with little lanterns,
> Throwing our tremulous arcs of light at random,
> Now here, now there, seeing a plane, an angle,
> An edge, a curve, a wall, a broken stairway
> Leading to who knows what; but never seeing
> The whole at once. . .We grope our way a little,
> And then grow tired. No matter what we touch,
> Dust is the answer—dust: dust everywhere.
> If this were all—what were the use, you ask?
> But this is not: for why should we be seeking,
> Why should we bring this need to seek for beauty,
> To lift our minds, if there were only dust?
> This is the central chamber you have come to:
> Turning your back to the world, until you came
> To this deep room, and looked through rose-stained windows,
> And saw the hues of the world so sweetly changed.

Intruder; however, the motif of death, the appearance of an elderly woman, the emphasis on a crowd, and the philosophical reflections about creation and creativity, seem to have provided a framework out of which certain dimensions of *Intruder* could have developed.   In one version of the setting copy, [474], Faulkner had written that Chick wanted to "release into that nothing what little of nothing he had which was all he had which was nothing: dust: who had wanted of course to leave [some] his mark on his time in man, some mark at least on his part of earth. . .to perform something passionate and brave and austere and found it all that remained was dust. . . ." There are a number of references to dust throughout the novel; none of them, however, is as telling as the above one. In this context, at least, dust refers to a void in Chick's life which would not support him.   Faulkner might have deleted this reference to dust (cf. page 193 of the first edition), because Chick was assisted by Miss Habersham and Aleck Sander when he went out to the graveyard to dig up, and intrude upon, Vinson Gowrie's grave.

A number of critics have made their own suggestions concerning the significance of the title. Joseph Gold believes

---

Well, in a measure, so only do we all.
I am not sure that you can be refuted.
At the very last we all put faith in something,—
You in this ghost that animates your world,
This ethical ghost,—and I, you'll say, in reason,—
Or sensuous beauty,—or in my secret self. . .
Though as for that you put your faith in these,
As much as I do—and then, forsaken reason,—
Ascending, you would say, to intuition,—
You predicate this ghost of yours, as well.
Of course, you might have argued,—and you should have,—
That no such deep appearance of design
Could shape our world without entailing purpose:
For can design exist without a purpose?
Without conceiving mind?. . .We are like children
Who find, upon the sands, beside a sea,
Strange patterns drawn,—circles, arcs, ellipses,
Moulded in sand. . .Who put them there, we wonder?

that Faulkner chose this title with care and maintains that
dust is metaphoric of time and that violating dead bodies is an
examination of the past, an interpretation that is favored by
Aaron Steinberg.[26] Elizabeth Kerr suggests that the title refers
to the body of Jake Montgomery in the grave of Vinson
Gowrie.[27] For her, Montgomery is the intruder. Hyatt Waggoner mentions the biblical notion that man is dust and will
return to dust unless regenerated by an afterlife.[28] Faulkner
made the connection between man as dust and the notion of
creativity: "Well, the individual is not too much, he's only a

Did someone draw them here before we came?
Or was it just the sea?—We pore upon them,
But find no answer—only suppositions.
And if these perfect shapes are evidence
Of immanent mind, it is but circumstantial:
We never come upon him at his work,
He never troubles us. He stands aloof—
Well, if he stands at all: is not concerned
With what we are or do. You, if you like,
May think he broods upon us, loves us, hates us,
Conceives some purpose of us. In so doing
You see, without much reason, will in law.
I am content to say, 'this world is ordered,
Happily so for us, by accident:
We go our ways untroubled save by laws
Of natural things.' Who makes the more assumption?

If we were wise—which God knows we are not—
(Notice I call on God!) we'd plumb this riddle
Not in the world we see, but in ourselves.

[26]Joseph Gold, *William Faulkner: A Study in Humanism from Metaphor to Discourse* (Norman: University of Oklahoma Press, 1966), p. 87.

[27]Elizabeth Kerr, *Yoknapatawpha: Faulkner's 'Little Postage Stamp
of Native Soil'* (New York: Fordham University Press, 1969), p. 222.

[28]Hyatt Waggoner, *William Faulkner, From Jefferson to the World*
(Lexington: University of Kentucky Press, 1959), p. 214.

pinch of dust, he won't be here very long anyway, but his species, his dreams, they go on. There's always somebody that will keep on creating the Bach and Shakespeare as long as man keeps on producing."[29]   Chick, by digging up Gowrie's grave, disturbs the normal patterns of existence in Jefferson; he is willing to explore the unknown and intrude into the void.   Of all the characters in this novel, only Chick has the resourcefulness to respond adequately to the demands made on him and retain a definite potential for future growth.

The ambiguity of the title, however, does not reveal the novel's main concerns.   In his book, *Go Slow Now: Faulkner and the Race Question,* Charles Peavy maintains that *Intruder* is Faulkner's most important fictional treatment of civil rights; he sees it both as a novel and a tract.   Peavy suggests that many of the sentiments of Gavin coincide with Faulkner's public statements in the mid-1950's: "Even such words as 'homogeneity,' 'outlander,' and 'to confederate,' which are so recurrent in the conversation of Gavin Stevens with his nephew, are repeated in the many non-fiction statements made by Faulkner on the civil rights issue."[30]   A number of critics, including Edmund Wilson, Elizabeth Hardwick, Irving Howe, and William Van O'Connor, see Gavin as Faulkner's mouthpiece: others such as Olga Vickery, Michael Millgate, and Cleanth Brooks say there is a distance between the author and his character.[31]   The problem of seeing

---

[29]*Faulkner in the University*, p. 286.

[30]Charles Peavy, *Go Slow Now: Faulkner and the Race Question* (Eugene: University of Oregon Press, 1971), p. 47.

[31]Edmund Wilson, "William Faulkner's Reply to the Civil Rights Program," *New Yorker,* 23 October 1948, p. 121ff.; Elizabeth Hardwick, "Faulkner and the South Today," *Partisan Review,* 15 (October 1948), 1133-1134; Irving Howe, *William Faulkner,* p. 99; William Van O'Connor, *The Tangled Fire of William Faulkner* (Minneapolis: University of Minnesota Press, 1954), pp. 136-142; Olga Vickery, "Gavin Stevens: From Rhetoric to Dialectic," *Faulkner Studies,* 2 (Spring 1953), 3; Michael Millgate, *The Achievement of William Faulkner,* pp. 224-225; Cleanth Brooks, *William Faulkner: The Yoknapatawpha Country* (New Haven: Yale University Press, 1963), p. 279.

Gavin as a spokesman for Faulkner is tricky because it should be remembered that most of Faulkner's pronouncements on civil rights were addressed to *ad hoc* situations beginning with the Turner-Whitt case in 1950. It might be anachronistic to hold that Gavin represents Faulkner's views when, at the writing of the novel, Faulkner had insisted on great privacy and rarely expressed himself publicly.

Faulkner initially thought of *Intruder* as a mystery story and seemed to have this fairly well plotted out in his mind before he began writing:

> Well, it began with the notion—there was a tremendous flux of detective stories going about at that time and my children were always buying them and bringing them home. I'd stumble over them everywhere I went. And I thought of an idea for one would be a man in jail just about to be hung would have to be his own detective, he couldn't get anybody to help him. The next thought was, the man for that would be a Negro. Then the character of Lucius—Lucas Beauchamp came along. And the book came out of that. It was the notion of a man in jail who couldn't hire a detective, couldn't hire one of these tough guys that slapped women around, took a drink every time he couldn't think of what to say next. But once I thought of Beauchamp, then he took charge of the story and the story was a good deal different from the idea of that—of the detective story that I had started with.[32]

In this quote, Faulkner makes two important statements about *Intruder:* the novel began with an idea and the nature of the novel changed once he realized Gavin's role in the novel. His initial Jamesian *donnée* was the image of Lucas in jail. What is most interesting about this is that Lucas provides the catalyst for the action in the story, much like Caddy in *The Sound and the Fury;* although he is featured in the first three chapters of the novel, Lucas becomes a major character more by his absence than by his presence.

In contrast to Lucas, Faulkner delayed the revelation of a

---

[32]*Faulkner in the University,* pp. 141-142.

number of his characters, notably Gavin Stevens, Miss Habersham, Mrs. Mallison, Jake Montgomery, and Crawford Gowrie;
the result, especially with Gavin and the two women, is that new
characters are gradually introduced who might be imporant in
solving the murder. In the case of Jake and Crawford, however,
the element of probability, so crucial to fiction in general and to
a murder mystery in particular, is diminished because these
two are little more than shadow figures who do not impress
themselves on the reader's mind. The ability to discern the truth
from that which is not true is at the heart of a mystery story;
the reader tries to match his wits against the unknown, but presumably rational pattern, composed, in part, of motive—effect—
explanation. As the reader begins to figure out what is happening, he must always be on guard lest the pattern become altered
in a way he least suspects, especially as Faulkner has structured
this novel with the delayed introduction of certain characters. A
too-facile pattern will disturb the reader because the suspense is
not sustained and the solution to the murder is adumbrated far
in advance of the actual conclusion of the story. On the other
hand, a mystery that is overly-complicated, with a pattern that
changes radically like a kaleidoscope, or with a pattern that
lacks symmetry based on how human beings probably respond
given the uniqueness of the situation before them, is equally
unacceptable. A murder mystery should normally unfold so that
the various factors can actually lead to a solution; the unfolding
should be done gradually, or organically, even though the significance of the solution might not be appreciated until the concluding summation.

As the mystery story is recounted by Gavin towards the
end of the novel, the reader can pinpoint rather precisely where
he failed to see a relationship or to understand the specific nature
of a clue that had been actually revealed. In all of this, timing,
suspense, revelation, locale, and motive, as well as the personalities of the protagonists, are crucial and each of these factors
should develop harmoniously with the others. Solving a mystery
often means discerning the relationship between what is obvious
and what is unexpected, so that the surprise factor is taken into
consideration and dealt with throughout. If the murderer is
known in advance, then the inevitable chase leading to his capture is important, and in the case of movies, the chase can be
enhanced by filming in a remote part of the world, or in the

labyrinthine streets of Old World cities. If the murderer is not known, as in *Intruder,* then clues must be given periodically so that, when put together at some key moment, they make reasonable human sense.

The murder-mystery aspect of *Intruder* is complicated because the alleged murderer, Lucas, is in jail during most of the novel and refrains from explaining completely what he has seen. He suffers the prejudice that exists against him mostly in silence. Although he does give a hint to Chick that the gun he owned was not the one that killed Vinson Gowrie, he does not offer further information about his involvement, at least initially. Thus, the three detectives, Miss Habersham, Chick, and Aleck Sander, are not quite sure what to do once they dig up Vinson Gowrie's grave. Faulkner created suspense not merely by the juxtaposition of these three individuals, but by their task of digging up a body in a deserted cemetery late at night. Yet what is most disturbing and even adds to the suspense is that we do not really know Vinson Gowrie, Crawford Gowrie, or Jake Montgomery. It is only later, when Gavin tries to piece everything together, that we learn, speculatively, that Crawford killed Vinson to prevent Vinson from learning that Crawford was stealing lumber and that he subsequently killed Jake to prevent Jake from revealing Crawford as Vinson's murderer.

It is precisely here that Faulkner, like Homer, nodded. In changing the nature of the novel from a murder mystery to the relationship between Chick and Gavin, he failed to dramatize or provide an adequate context in which to appreciate Crawford's motive for committing fratricide. In addition, he has done a sleight-of-hand by having Jake's body placed in a shallow grave and by having Vinson's body buried in quicksand. This makes no logical sense except to show that Crawford was confused as how to proceed. Also, placing Jake's body in Vinson's grave adds to the dramatic atmosphere of the novel but changes little the actual drama since the murder weapon is a decisive element in this novel and had Crawford destroyed this, it would have been difficult, it seems to me, to convict him in a court of law. It is ironic that the Luger used to kill Vinson is also the gun Crawford uses to commit suicide; yet, it is never described during the course of the novel and even eludes Crawford's jailers after he has been apprehended. One might speculate as to what would have happened if Crawford destroyed the gun after both men were murdered and Jake deposited in quicksand. Certainly Jake would have been forgotten in time, even though he would not have been found neither in Yoknapatawpha County nor Crossman County; and since neither Jake, nor the gun, would have been found, it would seem that the case would never be completely solved. The Gowries would know that Crawford had a Luger, but since fraticide was so repugnant to them, they might have dismissed it and thought that Jake had owned a gun or that one of Jake's enemies from Tennessee might have owned one. Since there was no previous history of antagonism between Vinson and Crawford, Faulkner has not patterned the murder scene with enough human motivation to make it all seem probable. To compensate for this, one might venture to say, Faulkner dealt with some larger issues surrounding this murder—especially the civil rights in the South, the growth of a young boy in his responsibilities towards a black man, and the relationship between philosophical reflection and concrete action in solving the problems of a Southern community.

Unlike some of the dimensions of this novel, particularly the dream sequences and the philosophy of Gavin, Faulkner knew the story line of the murder plot well enough so that he did not have to restructure much of it in the setting copy. While Faulkner did not initially delineate the solution to the mystery story to the point that Crawford is apprehended, he seemed to have known the results of finding the bodies of Vinson and Jake sufficiently to realize he could handle the implications of this in the latter chapters of the setting copy.

Although Faulkner's statement in the interview at the University of Virginia (13 May 1957) that he had an idea of this novel before writing it does not mean he had worked out all the details, since in the original draft, Lucas was arrested for the murder of Jake Montgomery, then later called in the setting copy a "white man," and finally Vinson Gowrie. This detail implies that Faulkner had not included the Gowries in his original conception of the story, although the rest of the story seems consistent with the setting copy version. In writing this novel, however, Faulkner explicitly stated that he was trying to write something other than a murder mystery and he did not want his characters accepted as "the puppet-play of a whodunit but as the protagonist-pattern of a belief that not government first but the white man of the South owes a responsibility to the Negro. . ." [18]. Faulkner was convinced that civil rights should not be bestowed upon the Negro solely for enduring the past, but rather "because of his present condition, whether the Negro wishes to accept it or not." Chick learns throughout the course of his relationship with Lucas that responsibility is based not on money, but on human commitment and human dignity. What Chick must recognize, too, is that Lucas is not a one-dimensional person, but is unique in that he is proud of his mixed white-black blood, and that he can grieve for a dead wife, just like a white man would do. Thus, Faulkner places the murder mystery in a larger fictive context while never losing sight of the significance of details.

In relating the events surrounding Vinson's death, the narrator states that Lucas had a pistol and, then rather matter-of-factly, that he waited until the youngest of seven brothers went into the woods and shot him, though later on [540 (V)] this was changed to six brothers. When revised in the setting copy, the narrator is less definite and says that no one was absolutely sure whether Lucas found or waylaid his victim [203], thus opening up the possibility that Lucas might himself be the victim of someone's scheming. Lucas' alleged action, however, seems appropriate since the townsfolk considered him arrogant. Not resisting in any way when he was captured standing over Vinson's dead body with a pistol in his hand, he was taken to the constable's home to prevent being lynched. Once Chick learns that the sheriff would bring Lucas to jail on Sunday morning, he dreads his confrontation with Lucas, though to his credit, he docs not hide nor escape from town on his horse. The ending of the first chapter of the original draft, which coincides with the ending of the second chapter of the setting copy, depicts Lucas asking Chick to request that his uncle come to see him.

Faulkner, in revising this material for the setting copy, used about half of it, as the first chapter of the setting copy ends with Lucas warning Chick to stay out of the creek. The second chapter of the setting copy, which had also been part of the first chapter of the original draft, structures more carefully Chick's repayment to Lucas and Lucas' gift of molasses delivered to Chick by a white boy. Since the chronology of events is important, not only for an insight into the way Chick matured, but in understanding the events concerning the murder, Faulkner in his revision clarified his chronology and slowed down the series of events to give fuller expression to them. For example, in trying to give a clue concerning Crawford, he reworked five times the description of the Gowries as stock- and timber-traders, two of whose members already had served in jail. Also in the setting copy, it is learned the Gowries were not immediately present after the shooting and thus a lynching never occurred; to prevent such a lynching the son of the store owner and the constable had spirited Lucas away. With this particular material and with the first three chapters of the setting copy, Faulkner clarifed the Lucas-Chick relationship to show ultimately the conflict within Chick as he decides to help Lucas.

Once Lucas is safe, the revised text focuses on new material as Chick wanders into his uncle's office and then finally goes home. At this point, Gavin is introduced and asks a major question: why did Lucas kill a Gowrie? In all, we really have no reason, except Lucas' indirect denial, to think otherwise, but at least Lucas will be safe until Sunday morning since the inhabitants of Beat Four will not act precipitously. Yet, Lucas is again considered guilty [224] as mentioned in the original draft, although Faulkner had previously seemed inclined not to be so explicit. When the text returns to the present, Chick is not only free again, he is there so Lucas can see him "not just from the edge of mere uniqueless death but from the gasoline-roar of apotheosis" [237]. Although Chick admits he is wrong [242], Faulkner decided not to use this realization in the final version of the story. Thus, Chick meets Lucas on Sunday morning sensitive to Lucas' predicament, but not with overt guilt feelings about helping him. The crowd, on the other hand, feels revenge, something that seems appropriate now since Faulkner in revising the original draft had put more emphasis on the citizens of Jefferson, the surrounding areas, and particularly on the Gowries. Also, we understand a bit more the parameters of Lucas' request to have Gavin visit him, since in the revised text Gavin has made his appearance and we know to some degree what to expect of him. Gavin is introduced in the second chapter of the setting copy briefly and then more fully in the next chapter. While this does not alter substantially the mystery plot, it does provide a smooth transition.

In the original draft, the second chapter started with Gavin and Chick walking on a Sunday evening in May and ends with Chick meeting with Lucas and deciding to travel nine miles to the cemetery to dig up Vinson's body. His mission is to check the bullet that killed Vinson. This chapter incorporates some of the views of the community, and while it provides a framework larger than just the Mallison family, it also shows Gavin pinpointing something that might make a crucial difference in solving this case. As the nephew and uncle enter into the jail, Faulkner notes "they had already passed out of the world of man, men, people who worked and had homes and raised families" [42] into a cell where Chick initially reflects his uncle's views that only *"a nigger could kill a man"* [44]. Having been refused legal assistance by Gavin, Lucas mentions merely that Vinson and another man were involved in dealing with lumber, but that the other man was stealing some of this lumber on his own at night; in the revised copy, Lucas refuses even to tell the name of this second man. Also, in the original draft, Lucas asks Chick to go to the cemetery and says that he will be paid for his efforts. The setting copy, however, emphasized Chick's realization of what his mission is all about, especially as Lucas would not reveal to any adult why his .41 Colt could not have killed Vinson. Ultimately, Chick knows before he has even started to pursue the facts of the case, Lucas has beaten him. In revising this material as Chapter Three of the setting copy, Faulkner did not modify the larger plot lines of the mystery story; rather, he focused on intensifying the atmosphere of the novel, particularly since the reader awaits the entrance of an unknown person who might possibly be Vinson's murderer. Although Faulkner changed slightly the meeting between Lucas and Chick when Chick returned to the cell, such as altering the name of Mount Hope Chapel to Caledonia Chapel, he seemed to stress rather the personalities of Lucas and Chick, emphasizing the apparent incompatibility of their relationship. Thus, within this framework, the conclusion of the second chapter in the original draft became the conclusion of the third chapter of the setting copy.

In Chapter Three of the original draft which became Chapter Four of the setting copy, Faulkner added three new elements that changed the nature of the murder mystery. First, Miss Habersham is introduced. She was depicted originally as a farmer in the original draft. Faulkner never seemed to know how old she was and thus her age vacillated from sixty to seventy to near-seventy in the original draft to sixty in the setting copy and seventy in the first edition. Secondly, at one point in the original draft, even though it appears to be an afterthought on Faulkner's part, Gavin almost solves one aspect of the mystery by asking Chick whether it was a rabbit, a tin can, or a mark on a tree that Lucas shot at, thus coming close to setting up a conjectural series of events that a master-sleuth might have more vigorously pursued, at least in his imagination. While in the original draft Chick initially wanted his uncle to help dig up Vinson's body, this was modified in the setting copy to where it was thought best that Sheriff Hampton be part of the operation. Thirdly, as Chick began to formulate in his mind the practical dimensions of proving Lucas' innocence, he ponders three modes of transportation: horse, car, or Miss Habersham's truck. Not only does Chick face immediate decisions, but Faulkner expanded Chick's motivation. In the original draft, Chick realized that he could dig up Vinson's body partly because no one would be there to apprehend him. In the setting copy, Chick realizes he needs the assistance of Aleck Sander, and thus Faulkner adds a more emotional component to Chick's decision-making process: "he flung himself bodily with one heave into a kind of deadly reasonableness of enraged calculation, a calm sagacious and desperate rationality not of pros and cons because there were no pros. . ." [297]-[298]. In addition, Faulkner in the setting copy indicated that Chick's commitment to Lucas and solving this mystery, as best he could, was total: "he could stop here and never pass it, let the wreckage of midnight crash harmless and impotent, against these walls because they were strong, taller than wreckage, stronger than fear. . ." [301]. Thus in the revised version, as Chick is joined by Aleck Sander and Miss Habersham, greater emphasis is put on the inner struggle that Chick undergoes as he contemplates the step he is about to take. Although Chick had forgotten about Miss Habersham in the original draft, this is not true in the setting copy where the encounter between Chick and Miss Habersham was significantly expanded.

Likewise in the setting copy, Faulkner integrated details with the overall action of the plot. It is clear in the setting copy, that Highboy smelled quicksand, planting in the reader's mind the fact that there is quicksand near the cemetery and that someone was definitely leading a mule or horse down from the

graveyard. One would expect that Faulkner might have drama-
tized even more the graveyard scene in rewriting it, but in fact,
he changed it slightly, merely altering the birth and death dates
of Amanda Gowrie and describing Jake Montgomery as "a shoestring timber-buyer over in Crossman County" [327], not from
Glasgow, Hollymount, or Holyvale, as he had indicated in the
original draft. Once a second body has been discovered, Miss
Habersham in the setting copy asks the question one would expect of a detective: "Now what? To find out if it wasn't his pistol—find out whatever it was he meant?" [306]. To this, Chick
responds by saying that they definitely need an expert to check
the bullet. At this point, the end of the third chapter of the
original draft and the fourth of the setting copy, Faulkner was
still in the process of adding complication to the murder-mystery
aspect of the novel, making sure in the setting copy, however,
not only that he gave sufficient clues but that he indicated the
direction the story would take, namely, to seek professional
assistance in determining the bullet that killed Montgomery. It
is with the fourth chapter of the setting copy that Faulkner, in a
sense, formally starts the action that will resolve the dilemma
Lucas finds himself in during the first three chapters of the
setting copy—an action that continues in a fairly linear imaginative pattern until the discovery of Vinson's body and the realization that Lucas is probably telling the truth.

With two murders to account for, one of which Lucas
could not have possibly committed since he was in jail at the
time of the murder, the three detectives, moving from a night-
time environment to an early morning situation, decide to enlist
the help of Sheriff Hampton and Gavin. Thus, by the time
Faulkner was more than half way through the original draft, he
brought the murder-mystery case into the light of day where the
proper public legal authorities could deal with it. Not only does
this mean that more people will become involved in the case,
with, at one point, a decided focus being put on the reaction of
the townsfolk, but that Gavin's pseudo-rational logic would
now be juxtaposed with the action, based on intuition, of the
two boys and an elderly woman. In making this transition,
Faulkner had to smooth out certain inconsistencies. For example, in the original draft, Gavin enters Sheriff Hampton's house
early Monday morning and the sheriff replies that Gavin would
not come so early if the tale Gavin told were not true. It is only

later in the text, however, that Gavin does actually recount the events of the case. In revising this material in the setting copy, Faulkner returns the focus to Lucas and away from the sequence of events that led up to the discovery of Montgomery's body. Although Faulkner hinted that Sheriff Hampton might dig up Montgomery's body himself without obtaining the proper permission from the court, he deleted this and decided rather that a telephone call to Harrisburg was necessary. Also, it is not clear in the original draft whether Montgomery and Vinson Gowrie were involved in the lumber business; this, too, was clarified in the revision. More significantly, and perhaps to remind the reader-detective of details and events, Faulkner narrates again in the setting copy [358]-[366], the story of Montgomery's exhumation; this retelling of the story partially reinterprets and redefines the episodes we have just read about. Now, the reader is more inclined to use deduction as a method for solving the murders. Since Lucas will be sequestered in Hampton's house and out of reach of the Gowries and any excited townsfolk, Gavin's task, as he sees it, is to verify as quickly as possible the findings of the three detectives.

When Faulkner started writing Chapter Six of the setting copy, he not only referred to some material in Chapter Four of the original draft, later designated as Chapter Five, but also added new sections. At this point, Faulkner does not advance the murder-mystery aspect of the novel, but probes instead Chick's interior state, especially as Chick after having been through such an exhaustive evening, has to deal with his mother. Faulkner did add another retelling of the exhumation scene, this time as recollected by a drowsy Chick (as found on the bottom of page 131 and top of 132 of the first edition) from the perspective of Chick who images himself riding Highboy out to the cemetery behind the truck. This revery, which is actually the beginning of one long sentence, is a fine example of Faulkner's style while rewriting the original draft of the novel; it contains a rhythmic pattern reflecting the specific act of riding a horse, yet retains about it a highly abstract quality: ". . .the truck lights not even in sight during the full half-mile until he slowed him into the long reaching hard road-gait and almost a mile before the truck overtook and then passed and the ruby tail-lamp drew on and away and then was gone but at least he was out of the pines, free of that looming down-watching si-

bilance, uncaring and missing nothing saying to the whole cir-
cumambiance: Look. Look. . . ." When Faulkner reused the
material he had written initially in Chapter Five of the original
draft, he placed the emphasis now on Gavin's philosophical reflections, though later he does mention a clue that the flowers
on the grave had been moved and not replaced, thus preparing
the reader for another surprise: an empty grave.

Thus in Chapter Seven of the setting copy, Faulkner prepared his reader for Nub Gowrie's moment of realization, when
he sees for himself that his son is not in the grave and that, in
fact, two men had been murdered instead of one. As Lucas
grieved for his dead wife, so too, Mr. Gowrie mourns for his dead
(and missing) son. In the original draft, Faulkner altered some of
the Gowrie-Hampton dialogue to achieve a better imaginative
juxtaposition between Lucas and Gowrie, perhaps to hint that
the murderer is the one person who could explain (in the original
draft, neither a black man, nor a note were used to inform Mr.
Gowrie of the situation at the gravesite) why Mr. Gowrie should
go to the cemetery; only this person could give an account of
the body switches and the empty grave. Thus in Chapter Seven,
in its original version and in the setting copy, the pattern again
shifts and a hidden figure is introduced. And when Crawford
is later identified just at the crucial moment before the grave is
found to be empty, two important facts are revealed: Crawford
owned a German automatic pistol and was involved in some timber business. By the end of the seventh chapter of the setting
copy, all the evidence, however circumstantial, is present for
solving the murder; it is just a matter of recognizing that the
pattern does have a definite shape.

Both in the seventh and eighth chapters of the setting copy,
Faulkner has remained relatively faithful to the murder-mystery
dimension of the plot as found in the original draft. In Chapter
Eight, those at the gravesite discuss the two trips made by the
presumed murderer and then stage their own reenactment of the
murders, though the logic behind the switching of the bodies
is never fully probed. The exact path the murderer took is not
clear and so Faulkner reworked this twice in the original draft,
making sure not to reveal prematurely the name of the murderer.
The sheriff shows remarkable perspicacity when Vinson's body is
finally discovered; even though the murder weapon has not been

located, the sheriff knows that it was a German Luger that shot Vinson. With this pseudo-information, it is clear even to Nub Gowrie that Crawford is the most likely suspect. Yet Faulkner has failed to demonstrate the exact relationship between the two Gowrie brothers and Montgomery. In all of this, Faulkner seems content not to alter substantially his original murder story, even though he has left a number of gaps in it.

Faulkner's seventh chapter in the original draft is incomplete, and at best, rather chaotic. We do know, however, that the townsfolk see the body of Jake Montgomery being transported to the undertakers and that Lucas definitely could not have killed Jake since Jake was at Vinson's funeral while Lucas remained in jail. In this original last chapter, Lucas is brought from the jail and put into a car though no satisfactory explanation for this is given. While trying to expand the murder story, Faulkner widened the horizons and intimated that he considered the town's reaction highly significant. Faulkner revised this material as Chapter Nine of the setting copy; it proved to be the most difficult section of the novel and went through at least nine modifications. It becomes clear that there is not time to have a bullet expert come from Memphis, since Vinson would be reburied soon and those in charge wanted to trap the murderer before he could flee. This explains why Lucas is seemingly being transferred by car. In Chapter Nine, Chick insists that the townsfolk ran to keep from having to lynch Crawford. Most of this chapter is devoted not to the murder story, but to a philosophical monologue by Gavin concerning civil rights in the South. From here to the conclusion of the novel, Faulkner is not overly concerned with the events surrounding the murders of Vinson Gowrie and Jake Montgomery. Word is sent to Crawford Gowrie that Lucas is to be transferred to Hollymount to testify at Jake Montgomery's inquest and that the car carrying Lucas would pass by the Whiteleaf cut-off. Eventually Gavin relates in his own idiom Lucas' involvement in the affair and his great reluctance to tell Mr. Workitt why boards of lumber were missing.

As Gavin summarizes his interpretation of the events concerning Vinson's death, he asks one question not found in the first edition: "Why did Crawford have to kill Vinson in order to obliterate the witness of his thieving? [565]-[566]. While

Lucas knew all along that Crawford was guilty, because he "cussed" Lucas so naturally, it is Gavin's question that demands attention and reflection. Unfortunately Faulkner does not do this. After Lucas related Vinson's death in the woods, in a passage which Faulkner deleted, perhaps because it shows an inability to handle this material and also because Gavin's speculations could add more confusion to an interpretation of the events, Gavin imagines Crawford telling Vinson: "I've got that nigger you caught watching that truck is out there in the woods waiting for you. Go talk to him if you still think it was [me] mine" [569 (V)]. Faulkner does compensate for not having Crawford actively present in the novel by having Gavin narrate some facts and impressions about Crawford. Gavin, however, cannot explain the "why" of the murder, though he can account for the "how." Since Crawford has not been a genuine, fully developed *persona* in the novel, it is quite appropriate for his capture to take place outside the drama of the novel, though in no way does it explain completely why he is desperate enough to commit suicide with a gun that should have been taken away from him. With this, however, the balance of justice can be restored, Lucas released, and Gavin paid for his legal services. Faulkner's last three chapters in the setting copy, like the first three, seem to provide a coherent context for understanding the murder-mystery aspect of the novel, rather than developing it as such.

In *Intruder,* as well as in certain other novels, Faulkner never hurried the revelation of his characters; he seemed to have such great respect for them that he allowed them to develop slowly and sometimes did not introduce a new character into a novel until the ones he had already introduced had been sufficiently developed and had some coherent identity in the reader's mind. In establishing the Lucas-Chick relationship in particular, Faulkner suggests right from the beginning that Chick ironically might be the one to save Lucas since he alone in the Jefferson community had a rather involved rapport with Lucas. In the setting copy, the first three chapters develop the Lucas-Chick relationship so as to include the unique quality of this relationship; the story begins in the present, goes through a number of flashbacks, and then returns to the present. The young, naive, white boy is confronted not once, but several times over a period of a few years, by an elderly, experienced black man, in what proves to be more than a student-teacher relationship since one enters into the life of the second in a profound way. Thus the flashback to Chick at age twelve demonstrates the particular nature of the tension between these two individuals and shows the inner emotions that Chick must deal with.

Since *Intruder* reflects a distinctive cultural, social, and historical environment as typically found in the novels of the Yoknapatawpha cycle, it takes time for the characters to interact with one another and reveal the various moods of the South in the late 1930's. Once Gavin has been introduced as the lawyer, the reader expects that Gavin should be the one to prove Lucas' innocence. Thus, a triangular relationship consisting of Lucas, Chick, and Gavin is tentatively suggested; however, when Miss Habersham is introduced this triangular relationship is soon altered, reminding the reader of Faulkner's thematical statements in the Ephraim story that "Young folks and womens, they aint cluttered. They can listen. But a middle-year man like your paw and your uncle, they cant listen. They aint got time. They're too busy with facks" [279]. With the entrance of Miss Habersham, a new triangular relationship is formed where one side of the triangle is progressively unbalanced relative to the other two sides:

1. Lucas
2. Chick
3. Miss Habersham

1. Old	1. Male	1. Black
2. Young 3. Old	2. Male 3. Female	2. White 3. White

Faulkner has put these three factors in tension with one another, so that while they remain clear and separate, they nevertheless form a unity, reminiscent of Coleridge's notion that the creative imagination reconciles opposites. While the work of the two detectives (not counting here Aleck Sander as a real detective) on Lucas' behalf is pitted against Gavin's philosophical speculations, it seems quite clear that Gavin cannot really offer more than the heroic activity of Chick and Miss Habersham.

As Faulkner was writing the original draft, he reminded himself formally that his story was more than a murder mystery; it may be that the story is fictional, imaginative, and even impossible, but it does have a literary theme, that "the white man of the South owes a responsibility to the Negro. . .because of his present condition. . ." [18]. Faulkner clearly believed that the responsibility of one race towards another goes beyond legal considerations and rests ultimately on interpersonal commitments whose bases are human respect and dignity. In the first chapter of the original draft, Faulkner dramatizes the Lucas-Chick conflict by placing Chick at a disadvantage in Lucas' home. Yet Chick reacts positively in perceiving that the odor in Lucas' house is more than a smell, it is "a condition: an idea: a belief: an acceptance, a passive acceptance of the idea that they were not supposed to have facilities with which to bathe properly. . ." [16]. Likewise, Lucas' face is "neither black nor white" [17]; he becomes a representative ("Sambo" in Gavin's terminology) of all the blacks who have been oppressed over the years, both before and after the Civil War.[33] And so Chick, inexperienced in the adult world, cannot blame the food Lucas serves as the source of his uneasiness since "his initial error, misjudgment, had been there all the time. . ." [19]. This sense of Lucas as a mythic person, on the one hand, and the separation of the races that Chick instinctively feels, on the other, become more subtle as Lucas rightly claims kinship to the white side of the McCaslin family; such a situation has created within Lucas, at least in the eyes of the whites, a superior, haughty attitude which they find unacceptable. Faulkner's revision of this material for the setting copy, however, definitely places Lucas' house and his person in a mythic perspective, especially as his face, the one human feature later to become symbolic of all people, seems to lack pigmentation; he is seen as "not arrogant, not even scornful; just intractible and composed," a phase modified later to indicate

---

[33]Cf. Margaret Walker Alexander's favorable discussion of Lucas in her article "Faulkner and Race," *The Maker and the Myth: Faulkner and Yoknapatawpha*, 1977 (Jackson: University Press of Mississippi), p. 112 ff.

that Lucas does have a degree of negroid pigmentation and, curiously enough, a hooked nose.

It is worth noting, too, that like Ike McCaslin, Chick's first genuine encounter with Lucas involves hunting, not deer or bear, but, in this case, mere rabbit. While Lucas is no Sam Fathers, he does initiate Chick into the *mores* of a community on the way to becoming quasi-urban. Even before Lucas had been brought into town for the alleged murder of Vinson Gowrie, he had been one of the catalysts in Chick's life and had manifested himself as a human being who is unique, adaptable, and definitely not a stereotype. Thus Chick must learn to react to and act with this new person and this new situation. He assumes that cigars and an imitation silk dress would normalize their relationship and appease his own sense of shame. Yet Lucas is Chick's match and the more Chick tries to treat Lucas as a "nigger," the more he meets his nemesis. Just as Rider in "Pantaloom in Black," Lucas' life is radically changed by the death of Molly, his wife. Because Chick is preoccupied with his efforts to dominate Lucas, he cannot perceive the depth of feeling in this black man he supposedly knows. When Lucas did not avert his eyes towards Chick on that cold January afternoon for the third time Chick saw him after their initial meeting, Chick felt that his relationship with Lucas had been terminated. Although he knows that he would like to flee from town and avoid any future confrontations, he knows he won't. At the end of the first chapter of the original draft which became the end of the second chapter of the setting copy, it is Lucas who speaks to Chick first, bidding him to summon his uncle, thus reinforcing Chick's premonition that their relationship would somehow continue.

In addition, Lucas is portrayed as a grandfather figure and consequently Chick has no desire to contradict him, especially when Lucas invites him home. From a psychological perspective, Chick's parents in this novel are replaced by grandparent figures (Lucas and Miss Habersham). It is almost as if Faulkner had to jump a generation so that the sins of the biological parents are not visited on their children. Faulkner breaks the genealogical link through this process of generation-distancing so that both grandparents and grandchildren (keeping in mind Aleck Sander) are able to view life from a larger context and not become imitators of the prejudices of their parents. Towards the end of the novel, Gavin seems to have assumed the role of father, not however, in a totally satisfactory way. Not only must Chick learn to deal with Lucas, but he must learn to integrate whatever dimensions of Gavin's philosophy he so chooses into his own framework of life. Furthermore, he must learn not to be smothered and manipulated by his too-comforting mother. Thus, this association of Lucas with Chick's grandfather, reinforced by the gold toothpick and beaver hat, suggests slightly different readings of the novel from the ones proposed by Cleanth Brooks and Olga Vickery, in that Chick has a family heritage that cannot be traced directly to his parents.[34]

This view of *Intruder* is not at odds with seeing the key events in Chick's life as the meal and later the offer to pay for the meal at Lucas' house, events we know as readers would take years for Chick to integrate into his life, precisely because Lucas is removed from him both by race and by one generation. It would take four years for Chick to understand this event, then it would take many more years after that to admit and accept it. It should be noted, in passing, that Molly, a grandmother figure who, like Aleck Sander, is relatively minor, is given a greater role in the setting copy, not only in her own right, but because of her relationship with Mrs. Mallison. In the original draft, there is no mention of Molly's death nor of Lucas grieving. These were part of the second writing of the novel and are revelatory of the fertility of Faulkner's imaginative way of writing a novel. These familial ties, though tenuous, when put together form a web, complicating Chick's motivation more than one might suppose. By ending the first chapter of the setting copy with Lucas refusing Chick's money, Faulkner is preparing us for the conclusion of the novel, one he had not written in the original draft, where Lucas himself pays his legal debt, a debt that could

---

[34]Though Cleanth Brooks and Olga Vickery see close relationships between "The Bear" and *Intruder*, neither one develops the notion of passing on the sins of one generation to the next in *Intruder*, though a comparison with "The Bear" would suggest such an approach. Cf. Cleanth Brooks, *The Yoknapatawpha Country* (New Haven: Yale University Press, 1966), pp. 279-94, and Olga Vickery, *The Novels of William Faulkner* (Baton Rouge: Louisiana State University Press, 1964), pp. 124-44.

ironically be paid only in money, though in this case it becomes absurd when one realizes the way Faulkner revised the number of coins involved in the transaction. As Lucas is observed in his own home, free from the pressures of the Jefferson community, his humanity is captured most vividly in the portrait of him and Molly kept above the fireplace. His gesture of providing a meal and then commanding the boys to shoot rabbit and stay out of the creek after his hospitality has been spurned, likewise point to his inner qualities, as a mulatto who is both gracious and forthright, and though insulted as a host and a human being, is not vindictive, but grandfatherly in the way he deals with an immature white boy and his friends.

In developing the character of Lucas, Faulkner usually put him in dramatic situations; for example, the scene in the country store where he antagonizes the local whites by his demeanor can only remind these men of a genealogical reality that they just as soon forget. This scene represents the lack of recognition that the white man gives the black man in the public forum, though in all honesty, it seems to me that Lucas provoked this particular attack. In addition, in the revisions concerning the three times Chick had seen Lucas since their meeting at Lucas' house, the emphasis on recognition is again stressed, this time, however, on the *non*-recognition of Chick by Lucas—almost a reverse act of parentage in the scriptural sense as when the Father conveyed sonship on Jesus by saying "This is my beloved son, with whom I am well pleased" (Matthew 3:17). When this recognition does not occur, Chick feels free morally and physically. Since Chick has not been acknowledged and recognized as a human being, neither by his own father, nor, in this case, by Lucas as a son or grandson, he lives in an emotional whirlwind which seems to quiet down once Lucas emerges from the car in front of the jail and obliquely offers some acknowledgment. It must be remembered that at the end of the first chapter in the original draft, Lucas recognizes Chick, but Chick has still not been called by name. He has been recognized, but not named. Although Chick feels a sense of freedom before he encounters Lucas at the jail (cf. "He was free." at the end of the first paragraph on p. 27 of the first edition), he is deceived, because in fact, he is far from being free; freedom cannot be static but is always in a forever-changing context. Throughout the novel Chick moves closer and closer to freedom, experiencing all the time its different modalities.

In terms of the entire novel, Chick's freedom is an illusion at this point in his life; he has no other norm to use for evaluating his freedom than his own sense of well-being. Like a musician, Faulkner repeats this motif of freedom in the subsequent episodes of the novel until it takes on a fugue-like pattern. In each of the following situations, Faulkner varies the modality of freedom:

Physical movement possible:	. . .but then he was *free,* hardly even pausing really, walking on to the corner where he would turn for home. . . .(28) . . .because he was *free:* and then he moved. . . .(30)
Possibility of planning for the future:	But then he was *free* and besides it was probably all over by now and even if it wasn't he knew what he was going to do and there was plenty of time for that, tomorrow would be time enough for that. . . . (31)
Psychological experience of liberation:	Because he was *free:* in bed: in the cool familiar room in the cool familiar dark because he knew what he was going to do. . . .(34-35)
Possibility of determining one's course of action:	. . .but then he was *free* and he would feel better after breakfast and he could always say he was going to Sunday school but then he wouldn't have to say anything by going out the back. . . .(38)
Determination of moral responsibility:	Because he was *free.* Lucas was no

longer his responsibility, he was no
longer Lucas' keeper; Lucas himself
had discharged him. (42) [Emphases
mine]

For Lucas, on the other hand, freedom seems to involve responsibility to listen, to imagine, and to be of service to another person. It is only in jail, where Lucas is completely deprived of his
freedom, that Chick gets a real sense of the score between the
two of them: *"He's not only beat me, he never for one second
had any doubt of it"* (73).   Once Chick faces the reality of
his situation with Lucas and admits it to himself, then he is able
to enter into a relationship with this elderly Negro that will
become a liberating experience for both of them.

        Faulkner is conscious of structuring Chick's future growth
once Chick is out of Lucas' house and several times indicates
when the growth will occur, thus giving important directional
signals for the reader. He thus sets up a sense of fluid time as
Chick grows towards greater maturity; there are specific moments of experience and then, over a period of time, the realization of the meaning of that experience:

   1. Real past (seen in the actual meal at Lucas' house).

   2. Flashback past (a conscious part of the present experience in-
       volving the past, but the significance of the past is in the
       present).

   3. Present action (events involved with going to the cemetery,
       digging up the grave, and reporting this to the sheriff).

   4. Revery sequence (the subconscious fusion of the past and pre-
       sent as seen in the recollection of the Mottstown football
       game).

   5. Projected future (the present situation seen from a future per-
       spective as articulated in Gavin's philosophical monologue).

The fusion of inner/outer, chronological/fluid human time,
something crucial to an appreciation of *The Sound and the Fury*,
helps provide a unifying literary device. It is in the interpenetra-

tion of these experiences of time that the novel receives some of its cohesion.

After the Lucas-Chick confrontation in front of the jail, Faulkner seemed impatient to have Chick consult with Gavin and twice in the setting copy ([198] and [206]) he began such a sequence. In this Faulkner departed to some degree from the original draft in that Chick goes to Gavin's office and sits behind his grandfather's desk, perhaps adumbrating his future role as well as the relationship between Gavin and the grandfather. The Mallison dinner scene, not in the original draft either, manifests the familial dimension of the story and provides a home environment as Gavin assumes more and more a father's role. Although Faulkner reworked this new material, he did not alter the nature of the original draft, changing it just enough to give the reader a deeper sense of Chick dealing with white adults. Ironically this meal is too hurried and lacks the graciousness apparent in Lucas' home. Yet, when Gavin and Chick meet, it is quite clear where Gavin stands: "It's Lucas' business, it's not mine" [515 (V)]. This Sunday in May is Chick's day of decision and though he admits in the original draft *"I was wrong. I was wrong all the time"* [32], an admission which provides the hidden impetus for Chick's susequent actions, he, unlike his uncle, ironically accepts Lucas as Lucas would like to be accepted. While Chick must absorb the opinions about Lucas that Gavin shares with him, he also goes ahead and hears Lucas' own abbreviated story; with this, he is in a position to make value judgments based on personal experience and intuition. This seems to be at the core of Faulkner's imagination: openness to what is, as it is, in all its complexity, as it confronts the individual in society. More than Gavin's opposition, however, it is money ("the man, the Negro, the room, the moment, the day itself— had annealed vanished into the round hard symbol of the coin" [181]) that weights Chick down, because it has become for him the substitute for a real human relationship. He needs to understand better the fabric of life and especially his false expectations in striving for "re-equalization, reaffirmation of his masculinity and his white blood" [197]. Thus, the half-dollar Chick threw into the creek is the same amount Ephraim accepts to find the ring. Does Chick, in a sense, pay for his insight into truth? Thus, in the early part of the novel, Gavin assists Chick in coming to such an understanding, not by encouraging him, but by blocking him.

In Chapter Two of the original draft which became Chapter Three of the setting copy, Gavin and Chick (father/son) encounter Mr. Lilley, the choral voice, the representative of the community who does not speak for himself, but whose ideas are voiced through Gavin, who has a penchant for doing this, as he did in interpreting events in Joe Christmas' life in *Light in August.* We feel confident that what Gavin reports is accurate, namely that Lucas should act simply like a "nigger" and the whites would accept him as such. Mr. Lilley's beliefs are written large on the walls of the courthouse where the agony and shame and grief of the South's battles and victories and defeats have been recorded. By isolating this story, Gavin has overlooked the other courthouse and jail stories; his romanticism is historic but cannot reconstruct the actual story involving Lucas waiting inside the walls of the jail.

In this section, Faulkner added an important facet to the text concerning the nature of language and its relationship to truth and how man can get by with a small vocabulary and a few clichés, a notion that he will develop later in the same chapter. Vocabulary is important. Since killing is a simple process, a few words suffice to describe it. Truth is universal and does not rely on figures of speech; all can learn truth—even a child and an old woman. This is corroborated in Miss Habersham's simple statement, which reinforces Gavin's own view of himself: "He's a Negro and your uncle's a man" [307]. Thus Chick at an early stage of the story has a good insight into the philosophical notions relating language and truth, more so than Gavin even at this point:

> . . .and now Miss Habersham in her turn repeating and paraphrasing and he thought how it was not really a paucity a meagreness of vocabulary, it was in the first place beacause the deliberate violent blotting out obliteration of a human life was itself so simple and so final that the verbiage which surrounded it enclosed it insulated it intact into the chronicle of man had of necessity to be simple and uncomplex too, repetitive, almost monotonous even; and in the second place, vaster than that, adumbrating that, because what Miss Habersham paraphrased was simple truth, not even fact and so there was not needed a great deal of diversification and originality

to express it because truth was universal, it had to be universal to be truth and so there didn't need to be a great deal of it just to keep running something no bigger than one earth and so anybody could know truth; all they had to do was just to pause, just to stop, just to wait. . . . [307]

These succinct ideas, so removed from Gavin's verbosity and glibness, indicate that wisdom and truth arise out of specific acts which repeat some universal design. For Faulkner, truth is a simple meditation on the significance of holistic experience.

When entering Lucas' cell, Chick is still under Gavin's influence. In the setting copy, the act of entering is intensified and reinforces the notion that Lucas' work is mythic: "But already they had passed out of the world of man, men: people who worked and had homes and raised families. . ." [256]. Likewise in the setting copy, Chick realizes that he has been appointed to serve Lucas: "It seemed to him that he had known all the time what it would be; he thought with a kind of relief *So that's all it is* even while his automatic voice was screeching with outraged disbelief: 'Me? *Me?*' " [275]. In the original draft [53], but not in the setting copy, it is at this point that Chick's name is given for the first time ("Charles Mallison junior"), suggesting again the correlation between insight, rebirth, and the process of naming—even if the birth is a type of autobirth. It is important, too, that the Ephraim anecdote occurs in the cell scene since the explicit moral which Faulkner likes to repeat is that women and young men are not weighed down by prejudice and can see simple, universal truth, and act accordingly. On [279] Faulkner added, "If you ever needs to get anything done outside the common run, dont waste yo time on the menfolks; get the womens and children working at it." Lucas seems to find comfort in Ephraim's reminder. Thus Chick emerges from the cell as the one in the spotlight since he alone at this point has the motivation and the insight, aided by personal contact with Lucas and the moral of the Ephraim story, to initiate the quest to save Lucas. Chick learns to believe in Lucas not because he is responding to a request, but because he realizes who Lucas is in this unique situation. And perhaps this brings Chick some peace of mind: *"He's not only beat me, he never for one second had any doubt of it"* [281], a realization not in the original draft.

While the middle chapters of the novel focus on the murder mystery as such, nevertheless they present four areas which, when considered from the viewpoint of textual revision, are dramatically important especially as they are linked with the last three, concluding chapters. First, Miss Habersham, introduced in Chapter Four of the setting copy, who, though she comes from an old family and, at present, sells vegetables and chickens for a living, does not fear town pressure or gossip because of her advanced age. In addition, Molly is the daughter of one of Miss Habersham's grandfather's slaves and grew up with Miss Habersham ("almost inextricably like sisters"), so in a sense, Miss Habersham, like Lucas, comes from a racially integrated family. She surprises Chick by her readiness to cooperate in digging up Vinson Gowrie's grave and confirms Chick's belief that this unusual act has rational human significance. Even when she is not in Chick's presence, he retains an image of her as he dreams of her finally going home. In Chapter Nine of the setting copy, her truck is caught up in traffic and she must travel out of Jefferson, almost in a symbolic way, in order to reroute herself back to town. She speaks with an imaginary man in a nightshirt and unlaced shoes:

> *Where you trying to go, lady?*
>
> *I'm trying to get to Jefferson.*
>
> *Jefferson's behind you, lady.*
>
> *I know. I had to detour around an arrogant insufferable old nigger who got the whole county upset trying to pretend he murdered a white man....* [490]

Chick can hardly keep from laughing as he imagines this dialogue and sees the reaction on the man's face as he deciphers what she is talking about. Even when the legal authorities have taken jurisdiction of the case, Miss Habersham continues to help Lucas by guarding the jailhouse door to prevent irate townsfolk from creating a disturbance, or even worse, attacking the jail itself. Throughout the tenth chapter, she remains alert, commenting occasionally in a ladylike fashion, and wearing eighteen-dollar gloves and thirty-dollar shoes. She does not capitulate to exhaustion, but maintains a calm, if somewhat eccentric, presence throughout the entire novel.

Secondly, Faulkner identifies the country Negroes with the land they inhabit. A ten-line description of them in the original draft [78] was expanded into approximately two and a half pages (cf. 95:4-97:10 of the first draft). Even though the Negroes remain out of sight because of the tension in Jefferson, their nervousness is felt. What happens to Lucas will ultimately affect lives and they know it. Unlike the whites who are often associated with weekend trips to the market, the Negroes are identified with the arid land where the road becomes its postulate "of the deliberate turning as with one back of the whole dark people on which the very economy of the land was founded, not in heat or anger nor even regret but in one irremediable invincible inflexible repudiation, upon not a racial outrage but a human shame" [318]. Faulkner is after the feeling, the ambiance, rather than the specific physical description of these people; he penetrates the unseen to what can be felt and understood. While Lucas and Molly are flesh and blood characters, the Negroes peering out fearfully from their windows at night are one step removed. And the Negroes whom Gavin describes in his monologue are even more removed. Faulkner does not include many blacks in this novel, perhaps to emphasize the symbolic role that Lucas plays. Yet, when the detectives expose the truth by digging up the graves, the prejudice against the Negroes is brought to light and can be corrected if the community so chooses. These Negroes, in a state of limbo, are waiting for just such a time when they can be appreciated as human beings and not as the repressed, negative side of the white race.

Thirdly, Faulkner's ideas on language and truth have theological implications as when Chick's insights are associated with "the deathless blood of our Lord not to be tasted, moving not downward toward the stomach but upward and outward into the Allknowledge between good and evil and the choice and the repudiation and the acceptance forever. . ." [322]. This grace note, more apt certainly for *A Fable,* reveals to some extent the dynamics of making a choice and seeking truth. Although Faulkner had included in the original the name of Jesus Christ, he preferred in the revision to delete this and substitute instead "our Lord" and "Allknowledge." Thus Chick's battle both within himself and without fuses the secular and the scriptural. Faulkner does not develop the Christ motif as he had in *A Fable;* however, he does refer in the sixth chapter of the setting copy to "Lucas' crucifixion" [373] and in the last chapter of the setting copy during Gavin's final philosophical excursion, he added a section concerning life's painful memories: "that in-evictible immortal memory awareness of having once been alive which exists forever still ten thousand years afterward in ten thousand recollections of injustice and suffering, too many of us know because of the room we take up but because we are willing to sell liberty short at any tawdry price for the sake of what we call our own which is a constitutional statutory license to pursue each his private postulate of happiness and contentment regardless of grief and cost even to the *crucifixion* of someone whose nose or pigment we dont like. . . ." (emphasis mine) [599]-[600]. When Chick returns home after filling up the grave, he thinks about the enemy in medieval terminology which reflects in a subdued way some of the biblical war imagery: "you believed you had captured a citadel and instead you found you had merely entered an untenable position and then found the unimpaired an unmarked battle set up again in your unpro-tected and unsuspecting rear. . ." [329], an insight not found in the original draft. As with the Mottstown football sequence and the references to World War I, particularly the British offi-cers in 1918, Faulkner compresses Chick's feelings into those of being under seige, yet of not naming the enemy precisely, since that would distort the congeries of feelings and attitudes. By the incremental repetition of these feelings in various images, Chick confronts these emotions within himself and has greater self-understanding.

In all, Faulkner seems to place the values depicted in this novel within a framework of the divinity of the continuity as man. After Chick responds about the young boys leading troops into battle in World War I, Gavin says, "There are some things we must always be unable to bear. Somethings we must never stop refusing to bear no matter how young or old we are. In-justice and outrage and dishonor and shame" [499], with vari-ants on [502] and [505]. As Faulkner revised this section in Chapter Nine, he inserted new pages of material. When Chick and Gavin discuss man's goodness, Gavin says: "He tries to be if they who use him for their power and aggrandizement let me alone. Pity and justice and conscience too—that belief in more than the divinity of individual man: in the divinity of his continuity as Man: think how easy it would [text stops]" [515 (V)]. This material was reworked twice more, deleting at one point the reference to man's divinity and adding it later on [515], and again reaching its final version on [516]-[517], setting copy pages which make up pages 202.1-204.11 of the first edition. Thus, this notion of the divinity of the continuity of man which puts Gavin's views in a far deeper philosophical and theological perspective bothered Faulkner and seemed to come to him as an afterthought.

Lastly, Faulkner emphasizes the reaction of the towns-folk who remain anonymous, afraid to articulate their feelings to one another, and prefer to see Lucas as a curious source of enjoyment. In the setting copy, but not in the original draft, Faulkner noted that Chick "remembered again the faces myriad yet curiously identical in their lack of individual identity, their complete relinquishment of individual identity into one We not even impatient, not even hurryable, almost gala in its complete obliviousness of its own menace, not to be stampeded by a hundred running children. . ." [372]. These onlookers who know the scenario are unwilling to admit that the scene is real and break through the cultural barrier and change their attitudes. Faulkner constantly repeats the refrain, "They ran." In Chapter Seven of the setting copy which is based on Chapter Five of the original draft, Chick, exhausted by his experience the night before, rests and tries to fight off sleep. His subconscious becomes active and Lucas' situation is squarely placed in a community context:

> . . .the whole white part of the county already there patient and biding and neither to be dispersed nor hurried since the county was theirs and hence the town which the county supported by sufferance, theirs the murdered white man and the bereavement of his vacating and the forfeit life of the black protagonist of the grief, theirs the right not to mere justice but to vengeance too to allot or withhold. . . . [111 (V)], [116 (V)]

Ultimately, the face of the white people in town is "just perspicuant jocular and without pity" [111], an image that seemed to obsess Faulkner in both the original draft and the setting copy mainly because it embodied generations of bitterness and hatred.

The last chapter of the original draft shows the direction the novel would take, particularly in describing the town's re-action to viewing Montgomery's body as it is brought in for preparation for burial. When Faulkner revised this material for Chapter Nine of the setting copy, he seemed even more con-cerned with the anonymity of the townsfolk, especially the "children of this lost *fabulous nation* which out of all earth could still afford to keep some of its own idle and sweatless—crowding the street in front of the jail from the blacksmith's to the Square. . . (emphasis mine) [102]. When repeated on [445], the fabulous nation "could still keep some of its own with no compulsion of them to earn their bread. . . ." As Faulkner dealt with the crowd, in Chapter Nine, he reworked scenes over and over, lengthening and expanding them. In his third attempt at the ninth chapter of the setting copy, he wrote, "one Face not even ravening, not even insatiate: just in motion, insensate, vacant of thought. . ." [446]. Likewise in the third revision of this chapter, Chick falling asleep sees himself as an intruder in the dust as he wants to "release into that nothing what little of nothing he had which was all he had which was nothing: dust: who had wanted of course to leave his mark on his time in man, some mark at least on his part of earth. . .to perform something passionate and brave and austere and found all that remained was dust. . ." [474], with variants on [551 (V)], [476], [477], [550 (V)], [472], and [481]. All these variants stress "the chronicle of man's brave passion." Faulkner wanted to perfect this passage, expanding it and making it more refined: Chick wanted to leave "some mark at least on his part of the earth but humbly waiting wanting humbly even not really hoping even nothing (which of course was everything) except one chance one right to perform something passionate and brave and austere not just into man's enduring chronicle, worthy of a place in it— who knew? perhaps adding even one little jot to the austerity of the chronicle of man's brave passion—in gratitude for the gift of time in it, wanting only that and not even with hope, willing to accept the fact that he had missed it forever because he wasn't worthy [text stops] ." Faulkner revised this four more times until he finally achieved the collocation of ideas he wanted on pages 193-194 of the first edition. This dramatic material is ironically enclosed within two separate sections which view the townsfolk as an amorphous "Face."

After Faulkner had finished his revisions and typed the final words concerning Lucas' request for a receipt, he had not put the story completely out of his mind. Robert Haas' letter to Faulkner, dated January 31, 1949, is significant because it shows Random House's willingness to insert new material into reprints of the novel, something, however, that was never done. Faulkner's February 7th reply indicates where he wanted the new material to go: in the middle of Chapter Seven of the first edition, at the conclusion of Gavin's lengthy monologue on "Sambo." Gavin asserts that once the black and white man confederate and an equilibrium is restored, and once the economic, political, and cultural privileges are integrated into the values implied in waiting, enduring, and surviving, then together both blacks and whites will prevail and dominate the United States. Chick pushes Gavin to articulate the conclusion to this thesis, namely that with total integration through racial intermarriages, the Negro would disappear, mainly because there are not enough Negroes to preserve their racial characteristics in any pure way. Curiously, the insistence on racial and social equality will ultimately mean miscegenation and racial extinction, though as Faulkner explains there will be isolated remnants of Negroes found throughout the world. Yet, for all practical purposes, the Negro will only be a record in some historical file, remembered in a revered way, comparable to the Briton recalling "his mystic trace of Norman."

By referring quite explicitly to himself as "a mild retiring little man over yonder at Oxford" where Oxford is as real as LeBourget and LaGuardia airports, Faulkner establishes himself as the authority in linking together *Intruder* with *Absalom, Absalom!*. It would seem that Shreve's tag line that in a few thousand years, he too "will also have sprung from the loins of African kings," is consistent with Gavin's views. Shreve maintains that though the Negro will loose some of his racial characteristics, just as rabbits and birds in the polar regions of the world turn white, the final product "will still be Jim Bond." Gavin's argument is slightly different in that he implies a fusion of the races, without any identifiable final Negro. Shreve's comments in context are simpliste especially when he contends at the end of *Absalom, Absalom!* that "it takes two niggers to get rid of one

Sutpen, dont it?"[35] Ironically Shreve does not see the conclusion to his notion, that his projected progeny too will share in royal African blood.

The specific content of the tag line that Shreve makes refers to miscegenation and the assimilation of the races, and since it occurs at the end of the novel, it should be viewed in terms of some of the preceding action. While Lucas Beauchamp does not bear any inner resemblance to Jim Bond, he does partake of a common ancestry that has had diversified results. Lucas pays his debt to Gavin and is assimilated back into Jefferson society. Jim Bond, on the other hand, like Benjy Compson, is the last of a family that has collapsed and shows little regard to the future. Yet Gavin, in citing this tag line, seems to brush aside Bond since the reality of Bond would disprove his thesis. Has Gavin read *Absalom, Absalom!* carefully? In any case, the naïveté of Shreve's remarks do seem congruous with Gavin's uncritical optimism, and thus, this citation is somewhat consistent with the way Gavin has so far developed his thesis.

To a degree, both novels center around real and alleged murderers (Henry/Lucas) and those who change internally because of the murders (Quentin/Chick). In *Intruder,* the problem is to prove the innocence of Lucas as the alleged murderer of Vinson Gowrie. In *Absalom, Absalom!,* while the problem is more complex, particularly since we have to account for the tellers in the tale, there is little doubt that Henry Sutpen killed Charles Bon. Unlike *Intruder,* more of an emphasis is put in *Absalom, Absalom!* on the family background of the one murdered. What was Henry Sutpen told by his father in the famous library scene? That Charles was part Negro, or that Charles was his half-brother, or both? In the process of vindicating Lucas, Chick grows tremendously, whereas Shreve who has magnificently speculated about the Sutpens and particularly the library scene does not realize that Quentin will commit suicide in the near future. Charles and Henry fuse into the personalities of Shreve and Quentin so that, deep down, the storytellers

---

[35]William Faulkner, *Absalom, Absalom!* (New York: Random House, 1936), p. 378.

assume the identities of the protagonists, perhaps modifying Gavin's view concerning the fusion of the races, to include the fusion of history and fiction, of story and the storyteller. Did Chick assume some of the identity of Lucas? While he manifestly appreciates Lucas' plight, something Gavin never does, Chick and Lugas never really merge into one personality.

Shreve's tag line is meant to synthesize humorously a very complicated story with many internecine relationships and we know he is far more perspicacious than this tag line reveals. His humor never does succeed in reversing the downward thrust of the novel's conclusion, with the discovery of Henry and the burning of Sutpen's mansion. His comment is an ironic jest—a throw-away line, one that he would himself hardly take seriously. Thus, if anything, the allusion to his tag line tempers the happy ending of *Intruder* since Shreve's remarks identify him not only with Jim Bond, but with Charles Etienne Saint-Valéry Bon and Charles Bon, three generations of tragic men who might fancifully be compared to Chick, Gavin, and Lucas. Were Chick to read *Absalom, Absalom!*, he would undoubtedly realize that the vision his uncle refers to in *Absalom, Absalom!* is highly nuanced and less neat than what Gavin has been proclaiming so far. Gavin's allusion to this tag line thus undercuts the pomposity of his own philosophical views since the tragedies of the Jim Bond, Charles Bon, and Charles Etienne Saint-Valéry Bon drain his views of any genuine optimism. Thus by writing a two-page insert, Faulkner refashioned the nature of the novel considerably.

APPENDIX A

There are 609 manuscript and typescript pages of William Faulkner's *Intruder in the Dust* in the Alderman Library of the University of Virginia, including the front material, the original draft of the novel, the setting copy, and miscellaneous pages. The following pages enumerate and describe this manuscript and typescript material. The numbers in the far left column which are in brackets refer in order to each of these 609 pages. The numbers listed in the A columns are the page numbers Faulkner typed on these pages (an asterisk after a number denotes that this number was not typed but is in Faulkner's handwriting). It should be noted that Faulkner renumbered some of these pages. The B columns tell approximately how many lines Faulkner crossed off on a particular page, whether on the upper (U), middle (M), or lower (L) part of the page. This will help identify those pages which contain similar material and give a general idea of the appearance of these pages. The C columns, labeled RECTO and VERSO, describe the front and back of each of the 609 pages. The pages of the setting copy are marked with the job number "40972." Thus "34 40972" refers to the thirty-fourth page of the setting copy which the printer stamped with a red stamp. The numbers in brackets in the C columns always refer to the bracketed number in the far left column. I have not attempted to give a full description of each of these 609 pages; rather I have listed only that information which I considered important to identify each page in order to show its relationship to other pages in this material.

	A	B	C RECTO	A	B	C VERSO
[1]-[11]			This material is explained in Chapter II of this book.			
[12]	1		This entire page is canceled by a red pencil line down the front.	4		The upper half of this verso is crossed off. The lower half has some manuscript writing beginning with "And he would remember . . . .": this is a version of Chapter Ten.
[13]	2- 230	Entire page	The manuscript writing on this page is a version of the original Chapter Ten of the setting copy.			
[14]	3	19 (U)	The manuscript writing has two versions of the original Chapter Ten of the setting copy.	—	14	This verso begins with the words " 'Lucas Beauchamp. . . .' "
[15]	5	1				
[16]	6		The entire page is canceled by a pencil line down the front.	—		This verso begins with the words "nity nor even suspension of a sentence. . . ." Cf. [171 (V)].

	A	B	C RECTO	A	B	C VERSO
[17]	7	9 (L)	The entire page is canceled by a pencil line down the front.	224		This verso begins with the words "was used to it by now...."
[18]	—	1	This page begins with the words "his pocket and old woman...."			
[19]	8	2 (U)	This page is canceled by a pencil line down the center and has the division of Chapters One and Two as they occur in the setting copy. At this point, however, Faulkner did not make this division. The manuscript writing is related to [19 (V)], and begins with "*say aloud that they were wrong....*"	226A		This verso begins with the words *say aloud that they....*
[20]	9		This page is canceled by a red line down the front.	210A		This verso begins with the words "and monstrous...."
[21]	10			209A		This verso begins with the words "boiled into the alley...."
[22]	11		This page is canceled by a red line down the front.	209		This verso begins with the words "anyway stricken...."

	A	B	C RECTO	A	B	C VERSO
[23]	12	14 (U)	The first part of the manuscript writing is like the original Chapter Ten of the setting copy. The second part is like Chapter Ten of the setting copy and begins with the words "Perhaps eating had something. . . ."			
[24]	13	8 (M+L)	The entire page is canceled by two vertical lines.			
[25]	14	11 (U)	The lower half is canceled by one pencil line.			
[26]	15	1				
[27]	L6 [sic]					
[28]	17	6 (L)				
[29]	17A		An inserted page.			
[30]	18	3 (M)				

	A	B	C RECTO	A	B	C VERSO
[31]	19					
[32]	20					
[33]	21		This concludes the first chapter of the original draft.			
[34]	22	8	This page begins Chapter Two of the original draft which is like Chapter Three of the setting copy. This page is canceled by a red line down the front. There is a marginal note: "[one undecipherable word] *get through to daylight* motif."	—		This verso begins with the words, "used instead the cafe there. . . ."
[35]	22A	2	This page is canceled by a red line down the front. An inserted page.	208		
[36]	23			209		This verso is a version of Chapter "IX", and begins with the words: "should have been dust [sic] after twenty-odd. . . ."
[37]	24					

	A	B	C RECTO	A	B	C VERSO
[38]	25		This page is canceled by a red line down the front.	208		This verso is a version of Chapter "IX".
[39]	26					
[40]	27					
[41]	28					
[42]	29					
[43]	30	3 (M+L)				
[44]	31					
[45]	32					
[46]	33					
[47]	34	1				
[48]	35					
[49]	36					

	A	B	C RECTO	A	B	C VERSO
[50]	37	3 (M)				
[51]	38					
[52]	39					
[53]	40	2				
[54]	41	Entire page				
[55]	42	Entire page				
[56]	41A	3 (U)	An inserted page.	—	11	This verso begins with the words "chair in the sun on Paralee's front gallery...."
[57]	43		An inserted page.	—	10	This verso begins with the words "save for his faint...."
[58]	43A	2				
[59]	44	9 (U)	This page ends this chapter.			

	A	B	C RECTO	A	B	C VERSO
[60]	45		There is a marginal note at the top: "[one undecipherable word] *get through to daylight.*"			
[61]	47		Faulkner typed [61] before [62]. He then continued and inserted [62] and [63]. Thus [61] as p. 47 was a mistake since he should have crossed it off and numbered it p. 46. Most of this page has manuscript writing on it relating to this chapter and was probably written when Faulkner was composing the setting copy.			
[62]	46		There are eight lines of manuscript writing on this page which follow the manuscript writing on [61]. An inserted page.			
[63]	46A		The final sequence of these pages is [61], [64], [62], [63], [61 (mss.)], [62 (mss.)]. An inserted page.			

	A	B	C RECTO	A	B	C VERSO
[64]	48	9 (M)				
[65]	49	1				
[66]	50					
[67]	50A		An inserted page.			
[68]	50B		An inserted page.			
[69]	51	7 (U)		—		This verso begins with the words "You can ax [sic] him...."
[70]	52		This page seems to follow [69] since the last word on [69] and the first two words on [70] are crossed off; the new words fit the context.	50		This verso is the original [66].
[71]	53					
[72]	53A	2 (U) 8 (L)	An inserted page.			

	A	B	C RECTO	A	B	C VERSO
[73]	53B		An inserted page.			
[74]	54	13 (U)				
[75]	55		Note the relationship between the first line of this page and the first line of [72] where the word "long" is repeated.			
[76]	56					
[77]	57					
[78]	58					
[79]	59					
[80]	60					
[81]	61					
[82]	62					
[83]	63					

	A	B	C RECTO	A	B	C VERSO
[84]	64		This is the last page of this chapter.			
[85]	65		This chapter was originally labeled "IV", but was later changed to "V".			
[86]	65A		An inserted page.			
[87]	66	6 (U) 6 (L)				
[88]	67	2 (U)		—	19	This verso begins with the words "boy...'then...."
[89]	68	2 (L)	Faulkner crossed off the last two lines of [89] and linked "his uncle moved, started" with "and he watched" on [90 (V)], thus making one sentence.	67		
[90]	69		An inserted page.	69	Entire page	

	A	B	C RECTO	A	B	C VERSO
[91]	69A	12		68A		
[92]	70	3 (U)				
[93]	71 221* 212*		The entire page is covered with manuscript writing in blue ink between the typed lines.	69A	1	This verso is canceled by a single pencil line.
[94]	71A		An inserted page.	70		This verso is canceled by a single pencil line.
[95]	220* 71B		From [95] to [106] there is manuscript writing in blue ink between the typed lines.			
[96]	72 219*					
[97]	73 218*					
[98]	74 217*					

	A	B	C RECTO	A	B	C VERSO
[99]	75 216*					
[100]	76 215*					
[101]	77 214*					
[102]	78 212*		Note that there are two p. 78's.	|		This verso begins with the words "self anything but" and is a rough draft of [369].
[103]	78 211*					
[104]	79 210*					
[105]	80 209*			80		
[106]	81 208*					

	A	B	C RECTO	A	B	C VERSO
[107]	82					
[108]	83					
[109]	84	3 (L)	This is the last page of this chapter.			
[110]	85	11 (L)	This chapter was originally labeled "V", but was later changed to "VII". An inserted page.			The following letter is found on this verso with a line through it.

C VERSO:

The following letter is found on this verso with a line through it.

Feb. 9, 1948

Dear Mr. Russell:

Have been hoping to see you in town or hear from you in regard to my corn patch and your cattle when they broke through the lane fence you and I agreed for you to run down to the creek on my place.

All of us on the creek had a short feed crop last year and it will soon be time to feed work stock again. I suggest we meet at some time soon convenient to you, with whatever judges or

(Cont'd)

	A	B	C RECTO	A	B	C VERSO
[110]	85	11 (L)				(Cont'd) umpires meet your appoeval [sic], and let us reach an agreement on how much corn was lost [end of text]
[111]	86	12 (U)	This page begins with the words "able May", part of the phrase "ineffable May," which was started on [109] as p. 85. Faulkner typed half of [111] as p. 85, then discarded it, and finally used it for p. 86.	86		
[112]	87	3 (L)		—		
[113]	88	7 (L)				
[114]	89	4 (U)				The words "was who" are linked to the last line of [110], thus making the phrase "He was as wide awake now as his uncle was who had slept. . . ." This page is canceled by a pencil line down the front.

	A	B	C RECTO	A	B	C VERSO
[115]	90					This side begins with the words "doors a thin" and has a pencil line down the front.
[116]	91			87		This page follows [111 (V)] and has a pencil line down the front.
[117]	92					
[118]	93		An inserted page.			
[119]	94	11 (U)	The first half of this page was intended as p. 93, then it became p. 94 after Faulkner had inserted [118].			
[120]	95	7 (L)				
[121]	96	5 (L)				
[122]	97					

	A	B	C RECTO	A	B	C VERSO
[123]	98		Cf. [147] for similar manuscript writing. [123] begins with the words "Square, across the mouth of the street moving parallel. . . ."			
[124]	99		A marginal note concerns Nub Gowrie explaining "I got word from a Nigra at breakfast this morning that some kind of bibby sheelying [?] was going on up here. But he ran. I couldn't fetch him or I'd whupped the rest of it out of him. What are *you going to do?*" This note was never incorporated into the text.			
[125]	100	8 (L)				
[126]	101	13 (L)				
[127]	102					
[128]	103					

	A	B	C RECTO	A	B	C VERSO
[129]	104					
[130]	105					
[131]	106		This is the last page of this chapter.			
[132]	107		This chapter was originally labeled "VI" and then changed to "VIII".			
[133]	108					
[134]	109					
[135]	110					
[136]	111	12 (L)				
[137]	112	2 (U)				
[138]	113					
[139]	114					

	A	B	C RECTO	A	B	C VERSO
[140]	115					
[141]	116	2 (M)				
[142]	117					
[143]	118		This is the last page of this chapter.			
[144]	119	17 (L)	The lower half of this page has been crossed off by four vertical pencil strokes.			
[145]	—		This page begins with the words "last were dispersing. . . ." The typing upside down begins with the words "in fact since the street light. . . .": this section is a version of [546].			
[146]	119A			—	4	This verso begins with the words "in a little lost Mississippi. . . ."; these words are all crossed out.

	A	B	C RECTO	A	B	C VERSO
[147]	119B	Entire page	Faulkner crossed off the typed text and wrote in between the lines. Cf. [123] for similar manuscript writing. [147] is an early draft of [123].			
[148]	———		This page begins with the words "waiting to recognize" and is canceled by a pencil line down the front.			
[149]	———		This page begins with the words "waiting to recognize. . . ." It has no pencil line down the front.			
[150]	120	10 (L)	This is the concluding page of the original draft of *Intruder*.			
[151]-[155]			These five pages are the preliminary material for the setting copy.			
[156]	1		2 40972			

	A	B	C RECTO	A	B	C VERSO
[157]	2		3 40972			
[158]	3	3 (M) 2 (L)	4 40972	—		This verso has the date: "Jun 18, 1948", with an arrow pointing to "7" on a scale of 1-12, indicating either 7 A.M. or 7 P.M. This type of stamp was used by The Haddon Craftsmen, Inc., Scranton, Pennsylvania.
[159]	4		5 40972			
[160]	5		6 40972			
[161]	6		7 40972			
[162]	7	1 (M)	8 40972			
[163]	8		9 40972			
[164]	9		10 40972			
[165]	10	3 (U)	11 40972			

	A	B	C RECTO	A	B	C VERSO
[166]	11	1 (M) 3 (L)	12 40972			
[167]	12	2 (U)	13 40972			
[168]	13		14 40972			
[169]	14		15 40972 The last two words are crossed off.			
[170]	15	16 (U+M)	This page is a late version of p. 15. The manuscript writing in red and blue ink is two versions of "Without moving nor even opening his eyes. . ."			
[171]	15	20 (U+M)	This page is an early version of p. 15. This page is canceled by a pencil line down the front.	—		This verso contains a speech of Mrs. Mallison urging to "just let's go." The typing here ends with the word "indig" and is therefore linked with [16 (V)].
[172]	15		16 40972 The last word is crossed off.			

	A	B	C RECTO	A	B	C VERSO
[173]	—		The word "later" is the first word on the page. There is a red line down the middle of the page. This page follows [171] which ends with the words "minutes" and then continues here with "later on".	—		This page is divided into two sections. The first words are "I know all that...." a) This material follows [559]. b) Cf. [19 (V)], [497], [498] for related material.
[174]	16		This page follows [173] and is a second version of [173]. [177] follows this page. This page is canceled by a pencil line down the front.	—		This page is divided into two sections. a) This material follows [202]. The first words are "and the Ingrums...." b) This material seems to follow [497]. The first words are "But still he didn't...."
[175]	15*	6 (M)	17 40972 The marginal note in blue pencil "four of them" is an attempt to make Faulkner's script more legible. An inserted page.			

	A	B	C RECTO	A	B	C VERSO
[176]	16		18 40972 This page is labeled "II" and is a later version since [174] is the original. An inserted page.			
[177]	16A		19 40972 An inserted page.			
[178]	17	1 (M)	20 40972			
[179]	18	1 (U) 3 (M)	21 40972			
[180]	18A		22 40972 An inserted page.			
[181]	19	12 (U)	23 40972			
[182]	20	1 (U)				
[183]	21	9 (L)	25 40972 This page is linked with [194].			
[184]	21A		26 40972 An inserted page.			
[185]	21B		27 40972 An inserted page.			

	A	B	C RECTO	A	B	C VERSO
[186]	22	5 (U)	This page is the original of [194]. The manuscript begins with "But still he didn't move...."			
[187]	22		This page is a carbon on Clearcopy Onion Skin of [186].	—		This verso is a carbon of the first nine lines of [194].
[188]	—	4 (U)	There is a diagonal line through half this page. There are three sections on this page: a) This is the first draft of a section about the events of Sunday morning about 9 A.M. b) This section beginning "So it was all" is a version of [184] at the bottom. c) This section beginning "was the grief" is a version of [184] at the top.			This page resembles [231]; cf. [230 (V)] also. The first words are "around with his nose in the air...." This page is canceled by a pencil line down the center.
[189]	22A		This page begins with the words "firmation of his" and is canceled by a pencil line down the front.	—		This verso is labeled "insert 27".

	A	B	C RECTO	A	B	C VERSO
[190]	—		This page is like [207] because the phrase "men (and some)" is common to both.			
[191]	22A		This page is canceled by a pencil line down the front.			
[192]	22A		This is a carbon copy on Clear-copy Onion Skin of [191]. The typing upside down is labeled p. "45". The manuscript writing repeats what has become unreadable because of the double typing.	—		This verso is a carbon and begins with the words "smear down...."
[193]	23	1 (U) 5 (L)	Two diagonal pencil lines cancel this page.			
[194]	22	9 (U)	28 40972 This page follows [183].			
[195]	23		29 40972			
[196]	24	1 (L)	30 40972			

	A	B	C RECTO	A	B	C VERSO
[197]	25	1 (L)	31 40972			
[198]	26	4 (L)	It looks like Faulkner stopped and then continued in the middle of the page. The conclusion of what was intended as a short story is indicated: "End of suggested story."			
[199]	27	20 (U+M)	This page begins with the words "judgment would have chosen . . . ." This page also has manuscript writing in blue ink in the upper portion of the page which begins with the words "without moving yet nor even opening. . . ." There is a marginal note: "insert 27." Cf. [189 (V)].	22		There are two versions of the section beginning "without moving" in blue and red ink.
[200]	28	24	There are three versions of the section beginning "without moving" in red and blue ink.	22 208		The entire verso is crossed off in red and blue ink. There are two sections in manuscript writing beginning with the following words: a) "without moving. . . ." (Cont'd)

	A	B	C RECTO	A	B	C VERSO
[200]	28	24				(Cont'd) b) "He would remember. . . . [Lucas leaving jail]"
[201]	29	21 (U+M)	There is manuscript writing on page beginning with the words "without moving. . . ."	—		This verso is canceled by a diagonal line. The first words are "he saw him then was not that Lucas' presence. . . ." Cf. [189].
[202]	30	1 (U)	This page begins with the words "Does that matter. . . ." The page is canceled by a pencil line down the front.	—	4	This verso is like [185] and [194], concerning the gift of molasses to Chick and Molly's death.
[203]	26A	2 (U)	This page begins with the words "judgment would have chosen . . . ." The last part of this page is crossed off; this crossed off section begins with the words "a violence. . . ." Cf. [225], [226], [223] for similar references.			

	A	B	C RECTO	A	B	C VERSO
[204]	27		This page begins with the words "judgment would have chosen" and ends with the words "flash at his".			
[205]	28	3 (M)	This page is a version of [208].			
[206]	27		This page begins with the words "judgment would have chosen . . . ." It resembles [207], [214], [216]. There is no dialogue on this page, unlike [204]. This page ends with the words "people knew".			
[207]	27		33 40972 An inserted page.			
[208]	28		34 40972 An inserted page.			
[209]	28A		35 40972 An inserted page.			
[210]	29	14 (U) 2 (L)	36 40972 The lines crossed off are repeated on [209]. Therefore this page is prior to [209]. An inserted page.			

	A	B	C RECTO	A	B	C VERSO
[211]	29		This is the original of [210] since [213] follows this page exactly. This page begins with the words "his and hence" and ends with the words "and cig-".			
[212]	29A	3 (U)	37 40972 This page was written directly after [210] since the crossed-off line on this page follows [210]. An inserted page.			
[213]	30		38 40972 This page follows directly from [211] and begins with the words "arette stubs. . . ."			
[214]	31		39 40972			
[215]	32	4 (M)	This is the original of [216]. This page is canceled by a line down the front.	230	10 (U) 6 (L)	This verso is labeled Chapter "X".
[216]	32		40 40972 An inserted page.			

	A	B	C RECTO	A	B	C VERSO
[217]	33		41 40972			
[218]	34	6 (M)	This is the original of [221].			
[219]	35	4 (L)				
[220]	36		The last line leads into [224].			
[221]	34		42 40972 An inserted page.			
[222]	35		43 40972 An inserted page.			
[223]	36		44 40972 An inserted page.			
[224]	37		45 40972			
[225]	27	12 (U)	The first two words on this page are "a synonym".			
[226]	—		This page resembles [223]. There are only four lines on the page and the first words are "a synonym. . . ."			

	A	B	C RECTO	A	B	C VERSO
[227]	—	9 (U)	This page resembles [223] and [222]. The first words on the page are "where Gieero [sic]...." The manuscript writing begins "sixteen and an old white spin-ster on the way to eighty...." Cf. [313] and [524] for similar passages.			
[228]	—	2 (U)	This page resembles [231] and is canceled by a pencil line down the front. The first three words of the page are "sooner or later [sic] ...."			
[229]	—	Entire page	This page resembles [224]. The first words of the pages are "a Negro. And this [sic]...."			
[230]	—		This is a carbon on Clearcopy Onion Skin of [229].			This verso is a carbon of [188 (V)]. The verso is crossed off by three vertical pencil lines.
[231]	38		46 40972			

	A	B	C RECTO	A	B	C VERSO
[232]	39		47 40972			
[233]	39A		48 40972 An inserted page.			
[234]	40	8 (U)	49 40972 This page follows [232].			
[235]	41		50 40972 The last four words are crossed off.			
[236]	42		51 40972 The first seven words are crossed off. This page follows [234].			
[237]	43		52 40972			
[238]	44		53 40972			
[239]	45					
[240]	—		The first words are "smear down one...." Cf. [192 (V)].			

	A	B	C RECTO	A	B	C VERSO
[241]	45		54 40972 After writing [239] and [240], Faulkner discarded them and went back to this page to begin p. 45 again.			
[242]	46		55 40972			
[243]	47		56 40972			
[244]	48		57 40972			
[245]	49		58 40972			
[246]	50		59 40972			
[247]	51		60 40972			
[248]	52		61 40972			
[249]	53		62 40972			
[250]	54		63 40972			
[251]	55		64 40972			

	A	B	C RECTO	A	B	C VERSO
[252]	—		This page begins with the words "I hope to hell" and is the original of [253].			
[253]	56		65 40972			
[254]	57		66 40972			
[255]	58		67 40972			
[256]	59		68 40972			
[257]	60	1 (U)	69 40972			
[258]	61	3 (M)	70 40972			
[259]	62		71 40972			
[260]	63		72 40972			
[261]	64		73 40972 The last three words are crossed off.			

	A	B	C RECTO	A	B	C VERSO
[262]	65		74 40972 The first three words of this page are the same as the last three of [261].			
[263]	66		75 40972			
[264]	67		76 40972			
[265]	68		77 40972			
[266]	69		78 40972			
[267]	70		79 40972			
[268]	71		This page is the original of [271].			
[269]	72		This page follows [268].			
[270]	72	3 (U)	This page is a second version of [269]. Note that the last word of this page "uncle" continues with "said of" on [273].			
[271]	71		80 40972 An inserted page.			

	A	B	C RECTO	A	B	C VERSO
[272]	72		81 40972 An inserted page.			
[273]	73		82 40972			
[274]	74	3 (M) 6 (L)	83 40972			
[275]	75		84 40972			
[276]	76		85 40972			
[277]	77		86 40972			
[278]	78		87 40972			
[279]	79		88 40972 Note the two green check marks.			
[280]	80		89 40972			
[281]	81		90 40972			
[282]	82	1 (M)	91 40972			

	A	B	C RECTO	A	B	C VERSO
[283]	83		92 40972 There is an insert taped to this page.			
[284]	84		93 40972			
[285]	85	3 (L)	94 40972 There is an insert taped to this page. This page is continuous with [292] where the first eight lines have been crossed off.			
[286]	—	4 (M)	The first two words are " 'Good evening" and the last word on the page is "you".			
[287]	—		The first three words are " 'So is Miss" and the last word on the page is "him".			
[288]	—		The first three words are " 'So i̇s [sic] Miss" and the last word is "do?' ".			

	A	B	C RECTO	A	B	C VERSO
[289]	—		The first two words are " 'Good evening" and the last word on the page is "all".			
[290]	86		95 40972			
[291]	87	9 (L)	96 40972 This page follows [290].			
[292]	87A	8 (U)	97 40972 This text follows [291] in an expanded form.			
[293]	88		98 40972			
[294]	89	2 (L)	99 40972			
[295]	90	10 (L)	100 40972			
[296]	91	4 (U)	101 40972			
[297]	92	5 (L)	102 40972			
[298]	93	5 (U)	103 40972			

	A	B	C RECTO		A	B	C VERSO
[299]	93A		104 40972 An inserted page.				
[300]	94	9 (U)	105 40972 This page follows [298].				
[301]	95		106 40972				
[302]	96		107 40972				
[303]	97		108 40972				
[304]	98		109 40972				
[305]	99		110 40972				
[306]	100	2 (U)	111 40972				
[307]	101		112 40972				
[308]	102		113 40972				
[309]	103		114 40972				
[310]	104		115 40972				

	A	B	C RECTO	A	B	C VERSO
[311]	105		116 40972			
[312]	106		117 40972			
[313]	107	3 (L)	118 40972			
[314]	—		This page begins with the words "orchards) so maybe" and follows [313: line 26].			
[315]	108	12 (L)	This page follows [314].			
[316]	—		This page begins with the words "the men, the young" and is the original p. 108.			
[317]	109		120 40972 This page picks up from the middle of [315].			
[318]	110		121 40972			
[319]	111		122 40972			
[320]	112		123 40972			

	A	B	C RECTO	A	B	C VERSO
[321]	113		124 40972			
[322]	114		125 40972			
[323]	115		126 40972			
[324]	116		127 40972 Note the change of Amanda Gowrie's dates: 78 1892--1926 [sic]			
[325]	117		128 40972			
[326]	118		129 40972			
[327]	119		130 40972			
[328]	120		131 40972			
[329]	121		132 40972			
[330]	122		133 40972			
[331]	123		134 40972			

	A	B	C RECTO	A	B	C VERSO
[332]	124		135 40972			
[333]	125		136 40972			
[334]	126		137 40972			
[335]	127		138 40972			
[336]	128	3 (L)	139 40972			
[337]	129		140 40972 This page follows [336]. The crossed-off lines on [336] are included on the top of this page.			
[338]	130		141 40972			
[339]	131		142 40972			
[340]	132		143 40972			
[341]	133		144 40972			
[342]	134		145 40972			

	A	B	C RECTO	A	B	C VERSO
[343]	135	7 (M)	146 40972			
[344]	136	2 (L)	147 40972			
[345]	136A		148 40972 This is an inserted page with only three lines.			
[346]	137		149 40972 This page follows [344].			
[347]	138		150 40972			
[348]	139	10 (L)	151 40972			
[349]	140	1 (L)	152 40972			
[350]	141		153 40972 An inserted page.			
[351]	—		This page begins with the words "her: 'thinking....'" This page follows [349].			
[352]	142		154 40972			

	A	B	C RECTO	A	B	C VERSO
[353]	143	14 (L)	155 40972			
[354]	143A		156 40972 An inserted page.			
[355]	144		157 40972 This page follows the crossed-off portions of [353].			
[356]	145		158 40972 This page follows [355] as the first three words are crossed off and continues the thought of the last three words on [355].			
[357]	146		159 40972 The last word is crossed-off.			
[358]	147		160 40972 This page follows [357] as the crossed-off word on [357] is repeated on this page.			
[359]	148		161 40972			
[360]	149		162 40972			

	A	B	C RECTO	A	B	C VERSO
[361]	150		163 40972			
[362]	151		164 40972 The last word is crossed off.			
[363]	152	2 (L)	165 40972 The word crossed off on [362] is repeated on this page.			
[364]	~~153~~ 213*	Entire page	This page follows [363]. There is manuscript writing on this page which is part of the original draft sequence of pages [93]-[106].			
[365]	154	1 (L)	This page follows [364].			
[366]	153	5 (U)	166 40972 The crossed-off lines follow from [365]. After this, the text picks up from [363].			
[367]	154		167 40972			

	A	B	C RECTO	A	B	C VERSO
[368]	155	5 (M&L)	168 40972			
[369]	—		This page follows [368]. Note that the lower portion of the page with phrases like "behind his uncle's car he could," "steady flow," and "midway carnival" are similar to those on [370]. Cf. [102 (V)] for similar phrases.			
[370]	156		169 40972 This page was inserted after [369] was discarded.			
[371]	157		170 40972 The last four words are crossed off.			
[372]	158		171 40972 This page follows [371] since the four words crossed off on that page form a poorly phrased idiomatic expression which was corrected on [372].			
[373]	159		172 40972			

	A	B	C RECTO	A	B	C VERSO
[374]	160		173 40972			
[375]	161		174 40972			
[376]	162		175 40972			
[377]	163		176 40972			
[378]	164		177 40972			
[379]	165		178 40972			
[380]	166		179 40972			
[381]	167		180 40972			
[382]	168		181 40972			
[383]	169		182 40972			
[384]	170		183 40972			

	A	B	C RECTO	A	B	C VERSO
[385]	171		184 40972 The first two words of this page are crossed off; it looks like this page follows [384] since the crossed-off words are synonymous with the ones actually used.			
[386]	172	1 (L)	185 40972			
[387]	173		186 40972			
[388]	174		187 40972			
[389]	175	1 (L)	188 40972 Note that the word "teeming" on [389] and [390] gives continuity to the text.			
[390]	176		189 40972			
[391]	177		190 40972			
[392]	178		191 40972			
[393]	178A		192 40972 An inserted page.			

	A	B	C RECTO	A	B	C VERSO
[394]	179	14 (U)	193 40972 This page follows [392].			
[395]	179A		194 40972 An inserted page.			
[396]	180	12 (U)	195 40972 This page follows [394].			
[397]	181		196 40972			
[398]	182		197 40972			
[399]	183		198 40972			
[400]	184		199 40972			
[401]	185		200 40972			
[402]	186		201 40972			
[403]	187		202 40972			
[404]	188		203 40972			

	A	B	C RECTO	A	B	C VERSO
[405]	189		204 40972			
[406]	190		205 40972			
[407]	191		206 40972			
[408]	192		207 40972			
[409]	193		208 40972			
[410]	194		209 40972			
[411]	195		210 40972			
[412]	196		211 40972			
[413]	197		212 40972			
[414]	198		213 40972			
[415]	199		214 40972 The last four words are crossed off.			

	A	B	C RECTO	A	B	C VERSO
[416]	200		215 40972 This follows [415] since the crossed-off words on [415] are synonymous with the words on [215].			
[417]	201		216 40972			
[418]	202		217 40972			
[419]	203		218 40972			
[420]	204		219 40972			
[421]	205		220 40972			
[422]	206		221 40972			
[423]	207		222 40972			
[424]	208		223 40972			
[425]	208		This page begins with the words "The truck was another pick (Cont'd)			

	A	B	C RECTO	A	B	C VERSO
[425]	208		(Cont'd) up." This page is labeled Chapter "IX" and is similar to [35 (V)], [38 (V)], [543 (V)], [547 (V)], and [549 (V)].			
[426]	208		This page is a carbon of [425] on unmarked carbon paper.	—		This verso begins with the words "thirty years ago" and concerns British soldiers and man's enduring chronicle. Cf. [486] and [531] for similar passages.
[427]	209-213*		This page follows [425]. The typing is crossed off and manuscript writing fills the entire page. The manuscript is connected with p. 213, as numbered at the bottom; both the manuscript and the number are in blue ink. The manuscript resembles [465].			
[428]	209		This page follows [424] and is the original p. 209 of the setting (Cont'd)			

	A	B	C RECTO	A	B	C VERSO
[428]	209		(Cont'd) copy. The page begins with the words "after twenty-odd miles ...."			
[429]	210	14 (U)	This page follows [428].			
[430]	211	16 (U) 1 (L)				
[431]	211		This is a carbon of [430] on unmarked carbon paper.	cf. note	3 (U)	Note: this verso is numbered "212-210*-211*-212*." This page is canceled by a red line down the front. This is a carbon of [469].
[432]	211A		This page follows the next-to-last line of [430].			
[433]	212	15 (U)	This is another version of [432].			
[434]	212	15 (U)	This is a carbon of [433] on unmarked carbon paper.	2143		This is a carbon of [449]. This page is canceled by a red line down the front.

	A	B	C RECTO	A	B	C VERSO
[435]	213		This page follows [434] and begins with the words "across it toward...."			
[436]	213		This is a carbon of [435] on unmarked carbon paper.	214		This verso is a carbon of [450] and is canceled by a red line down the front.
[437]	214-215*	12 (U) 3 (L)	This page follows [435].			
[438]	2145		This page follows [437].			
[439]	216	2 (M)	This page follows [438]. Cf. [470].	—		The verso has only two words: "covered that".
[440]	—		This page is a version of [439] and begins with the words "ting out of it...."	—		
[441]	209		224 40972			
[442]	210		225 40972			

	A	B	C RECTO	A	B	C VERSO
[443]	209	1 (L)	This page begins with the words "thought we already. . . ."			
[444]	210	10 (L)	This page begins with the words "in front. . . ."			
[445]	211		This page begins with the words "lowing in its turn. . . ."			
[446]	212		This page begins with the words "them in one inextricable. . . ."			
[447]	212		This is a carbon of [446] on unmarked carbon paper.	—		This verso is a carbon of [536].
[448]	213		This page begins with the words "people yet with nobody. . . ."			
[449]	214⁄3		The manuscript writing on this page is a continuation of the manuscript writing on [427].			

	A	B	C RECTO	A	B	C VERSO
[450]	214		This page begins with the words "in the maroon earthenware pot...."			This verso is a carbon of [437].
[451]	215	3 (L)	This page begins with the words "which had held him...."			
[452]	215	3 (L)	This is a carbon of [451] on unmarked carbon paper. This page is canceled by a line down the front.	214		
[453]	216		This page begins with the words "of them both [sic] slender...."			
[454]	217	1 (U)	This page is continuous with [453] according to the first edition, though the text itself does not seem to read smoothly. This page begins with the words "a turn to the left...."			
[455]	218		This page begins with the words "Miss Habersham...."			

	A	B	C RECTO	A	B	C VERSO
[456]	209		This page begins with the words "the other the normal...."			
[457]	209		This is a carbon of [456] on unmarked carbon paper.	—		This verso is a carbon of [461] and begins with the words "muscled and asleep...." This page is canceled by a line down the front.
[458]	211* 211-209*	12 (U) 2 (L)	This page begins after the crossed-off section with the words "merchants and cotton buyers" and follows [543 (V)].			
[459]	212* 212-210*	3 (L)				
[460]	211	7 (U)				
[461]	—		This page is related to [459] and begins with the words "muscled and asleep...." An inserted page.			

	A	B	C RECTO	A	B	C VERSO
[462]	210A		Cf. [548 (V)] for a similar page.			
[463]	211		226 40972			
[464]	212		227 40972			
[465]	213		228 40972			
[466]	214		229 40972			
[467]	215		230 40972			
[468]	216		231 40972 An inserted page.			
[469]	cf. note	13 (U)	Note: this page is numbered "210*-211*-212-214*." There is manuscript writing in red and blue ink in the upper half of this page. Cf. [427] since the page number "214" above follows "213" on [427].			
[470]	217		232 40972 This follows [439].			

	A	B	C RECTO	A	B	C VERSO
[471]	216	8 (L)	This page is a version of [480].			
[472]	217	9 (L)	Cf. [550 (V)] and [481] since both pages begin with "ling by the hand...."			
[473]	—		This page begins with the words "That damned Gavin...."			
[474]	—	3 (M)	This page begins with the words "how to xxxxx [sic] escape...."			
[475]	224	3 (M)	This page follows [492].			
[476]	—		This page begins with the words "one chance...." Cf. [426 (V)] for a similar passage about "man's enduring chronicle."			
[477]	—		This page begins with the words "it could possibly...."			
[478]	214		This page begins with the words "flick! again...."			

	A	B	C RECTO	A	B	C VERSO
[479]	215		This page begins with the words "ing or rather...."			
[480]	216	3 (L)	This page begins with the words "'You see?'" Cf. [471] for a similar page.			
[481]	217		This page begins with the words "ling by the hand...." Cf. [472] and [550 (V)] for similar passages.			
[482]	cf. note	6 (U)	233 40972 Note: this page is numbered "222* 219 218*-219*." This page follows [455].			
[483]	cf. note	3 (U) 4 (L)	234 40972 Note: this page is numbered "223* 220 220*."			
[484]	221	1 (M)	The first words on this page are "Blow the horn.'"			
[485]	222	7 (L)	Notice the reference to "birth-mark" as on [475].			

	A	B	C RECTO	A	B	C VERSO
[486]	223		This page begins with the words "thirty years ago. . . ." Cf. [531], [426 (V)], and [476] for similar passages.			
[487]	224		This page begins with the words "form something passionate. . . ."			
[488]	225	1 (L)				
[489]	220A		235 40972 An inserted page.			
[490]	221	9 (U)	236 40972			
[491]	222	9 (M&L)	237 40972			
[492]	223		238 40972			
[493]	224	7 (L)	239 40972			
[494]	224A		240 40972 An inserted page.			
[495]	225		241 40972			

	A	B	C RECTO	A	B	C VERSO
[496]	226	11 (L)	242 40972			
[497]	226A		This page begins with the words *say aloud....*			
[498]	226A		A longer version of [497].			
[499]	226		This page begins with the words "'Yes,' his uncle...."			The verso is labeled Chapter "X" and begins with the words "But time or not...."
[500]	226	1 (M)	This is a version of [499] and begins with the words "'Yes,' his uncle...."	—		
[501]	226	11 (L)	This page begins with the words "'It's gone,' he...."			
[502]	227		This page follows [501].			
[503]	226AB	5 (U) 4 (L)	Cf. [535 (V)] for a carbon. An inserted page.			

	A	B	C RECTO	A	B	C VERSO
[504]	226BC	7 (L)	This follows [503]. Cf. [520 (V)] for a similar passage. An inserted page.			
[505]	226GD	1 (U) 5 (L)	Part of this page is related to [504] and part to [502]. An inserted page.			
[506]	227	1 (U)	243 40972			
[507]	228		244 40972			
[508]	229		245 40972			
[509]	230		246 40972			
[510]	231		247 40972	—	5 (U)	This verso is a version of [175] where Chick is trying to give Lucas coins. The first words of this page are "at least he...." The page is crossed off in red ink and plain pencil.
[511]	232		248 40972			

	A	B	C RECTO	A	B	C VERSO
[512]	233		249 40972	226A-1		This verso is crossed off in red ink and plain pencil.
[513]	234	1 (L)	250 40972			
[514]	234A		251 40972 An inserted page.	—	12 (U)	This verso begins with the words "safely only. . . ." It is a rephrasing of the material on [532].
[515]	234B		252 40972 An inserted page.	234B	18 (U&M)	a) The upper part of this page concerns Chick's inability to get to sleep quickly and not count sheep and is a preliminary version of [219]. b) the lower part is about Gavin's theory of the divinity of the individual man and comes before [533].
[516]	234C		253 40972 An inserted page.			
[517]	234D		254 40972 An inserted page. The last three words are crossed off.			

	A	B	C RECTO	A	B	C VERSO
[518]	235		255 40972　The first two words are crossed off.			
[519]	236		256 40972			
[520]	237		257 40972	cf. note	8 (U)	Note: this verso is numbered "226-C-1". Cf. [504] for a similar passage.
[521]	238		258 40972　This page is labeled Chapter "XI", but should really be Chapter "X". This was a typing mistake by Faulkner. An inserted page.	230	13 (L)	This verso is labeled Chapter "X".
[522]	228		This page is a carbon of [539 (V)] on unmarked carbon paper. The page begins with the words "Or perhaps it was the eating. . . ." This page is canceled by a red line down the front.	——	4 (U)	This page is a carbon of [538 (V)].
[523]	229		This page begins with the words "you see. . . ."			

	A	B	C RECTO	A	B	C VERSO
[524]	229		This page begins with the words "sixteen and an old...."			
[525]	230	13 (L)	This page is labeled Chapter "X" and begins with the words "Without moving...."	—		This verso is labeled Chapter "X" and begins with the words "Without moving...." There are seven lines on this page.
[526]	—		This page is labeled Chapter "X" and begins with the words "Without moving...." The last words on the page are "dar's vast diastole."	—	5 (M)	This verso is labeled Chapter "X" and begins with the words "Still not moving...."
[527]	—	5 (M)	This page is a carbon of [526] on unmarked carbon paper. This page is canceled by a red line down the front.	—		This verso is a carbon of [525 (V)].
[528]	—		This page is labeled Chapter "X" and begins with the words "Without moving...." It ends with the words "further awake."	—	7 (L)	This verso is labeled Chapter "X" and begins with the words "Still not moving...." It ends with the words "supper too."

	A	B	C RECTO	A	B	C VERSO
[529]	—		This page is a carbon of [528] on unmarked carbon paper.	—		This verso is a carbon of [514 (V)] and begins with the words "safely only...." This verso is canceled by a red line down the front.
[530]	230-	12 (L)	This page is labeled Chapter "X" and begins with the words "Without moving...."	238		This verso is labeled Chapter "XI" and begins with the words "Perhaps eating...."
[531]	—		This page begins with the words "thirty years ago...." Cf. [486].			
[532]	231	16 (L)	Cf. [514 (V)] for a version of the crossed-off lines.			
[533]	234C		This page begins with the words "anyway of one serene...."	—		This verso has three lines beginning with the phrase "in the same chew...." Cf. [521] for a similar phrase.
[534]	235	8 (U)	After the crossed-off words, this page begins with the words "the stores and...."			

	A	B	C RECTO	A	B	C VERSO
[535]	235		This is a carbon of [534] on un-marked carbon paper.	226AB	5 (U)	This verso is a carbon of [503] and is canceled by a red line down the front.
[536]	—		This page begins with the words "purpose was to keep Willy Ingrum's nocturnal...."			This verso begins with the words "on the outside wall...."
[537]	238A	10 (U)	259 40972 An inserted page.			
[538]	239		260 40972	—	7 (U)	This verso begins after the crossed-off words with the words "But he didn't move...." Cf. [522 (V)] for the carbon.
[539]	240		261 40972	228	15 (M&L)	This verso is labeled Chapter "X" and is the original of [522 (V)]. It begins with the words "Or per-haps it was the eating...."
[540]	241	10 (L)	262 40972	—	15 (U&M)	This verso begins with the words "judgment would have chosen...."
[541]	242	5 (U) 1 (L)	263 40972			

C VERSO	B	A	C RECTO	B	A	
			264 40972	6 (M)	243	[542]
This verso is labeled Chapter "IX".	13 (L)	208	265 40972 An inserted page.		243A	[543]
This verso begins with the words "But not tonight; two oclock this afternoon...." This verso is a longer version of the lower part of [444].	12 (U&M)	210A	266 40972 An inserted page. Cf. [536 (V)] as both pages deal with the telephone system connected to the bell on the outside wall.	7 (M)	243B	[544]
			267 40972 An inserted page. The "B" was typed by mistake and then changed to a "C".		243BC	[545]
This verso begins with the words "Yes, there are some things...." The text concerns Gavin stating that it is 9:30 [P.M.] and there is time for Chick to take a shower and eat supper. Cf. [502] and [505].	11 (U&M)	—	268 40972	5 (U) 4 (L)	244	[546]
This verso is labeled Chapter "IX". and differs from [543 (V)].	16 (L)	208	269 40972 An inserted page.		244A	[547]

	A	B	C RECTO	A	B	C VERSO
[548]	cf. note	6 (U) 8 (L)	Note: this page is numbered "24*b* 3-B." The middle section refers to "Willy Ingrum's nocturnal counterpart." Cf. [536] for a similar passage.	210A		This verso is a version of [462].
[549]	245	3 (L)	270 40972	208	16 (L)	This verso is labeled Chapter "IX" and differs from [547 (V)].
[550]	246	2 (U)	271 40972 This page follows [549].	——	13 (U&M)	This verso begins with the words "ling by one hand. ..." The text concerns Chick trying to go to sleep and rid himself of thoughts about Lucas. Cf. [472] and [481] for similar passages.
[551]	247		272 40972	——	13 (U&M)	This verso is a later version of [473]. It resembles [475] also.
[552]	247A		273 40972 An inserted page.			
[553]	248	14 (M)	274 40972 This page follows [551].			

	A	B	C RECTO	A	B	C VERSO
[554]	249		275 40972	—	1 (U)	This verso has part of one sentence on it: "heavily sighing voice; 'I thought we settled this three times this afternoon.'" It is related to [443] and [555].
[555]	250	4 (U)	276 40972			
[556]	251		277 40972			
[557]	252	1 (L)	278 40972			
[558]	253		This is the original of [559].			
[559]	253		279 40972			
[560]	254		280 40972			
[561]	255	8 (L)	281 40972			
[562]	—		This page begins with the words "watching him...." It is the original of [563].			

	A	B	C RECTO	A	B	C VERSO
[563]	256		282 40972 This page follows [561].			
[564]	257	1 (U) 14 (L)	283 40972			
[565]	257A		284 40972 An inserted page.			
[566]	257B		285 40972 An inserted page.			
[567]	257C		286 40972 An inserted page.			
[568]	258	11 (U)	287 40972 This page follows [564].			
[569]	257A		This page begins with the words " ' "And you let...." "	259A		This verso begins with the words " ' "No. He cussed [sic]...." "
[570]	259	3 (L)	288 40972 This page is related to [569 (V)].			
[571]	259A		289 40972 An inserted page. This page is related to [569 (V)].			

	A	B	C RECTO	A	B	C VERSO
[572]	260		This page is the original of [573].			
[573]	260	9 (L)	290 40972 An inserted page.			
[574]	—		This page begins with the words "but almost" and ends with the words "a natural." It is the original of [575].			
[575]	261	3 (M)	291 40972			
[576]	262	1 (L)	292 40972			
[577]	263		293 40972	—	8 (U)	This passage concerns Crawford Gowrie's background, his deserting the army and serving time in Leavenworth and Parchman.
[578]	264		294 40972			
[579]	264A		295 40972 An inserted page.			
[580]	265	5 (U)	296 40972 This page follows [578].			

	A	B	C RECTO	A	B	C VERSO
[581]	266		This is the original of [582].			
[582]	266		297 40972			
[583]	266A		298 40972 An inserted page.	——	4 (U)	This verso begins with the words "out, what would you do first, want to do first before you left for good never to come back, if your name was Gowrie. . . ."
[584]	266B		299 40972 An inserted page.			
[585]	267		300 40972 This page is labeled Chapter "XII"; it should be labeled "XI".			
[586]	268	2 (M)	301 40972 The last two words are crossed off.			
[587]	269	10 (L)	302 40972 The last four words are crossed off in blue ink.			
[588]	269A		303 40972 An inserted page.			

	A	B	C RECTO	A	B	C VERSO
[589]	270	2 (L)	304 40972 It looks like this page originally followed the crossed-off words on [587].			
[590]	270A		305 40972 An inserted page.			
[591]	271	5 (U)	306 40972 This page follows [589].			
[592]	272		307 40972			
[593]	273		308 40972			
[594]	274		309 40972			
[595]	275	11 (L)	310 40972			
[596]	276					
[597]	276		311 40972 This follows [595] an inserted page.			
[598]	276A		312 40972 An inserted page.	——	11 (U)	This verso follows [596] and is a version of [599].

	A	B	C RECTO	A	B	C VERSO
[599]	277	4 (U) 3 (M)	313 40972 This follows [597].			
[600]	278		314 40972			
[601]	279		315 40972			
[602]	280	4 (M)				
[603]	281					
[604]	280		316 40972			
[605]	281		317 40972	—		There is a date on the verso: "Received June 1, 1948."
[606]	156A		This page and the following two form a part of the novel which Faulkner wanted included in the second printing of *Intruder*. The page number "156A" refers to the first edition pagination.			

	A	B	C RECTO	A	B	C VERSO
[607]	B					
[608]	B		This is a carbon of [607] on un-marked carbon paper.			
[609]	—		Blank sheet.			

APPENDIX B

This is a list of corrections made by the Random House editorial staff on the setting copy pages. The column on the left indicates the page on which the correction occurs and the column on the right indicates the page in the first edition where the correction was made, if a correction was made at all. A number of marginal notes have been included in the column containing the corrections.

Setting Copy Page	Corrections	First Edition Page
2 40972.5	He ——→ Chick ["Author: Should this be Chick Mallison?" (Correction not made)]	3.5
4 40972.1	atartled ——→ startled	4.23
4 40972.3	immanent ——→ immanent	4.25
4 40972.4	with the their ——→ with their	4.26
5 40972.19	almost a log/, whose ——→ almost a log whose	6.2
6 40972.17	except for the hat/, and ——→ except for the hat and	6.31
6 40972.23	intractible ——→ intractable	7.3
8 40972.9	intractible ——→ intractable	8.15
8 40972.24	as they ——→ as the	8.31
9 40972.15	intractible ——→ intractable	9.18
9 40972.25	where people /, with ——→ where people with	9.28

Setting Copy Page	Corrections	First Edition Page
10 40972.8	calender ⟶ calendar	10.7
10 40972.26-27	even the having been told he had remembered ^ sitting ⟶ he had remembered even the having been told, sitting	10.28-29
11 40972.20	something ⟶ something	11.15
12 40972.22	whi h ⟶ which	12.13
13 40972.7	eccept ⟶ except	12.21
13 40972.12	entere ⟶ entered	12.27
17 40972.18	[Reference to "four of them" (Marginal note to clarify Faulkner's handwriting)]	16.14
18 40972.6	yap ing ⟶ yapping	17.6
20 40972.7	whom ⟶ who	18.14
20 40972.14	afternnon ⟶ afternoon	18.20
21 40972.5	purchse ⟶ purchase	19.6

Setting Copy Page	Corrections	First Edition Page
22 40972.9	himself youngish ⟶ himself a youngish ["OK/?" (Marginal note)]	20.5
24 40972.13	dcarcely ⟶ scarcely	21.19
25 40972.18 26 40972.1	was was the ⟶ was the	22.21
26 40972.13-15	...gone? Why didn't... [Deletion of a sentence by Faulkner]	23.2
28 40972.11	intractible. ⟶ intractable,	23.28
28 40972.15	before before he ⟶ before he ["?" (Marginal note)]	23.32
28 40972.26	countrt ⟶ country	24.2
29 40972.16	sytaight ⟶ straight	24.30
30 40972.13	youched ⟶ touched	25.23
31 40972.17	inesthetisable ⟶ inanesthetisable ["Author: inanesthetisable?" (Marginal note)]	26.24

Setting Copy Page	Corrections	First Edition Page
32 40972.2	Lucas saying ——→ Lucas: saying ["'Author: saying: (?) as line 5 infra p. 26?" (Correction not made)]	27.2
32 40972.5-7	..that me? Because it was. . . [Deletion of a sentence by Faulkner]	27.5-6
32 40972.8	["End of suggested story." (Marginal note: Not in Faulkner's handwriting)]	27.7
33 40972.2	to shoot anybody/, least of all one named Gowrie/, before ——→ to shoot anybody least of all one named Gowrie before	27.24-25
33 40972.7	or land- / and ——→ or land- and ["'land=/" (Marginal note)]	27.30
35 40972.12	steube ——→ stübe	29.29
37 40972.11	they had ——→ (they had	30.26
41 40972.24	Sundayin ——→ Sunday in	34.2

Setting Copy Page	Corrections	First Edition Page
42 40972.6	for for being ⟶ for being [This correction was made by the typesetter in plain pencil]	34.13
42 40972.15	Feaser ⟶ Fraser	34.23
43 40972.6	excrutiation ⟶ excruciation	35.9
43 40972.9	penententiary ⟶ penitentiary [This correction was made by the typesetter in plain pencil]	35.12
46 40972.10	graitutous ⟶ gratuitous	37.32
47 40972.24	have ^been thick ["Author: ?/been" (Marginal note)]	39.11
48 40972.9	bachekor ⟶ bachelor	39.23
49 40972.14	or lack ⟶ of lack	39.32
49 40972.21-22	...to bury. They have... [Deletion of a sentence by Faulkner]	40.6
50 40972.15	goimg ⟶ going	40.25

Setting Copy Page	Corrections	First Edition Page
53 40972.5	some of then ⟶ some of them	42.32
53 40972.5	had even see ⟶ had even seen	42.33
53 40972.8	barnership ⟶ barbershop	43.3
53 40972.15	reslly ⟶ really	43.8
55 40972.9	intractible ⟶ intractable	44.28
57 40972.11	pausing the ⟶ pausing to ["Author: anything left out or OK/?" (Marginal note)]	46.12
58 40972.13-14	where cant ⟶ where you cant ["Author: OK/?" (Marginal note)]	47.10-11
58 40972.26	Lawyer? Them ⟶ Lawyer? Them	47.25
59 40972.20	de½end ⟶ depend	48.12
60 40972.23	faint with ⟶ faint with ["Author: bulb? light? /?" (Marginal note: Correction made to "faint bulb with")]	49.12

Setting Copy Page	Corrections	First Edition Page
61 40972.8	brick. ⟶ brick,	49.24
63 40972.13	no tonight ⟶ not tonight	51.22
64 40972.15	waits ⟶ waist	52.21
65 40972.20	Hampton (/.'s ⟶ Hampton's	53.22
67 40972.6	hanges ⟶ hinges	54.29
68 40972.21	steps a ⟶ steps a ["Author: OK? or in, into?" (Marginal note: Correction made to "steps and into a")]	56.11
68 40972.24	fuve ⟶ five	56.15
73 40972.19	watchinh ⟶ watching	60.10
75 40972.16	Now.. ⟶ Now.	61.30
75 40972.18	intractible ⟶ intractable	61.33
77 40972.13	vale Hollymount ⟶ Hollymount ["Hollymount/" (Marginal note)]	63.10

Setting Copy Page	Corrections	First Edition Page
78 40972.19	self defense ⟶ self-defense ["=OK/?" (Marginal note)]	64.8
79 40972.22	penetentiary ⟶ penitentiary	65.6
80 40972.2	door/,. ⟶ door.	65.13
80 40972.16	corborundum ⟶ carborundum	65.27
84 40972.22	mead ⟶ meat	68.25
84 40972.25	insuoerable ⟶ insuperable	68.29
85 40972.12	face ⟶ faced ["Author: faced?" (Marginal note)]	69.10
85 40972.21	Mount Hope ⟶ Caledonia	69.17-18
88 40972.16	In fact ⟶ In fack ["Author: In fack?" (Marginal note: Correction not made)]	71.31
91 40972.15	cow ot ⟶ cow or	74.15

Setting Copy Page	Corrections	First Edition Page
92 40972.25	"even before he saw the watch—small gold in a hunting case suspended by a gold brooch on her flat bosom like and in almost exactly the same position as the heart sewn on the breast of the canvas fencing vest—because since his grandmother's death no other woman in his acquaintance wore even owned one and in fact" ["insert on p. 83" (Marginal note)]	75.20-26
93 40972.1	Hanersham ⟶ Habersham	75.29
93 40972.13	speng ⟶ spent	76.9
94 40972.16	"with the neat small gold watch pinned to the flat unmammary front"	77.9-10
96 40972.10	rabbit of ⟶ rabbit or	78.23
98 40972.23	exhume up ⟶ exhume it ["OK/?" (Marginal note)]	80.4
99 40972.11	said/. again ⟶ said again	80.19
101 40972.20	oicked iy ⟶ picked it [This correction was made in plain pencil by typesetter]	82.2

Setting Copy Page	Corrections	First Edition Page
106 40972.13	fury andd. ⟶ fury and	85.6
112 40972.4	paucity/, a ⟶ paucity a	89.16
112 40972.6	humen ⟶ human	89.18
113 40972.10	comptehended ⟶ comprehended	90.18
114 40972.5	rove ⟶ untied [This correction probably made by the typesetter, since the typesetter used a plain pencil to put a check mark on each of the galley pages. There is a question mark in plain pencil in the margin, not in blue pencil as has been used by Erskine: rive = "to tear out"]	91.7
118 40972.1-2	to two ⟶ to do two ["OK/?" (Marginal note)]	94.14
121 40972.1	bothw ould ⟶ both would	96.16-17
121 40972.12	desert amd ⟶ desert and	96.28
122 40972.19	donw ⟶ down	97.33

Setting Copy Page	Corrections	First Edition Page
123 40972.7	stromg ——→ strong	98.15
124 40972.3	in int the ——→ it in the ["?" (Marginal note in plain pencil probably made by typesetter)]	99.3-4
124 40972.18	head/, among ——→ head among	99.18-19
126 40972.23	Lucas sais ——→ Lucas said	101.15
129 40972.5	took/, jerked ——→ took, jerked	103.16
135 40972.20	lat ——→ last	108.33
139 40972.4	slicing ——→ slicing	111.25
141 40972.8-12	[Reference to Aleck Sander saying that Miss Habersham and Chick thought he had no doubts about going with them. "Author: On 103, A.S. is on horse and going before he knows about truck or Miss H." (Marginal note)]	113.20-25
142 40972.1	over ——→ oven	114.9
142 40972.11	to, look ——→ to look	114.20

Setting Copy Page	Corrections	First Edition Page
145 40972.4	do it / ⟶ dc it--	116.30-31
145 40972.16	rest/. ⟶ rest.	117.11
145 40972.20	an ⟶ any	117.15
152 40972.4	listening /, , he ⟶ listening, he	121.25
153 40972.3	["Author: fifty,?" (Marginal note: no change made)]	122.19
154 40972.12	got?)) ⟶ got?"))	123.25
154 40972.19	ao ⟶ so	123.32
157 40972.17	him/.'/ that ⟶ him that	126.1
157 40972.26	too/. Paralee ⟶ too. Paralee	126.11
159 40972.19	horried ⟶ horrified ["Author: Horrified harried worried see *MS*?" (Marginal note)]	127.27
159 40972.24	. . jail:' ⟶ already. . . . [A phrase has been deleted]	127.32

Setting Copy Page	Corrections	First Edition Page
160 40972.20	it /,:tasting ⟶ it: tasting	128.22
162 40972.21	lound ⟶ loud	130.11
162 40972.27	too lound ⟶ too loud	130.17
163 40972.19	unto ⟶ into	131.4
167 40972.11	dense--rank ⟶ dense rank	134.4
167 40972.16	linament ⟶ liniment	134.9
168 40972.4	dirt of ⟶ dirt or	134.26
168 40972.10	a) where had ⟶ where he	134.33
	b) in, of a ⟶ in, a ["OK/?" (Marginal note)]	134.33
169 40972.6	Sure ⟶ Square	135.16
169 40972.8	curn ⟶ curb	135.19

Setting Copy Page	Corrections	First Edition Page
171 40972.5-6	was was out ——→ was out [Typesetter's correction in plain pencil]	137.9
174 40972.7	Jury's ——→ Jury'll ["Author: Jury'll?" (Marginal note)]	139.28
176 40972.9	ehad ——→ ahead [Typesetter's correction in plain pencil]	141.14
176 40972.14	----- ——→ $\frac{2}{em}$	141.19
176 40972.16	sgain ——→ again	141.20
178 40972.3	----- ——→ $\frac{2}{em}$	142.26
179 40972.12	a) ----- ——→ $\frac{1}{em}$	144.13
	b) ----- ——→ $\frac{1}{em}$	144.13
181 40972.18	withhold ——→ withhold	146.8
184 40972.22	----- ——→ $\frac{2}{em}$	148.33

Setting Copy Page	Corrections	First Edition Page
185 40972.6	[Reference to Armstead. "Author: Not Armstid, as in Hamlet, Light in August?" (Marginal note: Faulkner did not make this suggested change, though it is "Armstid" in the original draft which was later crossed out and retyped "Armstead" [116])]	149.10
185 40972.7	—→ $\frac{2}{em}$	149.11
186 40972.2	a) ---→ $\frac{1}{em}$	150.2
186 40972.2	b) ---→ $\frac{2}{em}$	150.3
186 40972.19	c) agin —→ again	150.21
187 40972.24	horison —→ horizon	151.23
189 40972.8	an —→ any	152.31
191 40972.6	priviledge ——→ privilege	154.22
191 40972.19	[Reference to "gasoline of another white man." "Author: as another. . .?" (Marginal note: changed to "gasoline as a white man")]	155.3

Setting Copy Page	Corrections	First Edition Page
191 40972.20	anywh en ——→ anywhen [Typesetter's correction]	155.3
194 40972.6	priviledges ——→ privileges	156.14-15
195 40972.21	a least ——→ at least	156.33
196 40972.5	intractible ——→ intractable	157.11
196 40972.23-24	perpindicular ——→ perpendicular	157.29-30
198 40972.19	——→ $\frac{2}{em}$	159.15
201 40972.20	name/, of ——→ name of	161.32
204 40972.18	[Reference to "firy." "Author: wiry fiery /?" [Marginal note: changed to "fiery"]]	164.12
207 40972.10	ineluctible ——→ ineluctable	167.11
210 40972.24	——→ $\frac{2}{em}$	170.3
211 40972.11	——→ $\frac{2}{em}$	170.16

Setting Copy Page	Corrections	First Edition Page
211 40972.20	bauk ⟶ back	170.25
214 40972.15	⟶ $\frac{2}{em}$	173.7
216 40972.18	set/, yesterday, ⟶ set yesterday,	174.31-32
217 40972.11	⟶ $\frac{2}{em}$	175.19
218 40972.5	stride ⟶ strides	176.7
218 40972.14	throufh ⟶ through	176.17
218 40972.22	lomg ⟶ long	176.26
224 40972.9	saturday ⟶ Saturday	180.24
225 40972.6	obto ⟶ onto	181.27
225 40972.16	[Reference to "uninsatiate." "Author: nor uninsatiate equals: insatiable? or does it? OK?" (Marginal note: no change made from setting copy to first edition.)]	182.4
232 40972.21	now south ⟶ not south ["Author: not/?" (Marginal note)]	187.33

Setting Copy Page	Corrections	First Edition Page
233 40972.18	accelerator/, solitary ⟶ accelerator solitary	188.21-22
236 40972.11	him ⟶ he ["Author: he/?" (Marginal note)]	190.1
238 40972.4	[New paragraph indicated]	191.4
238 40972.21	⟶ $\frac{2}{em}$	191.21
241 40972.6	aint', ⟶ aint,'	193.9
242 40972.14	[Reference to "uninsatiate." "Author: as on 210 [225 40972]" (Marginal note: no change made)]	194.14
243 40972.19	that ⟶ than ["Author: OK/?" (Marginal note)]	195.2
244 40972.21	th ⟶ to ["OK/?" (Marginal note)]	195.33
245 40972.24	unvle ⟶ uncle	196.25
246 40972.20	weee ⟶ were	197.22

Setting Copy Page	Corrections	First Edition Page
247 40972.12	⟶ $\frac{2}{em}$	198.10
247 40972.17	sox ⟶ socks ["Author: socks/?" (Marginal note: correction not made)]	198.15
247 40972.22	npw ⟶ now	198.20
249 40972.18	forseighted ⟶ foresighted	200.4
250 40972.11	kill/. and ⟶ kill and	200.23
255 40972.9	abd endure ⟶ and endure	204.20
256 40972.5	⟶ $\frac{2}{em}$	205.8
256 40972.24	⟶ $\frac{2}{em}$	205.30
256 40972.25	⟶ $\frac{2}{em}$	205.30
284 40972.4-8	[Reference to two phrases in the setting copy: " . . .who owned the trees and the resulting lumber and so could do what he liked with it and the mill crew who were hired by the day and therefore didn't care what went on at night as long as they got their money each Saturday. . .who owned	224.5-6
284 40972.12-16		224.11-14

Setting Copy Page	Corrections	First Edition Page
	the trees and the resulting lumber and so could do what-ever they liked with it and the mill crew who were hired by the day and so wouldn't have cared even if they had known what was going on at night as long as they got their pay every Saturday..", "Author:?↱" (Marginal note: this query concerns the duplication of the text. Ultimately, the first edition follows the text as modified by Faulkner.)]	
285 40972.13	———→ $\frac{2}{\text{em}}$	225.7
286 40972.2	———→ $\frac{2}{\text{em}}$	225.23
286 40972.15	———→ $\frac{2}{\text{em}}$	226.3
287 40972.17	Sat'dy ———→ Sat-dy ["Sat=dy" (Marginal note)]	226.11
288 40972.6	--———→ $\frac{2}{\text{em}}$	226.26
288 40972.10-11	almost before Lucas had left home good and now it for him ^was ———→ for him almost before had left home good and now it	226.31-32

Setting Copy Page	Corrections	First Edition Page
291 40972.3	----→ $\frac{2}{em}$	228.10
291 40972.9	it /. but ----→ it but	228.17-18
291 40972.22-23	[Reference to "insomnambulism." "?" (Marginal note: no change made.)]	228.27
291 40972.25	Cick ----→ Chick	228.30
292 40972.12	Ceawford ----→ Crawford	229.11
292 40972.17	----→ $\frac{2}{em}$	229.17
292 40972.21	it /, apparently, ----→ it apparently,	229.21
293 40972.7	[Reference to "within in." "Author: OK/?" (Marginal note: no change made.)]	230.2
293 40972.16	----→ $\frac{2}{em}$	230.12
294 40972.3	priviledge ----→ privilege [Typesetter's correction]	230.30
294 40972.13	----→ $\frac{2}{em}$	231.8

Setting Copy Page	Corrections	First Edition Page
296 40972.14	Qilly ——→ Willy	232.6
298 40972.7-8	beneath the weight of stopper-full gallon jugs so that for years ^ you could ——→ for years beneath the weight of stopper-full gallon jugs so that	233.20-21
299 40972.7	----- ——→ $\frac{2}{em}$	234.15
300 40972.8	slaes ——→ sales	235.9
301 40972.20-21	through their supercharged amplifiers than ever ^ to be heard ——→ than ever through their super- charged amplifiers to be heard	236.11-12
303 40972.	[Page number 289-A changed to 269-A]	
304 40972.10	corbon ——→ carbon	238.8
304 40972.13	[Reference to "what." "Author: t/? or something left out" (Marginal note: Faulkner deleted phrase "unified in what move-ment" and substituted "dowelled into one interlocked mosaic so infinitesimal of motion as to be scarcely worthy of the word," thus indicating that this correction and perhaps the one on [284 40972] were made after Albert Erskine's correction.	238.12

This would mean that Faulkner actually saw some of these corrections (as Erskine told me in a private interview), approved them, and made some additional corrections of his own.)]

Setting Copy Page	Corrections	First Edition Page
304 40972.16	even or ⟶ even on	238.16
304 40972.23	horse /, or ⟶ horse or	238.22
305 40972.6	automobile/; not ⟶ automobile: not	238.30-31
305 40972.12 306 40972.6	We we cannot ⟶ We cannot	239.4
306 40972.8	subrose ⟶ subrosa ["?" (Marginal note: correction made.)]	239.6
306 40972.11	out ⟶ our	239.8
306 40972.25	scract ⟶ scratch	239.26
307 40972.12-13	Lucas/, crossing the Square, probably at the same time/,— ⟶ Lucas crossing the Square, probably at the same time—	240.6-7
307 40972.16-17	afternnon ⟶ afternoon	240.10

Setting Copy Page	Corrections	First Edition Page
308 40972.10	button/, but ⟶ button but	240.28
308 40972.11	[Insert "and the worn gold loop of the watchchain—"]	240.30-31
308 40972.19	intractible ⟶ intractable	241.6
310 40972.13	⟶ $\frac{2}{em}$	242.14
311 40972.12	have/,. ⟶ have.	242.31
311 40972.21-26	[Reference to "Caledonia Church." "Author: OK that Lucas says (76) [85 40972] Chapel." (Marginal note: no change made.)]	243.5-6 243.11-12
311 40972.24	a voided ⟶ avoided	243.9
313 40972.6	Stevens's ⟶ Stevenses	243.19
314 40972.8	⟶ $\frac{2}{em}$	244.12
316 40972.7-8	the purse took a half dollar and laid it on the from ^ desk ⟶ from the purse took a half dollar and laid it on the desk	247.2
317 40972.19	intractible ⟶ intractable	247.2

INDEX

Absalom, Absalom!, xv, 9, 48-49, 52, 55-56, 116, 248, 281-83

Agee, James, 77

Aiken, Conrad, 249

Akers (film character), 235

Alderman Library (University of Virginia), xvii, 2-4, 24, 52, 55, 59-60, 64, 285

Aleck Sander, 36, 68-70, 72, 87-88, 94-96, 99, 116-17, 128-29, 152, 155, 156-61 (trip to cemetery), 167, 169, 175, 178, 185, 207, 225-26, 247, 250, 255, 260, 266, 268-69, 375, 391

Alexander, Margaret Walker, 267

Algonquin Hotel, 42

Ambler, Eric (*Uncommon Danger*), 10

America (film character), 235

American Academy of Arts and Letters, 48

Anderson, Sherwood, 44

Armstead (Armstid), 103, 378, 391

Art as Experience (John Dewey), xv

Ash, Old Man, 238-39

As I Lay Dying, 48

Bacher, William, 11, 16

Backhouse (Backus), Lieutenant, 237

Backhouse (Backus), Melisandra, 237

Baptiste, Simon Laroque (*Come in at the Door*), 230

Barnett, Ned, 22

Barr, Caroline (Callie), 46, 70

Basso, Hamilton, 41

"Bear Hunt, A," 238

"Bear, The," 43, 269

Beat Four, 34, 99, 132, 135, 138-39, 159, 171-72, 176, 179, 186, 188, 211, 258

Beauchamp, Lucas, 3, 7-8, 22-23, 31, 35, 47, 51, 66-76 (including Lucas' house), 77-81 (in jail), 105-06, 114, 117, 119, 126 (physical description), 127-29 (Lucas' house), 130-34 (encounters with Chick), 136-41, 142-49 (in jail), 152, 154, 169, 171, 177 (as "Sambo"), 181, 183, 186-88, 192, 201, 204, 208, 215, 219-26, 227-28 (pays legal fees), 231, 237, 238-39, 253, 257-62, 264-70, 272-75, 277-79, 283, 312, 348, 383, 386, 387, 390

Beauchamp, Molly, 74-75, 85, 88, 97, 128-31, 134, 156, 158, 238, 268-70, 276-77, 312

Berkeley, Jr., Edmund, xvii

Bessemer Foundry, 21

Bilbo, Theodore, 25

Birdsong, 3

Blankton (town in *A Fable*), 246

1. P. 1, supra 5:   Bob Haas feels this first He should be immediately identified. It doesn't bother me either way, but Chick Mallison could be put in in [sic] parentheses without violating the consistent pattern of reference that holds for the rest of the book—where *he* always means Chick.

2. P. 4, supra 1:   . . .have been expected and even excused for doing/ shd strictly be expected to do and even etc.

3. P. 4, center: neither cold or not/ nor?

4. P. 15, infra 5:   at last the man had something / had said something?

5. P. 21B, infra 2:   hers and Lucas' married daughter / not correct usage though it sounds better to me than *her* would

6. P. 25, infra 9:   inesthetisable / doesn't mean anything (unless it be "incapable of being made sentient"); meaning, I think, calls for in*an*esthetisable

7. P. 26, supra 2:   colon after saying would be uniform with similar form on 25, i 5.

8. P. 28A   *steube* / cant find anywhere

9. P. 30, supra 11:   Lucas would have been / wdnt this be clearer if *should* have been? /

10. P. 39, infra 3:   Sunday would have thick with dark hands / would have been?/ or what?

11. P. 48, infra 9:   pausing the speculate / to ?/ or something left out?

12. P. 49,   where cant hear / where you cant ? / or what then?

13. P. 51   lighted each other by a single faint with / faint bulb? / light ?/ or what?

14. P. 58

risette- / this stumps me not in any Eng or Am dict. Larousse is helpful: petit ris agréable. Yet somehow I think I've heard or read this word to mean some special kind of a curve. Surely it isnt simply smile-shaped hinges.

15. P. 59, infra 6:

mounted one last steps a passage / something missing?

16. P. 76, center:

while they face one another / faced?

17. P. 79, infra 11:

with facks. In fact. . ./ I figure a man who says facks will likely say in fack [unclear typing] too, but this may be based on a system instead of oversight.

18. P. 122

Uncle Gavin's theory of pants-buttoning / Chick earlier (p. 34) makes a similar observation of self-buttoning, apparently on his own, then later (p. 153) refers to it again as Uncle Gavin's. This is not important at all, and is explicable on the grounds that Uncle G is fond of saying this and does so often; but Chick's earlier use of it (for the reader) does take a little of the edge off Uncle G's remark on p. 122.

19. P. 130, supra 10:

Only when we got to the truck. . . ./ Aleck Sander's explanation here does not fit with original event (p. 103), in which he gets on the horse with apparently the intention already of going before he even knows about the truck and Miss H (unless he was only riding down to open the pasture gate, which seems unlikely), and I don't know if we are to take it he's forgotten why or is lying or what. It is of no great importance but seems worth pointing out in case it is an oversight.

20. P. 141, supra 3:

a bachelor of fifty thirty-five years free / comma after thirty ?

21. P. 146, infra 9:

horried /? a typo full of possibilities: harried, worried, horrified/ which is it? or is it something else still?

22. P. 161, supra 7:   the Grand Jury's get you / Jury'll ?/

23. P. 167, infra 4:   perspicuant / this invention is hard to get a hold on: its form seems to relate it more to perspicuity (transparency) than to perspicacity (discernment), though the latter signification seems more likely in the context. (Dict has an obs form perspicience, from which could be derived perspicient.)

24. P. 172, supra 6:   Armstead / Light in August and The Hamlet both have family name of Armstid, and in the Hamlet the name appears in a similar constellation of names.

25. P. 172, infra [sic] :   Anglo Saxons / Uncle Gavin could just as well include Anglo Saxons (whatever they are) as except them from this generalization, which is full enough of holes anyway without inventing Anglo Saxons to try to plug them up.

26. P. 178, infra 9:   gasoline of another white man / as another white man /?

27. P. 189, infra 9:   firy / wiry, fiery ?/ or what?

28. P. 210, infra 11:   nor uninsatiate / doesn't the *nor* in front of the double negative prefix cancel the *un-* and leave the *in-*in force?   So that we then have a sentence meaning that the Face is not ravening but *is* insatiable? It seems to me mean [sic] the opposite of this (though perhaps I misinterpret—it comes to be almost a mathematical problem in the addition of negative numbers).

29. P. 217, infra 8:   going now south but east now / going not south /?

30. P. 221, supra 2:   than him / he /?

31. P. 226, infra 2:   uninsatiate / (not even) same as note on 210

32. P. 227, infra 8:   more men that Garnett / than /?

33. P. 231, center: sox / why not socks?

34. P. 234A, infra 3:   conceptible / I thought at first this was a coinage (by analogy with susceptible) but dict has it as obs form meaning conceivable; it also has conceptive (capable of conceiving) and I wonder if that is not the meaning intended here?

35. P. 248, infra 2:   rang / this seems o k, but it might be a typo /? (turned and rang the short . . .dead empty block)

36. P. 257A, supra 4-7 and supra 12-16:   I wonder if the almost identical repetition of lines 4-7 is not an error made in copying from an earlier draft ??

37. P. 263, supra 7:   had been dug up within in— / ok /?

38. P. 270, center: unified in what movement / that /?

39. P. 276, infra 1 & 6:   I suppose it's all right for Uncle G to call it Caledonia Church, though Lucas (p. 76) says Caledonia Chapel.

40. P. 278, supra 10:   patina-ed / there *is* the word patinated, which is nice. Cf. 39 for use of this word relating to a gun.

[The following corrections were originally typed on a larger typewriter; the last correction indicates that Faulkner himself wrote these.]

41. Page 83, down through line 23. Change rest of page to read:

head such as his grandmother had used to wear and then he recognized her even before he saw the watch—small gold in a hunting case suspended by a gold brooch on her flat bosom almost like and in almost exactly the same position as the heart sewn on the breast of the canvas fencing vest—because since his grandmother's death no other woman in his acquaintance wore or even owned one and in fact he should have recognized the pickup truck: Miss Habersham, whose name was now the oldest which remained in

42. Page 85, down through line 15. Change line 24 to read [someone has circled "24" and written a question mark above it] :

dollars and ninety-eight cents with the neat small gold watch pinned to the flat unmammary front and the shoes and the gloves

43. Page 68. Line 13. Correct Hollyvale to read 'Hollymount'.

44. Page 76, line 21/. Correct Mount Hope Chapel to read 'Caledonia Chapel.'

45. Page 273, line 11. Change line 11 to read:

coat not soiled so much as stained under the black coat and the worn gold loop of the watch-chain—

46. Re Hollymount: It seems to me I named this town before, in Sartoris and Sancyurary [sic] both, but I have forgot what now. I think I have caught the only inconsistencies in this one thought, and Hollymount will do.

[There are check marks by these numbers: 6, 7, 9, 10, 11, 12, 13, 15, 16, 17, 20, 21, 22, 24, 26, 27, 28, 29, 30, 31, 32, 33, 37, 38, 39, 41, 42, 43, 44, 45. Some of the check marks are faint, though I think the list is accurate. There is a question mark before 46.]

APPENDIX C

This is a list of comments and suggested corrections made by Albert Erskine of Random House. The page numbers refer to the setting copy pages. The last six corrections were made by Faulkner.

Bleak House (Charles Dickens), 232

Blotner, Joseph, xiii, xiv, xvi, 1, 4, 5, 7, 15, 31, 34, 52, 53, 65, 232, 234

Bon, Charles, 282-83

Bon, Charles Etienne Saint-Valéry, 283

Bond, Jim, 55-56, 281-83

Bookwright, 103

Bowers, Fredson T., xv, 65

Brackett, Leigh, 12

Brandt, Carol, 36

Breit, Harvey, 45

Brooks, Cleanth, 252, 269

Brown, Clarence, 49, 56, 64, 91

Brown, John, 220

Burger, Knox, 35

Cagney Productions, 34

Caledonia Chapel, 84, 147, 259, 371, 387, 393

Campbell, Harry, 36

Campbell, William (*Come in at the Door*), 230

Carter, Hodding, 25, 43

"Centaur in Brass," 239

Cerf, Bennett, 9, 12, 28, 30, 32, 34, 36, 37, 42

Cerf, Phyllis, 30, 42

Chandler, Raymond (*The Big Sleep*), 12

Chase, Richard, 45

Chatto and Windus, 42

Chicago, Illinois, 135, 139

Christmas, Joe, 274

Cicero, Illinois, 135

Civil War, 14, 44, 267

Cobb, Humphrey (*Paths of Glory*), 11

Coldfield, Rosa, 55

Coleridge, Samuel T., 266

Collected Stories of William Faulkner, 45, 47, 237, 248

Collier's, 20, 35

Collins, Carvel, 36

Columbia University, 4

Come in at the Door (William Campbell), 230

Commins, Saxe, 26, 27, 28, 34, 42, 49

Compson, Benjy, 282

Compson, Caddie, 253

Compson, General, 90, 158

Compson, Quentin, 55, 282

Cooper, Minnie, 248

Corporal (*A Fable*), 46, 242-44

Cotton, Ernest, 248

Coughlan, Robert, 41

"Courtship, A," 33

Cowley, Malcolm, 13, 14, 15, 17, 18, 27, 41-48, 50, 56

Cowley, Muriel, 42

Crane, Joan St. C., xvii

Crossman County, 92, 161, 163, 225, 256, 261

Cullen, Hal, 234

Cullen, Linburn, 234

Dandridge, Maggie (Chick's grandmother), 129

Davis, Anne Louise, 35

Death in the Family, A (James Agee), 77

Dennis, Stephen, 65

Department of Justice, 245

De Spain, Major, 90, 158, 237, 238

Detroit, Michigan, 54

Devine, Eric "Jim," 42, 229

Dewey, John, xv

Dickens, Charles, 43, 231-33 (in-

fluence on Faulkner)
"Divorce in Naples," 237
Doctor Martino and Other Stories,
248
Don Quixote, 43
Double Dealer, The, 249
Downs, Mrs., 83, 148
"Dry September," 248
Dukinfield, Judge, 239
DuPre, Jennifer, 237

Edmonds, Carothers, 67, 70, 73,
127-28, 132, 136-37, 141, 158
Edmonds, Carothers "Roth," 238
Edmonds, Zack, 238
Ellery Queen Mystery Magazine,
14
Ephraim, 80, 83, 84, 146, 148,
163, 173, 266, 273, 275
"Error in Chemistry, An," 14
Erskine, Albert, 34-36, 133, 151,
153, 225-26, 373, 385, 385, 389
Exsultet, 187

Fable, A, xv, 1, 2, 7, 11-12, 41, 43,
46, 48, 61, 162, 175, 235, 242-47,
277
Fadiman, Regina, xiv, 65
Falkner, Dean Swift, 45
Falkner, Judge J. W. T., 235
Falkner, Maud Butler, 70
Farmer, Cecilia, 78-79
Fathers, Sam, 90, 158
Faulkner: A Biography, 5, 8, 16
Faulkner-Cowley File, The, 14,
15, 17, 18, 46, 50
Faulkner in the University, 1, 51,
252, 253, 256
Faulkner, John, 47
Faulkner, Malcolm, 36

Faulkner, Miscellany, A, 55
Faulkner Studies, 51
Faulkner, William, (allusion to
himself) 281; (corrections of
tye typescript) 393-94; (family)
5, 6, 36, 45; (financial pres-
sures) 4, 5, 7-10, 13-16, 18,
20, 24-25, 30, 32, 36, 39, 40,
41, 44, 49
Fieldstone Sanitarium, 45
Films, "Background to Danger"
10; "Barn Burning" 13; "Battle
Cry" 11, 235; "Big Sleep, The"
12; "Country Lawyer" 11;
"Damned Don't Cry, The" 12;
"Deep Valley" 11; "Fog Over
London" 12; "God is My Co-
Pilot" 12; "Liberation Story"
10; "Life and Death of a Bomb-
er" 11; "Mildred Pierce" 12;
"Southerner, The" 46; "Stallion
Road" 13; "Strangers in Our
Midst" 12; "To Have and Have
Not" 12
"Fire and the Hearth, The," 3,
238
Flags in the Dust, 27
Ford, Ruth, 45-46
Forkner, Benjamin, xvii
Forrest, General N. B., 237
Fraser, ------ (in "Monk"), 241
Fraser, Doyle, 103, 138-40, 221,
248, 368
Freudenberg, Anne, xvii, 60-61
Frost, Mark, 236

Glasgow (town in *Intruder*), 80,
92, 114, 145, 161, 163
Go Down, Moses, 2, 10, 40, 41,
52, 53, 238
Gold, Joseph, 232, 250-51

"Gold is Not Always," 3
Goodwin, Lee, 23
Gowrie, Amanda Workitt, 37, 92, 160, 261, 336
Gowrie, Crawford, 114-15, 177, 199, 208, 211-12, 215, 220-25, 230, 235 (possible source for Crawford), 248, 254-56, 258, 263, 264-65, 358, 384
Gowrie family, 105, 113-14, 131, 134-35, 139, 147, 150, 155, 180, 188, 193, 194, 204, 240-41, 256, 257-58, 262, 359, 367
Gowrie, Forrest, 105
Gowrie, Henry, 105, 114
Gowrie, "Nub," 31, 111-13, 115-19 (at gravesite), 178, 207-08, 210, 235 (possible sources for Nub), 263, 301
Gowrie, N. B. Forrest, 37
Gowrie, Vinson, 66, 80-83, 86-87, 91-93, 102, 104, 111, 114, 117-19, 122, 126, 129, 134, 136-37, 145, 153, 163, 176, 178, 183, 188, 208, 210, 230, 235 (possible source for Vinson), 251, 255, 256, 257, 259-65, 268, 276, 282
Great Expectations (Charles Dickens), 232-33
Green, A. Wigfall, 1
Greenville *Democrat-Times,* 25
Gresset, Michel, xiv
Grier family, 237
Grierson, Emily, 233
Guinzburg, Harold, 9
Gwynn, Frederick, 1, 232

Haas, Merle, 49
Haas, Robert, 3, 5-9, 12, 13, 15-19, 23, 24, 25-34, 36-41, 42, 45, 48, 49, 52-54, 123, 248, 281, 390
Habersham, Eunice, 31, 36, 80, 84-85 (age), 84-92 (trip to cemetery), 92-102 (after visiting cemetery), 151 (age), 151-53, 156-61 (trip to cemetery), 162, 164-65, 167, 169-72, 181, 183 (description), 186, 190, 195, 205, 207, 222, 223, 225-26, 230, 233, 237, 250, 254, 255, 259, 260 (age), 261, 266-68, 274, 276, 322, 341, 372, 374, 391, 394
Habersham, Dr. Samuel, 156
Haddon Craftsmen, Inc., 62, 305
Halford, Doyle, 48
Halladay, Jim, 94, 163
Hamlet, The, 3, 4, 9, 52, 158, 387, 391
Hampton, Sheriff Hope, 31, 55, 66-67, 76, 80, 85-86, 92-93, 100, 111, 112-14, 116-18, 120-21, 122, 125, 134, 137, 138, 153, 162-63, 166, 172, 178, 190, 192, 196, 210, 211, 212, 215, 217, 220-21, 223-24, 226, 260-63, 272, 370
"Hand Upon the Waters," 239
Hardwick, Elizabeth, 229, 252
Harper, Emmanuel, 40
Harper's Bazaar, 165
Harrisburg (town in *Intruder*), 94-95
Harris, Meloney, 237
Harvard University, 42 (Club), 52, 55, 125, 245
Hathaway, Henry, 11
Hawkshaw, 248
Havisham, Estella (Dickens' character), 233
Havishman, Miss (Dickens' charac-

ter), 233
Hawks, Howard, 12
Hemingway, Ernest, 12, 41, 51, 57
Henry, Prof., 99, 168
Herndon, William, 10, 11, 13
Higginbotham, Elwood, 234
Hodge, Russell, 230
Hodge, Thompson, 230
Hogganback, Boon, 90, 158, 238
Holland, Anse, 239
Holland, Virginius, 239
Hollymount (town in *Intruder*),
  80, 92, 145-46, 161, 220, 261,
  264, 370, 394
Hollyvale (town in *Intruder*), 92,
  145, 161, 261, 394
Hollywood, California, 2, 10-15,
  18, 19, 30, 36, 38, 64
Horton, Howard, 48
"Hound, The," 248
House of Dust: A Symphony, The
  (Conrad Aiken), 249-51
Houston, Jack, 248
Howe, Irving, 231, 252
Huck Finn, 231
Hurry, Chester (*Come in at the
  Door*), 230
Hurry, Robert (*Come in at the
  Door*), 230
Hutchens, John, 42

Ingrum, Willy, 171, 179, 187, 193
  195, 217-18, 200, 223, 225, 353,
  355
Internal Revenue Service, 2, 24-25
Intruder in the Dust, (additional
  material) 52-56; (filming of *Intruder*) 34, 36-38, 39, 40, 48-49,
  56, 63-64 (Ben Maddow), 91;
  (genesis of story) xv-xvi, 6, 8, 9,
  12, 15, 19, 21, 22-23, 29; (possible

sources) 229-42; Themes (*civil
  rights*), 22-23, 46-47, 51-52, 54-
  56 (new material), 71-71 (formal
  statement), 77 (Mr. Lilley), 79,
  102, 104-10 (Gavin's views), 137,
  143 (Mr. Lilley), 176-77 (Gavin's
  views), 219-20, 226-27, 233,
  253, 257, 267, 274, 277-78,
  281-83 (new material); (*generation-distancing*) 268-70; (*notion
  of freedom*) 137-39, 270-72;
  (*performing passionate and digni-
  fied acts*) 191, 200-02, 207-08,
  210, 250, 257, 280; (*vocabulary
  and truth*) 89, 98, 154, 157,
  162, 268, 274-75, 277; (*women
  and children*) 46, 83-84, 92, 95,
  97, 157, 158, 161, 168, 255,
  266, 275; (title) 26-30, 32-33,
  191, 248-53, 280
Issetibbeha, 248

Jackson, Charles (*The Lost Week-
  end*), 46
Jefferson (Yoknapatawpha County),
  22, 34 (title), 79, 82-83, 92,
  102-03, 142, 252, 258, 270,
  276, 277
Jenkins, Wilfred, 234
Jesus Christ, 11, 46, 92, 270,
  277-78
Johnson, Gregory, xvii
Jones, Sheriff Buddy, 235
Jonsson, Thorsten, 15
Joor, W. W., 40
Joyce, James, 21-22

Kerr, Elizabeth, 251
Klopfer, Donald, 28, 42
Klopfer, Patricia, 28, 42

"Knight's Gambit," 14, 15, 240
Knight's Gambit, 1, 2, 15, 49, 89, 239-40
Kroll, Leon, 48

LaGuardia Airport, 42, 54, 281
Leavenworth Prison, 222, 358
Lee, General Robert E., 220
Legate, William, 96, 144, 146, 153, 163
Les Amis Myriades et Anonymes à la France de tout le Monde, 243-44
Levee Press, The, 25, 28
Lewis, Clifford, 229
Lewis, Sinclair, 42
Life, 41, 50-51, 56-57
Light in August, xiv, 45, 274, 378, 391
Lilley, Mr., 77, 83, 142-43, 274
Linscott, Robert, 20
Lion in the Garden, 1, 7
Liveright, Horace, 44, 45
Longstreet, General James, 44, 213
Longstreet, Stephen, 10
Los Angeles, California, 54
Lost Weekend, The (Charles Jackson), 46
Louisiana State University, 35
Lyman, Guy, 41
Lyman, Helen Baird, 41
Lyman, James, 41
Lytle, Andrew, 229, 232

Maddow, Ben, 63-65
Magwitch, Abel (Provis), 233
Mahon, Donald, 236
Mahon, Joseph, 236
Mallison, Charles (Chick), 7, 29, 31, 36, 54, 67-76, 82 (name), 77-84 (visiting jail), 88 (name), 84-92 (trip to cemetery), 97-98 (football game), 92-102 (after cemetery experience), 104-10 (listening to Gavin), 116-17 (second trip to cemetery), 120-22, 125-29 (meeting with Lucas), 130-34 (process of maturing), 135-36 (with Gavin), 136-42 (anxiety before confronting Lucas), 142-49 (visiting jail), 150, 151-53 (with Gavin), 154-56 (interior state), 156-61 (trip to cemetery), 162, 165-70 (extremely tired), 172-73 (his views concerning the crowd), 174, 179-98 (standing in the Square), 199-212 (talks with Gavin and mother), 213-17 (Gavin talks to Chick), 218, 219 (revery), 220, 225, 228, 231, 236, 237, 239-42 (in other stories), 246, 247, 250, 252, 253, 255, 257-61, 264-74, 275 (name), 276-83, 312, 348, 349, 354, 364, 374, 384, 390, 391
Mallison, Mrs., 83, 97, 100, 128-29 (on family names), 131, 148, 153, 162, 166, 168, 172, 182-83, 185-86, 190, 193, 195, 198-99, 206, 237, 254, 269, 306
Mannie, 3
Marlor, Lawrence, 234-35
Marshal (*A Fable*), 243-45
Massey, Linton, xvii, 3, 60
Maycox, Judge, 95
Mayes, Will, 248
McCallum, Buddy, 119, 199
McCannon, Shreve, 52, 55, 56, 281-83
McCaslin, Ike, 90, 158, 268
McCoy, Ruby, 40
McMillan, Mattie, 234

Memphis, Tennessee, 35, 93, 151
Mencken, H. L., 24-25
Meriwether, James, xv, xvii, 1, 35, 36, 45, 55, 59-61, 65, 133, 231
Metro-Goldwyn-Mayer, 10, 36, 37, 38, 48, 49
Millard, "Granny," 237
Millgate, Michael, 1, 2, 40, 65, 229, 231, 252
Minmagary, 39
Mississippian, The, 249
Mississippi College, 48
Mistairy (*A Fable*), 244
Moby Dick, 43
Montgomery, Jake, 66-67, 91-92, 96, 104, 111-12, 114-15, 117-19, 121-22, 161, 163, 183, 188, 193, 200, 207, 220, 221, 251, 254, 255-56, 261-62, 264, 280
Monk, 240-42
"Monk," 240
Moore, Donald, 37
Mosby, Uncle Hogeye, 190, 195
Mosquitoes, 236
Mottstown (town in *Intruder*), 80, 97-98, 167, 272, 278
Mount Hope Chapel, 82, 84, 147, 150, 259, 371
Mullen, "Moon," 15
"My Grandmother Millard and General Bedford Forrest and the Battle of Harrykin Creek," 237

Nagano, Japan, 1, 231
National Institute of Arts and Letters, 48
Neuberger, Elsa, 37
New Orleans, Louisiana, 40, 44, 136, 245
New York *Herald Tribune Weekly Book Review*, The, 42

New York *Times*, The, 42, 44, 45, 48
Nigger Jim (in *Huck Finn*), 231
Nigger of the Narcissus, The (Joseph Conrad), 43
Nobel Prize, 15, 47, 110
Norton Publishers, 34

Ober, Harold, 3, 10, 11, 13-22, 27, 28, 31-35, 37-39, 48
Obringer, R. J., 13, 16
O'Connor, William Van, 252
O. Henry Memorial Award, 6, 48
Omnibook, 34, 42
Oxford *Eagle*, The, 15, 56, 234
Oxford, Mississippi, 1, 8, 9, 11-15, 18, 22, 36, 41, 42, 43, 44, 46, 47, 48, 52, 53, 55 (literary allusion), 56, 64, 234-35

Pan Michael (Henryk Sienkiewicz), 47
"Pantaloon in Black," 3
Paralee (Alex Sander's mother), 71, 80, 87, 97, 148, 163, 165-66, 291
Parchman Prison, 222, 235, 358
Parker, Margaret, 36
Partisan Review, 20-21, 31
Paths of Glory (Humphrey Cobb), 11
Patton, Nelse, 234
Peavy, Charles, 252
Perry, George (*The Southerner*), 13
Pickett, General George, 213
Pirrip, Philip ("Pip") (*Great Expectations*), 233
Plunkett, Michael, xvii
Polk, Noel, 65

Portable Forkner, The, 13, 17, 41, 43
Princeton University, 59
Pritchard, David, 234
Prose for Comparison, 34

Rahv, Philip, 20
Random House, 4, 5, 7, 9-10, 13, 15-18, 20-22, 23, 28, 29, 30, 32-43, 49, 52-53, 63, 124, 133, 281, 363, 389
Rankin, John, 25
"Red Leaves," 248
Reivers, The, xv, 5-6, 235
Renoir, Jean, 46
Requiem for a Nun, 78-79
Reynal and Hitchcock Publishers, 34
Richards, Lucille, xvii
Rider, 3
Rinheimer, Howard, 16
Ripley, Mississippi, 22, 36
Roberts, Glen, 234
Roberts, Ike, 234
"Rose for Emily, A," 233
Rowan Oak, 1, 36, 42, 50, 229-30
Rubin, Jr., Louis, xvii
Russell, Mr. (Faulkner's neighbor), 23, 35, 298

Saint Patrick's Cathedral, 42
Saki, 13
Samway, S. J., Patrick, 55, 133, 229
Sanctuary, 23, 48, 394
Sardis Reservoir, 40
Sartoris, 1, 27, 237, 394
Sartoris, Bayard, 237
Saturday Evening Post, The, 4, 20, 38

Sewanee Review, 33
Shakespeare, William, 43, 209, 252
"Shall Not Perish," 237
Shegog, Reverend, 23
Sherman, Connecticut, 45
Sidney, George, 235
Sienkiewicz, Henryk (*Pan Michael*), 47-48
Skipworth, ——, 138-39
Smith, Harrison, 34, 42
"Smoke," 239
Snopes trilogy, xv, 232
Soldiers' Pay, 44, 236
Sound and the Fury, The, 1, 23, 253, 272
"Southerner, The," 46
Southerner, The (George Perry), 13
Southern Review, The, 35
Southwell, Anne, xvii
Steinbeck, John, 48
Steinberg, Aaron, 229, 251
Stephens, Lamar, 36
Stevens, Gavin, 1, 2, 14, 15, 31, 46, 49, 51, 52, 54, 55, 68, 77-81 (visiting Lucas), 83-85, 93-101 (after cemetery trip), 104-10 (philosophical ideas), 115, 116-17 (at gravesite), 125, 134-36, 144-46 (visiting Lucas), 147-48, 151-53 (talks with Chick), 153-54, 157, 164-66, 175-77 (Gavin's reflections), 178, 182, 187, 189-92, 195, 198, 200, 200-06, 209-12 (with Chick), 213-17 (talking to Chick), 218-20, 221-24 (thoughts about the crime), 226 (on cars), 227-28 (accepts Lucas' money), 229, 230, 236, 239-42 (in other stories), 244, 247, 252, 253-55,

258-67, 269, 273-75, 277-78, 281-83, 344, 347, 354, 387, 391, 392, 393

Strother, Caspey, 237
Strother, Simon, 237
Sullivan, Senator W. V., 234
Summers, Jill Faulkner, xvi
Sutpen dynasty, 55
Sutpen, Henry, 282
Sutpen, Thomas, 282-83
Sutterfield, Reverend Tobe (Monsieur Tolleyman), 243, 244-47
Swanson, H. N., 10
Sweetbriar, Virginia, 148

Tagliabue, John, 229
Tatum, Jesse, 235
Terrel, Bill, 241-42
"That Will Be Fine," 237
These 13, 41
"To Have and Have Not," 12
Tommy's Turl, 239
Thompson, Ralph, 42-43
Thorpe, James, xv, 65
Tom Sawyer, 231
Tom-Tom, 239
Tubbs, Euphus, 79-80, 153
Turner-Whitt case, 253
Twain, Mark, 231-33
Twentieth Century-Fox, 16

"Uncle Willy," 237
Uncommon Danger (Eric Ambler), 10
Universal Studies, 39
University of Mississippi ("Ole Miss"), 36, 48, 49, 231, 245
Unvanquished, The, 5, 8, 9, 53

Van Doren, Mark, 48
Vangard Films, 37
Varner's store, 224, 248
Vickery, Olga, 51, 229, 252, 269
Viking Press, 9, 13
Villard, Henry, 42
Vinson, Adam, 235
Von Auw, Ivan, 37, 39

Waddle, Mary Betsy, 1
Waggoner, Hyatt, 251
Warner Brothers, 10, 11, 13, 15-18, 30, 34, 37, 38, 46
Wasson, Ben, 25
Webb, James, 1
Wild Palms, The, 9, 52-53
Wilk, Jacob, 16, 37-38
William Faulkner's Library—A Catalogue, 229-30
Wilson, Edmund, 252
Wishing Tree, The, 202
Witten, Maggie (or Whitten), 128-29
Workitt, Sudley, 221-22, 264

Yale University, 25, 42
Yoknapatawpha County, xiii, xvi, 56, 90, 109, 159, 242, 256, 266

Faulkner's Intruder in the Dust:

A Critical Study of the Typescripts

Composed in IBM Selectric Composer *Journal Roman*; printed offset, and sewn by McNaughton & Gunn, Incorporated, Ann Arbor, Michigan; and bound by Howard Dekker, Incorporated, Grand Rapids, Michigan. The paper on which the book is printed is the International Paper Company's *Bookmark*.

Faulkner's Intruder in the Dust is a Trenowyth book, the scholarly publishing division of the Whitston Publishing Company.

This edition consists in 500 casebound copies.

MONUMENT OF JOHN TRENOWYTH,